Baptist Sacramentalism

A Warning to Baptists

Baptist Sacramentalism

A Warning to Baptists

David H.J.Gay

BRACHUS

BRACHUS
2a Banks Road
BIGGLESWADE
SG18 0DY
UNITED KINGDOM
e-mail: davidhjgay@googlemail.com

Available on-line through Amazon, Waterstones, Barnes & Noble,
BookButler, PriceMinister, Google Books *etc.*

For multiple copies, please contact me direct.

BRACHUS 2011

Scripture quotations, unless otherwise stated,
are from the New King James Version

OTHER BOOKS BY THE SAME AUTHOR
UNDER DAVID GAY
Voyage to Freedom
Dutch: Reis naar de vrijheid
Christians Grow Old
Italian: I credenti invecchiano
Battle For The Church

UNDER DAVID H.J.GAY
The Gospel Offer is *Free*
Particular Redemption and The Free Offer
Infant Baptism Tested
Septimus Sears: A Victorian Injustice and Its Aftermath

Blow the trumpet in Zion, and sound an alarm in my holy mountain!

Joel 2:1

If the trumpet makes an uncertain sound, who will prepare for battle?

1 Corinthians 14:8

Contents

Acknowledgements

I am deeply indebted to several people. First and foremost, Nigel Pibworth. Nigel not only supplied me with extensive source material and made probing comments on the manuscript, but he constantly stimulated me in conversation which displayed a knowledge both wide and deep. I know no man more keenly and perceptively aware of the literature than he. Generous as ever, he made his precious store freely available to me. I thank him.

But others, too, have made their valuable contribution. I record my gratitude to Jon Bevan, Simon Gay, Jack Green, Andrew Rome and Colin Vincent who read the manuscript and made discerning and encouraging comments. My thanks also to Audrey Broomhall, Margaret Harvey (who also read the manuscript), Paul Lucas and Carol Saunderson who kindly read the typescript, and made helpful suggestions. My wife, Mona, not only read the manuscript but helped me check the extracts – no easy task, as only those who have tried it know. I thank her. The responsibility for every error which remains is, of course, entirely my own.

Note to the Reader

To those who are familiar with my writings, it will come as no surprise to find the usual extensive quotations in this book. 'Not again', do I hear somebody sighing? 'Surely not again! Why *does* he do it?'

Well, why do I persist in what many must consider an annoying quirk? To read my apology for it – that is, to read my *defence* of it; I am far from apologetic about it! – see my *Infant Baptism Tested*. But, if any further justification should be required, and to begin in the way I intend to go on, what about the following?

Richard Dawkins, that infamous arch-enemy of Christianity, and indefatigable promulgator of the virtues of 'science', in his *A Devil's Chaplain*, quoted the sermons of Frederick William Sanderson, sometime headmaster of Oundle before Dawkins was a pupil there. Dawkins wanted to show – to advertise – how the 'enlightened' Sanderson exalted 'science' and had a passion for truth. Dawkins' had a sub-text, of course. Nothing wrong with that. But what was that sub-text? He wanted to show that those who cling to the Bible stifle enlightenment.

Very well! But the innocent reader of Dawkins fails to get the whole Sanderson. In what way? By Dawkins' subtle and selective quotation – by his subtle and selective quotation without letting his readers know! That's how!

Let me show you what I mean. This is how Dawkins quoted Sanderson[1] praising the scientists:

Faraday, Ohm, Ampère, Joule, Maxwell, Hertz, Rontgen; and in another branch of science, Cavendish, Davy, Dalton, Dewar; and in another, Darwin, Mendel, Pasteur, Lister, Sir Ronald Ross. All these and many others, and some whose names have no memorial, form a great host of heroes, an army of soldiers fit companions of those of whom the poets have sung...
There is the great Newton at the head of this list comparing himself to a child playing on the seashore gathering of the pebbles, while he could

---

[1] Dawkins was quoting from Anon: *Sanderson of Oundle*.

xi

see with prophetic vision the immense ocean of truth yet unexplored before him...[2]

High praise indeed for science and scientists. Dawkins went on: 'How often did you hear that sort of thing in a religious service?' Quite! I wouldn't want to hear it myself in a sermon; the praise of God is what I want to hear. Sanderson's words, however, were music to Dawkin's ears. The headmaster was saying just what he wanted.

Or was he?

Note Dawkins' use of ellipsis '...'. Nothing wrong, of course, with using an ellipsis. I do it myself. Every author, unless he wants to quote his source entire, has to select, and has to show his omissions by an ellipsis. But – and here's the rub – what if the omissions actually work against the author's underlying theme? Unless he indicates that he has left out such contradictory sentiments – preferably showing it by sample quotation – he, to put it as kindly as I can, is being less than frank with his readers.

So Dawkins. Getting back to the extracts above, but now including – in bold type – what Dawkins omitted, this is what Sanderson *actually* preached:

Faraday, Ohm, Ampère, Joule, Maxwell, Hertz, Rontgen; and in another branch of science, Cavendish, Davy, Dalton, Dewar; and in another, Darwin, Mendel, Pasteur, Lister, Sir Ronald Ross. All these and many others, and some whose names have no memorial, form a great host of heroes, an army of soldiers fit companions of those of whom the poets have sung; **all, we may be sure, living daily in the presence of God, bending like the reed before his will; fit companions of the knights of old of whom the poets sing, fit companions of the men whose names are renowned in history, fit companions of the great statesmen and warriors whose names resound through the world.**
There is the great Newton at the head of this list comparing himself to a child playing on the seashore gathering of the pebbles, while he could see with prophetic vision the immense ocean of truth yet unexplored before him. **At the end is the discoverer Sir Ronald Ross, who had gone out to India in the medical service of the Army, and employed his leisure in investigating the ravishing diseases which had laid India low and stemmed its development. In twenty years of labour**

---

[2] Dawkins p55.

he discovers how malaria is transmitted and brings the disease within the hold of man. On the day in which he made this great discovery he writes, and in writing makes one muse the handmaid of the other:

> *This day relenting God*
> *Hath placed within my hand*
> *A wondrous thing; and God*
> *Be praised. At his command*
> *Seeking his secret deeds*
> *With tears and toiling breath*
> *I find thy cunning seeds,*
> *O million-murdering Death.*[3]

Interesting omissions, are they not?

And that is not the end of it. Dawkins did not see fit to let his readers know that his star witness, Sanderson, said such things as this to the boys in his care:

In the first place, and I think essentially in the first place, is the study of the Bible. I do not say the mere mechanical reading of it. I do not say the steady reading of the Bible through. I do not say the picking out of particular passages, but the regular, careful study of it, with all the material now before us available for its study. It is not too much to say that the help for us is ten times what it was ten years ago...

A careful study of the Bible is a great aid to meditation: and this meditation or prayer is very essential to a full life. We perish if we cease from prayer. Of course, true, earnest, helpful prayer is difficult. It is difficult to fix the attention, difficult to know what to pray for, what to pray about. Perhaps the best way is to meditate with a note-book. Pray and study. Write down your thoughts. Get your desires and aspirations definite...[4]

Or:

Scientific men might well bring themselves to the discovery of the Christian ideals; 'back to Christ' may be their motto. By so doing, and so acting, there will be evolved in action a new ethical code of laws.[5]

---

[3] Anon p205.
[4] Anon p194.
[5] Anon p348.

Reader, do not misunderstand me. I am not for a moment suggesting that Sanderson would have advocated my stance on Scripture. Not at all! Indeed, I have just quoted him saying what I profoundly disagree with. For instance, I *do* advocate 'the steady reading of the Bible through'. And more. *But that is not my point.* Rather, I am taking the medicine I want to spoon out to Dawkins. He failed to quote Sanderson, at least in the above-mentioned instances, where Sanderson spoke against his (Dawkins') viewpoint. And he failed to tell his readers what he had done. In this way, he did not play fair with his readers – *nor with Sanderson.*

In short, by means of this extended rigmarole about Richard Dawkins, I am trying to explain why I give extensive extracts from those I quote. It goes some way to protect me and protect my sources. Above all, I do it to protect you, reader, from having the wool pulled over your eyes, inadvertently or by design.

So... perhaps my eccentric predilection for extensive extracts is not quite so annoyingly pointless, after all?

Of course, if I have failed to keep to my rubric, I am not only sincerely sorry, but, if drawn to my attention, I will rectify the matter in any second edition, including a full admission of my error.

Enough of this. Serious matters are afoot. So let us begin!

Preamble

We are all sinners. So says the Bible. And the sinner is spiritually dead in his sins. So says the Bible. And this has huge consequences. The sinner, dead in his sins, has no sense of his eternal danger, is unable to feel his need of deliverance, unable to repent, believe, come to Christ, call upon him and so be saved. Spiritual things are foolishness to him. In his heart, as a natural man, he hates God and the things of God. He cannot please God, but is under his wrath. Even as he lives, he is under God's condemnation. If he dies in unbelief, he will be eternally condemned. So says the Bible (John 3:18,36; 6:44,65; Rom. 3:23; 8:5-8; 1 Cor. 2:14; Eph. 2:1-3).

The sinner, therefore, must be born again. Christ says so (John 3:3-8). The sinner needs a new heart, a new mind, a new will, a new disposition, a new spirit. He needs to be made to live! And God alone can give and do this (John 1:13; 3:6,8; 6:44-45,65; Jas. 1:18; 1 Pet. 1:23),[1] but he does promise to give and do such (Ezek. 36:26). This is what the Bible means by 'regeneration'. A sinner who is regenerated has been 'born again', 'born of God', 'born of the Spirit' (John 1:13; 3:8; 1 John 2:29; 3:9; 4:7; 5:1,4,18). Such a sinner feels his sin, and is enabled to repent and believe. He is taken out of Adam and put into Christ (Rom. 5:12-21). He is delivered from the kingdom of darkness, and translated into the kingdom of light, the kingdom of Christ (Col. 1:13). He is liberated from slavery

---

[1] 'There is a necessity that there should be a work of grace upon our souls, which shall come, not from ourselves, but distinctly from God... There must be wrought upon us, in order to our being truly [planted] in the courts of the Lord's house, a work of grace infinitely beyond the power of the will, or all the power that dwells in human nature. We must, in fact, be new-created. We must be born again. We must have as great a work wrought upon us as was wrought upon the body of Christ when he was raised from the dead. The eternal power and Godhead of the divine Spirit must put forth the fullness of its strength to raise you up from your death in sin, or otherwise you will be like sear branches and cast-off pieces of wood, but never will you be trees planted, made to live and grow in the courts of the Lord's house. There must be something done for us [and to us and in us], if we are [to be] planted' (Spurgeon: *Metropolitan* Vol.23 pp410-411).

to sin under his father, the devil, and made a child of God (John 8:31-47). He is a new creation, and everything has become new (2 Cor. 5:17).

Very well. That's the starting point. In what follows, there is no debate about any of that. None whatsoever. If any man does not accept these biblical facts, he has no part in the debate in which I now engage. My concern at this time is not with him, but with those who accept these biblical facts.

Taking it for granted, then, that we all are convinced that sinners are dead in their sins, and must be born again, and – until they are regenerated – they will never come to Christ for salvation – the great question in hand is this: How are these sinners regenerated? In particular – more precisely – when sinners, who are dead in their sin, are regenerated, are they regenerated by baptism? In other words: Does the New Testament teach baptismal regeneration?

That is the question. Does the New Testament teach baptismal regeneration?

So... what is the answer? Does the New Testament teach baptismal regeneration?

Well, yes and no.

Yes? Yes, indeed – as long as the baptism is *spiritual* baptism, baptism by the Spirit. But if we are talking about *water* baptism, then the New Testament does *not* teach baptismal regeneration; that is, it does not teach that as a person is baptised by water he is also baptised by the Spirit.

But, starting with the Fathers, many have wrongly believed in baptismal regeneration by water – sacramental baptism. Indeed, since the Reformation, not only Rome, but the Reformed – whether Lutheran, Calvinist, Anglican, Puritan or Presbyterian – have mistakenly taught that grace is conferred by means of the sacramental water.[2]

---

[2] See my *Infant*. To avoid over-repetition of this phrase, I wish it to be understood that in my *Infant* I have fully set out my views on Reformed sacramentalism and infant baptism. The reader should consult that volume

But in the last hundred years a new phenomenon, a staggering phenomenon, has arisen. Early in the 20th century, Baptists – of all people! – began to teach and practice[3] sacramental baptism. What is more, during the opening decade of the 21st century, the pace towards sacramentalism among Baptists has been increasing. And I am horrified. Hence this book.

Let me say at once what this book is not. I do not pretend to have written 'a scholarly tome', in which, apparently, you, reader, should find it 'impossible to reconstruct [my] personal theological convictions'.[4] Far from it! *They*, I hope, will be clear enough.[5] But I make no apology for having an agenda, and for spelling it out. Those I write against have one too, and they are not shy about it.

The fact is, as I have said, there is a cataclysmic shift taking place in Baptist circles. Alarmingly, although as yet most of them are 'blissfully' unaware of it, the earth has already begun to move under Baptist feet. And so far-reaching are the effects of this impending earthquake, I want to do – I must do – what I can to let Baptists (and others) know about it. Indeed, I want to do more. I aim not merely to inform, but to persuade. I am no disinterested bystander, simply reporting what is passing before my eyes. I am involved. I want to be involved. I must be involved. Eternal issues hang upon what is happening, and I cannot be neutral.

What, in particular, am I making such a song and dance about? What is this battle? What is it that disturbs me so much? What is it that makes me want to go into print to warn my fellow Baptists about?

---

to fill out details on those matters lacking in this present work. To a lesser extent, the same applies to my *Battle*.

[3] Let me admit my breaking of the 'rules'. I use 'practice' for both 'practice' and 'practise'. I apologise to any who might be offended by this.

[4] *British Reformed Journal*, no.49, Summer 2008 p36.

[5] The late David Wright told me he was saddened by what he saw as the failure of reviewers to understand what he was saying in his *What...?*. I asked him if I had mis-read him. He assured me not. What is more, he told me, they wouldn't make the same mistake with my *Infant* as they had done with his work. I was glad. I hope the same is true of this book. Incidentally, I will always fully denote N.T.Wright – to distinguish him from David Wright.

Baptist sacramentalism. That's the battle, and that's what this book is about. Baptist sacramentalism – an oxymoron,[6] if ever there was.[7] But there it is. Baptists – most of whom, I say, are 'blissfully' unaware of it – Baptists are being taken along the high road of sacramentalism to... to where? To Rome! Or, to put it more accurately, an increasing number of Baptist scholars have a sacramentalist agenda – which, if things go on as they are, will end up in wholesale Vaticanisation. And, so seriously do I regard this, I must do what I can to sound an alarm before it is too late.

Alarm? Alarmist, more like! Do I hear somebody say it? If so, read on!

Reader, let me make my purpose plain.

If you are a Baptist sacramentalist, with respect I am trying not only to inform you, but to challenge and change your mind.

If you are an anti-sacramentalist, I write to warn you of what is going on, and to confirm and encourage you in what you and I regard as the biblical stance.

And, if you do not know what I am talking about, I hope, changing the figure I used just now, to remove the scales from your eyes in order to let you see the gathering storm-clouds, and to prepare you for the coming downpour.

My purpose, therefore, is confessedly largely negative, exposing the errors and dangers, as I see them, of sacramental baptism; using yet another illustration, to act as a siren (in the opposite sense to Greek mythology!), warning the unwary of treacherous reefs ahead. In this regard, I make no apology for being strident – mariners kept from foundering on the rocks don't often complain of the clanging bell which disturbed their sleep. As to that, while some want only a

---

[6] An oxymoron is a phrase using two words which are contradictory; 'pretty ugly', for example. In my opinion, 'baptist' and 'sacramentalist' are mutually contradictory.

[7] Note the title of Stanley K.Fowler's contribution to Cross and Thompson – 'Is "Baptist Sacramentalism" an Oxymoron?: Reactions in Britain to *Christian Baptism* (1959)'. His answer was: No! Mine is: Yes!

positive approach, the Bible shows us how necessary – and God-honouring – a negative course can be.

D.Martyn Lloyd-Jones:

It is the business of a Christian teacher, as I understand it from the New Testament itself, not only to give a positive exposition but also to oppose wrong teaching. The New Testament itself does that, but this approach is not popular today. People say: 'Don't be negative, give us the positive truth; don't be controversial'. But if error is being taught it must be corrected. Paul does this constantly. He exposes the false, warns against it, urges Christians to avoid it; at the same time he gives the positive truth. So we must of necessity do the same. What we believe is of vital importance, because it is going to affect our whole life and conduct.[8]

And our eternity. Above all, I say, our eternity.

As I have explained, I aim to speak the truth, albeit trenchantly, in love. If I needlessly offend, I sincerely apologise, and ask those who disagree with my tone, to be kind enough to remember why I have written. *It is the care of souls which moves me.* I dread to have to confess with W.E.Gladstone (in a pamphlet published late in life): 'It has been my misfortune all my life, not to see a question of principle until it is at the door – and then sometimes it is too late!'.[9] I quote this with regard both to myself *and those who read what I write.* The same goes for Gerrard Winstanley's address to Oliver Cromwell in 1651: 'I must speak plain to you', he said, 'lest my spirit tells me another day: "If you had spoken plain, things might have been amended"'.[10] I have wrestled over 2 Timothy 2:23-26. But I do not think I have engaged in 'foolish and ignorant disputes'; nor have I set out to 'generate strife'; and I hope I have not been guilty of what Paul meant when he told us 'not to strive about words to no profit, to the ruin of [my readers]' (2 Tim. 2:14); that is, 'contentions and strivings' (Tit. 3:9). (See also 1 Tim. 6:4). John Gill's comments are apt:

Such an one ought not to strive about words *to no profit*, about *mere* words, and in a litigious, quarrelsome manner, and *for mastery and not*

---

[8] Lloyd-Jones: *Sons* pp92-93.
[9] A.N.Wilson: *Victorians* p474.
[10] Hill: *Defeat* p19.

truth; though he may, and ought to strive for the faith of the gospel; this is praiseworthy in him.[11]

John Calvin, too, I have found helpful on this, especially when he, even in his comments on the verse, was prepared to call the views of those he opposed, 'silly trifles' – not forgetting, also, his diatribes against the Anabaptists and others. On the main issue, he explained that the apostle calls the 'questions' 'foolish, because they are uninstructive; that is, they contribute nothing to godliness'. I am convinced that what I am writing about meets both of Calvin's criteria in the positive sense – it demands as much clear instruction as possible, it is instructive to think it through, and is of the utmost concern to godliness. 'When we are wise in a useful manner, then alone are we truly wise', said Calvin.[12] I hope my book comes under that 450 year-old commendation. Above all, I hope my attitude bears at least some semblance to 2 Corinthians 2:3-4.

And let us not forget Jude 3. In 1954, Lloyd-Jones addressed the annual meeting of the Inter-Varsity Fellowship. Douglas Johnson made some notes of what he said:

In Jude 3, we read: 'Beloved, while I was very diligent to write to you concerning our common salvation, I found it necessary to write to you exhorting you to contend earnestly for the faith which was once for all delivered to the saints'. Here we are given a stirring call to the defence of the faith. Such a call is not popular today. It is not popular today even in some Evangelical circles. People will tell you that it is all 'too negative'. They continually urge that we must keep on giving the positive truth. They will tell us that we must not argue, and we must never condemn. But we must ask: 'How can you fight if you are ever afraid of wounding an enemy?' 'How can you rouse sleeping fellow-warriors with smooth words?' God forbid that we find ourselves at the bar of judgement, and face the charge that we contracted out from love of ease, or for fear of man, or that we failed to do our duty in the great fight of the faith. We must – we must fight for the faith in these momentous times.[13]

---

[11] Gill: *Commentary* Vol.6 p636, emphasis mine.
[12] Calvin: *Commentaries* Vol.21 Part 3 pp232-233.
[13] Murray: *The Fight* p301. The full address was published in Lloyd-Jones: *Knowing the Times* pp51-60.

The bar of judgement! What a thought! I know I stand at man's bar today. But, and of far greater consequence, I am also conscious that before long I shall have to stand and answer at God's bar. Every day brings me closer to it. That being so, I must speak now, and speak in the way that I do.

Moving on from the *tone* in which I have written, as I said in my *Infant*, I ask those who think me deplorably divisive in my choice of subject, to bear in mind the issue – sacramentalism. I ask them to bear in mind the growing weight of evidence which shows an increasing emphasis upon it among both Reformed and Baptist scholars today. Papist sacramentalism has been around for 1700 years or more. We have had Reformed (Lutheran, Calvinist, Anglican, Puritan and Presbyterian) sacramentalism getting on for 500 years. And now we have a new phenomenon to contend with – *Baptist* sacramentalism. But, whichever variety we are talking about, sacramentalism is a colossal error, the cause of much harm; indeed, it is a great evil. I do not look upon sacramentalism as a peripheral issue. Far from it. Sacramentalism is ruinous to the gospel. It is pernicious, a poison injected into the jugular of the Christian religion. And, as such, it is disastrous to the souls of men.

So, there it is, reader. You know what this book is about, the tone in which it is written, and why. Do you want to read on? Assuming that you do, let us get down to it.

Introduction

Baptist sacramentalism. First, let me define my terms, so that we are all clear as to what we are talking about.

By a Baptist, I mean one who, in obedience to Christ's command, holds to the immersion of professing believers in water as a physical demonstration of the spiritual reality they have already experienced.

By sacramentalism, I mean the erroneous notion that spiritual grace is conveyed (or made effective) by an outward act.[1]

---

[1] 'Grace'. This is a difficult word, simply because we are so familiar with it, and use it so frequently, often without pausing to think precisely what we mean by it. I myself plead guilty. It can range in meaning from 'some kind of vague blessing' to 'all the benefits of everlasting salvation which God accomplished for the elect in Christ'. 'Means of grace', a non-biblical phrase in common use, is likewise pregnant with difficulty. So let me set out the way in which, in this book, I shall use 'grace', 'the conveying of grace'.

In this present volume, when I speak of 'grace', I am thinking mainly of regenerating grace, saving grace; and when I speak of 'the conveying of grace', I am thinking of the communication, the imparting, the transmitting of regeneration, of salvation. While I deny that water baptism conveys grace, I do not mean that there is no blessing or benefit in being baptised. Of course not! But I utterly repudiate the notion that God actually regenerates a sinner by water baptism, that he bestows, imparts, conveys, transmits his Spirit upon and to the sinner by means of water. Water baptism does not regenerate, does not save. It does not convey regenerating, saving grace. It represents it, but it does not transmit or convey it. I include the adjective 'water' because, as I shall argue, spiritual baptism does convey the regenerating, saving grace which water baptism represents.

As I have shown in my *Infant*, the Reformed believe that grace is conveyed in what they call the sacrament of baptism – their quarrel with Rome on the issue lies in *ex opere operato*; that is, the Reformed reject the notion of an automatic conveyance or 'magical' conveyance of grace in water baptism. See my *Infant* for my arguments showing why this escape-route will not satisfy.

Finally, in this book, while I concentrate on baptism, what I say also applies to the Lord's supper.

In short:

A Baptist baptises only those who profess (and give evidence of) inward spiritual grace, and does so to represent that grace.

A sacramentalist baptises to produce or convey the grace.

To me, therefore, a Baptist cannot be a sacramentalist; as I have said, 'Baptist sacramentalism' is an oxymoron. Actually, it is a contradiction – not merely in terms, but in fact. Or ought to be. Nevertheless, it exists. Oh yes, it certainly does! This, from one of its leading proponents, George Beasley-Murray, should make it clear enough:

God's gift to baptism and to faith is one: it is his salvation in Christ. There is no question of his giving one part in baptism and another to faith, whether in that order or in the reverse. He gives *all* in baptism and *all* to faith.[2]

And:

To be [water] baptised... is to become one with Christ through the Holy Spirit and a member of the body of Christ. It means union with Christ by the Spirit and in the Spirit.[3]

Reader, this is the sort of thing I am talking about, and, I am sorry to say, is being taught by an increasing number of Baptist theologians today. And, putting it mildly, I intensely disagree with it. So, as I have said, having tried to deal with *Reformed* sacramentalism, I now want to tackle this new and growing phenomenon of *Baptist* sacramentalism.

A word of warning, however. Just as with the Reformed, so Baptist sacramentalists have their qualifiers; that is, they are not averse to making a massive statement about the power and efficacy of baptism, and then adding a statement which virtually contradicts what they have just said, or at least 'qualifies' or withdraws it in some way. But it will not wash. Let's have done with double-speak. In any case, as I said when dealing with Reformed sacramentalism, how can we be sure that 'ordinary' believers understand the

---

[2] Beasley-Murray: *Baptism Today and Tomorrow* p37, emphasis his.
[3] Beasley-Murray, quoted by Cross: 'Spirit- and Water-' p124.

qualifiers? Indeed, do they simply listen to the agreeable bits, and ignore the rest?

Qualifiers! Let me give an example of a sacramental Baptist doing the sort of thing I refer to. First, the massive statement for the efficacy of baptism:

The transaction accomplished in [water] baptism is divinely authenticated by the gift... of the Spirit as the mark of divine possession. The connection is unmistakable in 1 Corinthians 12:13... Paul certainly means that a sufficient, even abundant, supply... of the Spirit of Christ is vouchsafed to all who are baptised [in water].

Pretty sweeping claims for baptism, are they not? Now for the immediate qualifier, the double-speak:

Yet here as always Paul is careful to avoid the impression that the rite of baptism itself conveys the Spirit. He never implies that the gift of the Spirit is conditioned by [water] baptism, and he often speaks of the Spirit's reception without any explicit reference to the rite.[4]

Which is it? I realise the left hand shouldn't know what the right is doing, but surely they shouldn't be doing contradictory things, should they?

Is there any danger, I ask again, of an 'ordinary' believer, despite the cautionary remarks, believing that by his baptism he has had the Spirit 'vouchsafed' to him? The answer is self-evident.

* * *

Before I tackle *Baptist* sacramentalism, let me sketch the rise and growth of sacramentalism itself – and the opposition to it.

In the New Testament, we read that the early believers, travelling far and wide, preached the gospel – commanding, inviting, urging, exhorting sinners to repent and trust Christ for salvation, warning them that if they refused they would perish. Some who heard the gospel did refuse; some procrastinated; but some – thousands – obeyed the gospel, repented and believed. All such were baptised by immersion, and added to the new body which Christ had set up – the church. From now on there were two groups in the world; the

---

[4] White pp203-204. White cited 1 Cor. 2:12; 2 Cor. 5:5; Gal. 3:5; 4:6; Phil. 1:19 *etc.*

church and the rest. Men were either believers or unbelievers; subjects of the kingdom of light or subjects of the kingdom of darkness. Christ, with his gospel, had brought about this profound cleavage in the human race. The words of the prophet had been fulfilled, and the old order of things had been well and truly shaken (Hag. 2:6-9,21-23; Heb. 12:18-29). Christ, through his own work, and through his people, had 'turned the world upside down' (Acts 17:6).

Until that time, societies had been homogeneous, 'sacral';[5] that is, all the citizens were incorporated into their particular society at birth by the performance of a rite or ceremony at the hands of a recognised priest, and were sustained and nourished in it by repeated priestly acts.[6] In this way, everybody automatically became a part of their society, lived in it and died in it. Indeed, death was the only way out of it – either natural, or violently enforced as punishment for any who dared challenge its over-arching homogeneity.[7]

But Christ, by founding his church, put an end to all that. By setting up his own kingdom, his unique kingdom with its own distinctive way of entering it, he forever destroyed the old homogeneity. Through the regenerating grace and power of his Holy Spirit, sinners came to individual, personal and voluntary repentance and faith in Jesus as Saviour and Lord. In this way, the Lord Jesus Christ *translated* these sinners out of the kingdom of darkness into *his* kingdom.

Sacral society, whatever form it took, reacted to this upstart kingdom within its very bowels – this new-fangled realm which was daring to challenge its universal homogeneity and power. Reacted to it? It hated it. It persecuted it to death. More precisely, it persecuted *Christ* in his members.[8] For Christ, by his gospel, had opened the last and decisive phase in the war which had begun with God's

---

[5] Sacral – 'of or for sacred rites' (*The Concise*).
[6] This was true both of pagan societies (witch doctors, initiating rites, and so on) and the Jews.
[7] Of course, there were many societies in the world – usually grossly intolerant of each other. But they were all sacral.
[8] Saul of Tarsus, before his conversion, persecuted believers, the church (Acts 8:1-3; 9:1-2,13-14,21; 22:4-5,19-20; 26:10-11; Gal. 1:13,23). But, in truth, he was persecuting Christ (Acts 9:4-5; 22:7-8; 26:9,14-15).

pronouncement in Genesis 3:15, and which will last until he returns in glory to judge the world.[9]

From the day of Pentecost, thousands – by being born again, and coming to repentance and faith in Christ and demonstrating it by obedience to him in baptism – were spiritually quitting their native society to join this separate, distinct society – the church. No longer thinking of themselves principally as citizens of any earthly realm, they knew and confessed themselves to be citizens of Christ's heavenly kingdom – even though such a profession brought down upon them the wrath of the sacral society they had forsaken. Rejecting Caesar as spiritual Lord,[10] they submitted to Christ as their spiritual king, acknowledging *him* as their sovereign Lord, their ruler, their law-giver in the spiritual realm. And when Caesar's (or any earthly ruler's) law clashed with that of Christ, it was Christ whom they would obey (Acts 4:18-20; 5:27-29). And Caesar didn't like it![11] He, in company with other earthly rulers (Acts 5:33), did not like it at all!

Is this not a fair summary of the New Testament?

Things continued thus for about 300 years.[12] During those centuries, the great universal sacral society of the time, the Roman Empire,

---

[9] I see the temptation of Christ (Matt. 4:1-11), many episodes in the Gospels and Acts, along with Rom. 16:20; 1 Cor. 7:5; 2 Cor. 2:11; 11:14; 12:7; Eph. 4:27; 6:11; 1 Thess. 2:18; 2 Thess. 2:9; 1 Tim. 3:6-7; 5:15; 2 Tim. 2:26; Heb. 2:14; Jas. 4:7; 1 Pet. 5:8; 1 John 3:8,10; Jude 9; Rev. 2:10,13; 12:9,12; 20:2,7,10 as part of this battle.

[10] Rejecting Caesar as spiritual Lord, but still obeying him in his role as an earthly king (Matt. 22:21; Mark 12:17; Luke 20:25; Acts 25:11; Rom. 13:1-7; Tit. 3:1; 1 Pet. 2:13-17).

[11] 'The charges brought against the Christians were atheism and anarchy. Their rejection of the old gods seemed atheism; their refusal to join in Emperor-worship appeared treasonable' (Williston Walker p43).

[12] But, almost from the start, serious innovations intrinsically destructive of Christ's order were introduced into the church – by its members (especially its leaders). The evidence for such even in the time of the New Testament itself is legion (Acts 15:1; 20:29; Rom. 16:17-18; 1 Cor. 15:12; 2 Cor. 11:3-4,12-15; Gal. 2:4-5,11-21; 2 Thess. 2:2-3,7; 1 Tim. 1:19-20; 5:15; 6:3-5,10; 2 Tim. 2:17-18; Tit. 1:9-16; 3:9-11; 2 Pet. 2:1-22; 1 John 2:18-23; 4:1-6; 2 John 7-11; 3 John 9; Jude 4-19 *etc.*). For prophetical warnings of

more-or-less continued to persecute the church – this minority outcast and upstart society – for daring to challenge its monolithic all-embracing power. It demanded conformity – or else. In the 4th century, however, a catastrophic change took place in the relationship between the two kingdoms.[13]

After a period of toleration of the church under the Emperor Constantine (following his so-called conversion), during the reign of Theodosius I, the State and the Church were fused to form a new monolithic sacral society[14] which replaced the old pagan sacralism,[15] yet retaining and adopting the old pagan principles. The Catholic Church, Christian sacralism, Christendom, had been invented.[16]

---

apostasy down the ages, see Matt. 24:3-28; Mark 13:4-23; Luke 21:7-17; 1 Tim. 4:1-3; 2 Tim. 3:1-9; 4:1-4 *etc*. For what follows in this section, in addition to particular references, see Boorman; Estep: *Revolution*.

[13] Many mistakenly take a diametrically opposite view of these events. They think Constantine was the best thing before sliced bread – and since. See my *Battle*.

[14] This was simply the logical outcome of Constantine. 'To Constantine's essentially political mind, Christianity was the completion of a process of unification which had long been in progress in the Empire. It had one Emperor, one law, and one citizenship, for all free men. It should have one religion' (Williston Walker p105). As in my *Battle* and *Infant*, I have the difficulty about church and Church. By the former I mean the New Testament concept; by the latter I mean one of the many inventions of men. I have found it impossible to be consistent – just one of the consequences of Constantine.

[15] 'Sacralism is the view that all the members of a particular nation should be bound together by loyalty to the same religion, which same religion gives political authority to the leaders of that nation. Religious dissent thus becomes the same as political subversion. Christian sacralism developed as Christianity became the official religion of the Roman Empire during and after the 4th century' (Bridge and Phypers p85).

[16] 'With the [so-called] conversion of Constantine in the 4th century... [the Church's] sacramental mission [which by then had been introduced into the Church] was ultimately co-opted by the earthly city... Christendom... initially presupposed the eschatology of the early church... church and secular rule as distinct structures... The Church responded... "by accepting this invitation to render a 'holy service' for the world". [Among the majority, there was a totally misguided] Christian jubilation over the Constantinian and Theodosian establishment of a Christian empire'

Christendom (the new sacral society) took over the Latin name – the *sacramentum*[17] – given to the initiating rite of the old pagan sacral society (remember, as I said, all sacral societies have their rites of

---

(Harvey pp102-103). Harvey is a Baptist sacramentalist. Hence my square brackets!

More accurately, the seeds of Christendom had been sown by Constantine; the full-flowering would take time. The story, naturally, is complicated. In addition to the east-west split of the Roman Empire, history is not so simple that we can say that on such and such a day, Christendom started. But in the 8th century, Charles the Hammer laid the ground work for it, and when Pope Leo III crowned the Hammer's grandson, Charlemagne, Emperor on Christmas Day 800, he signalled the founding of what would become known as the Holy Roman Empire, a powerful Catholic empire in the west. Hence Christendom. 'The Carolingian world [the Holy Roman Empire] first defined itself as "Christendom" over against the worlds of pagan barbarians and Muslim infidels... Christendom... derived [from the Roman Imperial state] its imperial ambitions, its religion, it central institution, the Church, and its written language, Latin... This new imperium, however, was no longer primarily defined in political terms; it was rather a society that fused the political and religious into one... defining itself by its religion, something that the... Roman Empire of Constantine and Theodosius had never done... imposing the Catholic orthodoxy of Rome throughout the west, and at the same time making the secular power sacred... Before Constantine, the church stood apart from, but was not hostile to, state power, in accordance with the biblical injunction to "render unto Caesar the things that are Caesar's, and to God the things that are God's" [Matt. 22:21. See also Rom. 13:1-7; 1 Pet. 2:13-17]. After Constantine, the Church remained separate from imperial power... With the Carolingians, Church and society became co-terminus, though with the Emperor supreme. With Gregory VII [1073-1085], the roles were reversed: Church and society were still one, but the spiritual power was now paramount... The clergy... increasingly became a sacerdotal caste separate from and superior to the laity... The central sacraments of baptism and the eucharist... [were thought to give] human beings support from birth until death' (Malia pp12-15,27-28). For the way this worked out until and including the Reformation, see Malia pp11-103.

[17] In about 200, 'Tertullian began to apply the term *sacramentum* to... baptism and the Lord's supper... Hence came the use of the word "sacrament" in Christian theology – a word which, as being at once ambiguous and figurative [let alone borrowed from pagans – DG], could well be spared... This term, misinterpreted or misunderstood[!], has assisted in introducing false doctrines and erroneous views' (Riddle p67).

passage, *all* of them);[18] hence 'sacrament'. Christendom applied the term to its own invented initiating rite – the so-called baptising of infants. The Church claimed that by this sacrament of infant baptism it effectively conveyed regenerating grace to infants, thereby making them Christians. This, of course, was a staggering and appalling – diabolical – corruption of the New Testament symbol of believer's baptism following faith. And in two ways: infants, instead of believers, were being baptised,[19] and the baptism was performed for the *conveying* of grace rather than the *representation* of the grace *already experienced.*[20] In short, baptism, in the hands of the Church, had come between the sinner and Christ.

As night follows day, sacramentalism led to – as it always will lead to – sacerdotalism; that is, priestcraft – the power to convey grace through the sacrament by the hands of a professional

---

[18] Sacramentalism detests a vacuum! I will give further examples of it – even in the 'enlightened' west. Even the Nazis and Communists had them. See the extended note on p300. This 'extended note' should be treated as though inserted at this particular point. Only in this way will sense be made of my use of 'earlier', below' *etc.* The same goes for all the 'extended notes'.

[19] I am not saying that Constantine was responsible for the introduction of infant baptism. It had been invented before his day – and it did not become all-powerful until 50 years, or more, after Constantine. (He himself was not baptised as an infant, but on his death bed). Augustine (even though he was not baptised as an infant) was the man responsible for making infant baptism the norm! 'It was he who provided the theology that led to infant baptism becoming general practice... in the later 5th century [or] more likely in the 500s or even later' (Wright: *What?...* p12). Christendom is always complicated!

[20] The second ordinance of Christ was also corrupted – the Lord's supper being made into the sacrifice of the Mass. 'With Cyprian [c200-258] the developed [corrupted!] doctrine of the Lord's supper as a sacrifice offered to God by a priest has been fully reached... The "Catholic" conception of the Supper was thus developed as... a sacrament in which Christ is really present (the *how* of that presence was not to be much discussed till the Middle Ages)... Much was still left obscure[!], but the essentials of the "Catholic" view were already at hand by 253'. 'Beginning in the late 12th century... the meaning of sacrifice was made dependent on the sacerdotal consecration of the bread and wine, with the actions performed by the cleric coming to have the dominant (and sometimes the sole) role in the proceedings' (Williston Walker p91, emphasis his; Harvey p105).

appointed to perform the ceremony.[21] And so it proved in the all-embracing State-Church.[22] The New Testament concept of church membership through repentance and faith in Christ as Saviour and Lord, followed by baptism and commitment to his church as a part of a life-long submission to Christ and his law, had been replaced by the sacramental concept of Church membership by infant baptism at

---

[21] No justification for sacramentalism or sacerdotalism can be found in Rom. 15:16. True, Paul uses ἱερουργεω, 'to minister in the manner of a priest, minister in priestly service' (Thayer). 'To be a minister of Christ Jesus to the Gentiles with the priestly duty of proclaiming the gospel of God, so that the Gentiles might become an offering acceptable to God, sanctified by the Holy Spirit' (NIV). But as Hodge said: 'Paul... no more calls himself a priest in the strict sense of the term, than he calls the Gentiles a sacrifice in the literal meaning of that word' (Hodge: *Romans* p438). The verse is best understood in the context of 'the priesthood of all believers' (Rom. 12:1; Phil. 4:18; Heb. 13:15-16; 1 Pet. 2:4-11; Rev. 1:6; 5:10; 20:6). See my forthcoming *The Priesthood of All Believers*. See also Haldane pp619-620.

[22] Tertullian had started the use of 'sacerdotal language', dividing the church into two – clergy and laity. He espoused the Latin *sacerdos*, a priest, to describe bishop, later to be applied to the minister; that is, he adopted another pagan word – *pagan*, mark you – to qualify, to corrupt, a biblical word. And it was not only the word which was ruined – so was the concept! In addition, 'Tertullian was much addicted to the adoption of Jewish phraseology with reference to the ministers and services of the Church; a practice which subsequently led to serious abuse... [He claimed] that Christian ministers are priests (such as the Jewish) in an exclusive sense – thus paving the way for the establishment of a false claim, by which the governors and teachers of the... Church arrogated to themselves peculiar gifts and privileges unknown to the early [that is, apostolic] church, including the sole power of offering to God an awful, but fictitious, sacrifice' (Riddle pp63,69-70,151-152,191). Seeing Cyprian regarded Tertullian as 'his master' (Bernard p224) – 'he was... a great admirer of Tertullian, whose works he used to call for with an intimation that he regarded them as models' (Riddle p94) – it is no surprise to learn it was he, Cyprian, who finally brought into the church the idea of a priesthood based on the Israelite system of the Old Testament. What a remarkable twisting of Scripture! What a distortion of the gospel! The writer to the Hebrews took great pains to prove that Christ had fulfilled and abolished the priesthood and sacrificial system of the old covenant. Cyprian, however, went completely against the Scripture and brought priestcraft into the church – into the church of all places! See Bernard pp215-262.

the hands of a priest. More than that, regeneration, itself, directly and sovereignly by the Holy Spirit – which Christ said is essential – had been replaced by so-called baptismal regeneration at the hands of a priest.[23] In this way, Christendom – the Church, its priests and their arrogated regenerating power in infant baptism – began its long history of shutting millions out from Christ and his salvation.

The monstrosity thus invented – an organisation, not an organism; an institution, not a spiritual body; a corporation, not a church – gained its 'shareholders' by so-called baptismal regeneration, as pagans were thus made into so-called Christians, even though they remained pagan in mind, heart and practice.

F.F.Bruce:

Christianity thus became fashionable... It meant a considerable ingress of Christianised pagans into the Church – pagans who had learned the rudiments of Christian doctrine and had been baptised, but who remained largely pagan in their thoughts and ways.[24]

In contrast to Christ's church, in which regeneration, followed by saving faith and repentance, ensured that converts abandoned their old paganism (Acts 8:9-12; 19:18-19; 1 Cor. 12:2; 1 Thess. 1:9-10), in the new-fangled Church, baptismal regeneration enabled the 'converts' to keep their old paganism and cover it with a veneer of institutionalised 'Christianity'.[25] It was Satan's master-stroke.

---

[23] 'The 2nd century Fathers are essentially unanimous in their understanding of [John 3:5] as referring to water baptism and spiritual regeneration... Justin [Martyr] articulated more clearly than had been done before the idea of baptismal regeneration... Justin engraved the doctrine of baptismal regeneration upon the history of the church... He suggests that although the miracle of regeneration takes place concurrently with baptism, it occurs as a result of personal choice, repentance, belief and a commitment to a life of obedience... Irenaeus... concur[red] with the earlier tradition of interpretation of John 3:5, as referring to outward baptism and inward (spiritual) regeneration' (Downing pp101,107-109,111). I will, of course, look at this scripture and expose the mistake of 2nd century Fathers.

[24] Bruce p295.

[25] Baptismal regeneration cannot eliminate paganism. Only the Holy Spirit by his supernatural power can do that. Right from the start, Christendom's 'converts', produced by baptismal regeneration, were allowed to continue with, for example, their use of beads, vestments, festival days. Indeed, the Church made a virtue out of necessity. John Henry Newman: 'Incense,

This new universal sacral society – Christendom, shortly to be dominated by the Catholic Church[26] ruled by its Pope – needed a theology to bolster or justify its sacramental system.

Cometh the need, cometh the man! Augustine, Christendom's leading theologian,[27] more than any other provided the required theology:

Augustine taught, and all adherents of Christian sacralism repeated after him, that society cannot hang together unless it is bound by a common

---

lamps, candles, votive offerings, holy water, vestments, images are all of pagan origin'. Monsignor O'Sullivan: 'Even after [Catholic] Christianity became the prevailing religion, it seemed impossible to root out the practice of using pagan charms. The Church, therefore, instead of trying to prevent it, endeavoured to turn it to [so-called] good ends by suggesting or tolerating the use of similar devices with Christian symbols'. The 20th century Roman Catholic scholar, Richard McBrien: 'The [so-called] conversion of Constantine... allowed the Church to be less defensive[!] about pagan culture, to learn from it and be enriched by it' (Jackson pp105-106).

[26] I am, of course, simplifying more than a thousand years of history. Space does not allow me to detail, for instance, the 2nd century east-west split brought about by the Pope of Rome who flexed his muscles but failed to impose his will on all the Catholic Church; the resistance of Milan (that is Lombardy, Piedmont and the southern provinces of France) to Rome over many centuries; and the papal schism when, for a time, there were two – and then three – rival Popes. The fact is, the Catholic Church would split into various other Catholic and Orthodox Churches. The west, which I am concerned with, would be dominated by the *Roman* Catholic Church (another oxymoron).

[27] 'He was to be the father of much that was most characteristic in medieval Roman Catholicism. He was to be the spiritual ancestor, no less, of much in the Reformation... The secret of much of Augustine's influence lay in his mystical piety... To Augustine... baptism and the Lord's supper are pre-eminently sacraments. By the sacraments the Church is knit together. [He stated that] "there can be no religious society, whether religion be true or false, without some sacrament or visible symbol to serve as a bond of union". Furthermore, the sacraments are necessary for salvation. [And again:] "Without baptism and partaking of the supper of the Lord it is impossible for any man to attain either to the kingdom of God or to salvation and everlasting life"' (Williston Walker pp160-166).

religion. And he taught that it is in the sacrament that the cohesive power of religion resides.[28]

Over a thousand years later, Calvin, himself strongly Augustinian, would endorse this:

To use the words of Augustine: 'In no name of religion, true or false, can men be assembled, unless united by some common use of visible signs or sacraments'.[29]

So said Calvin.

But this is to anticipate. The rise and spread of Christendom and its sacramentalism did not go unchallenged.[30] Voices were raised

---

[28] Verduin p139.

[29] Calvin: *Institutes* Vol.2 p505. For the history of sacramentalism from the time of the Fathers, the part played by Augustine and Aquinas, and how it led to sacerdotalism, see Grenz pp77-79; Harvey pp96-110. John E.Colwell quoted Aquinas: 'Augustine says... that the baptismal water touches the body and cleanses the heart. But the heart is not cleansed save through grace. Therefore it [baptism] causes [note the word!] grace; and for like reason so do the other sacraments of the Church... The instrumental cause works not by the power of its form, but only by the motion whereby it is moved by the principal agent; so that the effect is not likened to the instrument but to the principal agent... It is thus that the sacraments of the New Law cause grace; for they are instituted by God to be employed for the purpose of conferring grace'. Note Colwell's link of (Augustine) Aquinas and Calvin: 'I am increasingly impressed by the similarities', he said, 'rather than dissimilarities, between Thomas Aquinas and John Calvin at this point' (Colwell pp233-235). Reader, speaking for myself – but I know I am not alone – I am 'impressed' with the incomprehensibility of Augustine at times. What does he mean? See Appendix 2 in my *Infant* for Augustine's own words. This ought to be read! His 'defence' of infant baptism is, in my opinion, one of the best arguments against the practice.

[30] 'There was... the sacramental and sacerdotal system of the early Church [that is, from the time of the Fathers] and the Middle Ages; and there was the principle developed from Constantine onwards that the Church was co-extensive with society; a Church-society, called by the Carolingians, Christendom. In this sacred world, the spiritual and sacred swords were inextricably linked, with the former, of course, being the higher of the two. Thus revolt... began in Europe with the re-definition of the sphere of the spiritual; that is, with [so-called] heresy. Specifically, since eternal salvation [it was claimed] depended on sacraments... European [so-called] heresy perennially tended towards anti-sacerdotalism and anti-

against it. Let me cite some. In so doing, I am not saying that the people I mention reached full gospel light, but I am saying that they were, at least, a flickering candle in the gross and deepening darkness: 'The Paulicans, who flourished in the eastern Church during the 8th and following centuries, and the followers of the French priest, Peter of Bruys, who lived in the 12th century, definitely rejected infant baptism in favour of that of believers only'. The Paulicans 'rejected the priesthood, the sacraments... [They said that] baptism means only the baptism of the Spirit'. 'The Petrobrusians [argued that] the baptism of persons before they have reached the years of discretion is invalid. Believer's baptism was based upon Mark 16:16, and children, growing up, were [to be] re-baptised... The synod of Toulouse, 1119, [condemned] as heretics those who rejected... infant baptism' – thus showing the existence of such 'heretics'. Meanwhile, in 1025, in north-eastern France, some 'heretics' asserted that 'the mystery [the sacrament – the words are synonymous in this context] of baptism and of the body of the Lord are nothing'; that is, infant baptism and the Mass do not save: 'There are no sacraments in the holy Church by which one can attain unto salvation'. Another, that same year, was accused by Rome (pot and kettle!) of seeking 'to introduce ancient heresies into modern times', showing that anti-sacramental views were nothing new at the time.[31]

I said voices were raised against sacramentalism. Voices? If only it had been their *voices* which had been called upon to protest! These 'heretics', denying that salvation comes by the sacraments under priestly manipulation, suffered ferocious persecution even

---

sacramentalism. Over the long years after the Gregorian reform of the 11th century, it eventually emerged that the ultimate consequence of this position was the abolition of both clergy and sacraments in favour of direct contact of the believer with God... In this sacred world, any challenge to the ecclesiastical hierarchy was automatically a challenge to the secular hierarchy' (Malia p4).

[31] Underwood p20; Schaff Vol.4 p577; Vol.5 pp482-485; Verduin pp142-144; Cramp pp50-67; Williston Walker pp227-232; Atkinson pp43-45,50. Such 'heretics' (anti-sacramentalists) were called – confusingly, I am afraid – sacramentarians; I will avoid the term so as to minimise confusion. Moreover, since 'sacramentarian' seems to be a chameleon-like word, when quoting others I will translate.

unto death. No, let me put it bluntly! They were butchered – at the
hands of the sacramental Roman Church.[32]

And so to the 16th century and the Reformation. Martin Luther
was, in his early days, virtually one with the anti-sacramentalists.
But the Reformation rapidly polarised – even more strongly, if that
was possible – the divide between the sacramentalists and the anti-
sacramentalists. Luther, and all the other Reformers, including
Zwingli and Calvin – whatever they said when they started on
reformation (and later!)[33] – did not take long to come down on the
Constantinian, sacral, sacramentalist side,[34] leaving the Anabaptists

---

[32] I stand by my assertion even though some Baptist sacramentalists deny
this. Philip E.Thompson, for instance, dismissed John Leland for, as he
alleged, 'displaying inadequate historical awareness'. Thompson brushed
aside – as being guilty of characterisation – those Baptist writers who have
argued that the Pope has imposed upon the conscience of men: 'The
imposition upon the conscience by which Baptist interpreters have
characterised the Church of Rome...' (Thompson: 'Sacraments' pp50-52,
emphasis mine). It is no characterisation; it is a fact. Thousands have been
slaughtered for daring to challenge the sacramentalist Church. Thousands
upon thousands, I say.

[33] Luther, Zwingli and Calvin could argue biblically for faith before
baptism. For evidence for my claims in what follows, see my *Infant*. Luther
said of the Waldensians: 'These brethren hold to the idea that every man
must believe for himself and on the basis of his own faith receive baptism,
and that otherwise baptism... is useless. So far they believe and speak
correctly'. 'There is not sufficient evidence from Scripture that one might
justify the introduction of infant baptism at the time of the early Christians
after the apostolic period'. Zwingli: 'Nothing grieves me more than that at
the present I have to baptise children, for I know it ought not to be done'.
'If we were to baptise as Christ instituted it then we would not baptise any
person until he has reached the years of discretion; for I find it nowhere
written that infant baptism is to be practiced'. Calvin: 'It would appear that
baptism is not properly administered unless when it is preceded by faith'
(Verduin pp196,198-199,203-204; Calvin: *Commentaries* Vol.17 Part 1
p386).

[34] Luther: 'So much is evident that no one may venture with a good
conscience to reject or abandon infant baptism, which has for so long a time
been practiced'. Zwingli: 'One must practice infant baptism so as not to
offend our fellow men'. Calvin: 'Though infants are not yet of such an age
as to be capable of receiving the grace of God by faith', nevertheless 'it is

to maintain their anti-sacramentalist stance. The Reformers, in fact, set up a rival Christendom – Reformed as opposed to Roman – both maintaining the initiating rite of sacramental infant baptism. They might have congratulated themselves (and many of their followers still do) that they had reduced the Roman seven sacraments to two, but by retaining the very notion of a sacrament they effectively ensured the continuing deception of millions, especially by the first – sacramental baptism. Bill Jackson:

The inclusion of 'only' two of the sacraments might have seemed a victory, but in actual fact it was a defeat. The 'sacrament' of baptism was perhaps the more dangerous, for those with strong Reformation beliefs... Baptism was closely linked to becoming a member of the body of Christ, and the step from 'covenant' baptism of children of Christian parents to full-blown baptismal regeneration was but a small one, and it must be wondered if the Reformers ever grasped the evil of baptismal regeneration.[35] It certainly was a doctrinal folly, and paved the way for large denominations of baby-baptisers who, while professing the true facts of the gospel, perform at least confusing, and at most heretical, functions as they sprinkle water on babies to make them 'Christians'... C.H.Spurgeon said: 'Baptismal regeneration has sent more people to hell than any other false doctrine'.[36]

Precisely – but sadly – so.

But this is to get ahead of ourselves. We need to return to the 16th century.

While the Reformers kept the medieval practice of sacramental infant-baptism, the Anabaptists rightly rejected Christendom (both Romanist and Reformed) and its initiating sacrament.[37] For this,

---

not rash to administer baptism to infants' (Verduin pp198-199,203-204; Calvin: *Commentaries* Vol.17 Part 1 pp386).

[35] As I have argued in my *Infant*, and noted already in this work, it was the *ex opere operato* aspect of baptismal regeneration which the Reformers did not like, not baptismal regeneration itself.

[36] Jackson p112.

[37] The Baptist sacramentalist, Clark H.Pinnock, took the opposite view to the Anabaptists. He talked warmly of 'the remarkable and ancient consensus [in Christendom] that baptism and the Lord's supper were means of grace and works of God... to bestow the benefits of the work of Christ on the faithful'. He deplored Zwingli's rejection (when talking of the supper) of this 'remarkable and ancient consensus' in Christendom (Pinnock p9).

they were savagely abused by both parties. This grievous fact, I am glad to be able to say, is being increasingly recognised and admitted these days. In quoting the following, and I pay tribute to David Wright's frankness:

When the Anabaptist protest emerged... the new [that is, the Reformed] papalism alongside the old, as the Anabaptists [rightly] read it – joined ranks in suppressing the dissenters. The contemporary church still waits for appropriate acknowledgement by the Vatican and the worldwide Anglican and Reformed communions (the Lutherans of Germany have in good measure led the way, and the Swiss Reformed churches have followed more recently) of their forebears' scandalous mistreatment of the first significant modern advocates of long-lost dimensions of New Testament baptism. One legacy of the baptismal breach of the 16th century... has been the stubborn hauteur displayed towards Baptists and believer's baptism by infant-baptist churches and theologians... The obscuring [by infant baptisers] of a truer picture [of the history of baptism] derives ultimately from 16th century apologetic, both Catholic and Protestant, against the Anabaptists.

This testimony from David Wright is all the more important because of his own position as Emeritus Professor of Patristic and Reformed Christianity, Edinburgh – Wright was a Reformed historian holding to infant baptism. Because of this, his words have added weight. And, as he declared, it was their reaction 'against 16th century Anabaptists' and 'later Baptists', which drove infant baptisers to skew their theology and make 'exaggerated historical claims, especially about the New Testament era and the next centuries'. He went on:

The Anabaptists... opposed... infant baptism, including fundamentally the Church-State alliance and the use of the coercive powers of State authorities in defence of the new Protestantism... Rejection of infant baptism not only set the radicals against both the Old Church and the

---

Here we have a clear-cut choice. I make no bones about my opinion. I deplore Pinnock's preference for the medieval sacramentalism of Rome, and his passing over, as of no consequence, the many who gave their lives to oppose it in light of Scripture. On the basis of the 'remarkable and ancient consensus' he spoke of, we should, I suppose accept (and rejoice in) all sorts of diabolical nonsense – infant baptism by ventriloquism, transubstantiation, auricular confession, Mariolatry, prayers to saints, and a host of other anti-biblical corruptions.

new Evangelical Churches, but also put in jeopardy their belonging to the civil community [that is, they were to be – literally – exterminated!], co-terminus as it was with the infant-baptised Church of the city or the region. Religious dissent had inseparable social and political implications, and the Anabaptists suffered repression in many places. They interpreted their persecutions as a baptism of blood in which they were identified with the sufferings of Christ. Their afflictions were a further confirmation, a further seal, of their being members of Christ's body.[38]

The fact is, the Anabaptists did not only reject infant baptism. It was the entire Constantine set-up (Roman and Reformed) to which they were vehemently opposed.[39]

And, please note, it was not just *infant* baptism which the Anabaptists rejected; they rejected *sacramental* baptism.[40] While

---

[38] Wright: *What...?* pp4-6,18,29. As I have said, David Wright's own position lends weight to his just criticism of the Reformers. The same goes for Verduin.

[39] Indeed, Verduin, in part, using testimony from Luther, argued that at least some of the original Anabaptists were infant baptisers but rejected such a baptism when performed by a Constantinian Church (Roman or Reformed) – that is, the fallen Church (Verduin pp195-197). But, according to Wright, 'Verduin's evidence from Luther does not stand closer scrutiny' (Wright: 'One' p333). It goes without saying that Anabaptist thinking would have undergone a transition from that of the medieval Church to their settled position, but all the evidence I have seen shows that this period was exceedingly short. The Anabaptists rejected Constantine, yes, but they were opposed to infant baptism, full stop. Again, Verduin called 'the Donatists' 'the original Anabaptists' (Verduin p192), but this is too sweeping. The Donatists were infant baptisers who rejected Catholic infant-baptism. The Anabaptists rejected infant baptism and Constantine. The 16th century Constantine Churches (Rome and the Reformed) labelled the Anabaptists as Donatists, and this served as an atrocious excuse, wrongly to trap and then hammer the former with Justinian's laws against the latter. See Wright 'One' pp332-334. And protest against infant baptism and sacramentalism, as I have said, did not start with the Anabaptists. But earlier opponents of the Constantine system have for too long been ignored. Or, as has been said, 'one of the interesting [grievous, sad] aspects of Reformation polemics is that medieval heretics – as earlier opponents of the Papacy – have been much more favourably treated by church historians than have the Anabaptists, even though they may have shared ideas in common with the latter' (Friesen p143).

nobody could pretend that the Anabaptists spoke with one voice, anti-sacramentalism was clearly stated by the overwhelming majority of them. Leaving aside their stance against infant baptism – which is a byword – take Balthasar Hubmaier who, in 1525, could speak of baptism in terms of 'the meaning of this sign and symbol... the pledge of faith'.[41] No sacramentalism here. Later that same year, he wrote:

Every devout Christian who permits himself to be baptised with water should beforehand have a good conscience towards God through a complete understanding of the word of God; that is, that [he] knows and is sure that he has a gracious, kindly God, through the resurrection of Christ... Then afterwards follows water baptism; not that through it the soul is cleansed, but [it is] the 'yes' [of] a good conscience towards God, previously given inwardly by faith. Therefore the baptism in water is called a baptism... for the pardon of sins. Not that through it or by it sins are forgiven, but upon the strength of the inward 'yes' of the heart, which a man outwardly testifies to on submitting to water baptism,

---

[40] C.Arnold Snyder: 'Anabaptists everywhere were agreed that neither priests nor sacraments were capable of conveying God's grace *ex opere operato* (by the performance of the act)'. I pause. This needs nuancing. Calvin, as I have shown in my *Infant*, struggled hard to keep clear of *ex opere operato*. But this is not the point at issue here. Calvin was a sacramentalist; the Anabaptists were not. To let Snyder continue: 'This rejection of sacramental efficacy was the first step towards Anabaptist baptism, for if the water could not convey grace or confer salvation... on what basis was infant baptism to be defended?... Although different answers to this question came from Lutherans to Reformed to Anabaptists' – not least, as I have shown, by individual Reformed teachers who have contradicted (and still do contradict) themselves – 'the posing of the question was common to all Evangelical groups that questioned the medieval sacramental understanding... The anti-sacramentalism of the Anabaptists identifies their point of departure within the general Evangelical protest of the 16th century'. Even though, as always, it is a little risky to generalise concerning the radicals, 'all Anabaptists – excepting perhaps Pilgram Marpeck – were in essential agreement with Ulrich Zwingli in their radical rejection of the sacramental mediation of grace' (Snyder pp73,223).
[41] Estep: *Renaissance* p210.

saying that he believes and is sure in his heart that his sins are forgiven through Jesus Christ.[42]

As William R.Estep noted, 'according to Hubmaier, baptism is not a part of the saving process but an act in which the new disciple confesses his allegiance to Jesus Christ'. As Hubmaier said:

Baptism... is when a man first confesses his sins, and pleads guilty; then believes in the forgiveness of his sins through Jesus Christ and therefore proceeds to live according to the rule of Christ by the grace and strength given him by God the Father, the Son and the Holy Ghost. Then he professes this publicly, in the eyes of men, by the outward baptism of water.[43]

Hubmaier also spoke of 'the baptism of the Spirit'. 'It is an inward enlightenment of our hearts, given to us of the Holy Spirit, through the living word of God', he said. As for 'water baptism':

It is an outward and public testimony to the inward baptism of the Spirit. A man receives it [water baptism] by receiving the water, when he, in the sight of all, acknowledges his sins. He also testifies hereby that he believes in the pardon of these sins through the death and resurrection of our Lord Jesus Christ. Then he has outwardly designated and enrolled himself and has been incorporated into the community of the church by baptism.[44]

Take another Anabaptist, Conrad Grebel. In addition to his clear condemnation of *infant* baptism – expressed thus: 'Infant baptism is a senseless, blasphemous abomination, contrary to all Scripture' – Grebel made no less clear his anti-sacramental view of the baptism of believers:

The Scripture describes baptism for us thus: That it signifies that, by faith and the blood of Christ, sins have been washed away for him who is baptised, changes his mind, and believes before and after; that it signifies that a man is dead and ought to be dead to sin and walk in newness of life and spirit, and that he shall certainly be saved if, according to this meaning, by inner baptism he lives his faith; so that the water does not confirm or increase [his] faith, as the scholars at

---

[42] Estep: *Renaissance* p211. I will return to the passage Hubmaier had in mind; namely, 1 Pet. 3:21.
[43] Estep: *Renaissance* pp211-212.
[44] Estep: *Anabaptist* pp154-167.

Wittenberg say, and [does not] give very great comfort [nor] is it the final refuge on the death bed.[45] Also baptism does not save, as Augustine, Tertullian, Theophylact and Cyprian have taught.[46]

While Dirk Philips, another Anabaptist, did use the word 'sacraments' when describing baptism and the Lord's supper, even so, he was clear:

The penitent, believing and reborn children of God must be baptised, and for them the supper of the Lord pertains (Matt. 3:16; 28:19; Mark 1:9; Acts 2:41; 8:12; 10:48; 16:15; 18:8; 22:16). These two symbols Christ gave and left behind and subjoined to the gospel because of the unspeakable grace of God and his covenant, to remind us thereof with visible symbols, to put it before our eyes, and to confirm it. In the first place [he ordained] baptism, to remind us that he himself baptises within and in grace accepts sinners, forgives them all their sins, cleanses them with his blood (Matt. 3:11; John 3:5), bestows upon them all his righteousness and the fulfilling of the law, and sanctifies them with his Spirit (Rev. 1:5; 1 Cor. 3:23).[47]

In short, as Estep concluded, 'the Anabaptists could [would] not justify practicing baptism on sacramental grounds'.[48]

And so to the 17th century. The teachers of the new Reformed Christendom, whether Lutheran, Calvinist, Anglican or Puritan, continued to claim they could initiate infants into the Church – indeed, into Christ – by the so-called baptism of infants. Even so, with the rise of the Baptists in England/Holland in the early years of the century, anti-sacramentalist believer's-baptism stood rock-like in this sea of sacramentalism. And as the decades passed into centuries, Baptist anti-sacramentalism grew and seemed secure.

And herein, perhaps, the seeds of complacency were sown, germinated and grew. Sadly, with the coming of the 20th century, things began to change. Then began the rise of... all things... *Baptist* sacramentalism. Not only did it start; it grew, *and continues to grow*

---

[45] I will return to this vital point.

[46] Grebel in G.H.Williams p80. For Grebel, 'baptism signifies the forgiveness of sins, an inner transformation of mind and heart, and a pledge of a life of discipleship' (Estep: *Anabaptist* pp150-154). Signifies! Baptism signifies forgiveness of sins; it does not convey it.

[47] Philips in G.H.Williams pp242-243. Baptism confirms *the gospel*, not *us*.

[48] Estep: *Anabaptist* p172.

in influence. And, as night follows day, it will lead to a corresponding rise in sacerdotalism.

Such an assertion touches a sore spot for sacramental Baptists – witness the way they keep stressing that they are not sacerdotalists.[49] But they deny it in vain. Sacramentalism always leads to sacerdotalism. Already we are seeing clear signs of the development, among sacramental Baptists, of a priestly, professional class which administers the sacraments and can 'explain' what is happening to the uninitiated 'ordinary' believers who, left to themselves, would not be able to work it out for themselves.[50]

So Baptist sacramentalism. This is the oxymoron I wish to examine.

* * *

Stanley K.Fowler is one of these leading Baptists scholars promoting sacramentalism today. William H. Brackney, in his Foreword to Fowler's recently (2006) published *More than a Symbol*, wrote:

---

[49] Colwell's assertion that Aquinas' qualification – that since only God can cause the (supposed) grace in the sacrament – 'affirms the sacramental while avoiding the sacerdotal' (Colwell p235), is manifestly false in the light of history. But Colwell is not alone. Stanley J.Grenz in 2006: 'Although a large number of Baptists today... continue to eschew the language of "sacrament", recent decades have witnessed a growing interest among some to recapture a depth of [sacramental] meaning in the Church's rites that they sense their forebears had discarded in a more "rationalistic" era, without undermining the important [and proper] critique of sacramentarianism [sacerdotalism] offered by their [Baptist] tradition' (Grenz p83). A.C.Underwood had already made the claim in 1937, repeated ten years later: 'Baptists are "sacramentalists" though they reject sacerdotalism' (Fowler: *More* p98; Underwood p274). See also Thompson: 'Sacraments' pp37-38. This, in my view, is whistling in the dark. Sacramentalism, once adopted, takes over, and inevitably leads to sacerdotalism. I have fully argued this in previous works. Baptists, down the centuries, have seen the twin dangers, and published vehemently against them, as sacramental Baptists admit. See Michael Walker pp8,85-87.

[50] For more on this unbiblical dependence of the 'ordinary' believer on the explanations supplied by the professionals, see the extended note on p301.

Helpful to those in other traditions than the Baptists is Dr Fowler's coverage of responses to British Baptist sacramental thought, and his comparison of the Baptists to contemporary Protestant and Catholic thinkers. In so doing, he has renewed the dialogue over baptism, the Holy Spirit and ecclesiology. The Christian community in general will profit from the contrasts he draws with other usages of sacramental terminology. What is really important about this book is that it opens new possibilities of serious theological dialogue for a Christian community that values experience and symbol. It is to the credit of the British Baptist sacramentalist movement that they have carried forth an understanding of baptism as an act of powerful theological meaning. Along with a minority of North American Baptist thinkers, British Baptists have succeeded in providing an agenda[51] to restore meaning to an ancient practice of the Church, and to engage a movement known for its theological obscurantism and radical individualism.[52]

Let me translate: British Baptist sacramentalists have an agenda. They want to introduce (not 'restore', let me stress with as much force as I can – 'introduce') sacramentalism among Baptists. They want to tackle (and overcome) the arguments of those Baptists who, the sacramentalists allege, have no appetite for fresh light (which, of course, goes to prove that sacramentalism is a novelty among Baptists), but rather prefer to go on in their hide-bound, stubborn

---

[51] There is a Baptist sacramentalist movement, please note, and they do have an agenda, as I have claimed.

[52] Brackney: 'Foreword' in Fowler: *More* xiv. An 'obscurantist' is 'one who opposes knowledge and enlightenment' (see *The Concise*). So now we know. Sacramental Baptists regard anti-sacramentalists like me as being against knowledge and further light. Well, let me say in response that I am one with John Robinson in his farewell to those sailing to America in 1620, speaking of God having more light to break out of his word. Let's have all the biblical light that Baptist sacramentalists can shine upon us – we can't have too much of it! But light is one thing; darkness is another. The only light which is light is *biblical* light. As for labelling people like me, note how Freeman accounted for the 'real absence' of the symbolic view of the Lord's supper by linking the Radicals (Anabaptists) with Gnosticism, Marcionism and Donatism (Freeman pp203-204). Find as many clubs as you can to bludgeon anti-sacramentalists with, seems to be the watchword. If the last one didn't do the trick, the next might. It has been Rome's way, the Reformers' way, and now, it seems, the sacramental Baptists' way. There is nothing new under the sun (Eccles. 1:9)!

ways, cutting themselves off from the mainstream of the Church which stems from the Fathers.

So now we know.

Well, I am one of those so-called obscurantist, individualistic radicals. And, as I have said, I, too, have an agenda. Let me re-state it. I want to do what I can to warn Baptists of this sacramental tsunami which is about to engulf them. Like a literal tsunami, whose initial movements may occur unnoticed far out to sea, deep in the trackless wastes of the ocean, so the recent rising and swelling of Baptist sacramentalism has gone virtually unnoticed by the overwhelming majority of Baptists. But just as the tidal waves sweep remorselessly towards land – where they wreak massive havoc – so it will be in the spiritual sense. Because of this, I want to do what I can to prevent the scriptural practice of 'the baptism of believers' being swept away in a tide of sacramentalism. Maybe, changing the figure, I should have said I want to do what I can to prevent the contamination – the breakdown – of believer's baptism by the insidious injection of sacramental poison into the biblical blood-stream.

Let me tackle head-on a criticism levelled at people like me. Fowler deplored that 'the doctrine of baptism does not occupy a central place in Baptist theology' – Fowler taking 'doctrine of baptism' to mean 'the interpretation of the divine-human encounter which occurs in baptism'. Baptists, Fowler said, 'have been slow to develop a theology of baptism', with no 'positive statement of what is presumed to happen in baptism'.[53] Anthony R.Cross, similarly: 'Baptists have been strongest on the subjects and mode of baptism, but weakest on what baptism actually means'.[54]

Let me reply. Speaking for myself, I gladly own the charges. I am not in the least apologetic about it. I say nothing about what baptism *means* because it doesn't *mean* anything – in the sense that sacramentalists use the word. Baptism *represents* something – and, I

---

[53] Fowler: *More* p1.
[54] Cross: 'The Evangelical sacrament' p196. See also Beasley-Murray: *Baptism Today and Tomorrow* pp80-88.

think, most Baptists have been exceedingly clear about *that*.[55] I have tried to be.[56] Since Scripture does not teach any such encounter as the sacramentalists claim, there is, therefore, no biblical theology to explain it. The New Testament does not teach a 'theology of baptism';[57] it teaches a theology of regeneration and conversion.[58] Fowler, censuring this notion, was pleased (from his point of view) to record that Baptist sacramentalism 'provides a way to formulate a baptismal theology... as opposed to the common tendency to develop a theology of conversion'.[59]

Well, that's clear enough. The cat is out of the bag. The agenda is being spelled out. The battle lines are being drawn. We cannot complain. We know the crux. It is a theology of baptism *versus* a theology of conversion. Reader, I know which side I am on. How about you? On which side are you?

---

[55] And not only Baptists. Thomas Goodwin: 'The eminent thing signified and represented in baptism, is not simply the blood of Christ, as it washes us from sin; but there is a further representation therein of Christ's death, burial and resurrection in [our] being first buried under water, and then rising out of it... a representation of a communion with Christ in... his death and resurrection. Therefore it is said: "We are BURIED with him in baptism"; and "wherein you also are RISEN with him". It is not simply said, *like as* he was buried and rose, but *with him*. So that our communion and one-ness with him in his resurrection is [effected by spiritual baptism – regeneration – and is] represented to us therein [that is, in water baptism], and not only our conformity or likeness unto him therein. And so [water] baptism represents this to us' (quoted by Newton p20, emphasis his).

[56] In previous books and below.

[57] I will look at all the cardinal (and some other) passages cited by Baptist sacramentalists, and show why I think they do not teach that God is active in water baptism in the sense sacramentalists claim. In other words, why there is no 'theology of water baptism' in Scripture. Let me make my position clear. My main concern here is not to prove there is no theology of baptism. I simply do not find it in Scripture!

[58] Sinners need to be regenerated and converted before any talk of baptism. And this puts the finger on the spot.

[59] Fowler: *More* pp250-251. See my *Infant* where I trace out, under infant baptism, the drift away from the biblical idea of 'conversion' – especially involving some kind of 'crisis' – into a 'process', ill-defined at that. Sacramentalism is bound to lead to this result. Baptist sacramentalism will! It is already! I will return to this vital theme.

Before I move on, I need to raise a serious issue connected with this. I have just noted that Fowler could speak of 'the common tendency' among 'traditional' Baptists 'to develop a theology of conversion'. An excellent observation. But I wonder if this is continuing among 'traditional' Baptists, with the same confidence as in the past? I fear it is not. Let me explain. In churches which practice only believer's baptism, it is easy to develop a culture in which people 'ask to be baptised', young people in particular. So what's wrong with that? Nothing – as long as the emphasis is biblically placed; namely, on conversion. Otherwise, 'asking for baptism' might soon degenerate into a social affair. Might? I fear I see straws in the wind – hefty straws in a rising wind at that![60] I will return to this weighty point.

Let me anticipate another criticism. Some might dismiss my book as written by one with a very low view of baptism – the inevitable consequence, they might add, of my anti-sacramentalism.

Very well. Then I will briefly explain what I think about baptism. Baptism is a standing command – an ordinance. An ordinance, I repeat. There is nothing optional about baptism. It is an ordinance of Christ, an obligation which he has laid upon all his people throughout this age. I agree with those (sacramentalists or otherwise) who assert that the New Testament does not know of an unbaptised believer. I, too, am convinced that if someone in those days did not express his faith by baptism, he would not have been treated as a believer.[61] Of course, the exception – the thief on the

---

[60] A friend commented that it was happening in his mother's time – in the 1930s.

[61] Wright: *What....?* p36; Cross: 'Pneumatological' pp161,165,167. But I am puzzled by some sacramental-Baptist statements in this area. In light of Matt. 28:19-20; Mark 16:15-16; Acts 16:31-34; Rom. 10:9-10, how could Stanley E.Porter say: 'One might think of baptism as wholly symbolic in significance, but it is then odd that the only act associated with conversion-initiation is the singular rite of baptism' (Porter p125). Why is it odd? I don't get it. Sacramentalists mistakenly talk of baptism as a seal. Elsewhere, I have fully set out my reasons for denying this. But granting, for sake of argument, they are right, what else do they want or need in addition to a 'seal' to authenticate conversion? Beasley-Murray, Porter's fellow-sacramentalist, it seems, would not have agreed with him: 'The gospel exercises its radical influence in a man's life when he receives it in faith; he becomes one with Christ when he submits to him in faith; for Paul

cross – was unbaptised for obvious reasons! Similarly, I am persuaded that baptism in the New Testament was only for believers. A baptised unbeliever (Simon in Acts 8, for instance) got short shrift when discovered. Because of the importance of this question of 'ordinance', let me pause and say more about it.

Baptism is an ordinance, not a sacrament

First, the very notion of an 'ordinance'. Since, as will become clear, I have much to say by way of disagreement with Beasley-Murray, I am glad to be able to quote him – and endorse him – on baptism as an ordinance:

We should observe that the authority of... baptism is of the weightiest order. It rests on the command of the risen Lord after his achieving redemption and receiving authority over the entire cosmos [Matt. 28:18-20]; it is integrated with the commission to preach the good news to the world, and it is enforced by his own example at the beginning of his messianic ministry. Such a charge is too imperious to be ignored or modified. It behoves us to adhere to it and conform to it as God gives grace.[62]

Baptism is an ordinance because Christ commanded believers to be baptised. Ordinance – command. And we must never forget the stress laid by Christ upon obedience to his commands (John 13 – 16, for instance). In other words, by calling baptism an 'ordinance', I am stressing the biblical concept of 'obligation'. Believers are *obliged* to be baptised; there is, I repeat, nothing optional about it. Although, according to Mark 16:16, there is nothing saving in baptism, Christ commanded believers to be baptised as the outward testimony of an inward experience. Combining this with Rom. 10:9-10,[63] where we are taught that an outward confession is essential, as

---

the decisive expression of such faith is baptism' (Beasley-Murray: 'Baptism in the Epistles of Paul' p148). See also Gilmore p65; Fowler: 'Oxymoron' pp130-131.

[62] Beasley-Murray: *Baptism in the New Testament* p92.

[63] But as for Rom. 10:9-10, Beasley-Murray went further than justified. Fowler approved of his seeing baptism 'as instrumental in the reception of salvation'. In Beasley-Murray's own words: 'The enigma of the relation of the Pauline teaching on salvation by faith and his high estimate of the value

Spurgeon said: 'The promise of salvation is not made to a faith which is never avowed'. And: 'God requires [baptism in water], and though men are saved without any baptism... [and] though baptism is not saving, yet, if men would be saved, they must not be disobedient'.[64]

Secondly, we must never divorce *obedience* to Christ and *love* for Christ: 'If you love me', he declared, 'keep my commandments... He who has my commandments and keeps them, it is he who loves me... If anyone loves me, he will keep my word... If you keep my commandments, you will abide in my love... You are my friends if you do whatever I command you' (John 14:15,21,23; 15:10,14). As the apostle maintained: 'This is the love of God, that we keep his commandments' (1 John 5:3; see also 1 John 2:5; 4:12; 2 John 6). Just a moment ago, I spoke about the concept of 'obligation'. In truth, it is the concept (not concepts) of 'obligation' and 'love'. In the relation between believers and Christ, 'obligation' and 'love' are virtually synonymous; at least, you can't have one without the other. As for the ordinance of baptism, believers are *obliged* to be baptised, obliged because they *love* their Saviour. It is because they love him, that they submit to Christ's command.

Thirdly, this question of 'ordinances' brings us to the heart of the issue. Ordinances. Here we come to a great divide. It is not merely a question of words. I, and people like me, take baptism and the Lord's supper as Christ's two ordinances,[65] symbolic acts which Christ commanded his people to do in order to represent and demonstrate, by the physical, the spiritual realities they have already experienced. Sacramentalists, on the other hand, claim that God is at work in these two ordinances, actually conveying effective grace to those undertaking the acts. The former speak of 'ordinances', and

---

of baptism come most nearly to solution in this verse' (Beasley-Murray: 'Baptism in the Epistles of Paul' pp129-130; Fowler: 'Oxymoron' p134). I will have more to say on Paul's so-called 'high estimate' of baptism.

[64] Spurgeon: *Early* p147; Grass and Randall p59.

[65] R.F.Chambers, interestingly, thought preaching was the first ordinance, making three altogether (Wood, unnumbered pages, but taken from the second page of the text).

often abhor 'sacraments' (as I do); the latter much prefer 'sacraments'.[66]

I am struck by the subtle, gradual – but far-reaching – 'adjustment' which Grenz was able to pull off in a few words. Let me tease it out.

He started well: 'Baptism and the Lord's supper serve as symbols of the relationship of believers to God and to one another'.

I pause. Excellent. But see how things developed! 'These acts symbolise, vividly portray and ritually enact...'. Enact what? 'These acts... ritually enact the participation of the community as a whole in the divine story'.

I pause again. Here we have the notion of 'participation'. Now for the next stage:

Participation in baptism and the Lord's supper facilitates symbolic participation in the saving events to which they point... Participants in these acts enact the gospel declaration that they died with Christ... The connection between rite and reality is stronger than mere announcement, however... We symbolically experience both Christ's death and his resurrection.

This soon led on to:

Through the Church's rites, the Spirit confirms in us... mediating to us a sense of our ultimate identity...[67]

It was not long after this that Grenz was using words like 'effects... bestows... conferred... experienced... participation... enter... participation... experience'.

In conclusion:

When baptism and the Lord's supper truly function in this manner as Church rites... these ordinances are well able to carry the sacramental significance intended by the Lord.[68]

Hey presto! In short compass, a seamless transformation of a symbol into a sacrament![69] It reminds me of the children's word-

---

[66] See Grenz pp76-84,89.

[67] In addition to 'confirms in us', note the word 'media' or 'mediating'. We will meet it repeatedly. Media? 'The means by which something is communicated... the intervening substance' (*The Concise*).

[68] Grenz pp91-95.

game – change 'black' into 'white', one letter at a time, making a proper word at each stage.

Having addressed this question of baptism as an ordinance, let me now go on with setting out what I think about baptism, leaving you, reader, to judge whether or not I have a low view of it.

Baptism as I see it

Baptism is one of the two ordinances Christ established for his people; baptism is experienced but once – upon profession of faith[70] – whereas the Lord's supper is to be regularly repeated throughout the believer's life; while baptism is an individual experience, the supper is a corporate act of the local church, and serves to nourish its unity. Both are symbolic acts. But while the grace represented in the symbols is not conveyed by these symbols,[71] nor in the observance, this does not mean they are pointless. In the physical symbols, the believer sees – represented before his eyes – the spiritual realities of his redemption in Christ, and so finds spiritual

---

[69] See also 'conveying', 'bestowal', 'effects' and 'effective' in Fowler: 'Oxymoron' pp131,138-139,142,149.

[70] For more on the way sacramentalism skews the biblical order of faith before baptism, see the extended note on p303. Sacramentalism is the root of the trouble, as I keep saying, and shall keep saying.

[71] Contrary to Richard Sibbes: 'The sacraments are mysteries, because in the one, under bread and wine, there is conveyed to us the benefits of Christ's body broken and his blood shed' (Sibbes p462). Certainly not. *Salvation* is not *conveyed* to us by the Lord's supper! And I disagree with Calvin: 'I do not... deny that the grace of Christ is applied to us in the sacraments' (Calvin: *Commentaries* Vol.20 Part 2 p239). I do. Of course, I fully accept – as I have stated – that obedience to Christ in baptism (and the supper) brings benefit and Christ's blessing. But Calvin meant far more than that! And so, I say, I disagree with him. Words are important. Take the supper. Christ is *represented*, not *presented*. 'This is my body which is given *for* you; do this in *remembrance* of me' (Luke 22:19; 1 Cor. 11:24-25). It is **not**: 'This is my body which is given *to* you; do this to *receive* me'. 'The ordinances... are rightly described as a special means of grace – but [they] do not constitute a means of special grace' (*We Believe* pp28-29).

instruction, edification and encouragement.[72] There is, furthermore, enormous benefit to be gained by sheer obedience to Christ – 'Whatever he says to you, do it' (John 2:5) – even if this should mean being plunged in water! The ordinances also serve as a kind of physical preaching of the gospel to any unconverted who might observe them.[73] Baptism serves another purpose also; a very important purpose, at that. It leads the believer into local church membership,[74] including the Lord's supper.[75]

---

[72] Take the Reformed infant-baptiser, Richard L.Pratt: 'The visible rite of baptism is added to the preaching of the word in order to confirm what is preached and what we experience through the inward work of the Holy Spirit in connection with preaching' (Armstrong p62). While I dissent from the 'confirm' (if it is taken to mean 'confirm *us*'), there is no nonsense here (at least) about *conveying* grace – baptism confirms *what is preached*, and demonstrates *what has already been experienced*. This is undoubtedly the New Testament position. If this had remained the practice in the churches, my book would never have been written. See later for my comments on the isolated verses which are claimed to reverse this order between faith and baptism. I dispute the deductions sacramentalists make from the verses.

[73] But I do not place the ordinances above preaching; nor even equal to it. Furthermore, I think the word should be preached at the ordinances. Sacramentalism is bound to diminish preaching in favour of the sacraments. It happens among the Reformed sacramentalists as I have already shown in my *Infant*. It will happen among Baptist sacramentalists too. I will return to this. Earlier, in an extended note, I quoted Haymes: 'A theology that is sacramental produces a strong theology of preaching... a non-sacramental theology diminishes preaching' (Haymes p264). I said I would return to it. I do so now. I strongly disagree with it, and will have more to say on it in the final chapter. For now, however, I want to contradict myself and admit I find some of the things Haymes said strike a chord with me. I agree wholeheartedly, for instance, with his statement: 'The purpose of preaching is not fundamentally the giving of information. It is a different, yet related, task to that of teaching. It is not... the recalling of history alone. It is a work of God effecting a divine encounter, a meeting... So, argues H.H.Farmer: "Preaching is telling me something. But it is not merely telling me something. It is God actively probing me, challenging my will, calling on me for decision, offering me his succour"... Thus a sermon is not a lecture. It is an event' (Haymes p270). I empathise with this. See Prov. 29:18. See my forthcoming book on Sandemanianism.

[74] For more on baptism and local church membership, see the extended note on p304.

Let Spurgeon's comments on Ananias' command to Saul, 'Arise, and be baptised, and wash away your sins', sum this up:

The tendency with many good evangelists is to say nothing upon that point. The main thing is to get this man to be a believer in the Lord Jesus Christ, but to say: 'Arise, and be baptised', is not that far less important? Brethren, we have nothing to do with altering Christ's message, but are bound to deliver it as a whole, without addition or diminution. The tendency everywhere is to say: 'Baptism should not be mentioned; it is sectarian'. Who said so? If our Lord commanded it, who dares call it sectarian? We are not commanded to preach a part of the gospel, but the whole of the gospel; and this Ananias did. Is it not written: 'He that believes and is baptised shall be saved'? Why omit one clause? I question whether God's blessing has not been withheld from some teachers and preachers because they have failed to repeat their message in its entirety. A brother will write to me next week and say: 'I am sorry that I cannot circulate your sermon, because you allude to baptism'. My dear brother, if you cannot circulate the sermon, I must be content without your kind help; but I cannot amend the Lord's word to please the best man upon the earth.

Spurgeon went on:

What prominence is given to baptism here [in Acts 22:16]! We should greatly err if we believed in baptismal regeneration, or even in the efficacy of washing in water for the removal of sin; but, on the other hand, we are not to place in the background an ordinance which, by the language of Scripture, is placed in the forefront. Ananias said to Paul: 'Arise and be baptised, and wash away your sins'. And this tallies with that other text: 'He that believes and is baptised shall be saved'. In both of these passages, the Lord puts a special honour upon baptism, and it would be ill for us to neglect that which he so evidently esteems. Do not make any mistake, and imagine that immersion in water can wash away sin; but do remember that if the Lord puts this outward profession side by side with the washing away of sins, it is not a trifling matter. Remember that other text: 'With the heart man believes unto righteousness, and with the mouth confession is made unto salvation'. Faith must be followed by obedience, or it cannot be sincere; do, then, what Jesus bids you. That is not, however, my point. I want to urge upon you that you should always speak the Lord's word faithfully, and be true to that which the Lord reveals to you, even to the jots and tittles. In these days there is much talk about 'undenominationalism', and in

---

[75] For more on strict or closed communion, see the extended note on p305.

that talk there is much to be admired; but the danger is lest [that?] we should on all hands begin to pare away a little from the word of God for the sake of an imaginary unity. The suggestion is that one is to give up this, and another is to give up that; but I say to you – give up nothing which your Lord commands.[76]

Quite!

Beasley-Murray:

If we want apostolic baptism, we must have apostolic preaching; and that includes in the proclamation of the gospel an affirmation that the hearing of faith will express itself in the obedience of baptism.[77]

Whether or not all this is dismissed as a low view of baptism, although I have not stopped to set out the biblical arguments, it is, as I see it, the biblical position.[78]

Having said that much by way of introduction, it is high time we got to grips with Baptist sacramentalism.

I begin with its history. When did it start?

---

[76] Spurgeon: *Metropolitan* Vol.31 pp250-251.

[77] Beasley-Murray: *Baptism Today and Tomorrow* p96.

[78] I emphasise the 'biblical'. If I *was* writing about believer's baptism, I would not depend on history. It would be no part of my case to try to establish an unbroken line of believer's baptism from the apostles to the Anabaptists. I know there is little documentary evidence to support it. But there may be reasons. Leaving to one side – for the moment – the time of the very early Fathers, it is to acknowledge the obvious to say that for at least 1400 years after the apostles, the *biblical* ordinance was carried out only by the minority. Furthermore, it was the practice of a desperately persecuted minority. 'Heretics' on the run – and worse – can hardly be criticised for not retiring to the study (which they did not possess) to set out their case in writing, especially in those days without easy writing-facilities, PCs, CD ROMs, memory sticks, printers (indeed, a printing-press!), print-on-demand, internet, e-mails, mobile phones and all the rest. To cap it all, can it really be thought that Rome – who tried to destroy the 'heretics' – would have preserved their writings? In saying all this, however, I am not conceding that there was no witness to believer's baptism in those days. But my case would not depend on it.

But just to repeat myself: I am not setting out what I see as the biblical – the Baptist – position. See my earlier note on my confessedly-negative purpose.

Sacramental Baptist Claims Based on the
17th, 18th and 19th Centuries

I myself would not start with history. The Bible would be my starting point. Establish the biblical principles first! History, however, seems to play a very important part in the Baptist-sacramentalist's case. Take Fowler, for instance. In his *More than a Symbol*, because he hoped to show that, right from their rise in the 17th century, there have been Baptists who have taken a sacramental view of the ordinance, he opened with a long and detailed look at Baptist history.[1] Sometimes nearer the surface than at other times, sometimes more clearly stated, sometimes less so, this sacramentalism has always existed among Baptists. So Fowler claimed.

I dispute this.[2]

---

[1] I will be engaging principally with Fowler's *More* because, as far as I know, at the time of writing, it is the latest and fullest attempt to establish a sacramentalist Baptist line of descent from the 17th century. And sacramental Baptists seem to be using his work as an authority – see, for instance, Cross and Thompson: *Baptist Sacramentalism* pp4,10,82,84,129-150,154,159,174,263; Cross: 'Dispelling'.

[2] I suppose I come under Thompson's assessment: 'Many Baptists reject even the possibility of a historic sacramentalism in their heritage'. Speaking for myself, while I do not reject the *possibility* of sacramentalism among Baptists, I say it is a contradiction in terms. I am certainly included in what Thompson quoted from Cross: 'The juxtaposition of "Baptist" and "sacramentalism" is unthinkable to many Baptists. The dominant belief is that Baptists early and late have been either non-sacramentalist or anti-sacramentalist'. Thompson (continuing my earlier extract) went on to explain why 'many Baptists reject even the possibility of a historic sacramentalism in their heritage'. 'They do so because they tend to retroject their own sensitivities and sensibilities onto their forebears' (Thompson: 'Sacraments' p37). Oh? Might there not be other reasons? Nevertheless, it is good medicine, and I, and those like me, must not push it aside untasted. But may I suggest that sacramental Baptists take a sip of it, too, as well as

For a start, I find it significant that Fowler chose the 17th century as 'foundational'. What about the Anabaptists who were baptising believers-only nearly a hundred years before?[3] Again, why is it that the 20th century Baptist scholars who began and developed the sacramentalist movement, did not do as Fowler and start with their history? *Indeed, why did they never try to argue their case from this supposed history of sacramentalism among the Baptists?* Fowler himself admitted it.[4] But, having owned the fact, unfortunately he drew the wrong conclusion. Instead of recognising that there was so little sacramental literature for those 20th century sacramentalists to draw on – and what little did exist was so feeble compared to the sacramentalism which the sacramentalists now wanted to promulgate, and therefore would do their cause little or no good – he clung to his view that there *was* such a source, and deplored the fact that these 20th century Baptist sacramentalists did not use it by going back to their own history, but 'were... much more concerned to interact with scholars of other traditions than to interact with earlier Baptist literature. Consequently, they failed to demonstrate that they were legitimate heirs of an early Baptist tradition'.[5]

In other words, according to Fowler, the sacramentalists could have demonstrated – and should have demonstrated (it was remiss

---

ladling it out to anti-sacramentalist Baptists like me? It is to be hoped that none of us 'retroject our sensitivities and sensibilities onto our forebears'.

[3] Significantly, Fowler almost totally ignored the history of the Anabaptists which pre-dated the rise of the Baptists by 80 years. And in what he did say, he took the line which I will note when I set out my summary of his arguments (see below): 'It would be a mistake to conclude that since [the] Baptists shared the Mennonite rejection of infant baptism, they therefore shared their non-sacramental interpretation of the efficacy of baptism' (Fowler: *More* p11). Why? Why would it be a mistake? Incidentally, here is an admission that the Mennonites were non-sacramental. See the previous chapter for extracts from the Anabaptists themselves.

[4] Fowler also noted the same lack of appeal to history by the anti-sacramentalists of the 18th century (Fowler: *More* pp53-54,129). Could it be that these 18th century Baptists did not regard the 17th century as foundational – that Scripture was far more important to them? Could it be that they were not going down Fowler's route? Could it be that instead of starting with history and moving on to Scripture, they began with Scripture and left it at that?

[5] Fowler: *More* pp129,155.

of them not to have done so) – that *they* were the true heirs of the early Baptist tradition.

This can be challenged.

There is, I say, a very simple explanation for this lack of appeal to history – which Fowler could not, or did not want to see; namely, no such sacramental-Baptist literature – as that produced by infant baptisers in those centuries – exists. *There was no such 'early Baptist tradition' of sacramentalism.* Rather, there is only a minuscule amount of evidence to be found among the earlier Baptists for the kind of sacramentalism Fowler and his colleagues are calling for. This 'evidence' for a long-standing sacramentalism among Baptists is, to say the least, underwhelming! As he himself said – on the very same page – this 20th century Baptist sacramentalism was a 'modification of Baptist theology', a 'conceptual shift', a 'new Baptist paradigm';[6] a 'shift' and 'new' for the Baptists, but not, of course, for the Romanist, Orthodox, Reformed (Puritan and Presbyterian) and Anglican – where there is an abundant sacramentalist literature to draw upon. Indeed, this body of literature is swelling by the day – as it now is for Baptist sacramentalists. As above, Fowler noted that Baptist sacramentalists 'were... much more concerned to interact with scholars of other

---

[6] Fowler: *More* p155. Pinnock noted Grenz' assertion in 1994 of 'a willingness in the Free Churches to change on' sacramentalism (Pinnock p18). I stress the 'change'. Grenz (and Pinnock) were admitting that sacramentalism among the Free Churches is a 'change', a departure, something new. Grenz in 2006: 'Recent decades have witnessed a growing interest among some to recapture a depth of meaning in the Church's rites, that they sense their forebears had discarded in a more "rationalistic" era' (Grenz p83). Quite! The rise of Baptist sacramentalism, as I have said, is a 20th century phenomenon. I do not accept the implication that sacramentalism was the norm of the Baptists of the 17th century, and that the more 'rationalistic' Baptists of the 18th and 19th centuries rejected it. The sacramentalism the Baptists rejected was the sacramentalism of Rome and the Reformed, and they rejected it from the 16th century. Indeed, right from its rise, from the time of the Fathers, there have been believers who have rejected sacramentalism.

traditions'.[7] I am not surprised – there was so little sacramentalism among fellow-Baptists for them to interact with!

And, of course, there is the over-riding consideration – which will not go away; namely, that Scripture, not history, is 'foundational'. Indeed, Fowler made the very point on the following page to the above when, in his preamble to an analysis of what he called 'the biblical foundations' of Baptist sacramentalism, he said: 'For these [that is the sacramental] Baptists, as for Baptists in general, no ultimate appeal can be made to ecclesiastical tradition – only Scripture can be the basis for such an appeal'. And, once again, he admitted the newness of the Baptist sacramentalism which arose in the 20th century:

The Baptist sacramental exegesis represents an alignment of this Baptist thought with the consensus of the historic Churches... The idea that baptism is merely[!][8] a symbol giving testimony to a conversion already

---

[7] Interact? Fifty years ago, Ernest Kevan highlighted the way Baptist sacramentalists were *influenced* by non-Baptists: 'No one would ever have dreamed of interpreting sacramentally [texts like 1 Cor. 6:11; Eph. 5:26; Tit. 3:5] *unless the dilemma of infant baptisers* had brought them into the discussion' (Fowler: *More* p127, emphasis mine). Cross and Thompson admitted their use of 'non-Baptist writings' in setting out Baptist sacramentalism (Cross and Thompson: 'Introduction' p1). Pinnock owned it for himself: 'A fresh reading of gospel [Gospel?] texts, an appreciation of Catholic, Orthodox and Protestant traditions, and forms of charismatic renewal – these have brought me to... argue for a recovery[!] of sacramental theology for Free Church Protestants' (Pinnock p8). All this ties in with what I have just noted from Fowler; namely, that Baptist sacramentalists find it far more congenial to interact with infant baptisers than Baptists. And it all supports my claim that sacramentalism is the fundamental issue.

[8] I object to the adjective 'merely'. I hope the 'symbolic' (that is, the biblical) view of baptism does long hold sway. But, I fear, '*merely* symbolic', moving to 'effective sign', will end in full-blown sacramentalism. There are only two stable positions: The biblical – symbol; the sacramental – baptismal regeneration. And we have to choose; we cannot dither between the two (Josh. 24:14-15; 1 Kings 18:21). 'Mere' symbolism is pejorative. Taking the supper as a memorial, for instance, need not be the same as making it meaningless. See Newman p215 quoting Timothy George on the Anabaptists. I will not repeat this note every time the word 'mere' or 'merely' is introduced to dismiss those of us who treat the ordinances as symbols, but it should not be forgotten.

completed has been formally accepted only in the Anabaptist and Baptist traditions.[9]

Let me underscore Fowler's concession. Baptist sacramentalists are moving away their traditional Baptist past to take up the sacramentalism of the other Churches. I call that a fundamental change, a fundamental newness if ever there was!

Even so, in a tortuous – yet weak – passage, although Fowler conceded that these pioneering 20th century sacramental-Baptist scholars did not themselves claim to have recovered the (alleged) original (sacramental) Baptist view of baptism (though Fowler, of course, wished they had done the 'obvious' and made such a claim), he argued that *if* the New Testament does take a sacramental view of baptism, *then* – with Baptist commitment to Scripture – sacramentalism should have been the predominant Baptist view these past 400 years. In this roundabout way, Fowler justified his ransacking of Baptist history to try to establish that the early Baptists *were* sacramentalists, and claimed that this demonstrates – proves – that the New Testament is sacramental in its teaching on baptism.[10] This tortuous argument,[11] I say, is weak in the extreme.

---

[9] Fowler: *More* p156.

[10] Fowler: *More* pp4-5.

[11] Tortuous? Let me prise out the core of Fowler's argument with an illustration: If the earth really is flat, we should find the flat-earth view has predominated scientific thinking this past 400 years. This being so, let us look and see if this has been the case. If it is, then we may safely deduce that the earth is flat. But what if we come up with only a few who believed it? Would that justify the flat-earth theory? Leaving the illustration, the best that Fowler could come up with was a few sacramentalist sentiments from a tiny minority of earlier Baptists. To go back to the illustration for a moment: I suppose a few flat-earthers would 'prove' a stream of flat-earthism has always existed. Of course, it would be quite a leap to then go on and say this has been the *dominant* notion these past 400 years. Finally, how ever many believed in a flat earth, it still wouldn't make a scrap of difference to the fact that the earth is 'unflat'. And, when all is said and done, before we go looking to see who has believed the earth is flat, shouldn't we start with the science and discover or prove whether or not the earth is flat? How much more so for theology. After all, in science we ought to observe the phenomena and try to deduce the governing law before we start looking at the various things men have believed. And when we

The fact is, we do not start with history; we start with Scripture. If sacramentalism is biblical, let us read it in the Bible, whether or not Uncle Tom Cobley in 1625, 1725, 1825 or 1925 believed it.

But there it is. That, in a nut-shell, is Fowler's thesis. Find sacramentalism in the writings of Baptists down the centuries and, hey presto, obscurantist Baptists[12] like me, who maintain that the Baptist sacramentalism of the 20th century is a novelty among Baptists, and, above all, a sinister departure from Scripture – then, Bob's your uncle, we have our feet knocked from under us. Sacramentalism is scriptural after all!

So what did Fowler claim to have found in the 17th, 18th and 19th centuries?

I can give my impression in a few words! Fowler, whistling in the dark! In my view, he was trying to keep his spirits up when he made his startling claims, and do it with such seeming (but misplaced) assurance: 'When the earliest Baptists [that is, the 17th century Baptists] addressed the question of efficacy of baptism, they spoke in sacramental terms... The dominant strain of early Baptist thought conceptualised baptism as both a sign and a seal of saving union with Christ, a divinely-ordained ritual which mediates the conscious experience of entrance into a state of grace'. He further tried – in vain, in my opinion – to establish that the sacramental view of baptism had indeed been 'the dominant strain of early Baptist thought'.

But then came the snag. Apparently, this dominant 17th century sacramentalist stream virtually ran dry for 200 years. 'For a variety of reasons... [it] was modified in a non-sacramental direction during the 18th and 19th centuries'. Even so, argued Fowler, no real harm was done. After all, he could 'explain' how this 'deviation' from the dominant sacramentalism came about. And, to crown it all, let us never forget, for Fowler it was the 17th century which was – and remains – 'foundational' for Baptists. And that, he maintained as he concluded his book, was sacramental in its view of baptism:

---

come to theology, since we have the definitive revelation to hand, it is *there* that we must look before doing anything else. Start with the Bible, and then look at history.

[12] See the previous chapter.

59

'Reformed sacramentalism was the essence of the mainstream baptismal theology of the 17th century English Baptists'.[13]

I dispute these claims, and dispute them vigorously.

But, reader, I have no intention of engaging in a blow-by-blow slugging match over who said what or why, or what they meant in saying it, in an attempt to establish or disprove that Baptists have always been – at heart – sacramentalists. The reason is simple. It is pointless. No doubt, if we look hard enough, we can find Baptists who have said the strangest things on all sorts of subjects. So what? What does *that* prove? That Baptists like everybody else can hold and express odd and inconsistent views from time to time, or fail to see the logical conclusions of what they have said?

Again, it would be wearisome, somewhat profitless and worse, to pore over countless pages of scores of manuscripts in order to establish whether or not some Baptists have been sacramentalists, or occasionally used sacramental expressions in writings or in their hymns or whatever. Why? Because of the absolute and fundamental principle which all Baptists adopt – at least, they used to adopt – and which all believers ought to adopt, and which I have stressed repeatedly; namely: in establishing any doctrine or practice in Christ's church, history is secondary, and Scripture is paramount. I remind you, reader, of what Fowler himself said: 'No ultimate appeal can be made to ecclesiastical tradition – only Scripture can be the basis for such an appeal'.[14] So why do we have to read through 155 pages of 'ecclesiastical tradition' before we get to it?[15]

---

[13] Fowler: *More* pp4,5,57,86-87,249. I say whistling in the dark. It reminds me of the preacher's notes: 'Argument weak here. Shout!'.

[14] Fowler: *More* p156.

[15] And sauce is sauce for sacramental goose as well as Baptist gander. What do I mean? Just this. George, when dismissing Baptist claims for an unbroken line of descent of Baptist churches from the apostles – which, as I have explained, I do not claim – George in dismissing this, said it was 'not only historically incredulous, but also theologically unnecessary' (George p30). Quite! So why don't we apply this principle to Fowler's extended effort to establish a line (even on his own terms, admittedly a badly broken line) of Baptist sacramentalism? It is 'theologically unnecessary', and worse.

For these reasons, I will not engage with Fowler's detailed raking over of the history of the Baptists of the 17th, 18th and 19th centuries.[16] Rather, I will sum up my reasons for rejecting his thesis. I emphasise this. I am simply summarising my objections, and only summarising them. I am not fully arguing my case. Although I will offer samples of the sort of thing I have in mind, for the reasons I have given, I am not trying to engage in a line-by-line battle with Fowler over the history.

I admit, at once, that some Baptists (and others who would not call themselves 'Baptists' but, nevertheless, baptise only believers) have used the word 'sacrament'. It would be pointless to deny it.[17] I also admit the evidence which Fowler produced to show that some (Benjamin Keach,[18] Anne Dutton[19], Charles Stovel,[20] and Baptist

---

[16] Fowler: *More* pp10-88,248-249. I make an exception in the case of Thomas Helwys who was quoted by Thompson. See below.

[17] Robert Anderson: 'All Christians recognise that baptism is... a sacrament'. In the omitted words, Anderson added a rider: 'In the true, as distinguished from, the superstitious sense of the word' (Anderson p221). Anderson was mistaken in his assertion, *I*, for one, do not recognise 'baptism as a sacrament'. Since it is an invented, non-biblical word which has such appalling overtones and consequences, it should be avoided. It has no 'true' – that is, New Testament – meaning. Again, I am sorry that Spurgeon was prepared to talk about 'the sacramental table' (*Metropolitan* Vol.31 p223, for instance), and 'the real presence', though he was careful to deny the corporeal or actual presence of Christ at the Lord's supper (see *Till He Come* on Google Books).

[18] Fowler: *More* pp29-30. Fowler quoted Benjamin Keach's Catechism: 'The outward and ordinary means whereby Christ communicates to us the benefits of redemption are his ordinances, especially the word, baptism, the Lord's supper and prayer; all of which means are made effectual to the elect, through faith, for salvation'. This – whether by design I cannot say – was copying, almost word for word, Westminster pp246,311. Yet, even in this, note Keach's omission of 'sacraments'. Nevertheless, I concede Fowler was right to say that 'this statement should make it perfectly clear that baptism was regarded [by Keach] as instrumental in some sense in the personal experience of salvation' (Fowler: *More* pp18-19). However, see below for my views of the reliance of the 1689 Particular Baptist Confession on the Westminster documents. But I accept, as even stronger evidence, Keach did quote Stephen Charnock to the effect that 'baptism is a means of conveying... grace, when the Spirit is pleased to operate with it' (Fowler: *More* pp29-30). In short, let us agree – Keach was a sacramentalist

W.Noel[21] – I think it fair to say these were Fowler's strongest witnesses) spoke in terms somewhat closer to sacramental baptism than the overwhelming majority of Baptists of the period. But not even four swallows (if indeed they are all swallows) make a summer.

– of some kind. According to Fowler the evidence was 'clear', but, as he also admitted, it was 'modest' (Fowler: 'Oxymoron' p145). Certainly it is a long way from the sort of thing Baptist sacramentalists are saying today. For more on Keach, see below.

[19] Fowler: *More* pp46-48. Fowler showed that Anne Dutton held that baptism is a seal. But in her pamphlet she did not use the term 'sacrament' (as Fowler admitted), and gave most space to baptism as a representation of the spiritual union of the believer with Christ. I do not concede that Dutton was a sacramentalist.

[20] Fowler: *More* pp65-72. With his idiosyncratic distinction between regeneration and the new birth, Charles Stovel thought John 3:1-12 refers to baptism – being born again by baptism, indeed. But, according to Stovel, being born again is not the same as regeneration – regeneration is the secret work of God; being born again is an open profession of a walk with Christ. So, although Stovel could be thought (on a superficial glance) to be teaching baptismal regeneration, he most definitely was not; he was teaching that by baptism a believer begins his open testimony of Christ before the world. I do not concede that Stovel was a sacramentalist.

[21] Fowler: *More* pp72-75. Baptist W.Noel, who left Anglicanism to adopt Baptist views, but showed signs of bringing some kind of sacramentalism with him (mostly, in my view, shown in a lax use of terms), did say that 'when a person who has received spiritual life manifests it by confessing Christ before men by immersion, then he is born of water and of the Spirit – his new birth is complete... Baptism is the profession of faith, the public confession of Christ, without which confession there is no true faith and no salvation... It is not enough to believe in Christ, but we must also profess... which it is the will of Christ that we should do by baptism... Baptism is thus necessary to remission of sins'. Rom. 10:9-10 springs to mind. Let me re-quote Spurgeon on this: 'The promise of salvation is not made to a faith which is never avowed'. And: 'God requires [baptism in water], and though men are saved without any baptism... [and] though baptism is not saving, yet, if men would be saved, they must not be disobedient' (Spurgeon: *Early* p147; Grass and Randall p59). Noel was, in my view, saying and meaning nothing more. It was a far cry from the sacramentalism which Fowler was trying to establish. Noel was lax in his terms, I say, but hardly anything more. I do not concede he was a sacramentalist.

My objections to Fowler's (and others') thesis[22] can be summarised as follows:

- The 17th century was not foundational. It was transitional.
- How did he select his historical examples? And in the ones he selected – presumably the strongest – why were there so few with even a hint of the sacramentalism he was talking about?
- In many of his deductions he was clutching at straws.
- He repeatedly argued from what writers did *not* say. Arguing from silence is not the best way to build a convincing case.
- He repeatedly read far more into words than is justified. Just now I said he was clutching at straws. I further say he made far more bricks than is warranted from the meagre amount of straw he managed to collect.
- He understated the strength of the non- or anti-sacramental statements he quoted.
- He attributed motives behind the words of those he quoted, often to explain away that which did not fit his thesis.
- He sometimes asserted without proof.
- He begged the question.
- He was not averse to making a sacramental suggestion and then withdrawing it – leaving the sacramental odour in the reader's nostrils.[23]

---

[22] For the sort of thing I am talking about, see the extended note on p306.

[23] To illustrate my meaning on this particular point, consider the following episode which took place in the English law courts. In 1931, Norman Birkett KC led for the Crown against Alfred Arthur Rouse for the alleged murder of an unidentified man in 'The Blazing Car Case'. An expert witness gave evidence which 'appeared at first sight to demolish a principal part of the structure of the Crown case. But Birkett immediately rose to the occasion. His cross-examination of the Cricklewood engineer was brief but deadly'. He asked the expert for the coefficient of expansion of brass. The expert did not know it. Later, another expert witness was put into the witness box. Birkett asked him if he knew the coefficient of expansion. He did not. 'This question, which effectively demolished the evidence of the defence's two expert witnesses, has been cited as the most devastating in its effect of any question ever put to a witness by Birkett in cross-examination. At the time, however, it was criticised in some quarters as a "trick" question which should not have been asked... Asked many years later what he would have done if the witnesses had given the correct answer

In short: In my opinion, Fowler did 'a Joachim Jeremias'; that is, he started with a thesis and found at least all the evidence he could to establish it.[24]

But in one thing he was absolutely right:

British Baptists who affirmed that baptism is a sacrament (that is, that baptism in some way mediates salvific union with Christ)... were definitely a [miniscule] minority. This began to change in the early part of the 20th century, when some influential Baptist leaders articulated the view that baptism is both an ordinance to obey and a sacrament of grace.[25]

Until the mid 20th century, therefore, we can definitely say that the overwhelming majority of Baptists were decidedly non-sacramentalist – if not anti-sacramentalist. They regarded baptism as a sign, a symbol – nothing more, nothing less – and they baptised believers on profession of their faith in obedience to Christ's command to represent their spiritual experience; it was, to them, an ordinance not a sacrament. Occasional passing remarks from certain writers can be cited which might point to a different stance, and there were some – like Barton W.Stone and Alexander Campbell in

---

(0.0000189), he said that he would have gone on to copper, then to aluminium and other metals, eventually leaving the subject as if it were of no particular importance' (Montgomery Hyde pp297-299,307-309). My point is this: By asking the witnesses these questions, which they could not answer, Birkett made them look unreliable, non-expert in the eyes of the jury. Yet a man can be an expert witness and not know these constants by heart – *as long as he knows where he can look them up and use them when he wants them.* His lack of precise knowledge of the particular coefficient does not in any way cast doubt upon his expertise – which is what Birkett had effectively (cleverly) done in this tangential way. I am convinced myself that the question should have been forbidden by the judge. Just for the record, in any event Rouse was found guilty and, on the eve of his execution, confessed to the murder.

Why did I say all this? Because, on occasion, Fowler, like Birkett, raised an issue to withdraw it. But the suggestion's odour is left in the nostrils.

[24] I have cited a wit. Let me stress his humour: Joachim Jeremias unearthed *at least all* the evidence for infant baptism. See Wright: *What*...? p18; Lane pp139-143.

[25] Fowler: *More* p88.

the mid 19th century (and their followers today)[26] – who did (and still do) teach that grace is actually conferred in baptism, but the overwhelming majority of Baptists thought that baptism is symbolic. Baptists were non-sacramentalist; indeed, they were anti-sacramentalist. May I remind you, reader, of something Fowler himself said:

The idea that baptism is merely[!] a symbol giving testimony to a conversion already completed has been formally accepted only in the Anabaptist and Baptist traditions.[27]

I acknowledge Fowler was here rightly saying that only Anabaptists and Baptists have maintained the anti-sacramentalist symbolic view of baptism – they alone of all the historic churches. Very well. I gladly own it. Indeed, this proves my point, which Fowler had himself vainly tried to disprove: *Baptists have been **anti-sacramental**.* Until the 20th century, that is.

It is now time to turn to that century, and on to the present day.

---

[26] See Castelein pp51-55,83-87,122-125,129-144.
[27] Fowler: *More* p156.

Baptist Sacramentalism
in the
20th and 21st Centuries

As I said at the close of the previous chapter, Fowler, in my opinion, failed to make his case for Baptist sacramentalism in the 17th, 18th and 19th centuries. The facts are against him. The overwhelming majority of Baptists in those centuries did *not* have a sacramental view of the ordinance and there was nothing approximating to what might be called 'a sacramental tradition' among Baptists.

Coming to the 20th century, however, Fowler was on surer – indeed, incontestable – ground. He was more than able to produce abundant evidence to support his case – except that his chapter is mis-titled.[1] It does not describe 'The Re-formulation of Baptist Sacramentalism'. Rather, it documents its *formulation*. Baptist sacramentalism *began* in the 20th century – it was not re-discovered or re-formulated then. But having begun, how it has grown – especially in the closing years of the 20th century and the opening of the 21st!

Let me trace its development.[2]

It was, I say, during the 20th century, with the renewal of the liturgical movement,[3] that some Baptist scholars began to put forward a sacramental approach to baptism. In 1953, J.M.Ross (an infant baptiser himself), speaking of Baptists, was able to say:

---

[1] Indeed, Fowler's book is itself mis-titled – it does not describe the *recovery* – but the *formulation* – of a Baptist sacramentalism.

[2] In reproducing these extracts from Baptist scholars, I do not mean to imply that these writers did not say other things; biblical things. But the fact is they said *this*. I have already described this as 'double-speak'. As I have noted in this work, and shown in my *Infant*, this is how Reformed infant-baptisers proceed; taking away – or trying to – with one hand, that which they have lavishly doled out with the other. It is a constant Evangelical-sacramentalist ploy. It will not do.

[3] I am speaking of 'the liturgical renewal felt by Baptists and others in the 1960s and perhaps most markedly in the 1980s' (Russell viii).

Baptism is being increasingly regarded not only as something the believer does, but as a means through which God acts upon him... In recent times, the philosophical background has changed, and we are able to see certain things in Scripture to which we were formerly blind[!]... It is no longer necessary for us to fear that we are sinking towards Rome if we follow Scripture in joining baptism with faith as the instrument of our salvation.[4]

Oh?

And if that was the situation in 1953, what now – a decade into the 21st century? Following something of a twenty-year hiatus from about 1970, during the closing years of the 20th century the sacramental drive among Baptists started to gather momentum.[5] And it continues to gather pace as the opening years of this century pass. If Derek Tidball, writing in 2006, was right: 'Baptists reject baptismal regeneration', I hope the same can be said five years later.[6] For the majority of Baptists, I think it can – still. But for how much longer? As he himself said:

There has certainly been a move among Baptist theologians to inject sacramental meaning into baptism without losing the element of personal faith as essential. Many Baptists preach it as an 'effective sign' not 'merely symbolic',[7] though perhaps the popular culture of Baptist churches means the latter often wins out over the former in the minds of the congregation.[8]

David Wright, who was, as I have noted, Emeritus Professor of Patristic and Reformed Christianity, Edinburgh – a Reformed historian holding to infant baptism – spoke of what he considered to be 'several signs of hope' 'early in the third millennium'. These included 'the growing evidence of sacramental thinking among Baptist theologians'. Wright, deploring the long history of (as he

---

[4] Ross pp111-112.
[5] Porter and Cross pp33-39.
[6] That is, regeneration by water baptism. Tidball p159. I am publishing this in 2011.
[7] See my earlier note on the pejorative 'merely'.
[8] Tidball p160. Note the point. Many professional Baptist theologians and preachers are sacramentalists. Most of the όι πολλοι (hoi polloi – the common people), at present, are not. Most of the latter, however, usually follow the former, given a little time.

saw it) the debasing of baptism by the way infant baptism has been practiced (sadly, he did not recognise that baptism has been debased by infant baptism itself – not just by corruptions of it!), wished to see a more sacramental approach to it; in other words, that those who use the term, and argue for the effects of infant baptism, would mean it. Wright wanted and worked for greater rapport among sacramentalists – both Reformed and Baptist – and was glad to see it happening. Indeed, he contributed largely to it.[9] The same goes for the sacramental Baptists he spoke of. Sacramentalism is what these people are calling for. Sacramentalism is the issue.[10]

Fowler:

In the 20th century... some British Baptist scholars... shifted towards a sacramental understanding of baptism as an integral part of conversion and an instrument by which grace becomes operative in individual experience... A significant stream of recent [early 21st century] Baptist thought moves along the lines of... sacramentalism.[11]

And by 'sacramentalism', Fowler meant:

To say that baptism is 'sacramental' is to say that it mediates the experience of salvific union with Christ; that is, that one submits to baptism as a penitent sinner in order to experience the forgiveness of sins and the gift of the Holy Spirit, rather than as a confirmed[12] disciple in order to bear witness to a past experience of union with Christ.[13]

---

[9] Wright: *What...?* pp10-11,87-102. See my *Infant*.

[10] Wright: 'Christian' pp163-169. For all that, Wright when, a few months after the appearance of his *What...?*, published this article in which he tackled the question of what to do next, failed to mention sacramentalism. Given his own emphasis in his book, and the emphasis in the articles and advertisements in the edition of the journal which published his article, its omission, when dealing specifically with the way forward, was serious, and failed to convey the full picture. As for the advertisements, see *Evangelical Quarterly* April 2006 pp115-116 for recent 'books on [believer's] baptism and sacramentalism'.

[11] Fowler: *More* pp3-4. Note the 'shifted'. It was, as I have said, new.

[12] I am sure that Fowler did not use 'confirmed' here in the technical Roman, Reformed or Anglican sense. I take it he meant 'established', 'definite' or 'credible'.

[13] Fowler: *More* p6. Of course, as I said before, there is immense blessing in the baptism of a believer as he witnesses to his union with Christ, and

Now... if that doesn't set alarm bells ringing for Baptists, nothing will.

Let me trace the history of this Baptist sacramentalism.

The rot set in with Henry Wheeler Robinson, who played a major role in the rise of Baptist sacramentalism right from the early decades of the century. Indeed, he played the leading role.[14] Cross recorded that Robinson's 'college days' in the 1890s:

Brought him into constant contact with those of other traditions, and this clearly had a deep and lasting effect on his attitudes... In later life, Robinson was closely associated with the Quakers and had a keen interest in... the writings of J.H.Newman...[15] He believed in the need for clearer thinking and greater charity, and, for Baptists, this applied more to baptism than any other doctrine because baptism was the major stumbling block to the union/reunion movement being proposed at that time... Robinson was born in... 1872, when the overwhelming majority of Baptists understood baptism to be nothing more than[!] an ordinance, a symbol of conversion, a profession of personal faith in Christ, a witness to the gospel, an act of obedience, and in the majority of churches, a condition of membership...[16] If the Tractarians are viewed as adopting an extreme position in their theology of baptismal regeneration, the [traditional] Baptist reaction should... be seen as the opposite extreme... From the likes of E.B.Pusey and J.H.Newman claiming too much for baptism, many Baptists claimed too little for it... During a serious illness in 1913... 'the truths of "Evangelical" Christianity... failed to bring him [Robinson] personal strength'. Such

---

obeys his command (similarly for the Lord's supper) – but it is a leap of astronomical proportions to try to turn this into sacramentalism.

[14] For more on the leading part in Baptist sacramentalism played by Henry Wheeler Robinson, see the extended note on p310.

[15] For more on Henry Wheeler Robinson and John Henry Newman, see the extended note on p311.

[16] Quite a list for 'nothing more than'! In light of this list of the reasons for baptising when it is regarded as 'nothing more than an ordinance, a symbol', how could Wheeler Robinson speak thus: 'If water baptism is not a means of grace, why keep it up?' After all, he himself spoke of 'immersion as a "symbolic expression of the historical truths on which our faith rests" [and] personal union with Christ by faith' (Cross: 'Pneumatological' pp153-155). If I may be allowed to answer Robinson's question: 'If water baptism is not a means of grace, why keep it up?' Because Christ commanded it – that's why! *Not* because it conveys grace.

strength, however, he found in 'a more "sacramental" religion' mediated through a priest and 'sacred elements'.[17]

As Cross made clear, Wheeler Robinson wanted the Baptists to have their own 'Oxford Movement'.[18] He explained. Wheeler Robinson wanted what he called:

---

[17] Cross: 'Pneumatological' pp152-154. And, yet again, note the admission that 20th century sacramentalism was a novelty. Note also the contribution of non-Baptists (Quakers and Tractarians) to Wheeler Robinson's move to sacramentalism, and the part played by the drive for ecumenism. These seeds did not fail to germinate. I agree that we 'need... clearer thinking and greater charity', but that thinking must also produce greater *clarity*. Mark the unmistakeable and unashamed sacerdotalism in Robinson's words – 'a more "sacramental" religion' mediated through a priest and "sacred elements"'.

Ernest Payne set out Wheeler Robinson's experience: 'The truths of "Evangelical" Christianity which he had often preached to others, failed during his illness, to bring him personal strength. He thus describes what happened, in an important autobiographical passage: "They (that is, the truths) remained true to him, but they seemed to lack vitality. They seemed to demand an active effort of faith, for which the physical energy was lacking... He contrasted with this... that of a more "sacramental" religion... in which the priest would bring the sacred elements to the bedside, and with them the needed grace. The result of this experience was not to change a "Protestant" into a "Catholic", but to lead him to seek for the lacuna in his own conception of Evangelical truth. He found it in his relative neglect of those [so-called sacramental] conceptions of the Holy Spirit in which the New Testament is [said to be] so rich"' (Payne: *Henry Wheeler Robinson* pp56-57). This speaks volumes!

[18] Cross: 'Pneumatological' p156. The Oxford Movement was a 19th century attempt by some within the Church of England to put a stop to liberalism. Its leaders, J.H.Newman, J.Keble and E.B.Pusey, were all members of Oriel College, Oxford in the 1820s. Keble's 1833 sermon, 'National Apostasy', marked the opening of the movement, and the first of the Tracts soon followed. Hence the alternative title the 'Tractarian Movement'. The Tracts, while anti-Reformation, also opposed Roman Catholic teaching. But from 1840 on, J.H.Newman led the movement increasingly towards Rome, his *Tract XC* in 1841 arousing a storm of protest. In 1845, Newman 'converted' to Rome. Pusey stayed within the Church of England, and 'Anglo-Catholic', 'Ritualist' and 'Puseyite', entered the lexicon (see Douglas p739). And Wheeler Robinson wanted the

The genuine sacramentalism of the New Testament... believer's baptism by which he meant the entrance of believers into a life of supernatural powers... Believer's baptism is actually a centre round which other doctrines can be logically and naturally grouped. We have made baptism our centre... [Wheeler Robinson saw the] sacraments as vehicles of a spiritual benediction on humanity, ordained by Christ as a means of union with him. More precisely, a sacrament is 'something which is a means by which the divine Spirit becomes active in the heart of reader or hearer... sacrament... means of grace'... [Baptism is no] 'mere symbolism... but [a] very real accomplishment of a divine work, the work of the Holy Spirit'... To be baptised into Christ is to put on Christ; that is, to enter that realm of the Spirit under Christ's Lordship.[19]

Wheeler Robinson made his position clear:

The symbol in the ancient world usually carried an effective as well as a declaratory or expressive meaning... Baptism in the New Testament certainly means... it is associated with the gift of the Holy Spirit... an experiential union with Christ in his redeeming acts... Does not baptism express much more than a personal act? Is it not, by virtue of being that, the New Testament door of entrance into a life of supernatural energies, the surrender to that 'law of the Spirit' which the apostle set in strongest contrast to the common life of men?... How closely it is related to the gift of the Holy Spirit... It needs to be said, of course, that the connection between water baptism and the baptism of the Spirit is of no mechanical kind,[20] such as quasi-magical ideas of the ceremony would suggest... There could be no risk of encouraging the idea of 'baptismal regeneration' (in the modern sense),[21] because all who were baptised were already believers... Indeed, it was the very divorce of baptism from personal faith which has made 'sacerdotalism' possible...
Baptists have been reluctant to recognise this 'baptismal grace', just because, in their judgement, it is utterly misrepresented and distorted when ascribed to unconscious infants. The reaction from a false doctrine of divine grace in baptism has made them suspicious even of the genuine [so-called] sacramentalism of the New Testament. We have been saying *believer's* baptism so emphatically that we have failed, or

---

Baptists to have their own Oxford Movement. Enough said! See the earlier extended note for more on Wheeler Robinson and J.H.Newman.

[19] Cross: 'Pneumatological' pp155-163; see pp151-176.

[20] Echoes here of Calvin and the Lord's supper, as I have shown elsewhere.

[21] Vain hope! Modern? This appalling notion has been ruining millions for 1800 years and more!

at least are failing now [1927], to say with anything like equal emphasis, believer's *baptism*; that is, the entrance of believers into a life of supernatural powers... If any Baptist reader is afraid that this may mean a sacramentalism of the lower kind, with consecrated water... let it be said quite distinctly that I am pleading for the connection of water baptism with the Spirit in *exactly the sense* in which all Baptists plead for its connection with personal faith... At the present time, and in this country, the Baptist future seems to depend on the relation to the distinctive feature of believer's baptism. Baptists must make either more or less of it.[22]

Wheeler Robinson had no doubt which he would opt for:

We must make more of baptism... If we teach... that water baptism is of real value... may we not teach that it is... possibly a real occasion... of that baptism of the Spirit...?... Baptism is a sacrament of grace... Water baptism was in the New Testament times the... occasion and experienced-means of the Spirit baptism of believers... I believe that the future of the Baptist Church in this country does largely depend on the recovery of a lost sacramental emphasis; on our making more, not less, of believer's baptism.[23]

Thus the spade work for Baptist sacramentalism was done by Henry Wheeler Robinson. The course was now set.

A.C.Underwood carried on the theme in 1937: Baptists are 'sacramentalists though they reject sacerdotalism'.[24] Sacraments are 'efficacious symbols which mediate the grace of God... At their baptism they receive a further accession of the Spirit in response to their faith'. Again, in 1947: 'Baptists... today... advance the... claim that they alone preserve the full sacramental value of believer's baptism as a means of grace... Baptists can offer high-churchmanship without clericalism, and sacramentalism without sacerdotalism'.[25]

---

[22] Wheeler Robinson: *The Life* pp79-80,175-179, first two emphases original; third, mine. Reader, let the words of the third emphasis sink in; that is, 'in exactly the sense'.

[23] Fowler: *More* pp89-97. Note the 'the Baptist Church in this country'. Such little unbiblical-phrases, such medieval (and Reformed) concepts, creeping in unnoticed today, become the definitive view tomorrow.

[24] Vain hope. See my earlier comments. The record of Wheeler Robinson's own experience – see above – exposes the futility of this hope.

[25] Underwood pp270,274; Fowler: *More* pp98-100.

Coming to the 1940s, Robert C.Walton spoke of 'an intimate relationship between the gift [of the Spirit] and the sacrament' of baptism; 'the gift of the Spirit to the Christian community, in which a man shares because he has entered that community through baptism'. 'New life is the gift of the Spirit; no man can achieve it by himself. To be born again "of water and of the Spirit" is to enter the community' by baptism. 'Faith in Christ and his benefits... is sacramentally expressed in believer's baptism'. 'If [since, he meant]... believer's baptism is a sacrament in which God acts, and an ordinance we are bound by our allegiance to obey, then to make it an optional extra means that the Baptist community sins grievously, misleading the flock committed to its charge, and by its neglect stops up one channel through which the divine blessing is meditated'.[26]

In 1947, Henry Cook:

The Baptist reason for avoiding the word 'sacraments' is... quite intelligible, but it is at the same time unfortunate, since the word 'ordinances' hardly does justice to all that is involved in baptism and the Lord's supper. These are ordinances undoubtedly, but they are surely very much more, and their significance lies not merely in the fact that they were enjoined upon us by Christ, but that they become to the man of faith an actual means of grace... [In baptism there is] a vitalising and enriching of his [God's] grace and power... [Baptism is] sacramental... that is, through which God in saving grace is able to come to the soul.[27]

Again, in 1947, F.Townley Lord, President of the Baptist Union,[28] writing about the Lord's supper, in part quoting others, showed his sacramental hand:

'The Church', says Dr Micklem, 'proclaims its good news by administering the sacraments no less than by preaching the word'... While it would doubtless be true to say that the majority of worshippers in Baptist... churches regard the Lord's supper chiefly as an act of remembrance, there are many who are emphasising more and more the

---

[26] Fowler: *More* pp100-105. I agree, of course, that baptism is not an optional extra, and to neglect it is 'to sin grievously'. But to be an anti-sacramentalist is not the same as treating baptism as an optional extra.

[27] Fowler: *More* pp105-107.

[28] By 'Baptist Union', I mean the Baptist Union of Great Britain.

real spiritual presence of the risen Lord – not in the elements, but in the believing heart of the worshipper. Thus Dr Wheeler Robinson could quote with approval [the Anglican] Richard Hooker's words: 'The real presence of Christ's most blessed body and blood is not... to be sought for in the sacrament, but in the worthy receiver of the sacrament'[29]... The [so-called] inadequacy of a merely 'commemorative' interpretation of the Lord's supper has been fully recognised... by... [some] Congregationalist and Baptist writers... 'Let us get rid of the idea', wrote P.T.Forsyth, 'which has impoverished worship beyond measure, that the act is mainly commemorative. No Church can live on that. How can we have a mere memorial of one who is still alive, still our life, still present with us, and acting in us?'... W.W.B.Emery: '... I have known good Christian folk to own that they found a note of dreariness and sadness in the Lord's supper which made it depressing and unhelpful. This is not surprising when it stands for remembrance alone. Unquestionably there is something dreary in an effort of memory to reach back over the centuries and recover touch with an event and a person who belong to the past'[30]... It is sometimes pointed out that

---

[29] I do not for a moment question the spiritual presence of Christ in every believer, but sacramental talk like this, whatever the subtle distinctions made by theologians, has been significant in the Romeward-drive. Reader, we must keep our eyes skinned for such subtle glosses.

[30] What a woeful ignorance of Scripture Forsyth and Emery here displayed. Christ did not institute his supper for the purpose Forsyth claimed. Christ spelled it out. He established the supper as a memorial of a historical, once-for-all-time event. When he said: 'Do this in remembrance of me', he was clearly speaking of his crucifixion – 'this is my body... this is my blood of the new covenant, which is shed for many for the remission of sins' (Matt. 26:26-28; Mark 14:22-24; Luke 22:19-20; 1 Cor. 11:24-26). On Christ's authority, and on apostolic authority, the Lord's supper is a commemoration of the historical event of his death. There is, also, the vital note of looking forward to Christ's return in the 'till he comes'. Of course, if men such as Forsyth and Emery thought and taught that remembering Christ's death meant that we should constantly rehearse the harrowing physical details of Christ's sufferings, and that is all, no wonder 'good Christian folk' did not like it. But if I realise – as Scripture teaches – that all my hope is bound up in the death of Christ, what should be more exhilarating to me than to have my heart reminded again and again of the event – above all, the person – which secured my everlasting salvation? And was Forsyth not in danger, to put it mildly, of belittling the command of the apostle? Are we not commanded to 'remember Jesus Christ' (2 Tim. 2:8, NIV, NASB)?

whereas many branches of the Christian Church put the altar in the centre, the Baptists... like most Free Churchmen, direct attention to the pulpit. If by this is meant that greater attention is necessary in Baptist... churches to the sacrament of the Lord's supper, there is point in the criticism. Undoubtedly, our churches should do more to give the Lord's table the place is has historically occupied in their theology[31] – the central place in the worship of the Church. But this is not to detract in any degree from the ministry of the pulpit.[32]

Oh no? The truth is quite the opposite. As I have argued – and I will return to it – sacramentalism always diminishes preaching.

In 1948, the Baptist Union published 'The Baptist Doctrine of the Church' in which it stated: 'The New Testament clearly indicates a connection of the gift of the Holy Spirit with the experience of baptism'.[33]

In 1956, and again in 1965, Neville Clark:

Baptism... is effective rather than merely symbolic... In baptism the disciple enters into the whole redemptive action of his Lord, so that what was once done representatively for him [by Christ] may now be done in actuality in him [by water baptism]... The point at which redemption becomes effective for us is at baptism... Baptism and [the] new birth are inseparably bound together.[34]

Clark again, in 1959, in his contribution to *Christian Baptism*,[35] edited by Alan Gilmore:

---

[31] Reader, beware! That the Lord's supper has historically occupied a central place in Baptist theology, requires proof, not mere assertion. Proof is also needed that it is *biblical* to place the Lord's supper before preaching, and that it should occupy the central place in worship. Will a sacramentalist give us that proof? I think we shall have a long wait.

[32] Lord pp85-98. See the tentative moves towards liturgy in this same article.

[33] Fowler: *More* p151.

[34] Fowler: *More* pp107-108.

[35] I have taken several of the extracts above from the contributions made by the various authors to *Christian Baptism*. For Fowler's extracts and summaries, see Fowler: *More* pp113-133; 'Oxymoron' pp129-150. Various other extracts appear at other places in my book. I repeat Kevan's criticism of *Christian Baptism*: 'No one would ever have dreamed of interpreting sacramentally [texts like 1 Cor. 6:11; Eph. 5:26; Tit. 3:5] unless the dilemma of infant baptisers had brought them into the discussion... It is

Baptism... implies, embodies and effects forgiveness of sin, initiation into the church and the gift of the Holy Spirit... Baptism effects initiation into the life of the blessed trinity and all the blessings of the new 'age', and so embodies the wholeness of redemption. It is 'into Christ', into the crucified, risen and ascended Lord, into the whole drama of his redemption achievement. We are incorporated into Christ that we may be crucified with Christ. We are crucified with Christ that we may share his resurrection... Baptism effects regeneration and new birth because and only because it sets us at Golgotha and the empty tomb... Baptism is a sacrament of the gospel... So it is that the story of our redemption contains three great 'moments'. Our redemption was accomplished at the cross and resurrection; it is accomplished at baptism; it will be accomplished at the parousia [Christ's return]. It is the maintenance of the separateness and the unity of these 'moments' that provides us with our problem and our task.[36]

Fowler summarised Clark's view:

Baptism is 'a sacrament of inaugurated eschatology', effecting the believer's entrance into the benefits presently attached to the kingdom of God... 'How is this union with Christ accomplished; how does baptism effect it? The answer is given in terms of initiation into the church. Baptism accomplishes union with Christ because it gives entry into the church, which is his resurrection body. Into that body, the baptised are incorporated as "members"... In baptism the Holy Spirit is given... In one sense, baptism effects what it signifies'... Christians die and rise with Christ in baptism.[37]

Beasley-Murray, in 1959, in his contribution to *Christian Baptism*, stated that 'the baptismal act... is the supreme moment in the believer's experience of salvation'.[38] Fowler summarised Beasley-

---

astonishing... to find that the authors [of *Christian Baptism*] are willing to concede a reference to baptism in these passages' (Fowler: *More* p127). Of Clark's chapter, Kevan said: 'Anything less Baptist would be hard to find'. Kevan deplored the sacramentalists' use of 'convey, effect, incorporate, and an unqualified allusion to the "efficacy" of the rite' (Cross and Thompson: 'Introduction' p4). For more on Baptist sacramentalists and history, see the extended note on p313.

[36] Clark: 'The Theology' pp308-309,313,316,318.
[37] Fowler: *More* pp110,112.
[38] Beasley-Murray: 'Baptism in the Epistles of Paul' p129. In light of the part played by Beasley-Murray in the rise of Baptist sacramentalism, the fact that he started as a student at Spurgeon's College in 1936, was its

Murray: 'Baptism is, for Paul, an effective sign... To assert that baptism saves by virtue of being the vehicle of faith is to take seriously what Paul says about both faith and baptism'.[39]

Replying to continued criticism of the sacramentalist claims, Beasley-Murray wrote again:

We are not contending that God justifies by faith, but gives the Spirit and unites to Christ by baptism, as though baptism was a 'work' alongside faith. That would be a perversion of the gospel. Our plea has been that in the New Testament, baptism is inseparable from the turning to God in faith, on the basis of which God justifies,[40] gives the Spirit, and unites to Christ.[41]

Principal 1958-1973, and then Professor of New Testament at the Southern Baptist Theological Seminary 1973-1980 (see http://archives.sbts.edu), says much.

[39] Fowler: *More* p119. In his reply to criticism of *Christian Baptism*, Beasley-Murray distanced himself from 'baptismal regeneration' because it is 'a slogan with an unpleasant odour about it'. What odour? 'Automatic production of spiritual and moral ends by going through external motions according to prescription'. Reading this, of course, I am reminded of Calvin's efforts to get off the hook when taunted by Romanists – it was, as I have fully explained, the mechanical *ex opere operato* which he objected to. But whoever tries it – Calvin or Beasley-Murray – all the weaving and dodging in the world will not avoid the just charge. I am not worried whether or not the thing is automatic; baptismal regeneration by water is what is taught by sacramentalists, and such baptismal regeneration – automatic or not – is an abomination. Beasley-Murray, arguing that the biblical texts – Matt. 28:19; Acts 2:38; 22:16; Rom. 6:1-5; Gal. 3:26-27; Col. 2:12; 1 Pet. 3:21 – support the view expressed in *Christian Baptism*, stated that baptism is 'the climax of God's dealing with the penitent seeker and of the convert's return to God'. Fowler repeated this remarkable – literally climacteric – statement (Fowler: 'Oxymoron' p147). Reader, is this really the impression a man from Mars would get on reading the New Testament? See my earlier works, and below, for my views on these verses.

[40] This will not do. It is in itself 'a perversion of the gospel'. Did you spot the subtle gloss, reader? 'Faith, on the basis of which God justifies'. Basis? Faith the *basis* of justification? Utter nonsense! And worse! When talking about justification, to put anything in front of, alongside or even after God's free and sovereign grace, as its 'basis', is to pervert the gospel (Acts 15:11; Eph. 2:5,8-9). It is *grace* which is the *basis* of salvation – not *faith*. As Fowler noted, quoting T.F.Torrance: 'We are justified by faith, [but] this does not mean that it is our faith that justifies us; far from it... We in faith

77

In 1960, Ernest Payne and Stephen Winward published a liturgy – a Service Book – for Baptists: *Orders and Prayers for Church Worship.*[42] According to this, in a baptising service, the minister is to say:

Let us now set forth the great benefits which we are to receive from the Lord, according to his word and promise, in this holy sacrament. In baptism we are united with Christ through faith, dying with him unto sin and rising with him unto newness of life... The Holy Spirit, the Lord and giver of life, by whose unseen operation we have already been brought to repentance and faith, is given and sealed to us in this sacrament of grace. By this same Holy Spirit, we are baptised in one body and made members of the holy and Catholic and apostolic Church, the blessed company of all Christ's faithful people.

Payne and Winward then 'suggested' that the minister should pray for those about to be baptised that they 'may by faith be united with Christ in his Church, and receive according to your promise the forgiveness of their sins, and the gift of the Holy Spirit'.[43]

That same year, R.E.O.White published *The Biblical Doctrine of Initiation*, arguing for what he called 'dynamic sacramentalism':

In the total human act of repentance-belief-baptism, divine things happen; the blessings offered in the gospel are not merely assured but given to whomsoever would respond in penitence and faith to the kerygma [preached] message, and the appointed response was baptism upon confession of faith, calling upon the name of the Lord... The dynamic... sacramentalism of the New Testament seizes upon the fact that divine activity and human response meet in sacramental action. The sacramental effect – enduement, gift, remission, reception, incorporation, death-resurrection – occurs within the personal relationship which the act expresses. This efficacy belongs strictly

---

flee from our own acts even of repentance, confession, trust and response, and take refuge in the obedience and faithfulness of Christ... That is what it means to be justified by faith' (Fowler: *More* pp206-207). Faith is not the basis of justification. And, in the context in which I am writing, the basis of justification is certainly not baptism! Faith (and repentance) are the *means* of salvation *based* on grace (Eph. 2:8-9). Baptism plays no part in justification whatsoever. No part whatsoever, I say again.

[41] Fowler: *More* pp131.

[42] See my reference to the liturgical movement at the start of this chapter.

[43] Fowler: *More* pp152-154.

neither to the element, nor to the rite, but to the action of God within the soul of the baptised who at that time, and in that way, is making his response to the grace offered to him in the gospel... God... in fulfilment of his promise in the gospel invests the rite at that moment, for that convert, with sacramental power. Such a conception of objectively disciplined sacramental encounter with God provides the basis for a truly realistic sacramentalism... retrieving the great New Testament sacrament from being reduced to an idle form or traditional symbol performed without spiritual profit.[44]

Again:

Paul's statements about baptism leave no doubt that in his mind baptism accomplishes things – does not merely express them figuratively... but marks their happening. Paul is a sacramentalist if it is remembered that for him the sacrament is a faith-sacrament... Because baptism expresses such faith, it is 'actually effective in uniting a man to Christ... placing him within the divine family'.[45]

Beasley-Murray in his *Baptism in the New Testament* published in 1962:

The idea that baptism is... purely symbolic... must be pronounced not alone [only] unsatisfactory but out of harmony with the New Testament itself.[46] Admittedly, such a judgement runs counter to the popular tradition of the [Baptist] denomination to which the writer [Beasley-Murray] belongs... The apostolic writers... view the act as a symbol with power; that is, a sacrament. 'Whoever says sacrament says grace', wrote H.J.Wotherspoon, 'for grace is the differentia of the sacrament, by which it is more than a symbol'... Adolf Schlatter... stated: 'There is no gift or power which the apostolic documents do not ascribe to baptism'. He meant, of course, that there is no gift or power available to man in consequence of the redemption of Christ that is not available to

---

[44] White pp274,308-309; Fowler: *More* pp133-139. This is not the choice. Taking the ordinance as a symbol is not the same as having 'an idle form... without spiritual profit'.

[45] White p276; Cross and Thompson: 'Introduction' p6. 'Because baptism expresses... faith, it is "actually effective in uniting a man to Christ"'. Does this mean that it is the *expression* of faith – baptism – and *not* the *reality* – *the faith itself* – which counts?

[46] Compare his words four years later: 'The question as to whether baptism is a symbol or a sacrament is ambiguous. Moreover, it poses an unreal opposition' (Beasley-Murray: *Baptism Today and Tomorrow* p13).

him in baptism... The sacrament is the occasion of God's personal dealing with a man in such a fashion that he henceforth lives a new existence in the power and in the fellowship of God... In the New Testament, precisely the same gifts of grace are associated with faith as with baptism. Forgiveness, cleansing and justification are the effect of baptism... forgiveness and cleansing... union with Christ comes through baptism... identification with Christ in his death and resurrection is rooted in baptism... participation in Christ's Sonship[47] is bound up with baptism... God's gracious giving to faith[48] belongs to the context of baptism, even as God's gracious giving in baptism is to faith... Baptism is... the divinely appointed rendezvous of grace for faith... [Water] baptism in the name of Christ... cannot be other than a baptism in the Spirit... Wheeler Robinson wrote: '... Baptism, in its New Testament context, is always a baptism of the Spirit'... Because of this association of baptism with the work of the Spirit, baptism in the New Testament is the true context for regeneration... Baptism is closely linked with the reception of the Spirit... It behoves us accordingly to make much of baptism. It is given as the trysting place of the sinner with his Saviour.[49]

Fowler said of Alec Gilmore's *Baptism and Christian Unity* which appeared in 1966: 'Gilmore articulated a Baptist sacramentalism... He defended a more Catholic kind of sacramentalism in which the operations of divine grace are more localised in material elements and physical actions'. Gilmore confronted those Baptists who were trying to resist the rise of sacramentalism:

Behind [their] self-defence, there obviously lies a fear. It is the fear that Catholic and sacramentarian [sacramental] teaching might be accepted by the growing generation of Baptists. It is more than that: it is the fear that some Baptists might run away with the idea that in the sacraments something happens. It is more even than that: deep down, it is the fear

---

[47] Beasley-Murray had 'sonship'.

[48] Leaving aside the question of baptism for a moment, it would have been better to express 'God's gracious giving to faith' along the lines of: 'The sinner receives from God through faith on the basis of grace'.

[49] Beasley-Murray: *Baptism in the New Testament* pp263-277,301,305. See also Beasley-Murray: *Baptism Today and Tomorrow* p41; Fowler: *More* pp139-145. Certainly nobody, after reading the above, could accuse Beasley-Murray of failing 'to make much of baptism'. Clearly, he made far *too* much of it.

that in the sacraments, God might do something...[50] Modern biblical scholarship finds much of the sacramental in Paul.[51]

Fowler:

Gilmore referred here to the work of A.Wikenhauser (1883-1960), a German Catholic New Testament scholar, on Pauline mysticism[!], in which he argued for baptism as the crucial objective component in Paul's concept of religious experience. Gilmore [quoted] Wikenhauser... 'Faith is the necessary condition for receiving baptism, which establishes union with Christ'.[52]

In 1996, Clark H.Pinnock:

God comes to us and deals with us through material signs... As bodily creatures, we need embodied expressions such as baptism and eucharist to make inward grace visible and tangible... Symbols... serve as channels of grace... In the sacraments, God offers grace that is effective when people receive it.[53]

Also in 1996, Paul Fiddes: 'The sacraments are pieces of matter that God takes and uses as special places of encounter with himself'.[54]

In 2006, Pinnock again:

Baptism is the act in which... there is the promise that [Jesus] will baptise us. Born of water and Spirit, we become members of his mystical body and receive the forgiveness of sins... Through the sign of water, people are baptised into Christ and put on Christ (Gal. 3:27).[55] They receive the washing of regeneration and renewal of the Spirit (Tit.

---

[50] I find this attack cheap and gratuitous. I fully acknowledge that I have fears. I fear that Baptists might become sacramentalists. I fear that Baptists might forsake Scripture and return to Rome. I fear that thousands – maybe millions – might be deluded and come to think that by their baptism God conveys grace to them and saves them. Although I am grieved that such fears are necessary, I am not ashamed of having them. Indeed, I ought to fear *not* having such fears. The same goes for you, reader.

[51] So much, then, for much 'modern biblical scholarship'!

[52] Fowler: *More* pp145-150. How sacramentalists can write such things in light of 1 Cor. 1:13-17, I fail to comprehend. I will return to that passage.

[53] Cross and Thompson: 'Introduction' p2.

[54] Cross and Thompson: 'Introduction' p2.

[55] Not Gal. 3:26, as printed.

3:5). Baptism in the New Testament is the moment when the Spirit is imparted... Sacraments are events where God acts to transform us.[56]

And this brings us up to the present.[57] Thus have Baptist sacramentalists spoken.

* * *

Fowler summarised his findings. Let me comment on his conclusions.

I have already noted Fowler's admission that these Baptist sacramentalists did not go back to their own history; this, as I have claimed, was because there was none to go back to. But, in addition, Fowler also admitted that Baptist sacramentalists – just like the Reformed – cannot agree on a common view of the so-called sacrament they write so much and so fulsomely about. This is highly significant. As, too, is his admission – again like the Reformed – that they are unable to give a clear simple plain statement as to what is happening in sacramental baptism, nor why it is happening, nor how it is happening.[58] Fowler:

There are still questions to be answered about the precise meaning of this sacramentalism... To say that baptism is instrumental in the application of redemption to the individual is not to say exactly how baptism conveys grace or what may be the nature of that grace, nor does it define the precise relationship between baptism and the faith of the individual. Sacramentalists draw various inferences about the connection between water baptism and Spirit baptism.[59]

---

[56] Pinnock pp15,20.

[57] More is coming out all the time. See, for instance, Michael Haykin (andrewfullercenter.org/'Baptist Life & Thought'/ 'A plea for solid reflection on the meaning of baptism', posted May 4th 2009), and the contributions which followed.

[58] Fowler: *More* pp154-155. Is it not significant that after 1800 years of sacramentalism, for all their claims about 'a theology of baptism', sacramentalists still haven't worked out what they claim is going on in baptism, nor how it is going on? See my *Infant*. See Holland for John Wesley's confusion.

[59] Fowler: *More* pp195-196.

Similarly, Timothy George, quoting Günther Gassmann on 'the Church[60] as sacrament, sign and instrument', confessed: 'There is no uniform understanding of what these terms mean in the various ecumenical texts in which they occur'.[61]

If I may translate: Baptist sacramentalists – like their Reformed counterparts – have no developed consistent theology of baptism after all. They complain about people like me for our lack of a 'theology of baptism' – but I have explained why I don't have one – yet they appear not to realise that they are in fact shooting themselves in the foot. If Baptist sacramentalists have a 'theology of baptism', why is it that although they are dogmatic that something happens in baptism, they cannot tell us what it is, or how it happens, or why? As they themselves admit, sacramentalists (let alone those who are part of the recent phenomenon of Baptist sacramentalists) have not yet worked it out! After 1800 years or more! Let Fowler set out this lack of clarity for himself and his fellow Baptist sacramentalists:

> To say that baptism is a sacrament is to say that it is a 'means of grace', but this is an assertion that demands definition, for all 'means' do not function in exactly the same way, and 'grace' is a somewhat elastic concept...

---

[60] Not merely baptism, notice, but the Church! For Pinnock on Vatican II, and **the Church** as *sacramentum mundi*, see the following chapter.

[61] George p23. Apparently, though, '"sacrament" is the most unambiguous [of the three], being used in the sense of effective mediation, representation or anticipation'. George continued: 'At the same time, "sacrament" is also the least frequently cited of these three terms. Apparently it is less of an ecumenical stretch to describe the Church as a "persuasive sign of God's love", or as an instrument for accomplishing God's purpose in Christ, than to claim that the Church is the "sacrament of God's saving work". At times, however, "sign" and "sacrament" seem to be used interchangeably as in the report of the World Conference on Mission and Evangelism, Melbourne, in 1980' (George pp23-24). This, as I understand it, means that the language is sufficiently vague and ambiguous to enable all ecumenists to make their assertions and then go happily on their way, everybody putting their own gloss on what they hear others saying. In other words, sacramentalism can drive on, conquering all before it, its advocates employing the tactics used by Second World War battleships: 'When in difficulties, make smoke'.

Are the benefits of Christ actually bestowed by God through baptism, or are they symbolically ratified as benefits given to faith? The language of Baptist sacramentalists has been varied on this [absolutely crucial] point, depending on what facet of theology they wanted to emphasise at any given time...

Baptist sacramentalists have recognised that there is some kind of normative connection between baptism and the reception of the Holy Spirit, although they have placed varying degrees of emphasis on this linkage and have seen varying degrees of consistency in the New Testament witness...

Are we in the Church because we are in Christ, or are we in Christ because we have been introduced into the Church which is the body of Christ?... Baptist sacramentalists have opted for each [both] of these logical orders...

The more perplexing question for Baptist sacramentalists is that of the relation between baptism and membership in the church (local), and this question is the most difficult test for the coherence of the system.[62]

In short, on 'the theology of baptism', 'there is still a lot of work to be done'.[63] Why, I ask again, after 1800 years or more?[64]

---

[62] Fowler: *More* pp209,211,219,223-224.

[63] Fowler: 'Oxymoron' p150.

[64] In my earlier work, I have noted the same kind of talk from Reformed sacramentalists. For further evidence, see Laning pp43-45. Those who are thinking of adopting Baptist sacramentalism, and uniting with infant baptisers, had better get used to this linguistic fog.
Just before going to press, I was introduced to P.Richard Flinn's 'Baptism, Redemptive History, and Eschatology'. I cannot resist summarising this work for the benefit of would-be Reformed-sacramentalists. According to Flinn, for the Reformers, 'baptism is... the symbol and seal of regeneration, of ablution [washing] for sin, of renewal by the Holy Ghost. [However,] when these aspects of the meaning of baptism are emphasised to the exclusion of others, it is only a matter of time before some qualification is required'. The Reformed have not been slow to provide such 'qualification'. For some, baptism is 'a seal, earnest and most sure pledge, creating faith in the things received or to be received... Under the Holy Spirit, baptism can be a powerful means of conversion and faith'. But – and there always is a 'but' – what about infants? 'Unfortunately, in the minds of many, the sacrament has become a sort of "dry run" in hopes that the real thing will transpire later. In an attempt to retrieve the power and significance of the sacrament administered to infants, at times the Reformed have slid towards... *ex opere operato*... There has been a long history of ambivalence and confusion among the Reformed on the meaning

And still they expect us to buy this pig in a poke. What pig? Fowler again:

Baptist sacramentalism is generally rooted in the concept of baptism as the vehicle of faith, the means by which faith becomes a conscious,

---

of the sacrament. Many, for example, have been uncomfortable with Calvin's formulation... The Reformed... have often been somewhat confused in trying to explain the power and efficacy of baptism, and the precise meaning of the sacrament when administered to infants', inventing such terms as 'vicarious faith, proleptic faith, objective faith *etc.*' to try to get off the hook. Flinn described G.C.Berkouwer's solution as 'very difficult to make sense of'. 'Meanwhile, many in the Reformed confession are left wondering what the Church really means when she baptises infants'. Flinn had little time for the solutions offered by John Murray and Meredith Kline. So what solution did Flinn (and his colleagues) suggest? It runs like this: 'When baptism is administered to the repentant sinner and his children, both adults and children are sealed into the covenant of grace. Their membership in the covenant is unconditional. The elements of baptism are not dependant upon faith for their efficacy... But... baptism is efficacious for salvation only through faith in the promises proclaimed in baptism. For the unrepentant, reprobate covenant child[!] who has been given the sign and seal of the covenant, or for the adult who has later apostatised, baptism remains extremely powerful and significant. Over each reprobate head, baptism seals and signifies the covenant of grace. But it is the negative aspects of the covenant with which the sinner has to do. These are powerfully sworn unto the individual as curses. His baptism testifies against him in the covenant lawsuit. He is sealed unto Christ's death in a negative sense. Christ's death is not merely of no saving significance: it utterly condemns him and heaps upon him divine vengeance... Having been formally sealed into the new age of the destruction of Christ's enemies, he himself will be most surely destroyed... Having been sealed into the new heavens and the new earth, baptism is powerful and efficacious over the one baptised, for the unrepentant becomes part of the dross burnt away by the refining fire of the Redeemer. In all these ways, baptism is powerful and efficacious, yet without the faith of the recipient. It is objectively significant to all to whom it is administered. It is significant unto salvation, however, [only] to those who believe' (Flinn pp111-151). Phew! It is to be hoped that those who administer baptism to infants on this basis will be completely open with all the parties concerned – and tell them that, in their view, God is using this baptism either to save or damn the baby, and that as the water is applied, the baptiser is sealing whichever it is, making it final.

tangible reality... If conversion were to be marked as a definite reality apart from baptism, what could serve as an adequate marker?...[65]
It is baptism in the Spirit, an act of the risen Christ, which makes the redemptive work of Christ transformative in the individual, and this encounter with Christ and the Spirit is assumed[!] to occur in [water] baptism...
The truth in the non-sacramentalist perspective is the affirmation that the gift of the Spirit is God's answer to faith in Christ,[66] but the error lies in the disjunction between faith and baptism. The biblical norm is not simply that there is some fresh experience of the Spirit in baptism, but rather that this is in fact the initiation into the life of the Spirit, inasmuch as it is initiation into Christ...
The burden of Baptist sacramentalism has been to assert that baptism is an event in which God truly acts and effects spiritual change in the [one baptised], and that this is so because it is the event in which there is a genuine and conscious divine-human encounter, a meeting of grace and faith.[67]

Fowler spoke of 'one of the common criticisms of Baptist sacramentalism from within the Baptist tradition has been that it makes baptism necessary for personal salvation, which elevates baptism to an unbiblical and unbaptistic level of significance and disqualifies the unbaptised from salvation'. Just so! He tried to escape the horns of this dilemma by calling the sacramental baptism he had been putting forward an 'ideal baptism', 'in the hope that the biblical paradigm will function as a norm to be approximated to the greatest possible degree'.[68] And Pinnock spoke of 'bad sacramentalism [and]... good'.[69]

It will not do! This kind of talk – 'ideal baptism' – reminds me of the infant-baptiser invention of the 'lapsed Christian'. And as for the notion of 'bad and good sacramentalism'... Not at all. There is only one sort of sacramentalism.

---

[65] For more on Fowler's thought that unless we think of baptism as a sacrament, we are left without 'an adequate marker of conversion', see the extended note on p313.

[66] This attribution to a non-sacramentalist like me needs careful nuancing.

[67] Fowler: *More* pp201-202,220,223,229. What a jumble! I agree, in the New Testament, baptism is one of the markers of conversion (see the previous note). A *marker* of conversion, I stress; it did not *produce* it!

[68] Fowler: *More* pp232-233.

[69] Pinnock p10.

The further away we get from Scripture the more inventive we have to become to cope with the mess we find ourselves in. With apologies to Sir Walter Scott: 'Oh what a tangled web we weave, when first we practice to devise'.

It will not do, I say again! When will sacramentalists give up their mealy-mouthed talk? Baptism is either a sacrament or it is not. If it is, it conveys grace; it *always* conveys grace. Full stop! And if Baptist scholars teach that baptism is a sacrament, it will not be long before thousands will come to believe that by their baptism they are saved.

Let us not mince words. I have stated my convictions on the subject. Let sacramentalists state theirs – with no recourse to get-out clauses and invented phrases. Let's have no more shrouding all the ramifications in a qualifying fog. The Bible is not written for philosophical lawyers and linguistic wizards. The 'ordinary' believer can read it, grasp it and obey it. Baptism cannot be so mysterious that only the metaphysicist can tell us what it means. In any case, judging by what I have read from sacramentalists – Baptist and otherwise – 'making it clear' is the last thing they seem able to do. Non-sacramental Baptists, however, are sure they know what they are doing when they baptise, and are prepared to state it for all to hear (or read) – and do so unequivocally. Speaking for myself, I do. Will the sacramentalists kindly return the favour?

There is only one way to get this fog to lift. Expose it to Scripture, and let the rays of *that* sun blaze upon it. We really ought by now to be seriously engaged with New Testament teaching on baptism. But, sad to say, we still have not finished with Baptist-sacramentalist skirmishes in their approach to the subject. Before we can get to grips with their claims in light of Scripture, and examine their expositions of Scripture, we have to look at some of the ideas, aims and practices which have been driving a growing number of Baptists towards sacramentalism.

And that will form the next chapter.

Baptist Sacramentalism – the Drivers

Baptist sacramentalism did not arise in a vacuum in England in the 20th century. In passing, I have already mentioned the liturgical movement. But there were other drivers, as I will now explain. I will do so under various headings. Not that everything can be neatly sewn up in this way, of course, but I do it to try to make things as clear as possible. Even then, much as I want to avoid it, inevitably there will be considerable overlap between the various sections.

Sacramentalism and ecumenism

The rise in Baptist (and the 'revival' of Reformed) sacramentalism has been coupled with the ecumenical movement. Indeed, it has been more than 'coupled with' it. Ecumenism has been one of its major drivers. J.D.Douglas: 'The ecumenical movement has... stimulated interest in baptismal and sacramental theology as the various branches of Christendom have attempted to work out a rapprochement'.[1] And Rome,[2] and beyond, is the terminus towards

---

[1] Douglas p101. See also, for instance, Beasley-Murray: *Baptism Today and Tomorrow* pp14-15; Fowler: *More* xiii pp4,7,105,145,149,154-155,248-249; 'Oxymoron' pp140,144-145; George pp21-23,32-35; Cross: 'Pneumatological' pp151-152,154,156-158; Newman pp213,219; Holmes p248. I find it of more than passing interest that James I.Packer (a Reformed Anglican to use his own terms) was asked to write the Foreword to Cross and Thompson: *Baptist Sacramentalism*. It lends weight to my claim that ecumenism is a driver of sacramentalism. These sacramental Baptists seem to be in the van, conceding ground to the astonishment of those they are approaching. No wonder Packer said he was 'surprised as well as delighted to be asked' to make such a contribution, and admitted 'these essays have surprised me'. He spoke of what he saw as 'a modifying of popular Baptist [biblical] ideas as they have been for the best part of two centuries'. I would say four centuries, not two. And I also disagree with Packer's assessment that 'this modification... has been guided by biblical light' (Cross and Thompson: *Baptist Sacramentalism* xiii-xiv). But note Packer's recognition that Baptists are 'modifying' the traditional Baptist view of the ordinance. His acknowledgement actually destroys the Baptist sacramentalists' claim that they are simply re-formulating a longstanding

which this ecumenical train is powering. As I write, the sacramental firemen are working overtime, keeping up a good head of steam in the locomotive's boiler as it pulls tender, carriages, guard's van and all along the chosen track, gaining momentum all the time.

Several books on the burgeoning ecumenical movement, published in the 1960s, warned of it, even as it was happening. Take Donald Gillies, who saw the connection the other way round (chickens and eggs come to mind); that is, sacramentalism as a driver for ecumenism:

A... distinctive ecumenical principle is the emphasis on sacramental unity. *Ecumenism is sacramental rather than evangelical*... This sacramentalism is not so much the contribution of one segment of the movement as [it] definitely [is] an *ecumenical* phenomenon... The prevailing emphasis [in 1964] on sacramental unity gives great impetus towards the attainment of a world Church. Indeed, in many ways, the sacrament of the Lord's supper[3] is the real uniting force and hope in ecumenism. In consequence, the strong desire for common participation in this sacrament tends to overrule the consideration of serious differences of interpretation... Why this sacramental emphasis?... The sacramental emphasis... is a force for making unity. It is an outstanding example of a more general trend among the nominally[4] Reformed

---

sacramentalism among Baptists. As I have argued, they are doing nothing of the sort. As Packer said, they are 'modifying' their traditional (biblical) view. Payne, in 1959, speaking of the Baptist Union's desire to re-think its position on, among other things, the 'sacraments', wrote: 'It became necessary for British Baptists to expound and defend their attitude to baptism in the light of contemporary biblical scholarship, and the theological debate in other Christian communions. They could no longer rest content with the exposition of their principles put forward by Dr Wheeler Robinson in 1911, weighty and effective as that had proved to be for nearly two generations. A new generation of Baptist scholars must be found to share in the ecumenical quest for the truth of God' (Payne: *Baptist Union* pp252-253). It was! Hence my book.

[2] For a summary of events connected with Rome from 1960 on, see the extended note on p314.

[3] And sacramental baptism. Indeed, sacramentalism is 'the real uniting force and hope in ecumenism'.

[4] I cannot vouch for the 1960s. I know that in the closing decade of the 20th century, and the start of the 21st, some 'Westminster Confession men' – not all of whom are merely 'nominally' Reformed – speak, *and continue to speak*, warmly of Rome; *increasingly so*.

Churches towards the acceptance of Roman Catholic doctrines and practices; especially the latter... Sacramentalists are set to establish Catholicism as the faith of ecumenism.[5]

Gillies quoted D.M.Paton from 1962: 'If Catholicism is in a way to becoming biblical, Protestantism is in a way to becoming sacramental'.[6] Gillies concluded:

The Romeward trend is no longer a matter for denial or even debate. It is an established fact. Let us not be deceived. The ecumenical movement is an affront to truth... It is a grievous offence against the God of our salvation. Ecumenism is the enemy of the gospel of regeneration by the Spirit and justification by faith alone.[7]

The Romeward trend? It is not only Rome! Indeed, as long ago as 1964, David Hedegård documented the ecumenical drive to accommodation with more than the Papacy,[8] which, unless checked by a return to biblical Christianity, will lead to a world-wide religion embracing the Reformed, the Evangelical, Rome, Islam and all.[9] Who will come out on top remains to be seen.[10] He concluded his

---

[5] Gillies pp41-48, emphasis his. See the entire volume.

[6] Gillies p41.

[7] Gillies p106. Sacramental Baptists are in the forefront of this drive to Rome. See the extended note on p315.

[8] Hedegård pp90-109. See the entire volume.

[9] See the extended note on p316 for sacramentalists and all religions.

[10] For what it's worth, I think it will be Rome. For 1500 years, Rome has shown a remarkable flair for accommodating – and then swallowing – anything and everything it meets. Take just one instance of what I am talking about. Look how successfully Rome has adopted pagan festivals, customs, fetishes and rites, and 'Christianised' them in its development of the Constantinian invention; Christmas and Easter, for example, with all their paraphernalia. It is a fact that 99.999% of believers (many of whom would be appalled if they seriously thought for a moment about the pagan-Roman connection) regard such observances as semi-biblical. So much so, in my experience, even to raise the subject with them brings wrath upon one's head. Rome has extended her tentacles far wider than most Protestants admit. See my earlier note on the admission by Roman scholars, including John Henry Newman, that Rome has always adopted pagan culture, adapting and using it for its own ends (see Jackson pp105-106).
Getting back to my suggestion. How could Rome swallow Islam (or *vice versa*)? Rome and Islam are both authoritarian, and both claim that more

book: 'A remarkable fraternisation between Protestants and Roman Catholics is taking place... This fraternisation must promote an amalgamation of Roman Catholics and Protestants'.[11]
    H.M.Carson, writing in the 1960s:

In the ecumenical debate, baptism has become one of the primary issues. The Decree on Ecumenism of the Second Vatican Council and the subsequent Directory on Ecumenism show the way that Rome is taking. Her problem has been to find a place for Protestants who have been excluded by the Bull of Pope Boniface VIII which declared in

---

than Scripture is required to obtain the truth. Calvin spotted it 450 years ago: 'Mohammed and the Pope agree in holding this as a principle of their religion – that Scripture does not contain a perfection of doctrine, but that something loftier has been revealed by the Spirit... From this source, the sacrileges of Popery and Islam have flowed; for, though those two antichrists differ from each other in many respects, still they agree in holding a common principle; and that is, that in the gospel we receive the earliest instructions to lead us into the right faith, but that we must seek elsewhere the perfection of doctrine, that it may complete the source of our education. If Scripture is quoted against the Pope, he maintains that we ought not to confine ourselves to it, because the Spirit has come, and has carried us above Scripture by many additions. Mohammed asserts that, without his Koran, men always remain children' (Calvin: *Commentaries* Vol.18 Part 1 pp101,145; see also Vol.22 Part 2 p237). In addition, both religions have mandatory fasting, elevate Mary ('Mary' appears 34 times in the Koran, I understand), hold to salvation by works, claim that Christ is not enough (Pope or Prophet are required), use beads in worship, incorporate paganism, have relics, shrines and symbols, exalt pilgrimages, and so on. Alan Clifford: 'Even where Islam is concerned, the Papacy is no longer a defence against this equally-false religion... During his visit to Turkey in 2006, Pope Benedict stated that the virgin Mary is a figure who unites Christians and Muslims, as if the Muslim denial of Christ's deity counted for nothing!' (Alan Clifford: 'Can The Pope Bring Hope? The Case for Religious Reformation and National Resistance', an email attachment to me Feb. 10th 2010; *The Daily Telegraph*, Nov. 29th 2006). Clifford referred to the *Catechism of the Catholic Church*, #841, which reads: 'The Church's relationship with the Muslims. "The plan of salvation also includes those who acknowledge the Creator, in the first place among whom are the Muslims; these profess to hold the faith of Abraham, and together with us they adore the one, merciful God, mankind's judge on the last day"'. This *Catechism* may be found at scborromeo.org/ccc.htm
[11] Hedegård p228.

1302 that outside the Church of Rome there is no salvation. Now the way in for the 'separated brethren' is baptism. They may not yet explicitly acknowledge the claims of the Pope, but by baptism they are in the One Church. Here is a problem for the Evangelical who still practices the baptism of infants. It is hard to see the difference between his position and that of the Catholic.[12]

Here, too, is a problem for the sacramental Baptist.

In 1960, Payne wrote of the way sacramental Baptists were beginning to square up to the 'opportunities' offered by the ecumenical movement. He started cautiously, however:

Baptists are only beginning to face together the theological implications of the rite of baptism as they practice it. The need for a more articulated theology, which takes account of the variety of opinion, polity and practice among Baptists and other Christians, is increasingly recognised. Whether or not they share actively in the ecumenical movement, Baptists are challenged by it.[13]

But within four brief years, Payne was returning with greater confidence to the theme, quoting Calvin who, though he was 'unwilling simply to concede the name of Church to the Papists, [did] not deny that there are churches among them... under his [the Pope's] tyranny'. 'In one [a] word', said Calvin, 'I call them churches, inasmuch... as some symbols of the Church still remain –

---

[12] H.M.Carson: *Farewell* pp130-138. 'From Vatican II... the decree on ecumenism declared that: "Baptism constitutes a sacramental bond of unity, linking all who have been reborn by means of it". *The Ecumenical Directory*... gives detailed instructions to Roman Catholics on methods of furthering the cause of reunion at the grass-roots level of parish life. The basis of the approach is that baptism is "the sacramental bond of unity, indeed the foundation of communion among all Christians". This enabled Henry St John to say at the Heythrop ecumenical conference in 1967 that non-Roman Catholics are within the Roman Church because "they are sacramentally baptised even though, without realising it, they live outside the visible structure and full organic communion of the one Church"'. As Carson said: 'When baptism is interpreted in the very flexible way already noted, where "baptism of desire" covers almost any conceivable response, we can see how widely the ecclesiastical net is being thrown. In fact this is simply another way of expressing... universalism... [the] hope that all men will ultimately be saved' (Carson: *Dawn* pp23-25).

[13] Payne: 'Baptists and the Ecumenical Movement' pp128-129.

symbols especially whose efficacy neither the craft of the devil nor human depravity can destroy'. In other words, since Rome still had the sacraments – note Calvin's 'symbols... whose efficacy' – Calvin would acknowledge a – *the* – Church among them.[14] Payne eagerly

---

[14] I developed this in my *Infant* – which see. Calvin's blind rage against the Anabaptists drove him to concede not an inch on re-baptism, even for those baptised as infants by Rome – the Anabaptists 'who deny that we are duly [truly] baptised, because we were baptised in the Papacy by wicked men and idolaters; hence they furiously insist on ana-baptism'. Calvin dismissed this as 'absurdities'. 'Against these absurdities, we shall be sufficiently fortified if we reflect that by [Roman] baptism we were initiated not into the name of any man, but into the name of the Father, and the Son, and the Holy Spirit and, therefore, that baptism is not of man, but of God, by whomsoever it may have been administered. Be it that those who baptised us were most ignorant of God and all piety, or were despisers, still they did not baptise us into a fellowship with their ignorance or sacrilege, but into the faith of Jesus Christ, because the name which they invoked was not their own but God's, nor did they baptise into any other name... The objection that baptism ought to be celebrated in the assembly of the godly [which Rome is not!], does not prove that it loses its whole efficacy because it is partly defective' (Calvin: *Institutes* Vol. 2 pp313-314,504,521, 524-525). And, right to the end, in his last and unfinished work, Calvin was still maintaining his stance on the acceptability of Roman baptism, even though performed in so corrupt a system: 'In the Papacy, such declension has grown up through many ages, that they have altogether denied God. Hence they have no connection with him, because they have corrupted his whole worship by their sacrilege, and their religion... differs in nothing from the corruptions of the heathen. And yet it is certain that a portion of God's covenant remains among them, because... God remains faithful... God's covenant with [the Jews] is [was?] not abolished, although the greater part of the people had utterly abandoned God. So also it must be said of the Papists... although with regard to themselves... they are without it [the covenant], and show by their obstinacy that they are the sworn enemies of God. Hence, it arises, that our baptism [which we received from the Papists] does not need renewal, because although the devil has long reigned in the Papacy, yet he could not altogether extinguish God's grace; indeed, a Church is among them... The Church is indeed among them; that is, God has his Church there, but hidden and wonderfully preserved; but it does not follow that they are worthy of any honour; indeed, they are more detestable, because they ought to bear sons and daughters to God, but they bear them for the devil and for idols' (Calvin: *Commentaries* Vol.12 Part 1 pp120-121). See Calvin writing to John Knox (Calvin: *Letters* pp215-216).

grasped this life-line: 'This, I believe, gives at least a basis from which to start a conversation, and it is significant that from the Roman side it is baptism which is spoken of as providing a link between Christians'. Payne cited Cardinal Bea as evidence.[15]

In 1962, Geoffrey Curtis, a member of the Mirfield Community of the Resurrection – an Anglican Monastical Community in the Benedictine Order – wrote:

What is the unity which according to the New Testament is given us by baptism? Or, to put it more simply, what in God's eyes does our baptism mean? The answer is given in two words. Those who have been [water] baptised are *In Christ*...[16] It was Paul who most firmly linked... the forgiveness of sins in baptism with the death and resurrection of Christ... It is of vital importance to recover the theological and devotional focus of the New Testament; which is [water] Baptism. Without this, we cannot reveal the Evangelical roots of the sacramental system nor show baptism to our Protestant brethren as the key to the door leading to Christian unity... The [water] baptised are already in Christ... The deepest meaning[17] of our baptism is this – our participation in Christ, as members of his body, grafted in him. Thereby all who have been baptised into Christ, being one with him, are one also with one another, in a unity not constituted by men, but by God. But if this unity is already present, Christians must strive to apprehend it more fully and to express it more effectually, in the completeness of its visible form. The penitent, prayerful realisation of the truth to which baptism witnesses will lead us to a clearer and more genuinely theological understanding of all the sacraments, and of the Church, their home, which forms itself (on earth) the sacrament of the mystical body of Christ. Baptism, Eucharist, the Ministry, all the sacraments and the Church itself, proceed from the same source, convey the same power, and mediate the same truth – the gospel of the saving action of Christ; his Baptism, Ministry, Passion, Burial, Resurrection, Ascension, Heavenly Session and longed-for Appearing.[18]

---

[15] Payne: 'Baptists and Church Relations' pp140-141; Calvin: *Institutes* Vol.2 pp313-314.

[16] Bearing in mind what the New Testament means by 'in Christ', this is a phenomenal claim for water baptism.

[17] By 'meaning', Curtis was not speaking biblically in terms of symbol. He was talking sacramentally about 'consequence'.

[18] Curtis pp191-210, emphasis his. I have left many of the capitals to better indicate the tone of the paper.

And, as I have shown, much ecumenical water has flowed under the bridge this last half-century, all of it in a Romeward direction. And sacramentalism is at the heart of it. Note, not only the content, but the tone in the following from the Evangelical, Alister McGrath: 'Modern ecumenical discussions have centred upon identifying which doctrines are essential to Christian belief, and which are open to debate'. He listed some of these so-called 'secondary doctrines', upon which disagreement may be permitted in 'Christianity', including: 'Whether, and in what way, Christ is present in the sacraments? Whether baptism signifies or causes believers to be born again?'[19] Note the words and tone, I say again. Who has defined 'secondary', and who has granted this 'permission'?

Downing engaged in another current and connected trend among Evangelicals and Reformed; namely, a return to the Fathers and an admiration of their teachings.[20] Writing in 1990, and showing incredible confusion and misunderstanding – but giving the game away – he asserted:

Baptismal regeneration as articulated in the 2nd century does not appear to be incompatible with Evangelical theology today. Nowhere was it stated [in the 2nd century] that the act of water baptism produced regeneration, but only that water baptism constituted the sacramental means by which God illustrated to man the spiritual birth which takes place on the basis of repentance and faith... Therefore one finds no basis at all in the 2nd century for any doctrine of baptismal regeneration relative to infant baptism... The analogy of Noah's day (salvation taking place only by one's inclusion in the ark), suggesting that spiritual rebirth can take place only within the community of the Church, presents a notion worthy of our consideration. Although the idea was to be taken too far a century later, perhaps we overstate the personal and individual aspect of conversion to the point that many apparent converts are never effectively integrated into the corporate life of the Church... We as Evangelicals should be gratified to find our emphasis on personal scripture [scriptural, spiritual?] regeneration on the basis of repentance and faith so well represented in the post-apostolic Church. The Orthodox and the Roman Catholic Churches have effectively claimed the patristic period as their own by tracing their particular traditions

---

[19] McGrath: *Understanding* pp66-67.
[20] For more of the Evangelical and Reformed return to the Fathers, see the extended note on p318.

through its centuries, leaving Evangelicals with seemingly little heritage to claim between AD90 and 1517. Not only would we gain credibility in our dialogue with other branches of the Church, but we would also enrich our own tradition and broaden our appeal, if we were to claim and demonstrate the presence of our theological and spiritual heritage in every age of the Church's history.[21]

The best construction I can place on this is to call it naïve. If Evangelicals of the 1990s and the Fathers of the 2nd century had a compatible theology on baptism and regeneration, then things were far worse in the 1990s than even I had imagined. If Downing (and those who agree with him) could not, and cannot, see that the Fathers' talk of water and regeneration in the same breath was not sowing the seeds of the diabolical evil we have seen this past 1800 years or more, I despair of saying anything to convince them.

As for particular details in the extract from Downing, the ark does not represent the Church. It represents Christ! Outside of *Christ* there is no salvation. You can be a Church member and yet be damned! And regeneration is not on the *basis* of repentance and faith. Regeneration is a sovereign work of God – by his fiat (John 3:3-8; Jas. 1:18); repentance and faith flow from that sovereign regeneration – not the other way round. In any case, if regeneration is based on anything other than the sovereign will, grace and power of God, it must be regeneration on the basis of works! Ah... Rome all over again! And, deliberately mixing my metaphors, clutching at straws in order to paint as rosy a picture as possible, Downing wanted us to take comfort from the fact that the 2nd century Fathers did not speak of *infant* baptismal regeneration! True enough, but what a tiny crumb of comfort with which to nourish oneself and gain enough energy to try to shift the tons of sacramentalist rubbish piled on the church by the introduction of baptismal regeneration!

Above all, Downing let the cat out of the bag. Present-day Evangelicals, it seems, long for 'credibility', long to be accepted in the academic world, long to be treated with respect by sacramentalists, long to be liked by the Orthodox and the Roman Churches, and so on. No wonder contemporary sacramental Baptists are more than happy to join in this ecumenical drive towards Rome.

---

[21] Downing p112.

Indeed, as I have shown, they are in the van. Relations are getting closer, firmer and warmer by the day. Fowler:

The common Baptist assertion that baptism is a bare sign is difficult to correlate with the actual biblical language about baptism, and it seems to be an inadequate basis for the typical Baptist willingness to perpetuate division from other Christians [not excluding Rome] on the basis of baptismal practice. Perhaps Baptist sacramentalism would offer a more compelling alternative. Whatever may be the significance of this British Baptist sacramentalism for inter-denominational dialogue, the greater significance would lie in its potential to reshape Baptist thought on a wider scale.[22]

In other words, sacramental Baptists flatter themselves that they might play the leading role in reconciling all sacramentalists from Rome to Geneva to Lambeth to Didcot[23] – and beyond!

So much for sacramentalism and ecumenism. But there are other potent ingredients to be added to this ecumenical and liturgical mix, this gadarene rush for unity or tolerance at all costs – which has done so much to encourage sacramentalism in the 20th century, and has eroded resistance to it. As I move on to explain, I have to confess that the next section is a bit of a rag-bag. Much as I have tried, I have been unable to sort it out any better.

Anyway, these 'potent ingredients' – what are they?

Sacramentalism, mass evangelism, the charismatic movement, the New Perspective and mysticism

I have already mentioned mass evangelism – particularly, the Billy Graham Crusades, with Graham's embracing of all and sundry both on the platform and behind the scenes. This has been a powerful catalyst in the sacramental-ecumenical drive this past sixty years. The charismatic movement with its all-dominant emphasis on baptism with/in/by the Spirit which overrides its theological indifference, has been another. This in itself has proved a powerful

---

[22] Fowler: *More* p250. No doubt. Hence my book.
[23] Baptist Union House is at Didcot.

unifying force in the ecumenical realm,[24] with one of its wings – the Papist – already having been long-persuaded that baptism with/in/by the Spirit comes through water baptism. The New Perspective, with its altered view of justification,[25] is another virulent constituent in all this. As is the move towards mysticism.[26]

And they have not occurred in neat water-tight compartments. Pinnock:

A fresh reading of gospel [Gospel?] texts, an appreciation of Catholic, Orthodox and Protestant traditions, and forms of charismatic renewal – these have brought me to... argue for a recovery[!] of sacramental theology for Free Church Protestants... [Unless we adopt] the sacramental principle, along with... belief in the possibility of signs and wonders... religion is powerless in both its sacramental and charismatic dimensions... The Spirit... washes us in baptismal water, and gets our feet to dance. Worship is weakened by a loss of the sacramental dimension, a loss of mystery, of liturgical beauty and of traditional practices... I would not want to see a revival of sacramentality which was not a renewal at the same time of charismaticality... Effectiveness is bound up with the Holy Spirit [as] Calvin writes... The Second Vatican Council agrees... I am concerned [said Pinnock] that we become both charismatic and sacramental as the early[27] church was.

---

[24] Packer: *Keep* pp170-181. See also Jackson pp133-145. Beasley-Murray: 'If the Church had possessed a clearer understanding of the apostolic [in Beasley-Murray's view, sacramental] teaching on baptism, it would have long since possessed a surer grasp of what the apostolic age knew of the Spirit – and perhaps a better experience of it also' (Beasley-Murray: *Baptism Today and Tomorrow* pp8-9). But, apparently, if it had risen in the first half of the 20th century, sacramental Baptists of the time would have had reservations about the charismatic movement. Cross: 'There can be little doubt that 20th century charismatic renewal would not have met with his [the principal mover of Baptist sacramentalism, Wheeler Robinson's] approval' (Cross: 'Pneumatological' p173).

[25] For more on the New Perspective and justification, see the extended note on p319.

[26] See Jackson pp157-165. Mysticism? The spiritual apprehension of truths that are beyond the understanding (see *The Concise*). 'The belief that personal communication or union with the divine is achieved through intuition, faith, ecstasy, or sudden insight rather than through rational thought' (*Encarta*).

[27] Early? We must be accurate. The *apostolic* church was not sacramental; the *patristic* Church was.

Pinnock broadened the notion and number of sacraments far beyond the 'seven or two' Rome/Reformed debate.[28] Citing 'Vatican II [which] speaks of the Church as *sacramentum mundi*',[29] Pinnock spoke of what he called 'natural [ordinary, everyday?] and ecclesial [Church] sacraments', saying: 'Sacraments are whichever and whatever media transmit the grace of God to us... Sacraments are sacred signs... through which God bestows life on us by the Spirit'. In this, Pinnock included music and kissing the Bible.[30] He further spoke of what he called:

---

[28] Rome spoke of seven sacraments; the Reformed, two. Both Rome and the Reformed are sacramentalist. I know there are differences – and I have explained what they are – but the fact remains they are both sacramentalist.

[29] See also George pp21-35; Harvey pp102-116. Freeman recorded how Henri de Lubac noted the history of 'the migration of terminology whereby language describing the eucharist as the mystical body was gradually applied to the [Roman] Church [itself – and not only to the Mass]. The result is that by the 12th century the eucharist was understood as the true body (*corpus verum*) while the Church became known as the mystical body (*corpus mysticum*)... de Lubac's attention to the "real" presence located in the Church and the "spiritual" presence in the eucharist suggest new possibilities and contours for sacramental discussions between Catholics and Baptists. Interestingly, de Lubac's work was not mentioned in the bilateral Catholic-Baptist discussions on grace' (Freeman p196).

[30] Wheeler Robinson: 'The Bible itself is no more than a collection of ancient documents till it becomes... a sacrament; that is, something which is a means by which the divine Spirit becomes active in the heart of reader or hearer' (Cross: 'Pneumatological' p154). While there is truth in this, it doesn't take a Sherlock Holmes to detect the sub-plot. Haymes: 'Some Christians... also recognise other moments in our personal stories in which the grace of our saving God is known. Thus, without suggesting for a moment that these are of similar nature and significance to baptism and eucharist, many would say that marriage has a sacramental character as in the flesh the grace of God is known. So also, for some, ordination has meant more than the choice of the people, or their own decision, but God meeting in blessing the one whom God has called to a life of ministry focused on word and sacraments... On Sept. 11th 2001 [9/11], people sought "sacred space" and those churches which were open soon found people coming to pray and to reflect. The buildings were being used while symbolically they were speaking' (Haymes pp265,267). It doesn't take a prophet to see where this is going and where it will end up. Remember, reader, these things are being said by Baptists!

A nice example [in the] prayer in the order of baptism of the Armenian Apostolic Orthodox Church: 'We pray, Lord, send your Holy Spirit into this water, and cleanse it as you did cleanse the Jordan by your descent into it... prefiguring this font of baptism and of the regeneration of all men'.[31]

Since Anglicans play a not-insignificant part in the drive for Baptist sacramentalism, it is just as well to know what some Reformed Anglicans are thinking. Take Peter Toon, writing in 1987:

The rite of baptism is not only God's appointed way of his either bestowing or confirming... regeneration... but it is also the means by which the new Christian testifies to having been born from above and converted to the Lord Jesus Christ.[32]

What a dog's breakfast! Does water baptism have two (or three) purposes? Is it either/or/but also? Does baptism bestow or confirm or testify to? What *was* Toon talking about?

In the first place, the baptism of *infants*, which Toon described as 'God's appointed way of... *bestowing*... regeneration'. But he also spoke of the baptism of '*adults*' – the baptism of believers, he meant, of course – as 'God's appointed way of... *confirming*...

---

[31] Pinnock pp8-20. Note how Pinnock opened his case for sacramentalism with: 'It is *a priori* likely... it is likely', giving me, at least, the impression that the thesis came first, after which Pinnock went looking for the evidence. And he certainly made no secret of where he looked for it. Pinnock also liked the Ethiopic prayer at the Lord's supper, and cited Kilian McDonnell and George T.Montague: *Christian Initiation and Baptism in the Holy Spirit: Evidence from the First Eight Centuries*, published by the Liturgical Press. Pinnock's is not a lone voice; see also George pp23-24. Grenz: '"Mystery" remains the normal designation for the sacraments in the Orthodox Church... Hence baptism may be called the "mystery of water"' (Grenz pp77-78). Simon Tugwell 'views the role of Roman Catholicism as being one of synthesis in which the various gleams of truth are brought together into focus. So he writes: "All the fragments of our world are to be gathered into God's wholeness"... Tugwell does not shirk the final conclusion, though it is one which parts company with the convictions of historic Christianity. He says quite frankly that in this quest for the final truth, "Marxism, Zen, Transcendental Meditation, Pentecostalism, all sorts of things, may help us on our way as we seek to enter into our inheritance of wholeness"' (Carson: *Dawn* pp37-38).

[32] Toon p188.

regeneration', or 'the means by which the new Christian testifies to having been born from above and converted to the Lord Jesus Christ'.

I have dealt with the former – the baptism of infants – in my *Infant*. Talking of the latter – the baptism of believers – I strongly dissent from the notion that baptism *confirms* regeneration. I see no scripture whatever for it.

So let's come to the only part of Toon's statement which *is* biblical; namely, baptism is 'God's appointed way... the means by which the new Christian testifies to having been born from above and converted to the Lord Jesus Christ'. Grievously, even though Toon admitted it 'is the form of baptism described in the New Testament', if he did not forget it, he buried it in a welter of patristic rite and ceremony,[33] as he immediately moved on to the following remarkable passage:

If baptism were once again to be scheduled for Easter day or some other festival... and... if the actual baptism were set in an appropriate rich ritual and liturgy, the dynamic relationship between regeneration and baptism, so obvious in the New Testament[!] and patristic literature [quite!], would perhaps be recovered. Ritual is very important in human society (witness the extent of ritual at American political rallies and football games);[34] thus the early church [that is, the Fathers – not the apostolic church] showed profound insight in developing the rite of baptism... A further incentive for re-establishing certain elements of the ancient [patristic] ritual is that an appropriate policy for the baptism of the infant children of committed church members [note the watering down of infant-baptiser theology] cannot truly be worked out until a

---

[33] As I have said, Evangelicals and the Reformed are showing an increasing fondness for the Fathers. See the earlier extended note.

[34] I have already referred to this, with special mention of the Soviet bloc – see the Introduction. In the UK, think of 'Abide with Me' at the Cup Final, State ceremonies, and, especially, the demand for birth, marriage and funeral rites, even by those who all their life have professed no faith in God – and by some, even, who have professed not to believe in his existence! Think, too, of the way the Church (not excepting the Reformed and Evangelicals) has not been slow in meeting the demand for such services. Indeed, the Church has, at times, seemed quite eager to meet it, wheeling out that benign, hoary old gentleman, 'taking the opportunity', to justify the abominable practice. See below for more on inclusivism.

deep understanding of the relationship of baptism and regeneration is recovered by the western churches.[35]

And that's a Reformed Anglican speaking!

The experience of the Baptist scholar, Michael Walker (1932-1989), serves as a telling case in point as to this mystical, liturgical and Romeward trend. Walker spoke warmly of Baptists who, in the middle of the 20th century, were beginning to adopt Calvin's sacramentalism; indeed, he himself was one of the scholars promoting it among Baptists. His experience, I say, makes salutary reading. Of Walker, David Russell noted:

There was something of the mystic about him, and something of the monk... Michael was deeply influenced by the liturgical renewal felt by Baptists and others in the 1960s and perhaps most markedly in the 1980s... He laid emphasis on the observance of the Christian Year... the Three Hours Meditation... and midnight Communion Service to welcome Christmas and Easter days... In all this he stood for a form of Baptist 'high churchmanship' which disavowed sectarianism on the one hand, with its tendency to non-sacramental worship, and on the other hand looked to 'the coming Great Church' in which the sacraments... would become... the symbol of its unity. To him, baptism and the Lord's supper were not simply 'ordinances', but sacraments... In his later years in particular he was deeply influenced by the Anglo-Catholic and the Roman Catholic traditions. He has pointed out that, in the eyes of some Baptists of the 19th century, to see the sacraments as in any way 'a means of grace' was 'to flirt dangerously with Catholicism'... He [deeply regretted this, and] made no secret of his love of ritual and the expression of worship he found in churches of that ilk... Indeed, though faithfully [according to his lights – DG] preaching the gospel in Baptist chapels throughout the valleys of South Wales, and a member of Llandaff Road Baptist Church, he was occasionally to be found on a 'free' Sunday worshipping in the nearby... Anglo-Catholic church where his presence and preaching was welcomed. His funeral service was held [there, at which]... there were no fewer than thirty priests, standing cheek-by-jowl with Baptist worshippers.[36]

---

[35] Toon pp188-189.
[36] Russell vii-x.

All these roads lead to Rome, I say. And I don't like it. As a consequence, I am of the same mind as Spurgeon who, 120 years ago, addressed his students thus:

It is quite certain, dear friends, that now or never we must be decided, because the age is manifestly drifting.[37] You cannot watch for twelve months without seeing how it is going down the tide; the anchors are pulled up, and the vessel is floating to destruction. It is drifting now, as near as I can tell you, south-east, and is nearing Cape Vatican, and if it drives much further in that direction it will be on the rocks of the Roman reef. We must get aboard her, and connect her with the glorious steam tug of gospel truth, and drag her back. I should be glad if I could take her round by Cape Calvin [avoiding the reefs I noted in my *Infant* – DG], right up into the Bay of Calvary, and anchor her in the fair haven which is close over by Vera Cruz, or the cross. God grant us grace to do it. We must have a strong hand, and have our steam well up, and defy the current; and so by God's grace we shall save both this age and the generations to come.[38]

Whether or not we have steam enough in the tug's boiler to defy the rising tide, only time will tell.[39] I doubt it. I doubt it very much. I certainly think the Romeward tide is running stronger than in Spurgeon's day, and I not only fear that the fire in the tug's engine-room has been allowed to die down to a few smoking embers, but the hull has sprung a number of serious leaks of late. As for the ship itself, the officers of the watch are not so clear-sighted as once they were. Indeed, some of them have deserted the bridge, and are asleep – snuggled up in their bunks, the duvet over their ears, letting the vessel in their charge drift. Letting it drift, indeed! Some of the

---

[37] Baptists in general are drifting, but sacramental Baptists are not!

[38] Spurgeon: *Second* p53. For more from Spurgeon, see Michael Walker pp165-169,173. Spurgeon: 'If a brother were to undertake to preach the ordinances only, like those who are always extolling what they are pleased to call the holy sacraments – well, you know where that teaching goes – it has a tendency towards the south-east, and its chosen line runs across the city of Rome' (Spurgeon: *Metropolitan* Vol.21 p644).

[39] I have no doubt about the tug – 'the glorious steam tug of gospel truth'. My doubts are centred on those who should know how to use that tug to rescue, protect and guide the main vessel and its precious cargo. I realise my illustration has some inbuilt contradictions – but the point I am making is clear enough I think.

officers are actually steering the ship towards Rome, and stoking the boilers. Yes, and at the same time![40]

Reader, what do you think of this from Michael Eaton:

> When the Charismatic movement began in the 1960s, many of us listened to arguments asking us to go back to the New Testament, and include prophecy in the church... I was convinced this was right, and so were many others. The little booklet, *Prophecy: A Gift for the Body of Christ* (1964) by Michael Harper of Fountain Trust (who subsequently joined the Greek Orthodox Church!) was pondered by many of us line by line.[41]

I find this extract alarming. Why? What is its most significant aspect? To me it is not the talk about prophecy – although I do not accept the claim that New Testament prophetic gift is still with us (I will not digress to develop my arguments and questions). Nor is it the mention of the Greek Orthodox Church – although what I think of that must be clear enough by now. No, these are not my problems.

The most disturbing point for me, and most disturbing by far, is Eaton's use of '!'. Really? Yes, really. 'Michael Harper... subsequently joined the Greek Orthodox Church!'. To me the '!' speaks volumes. Here is a man – Eaton – who clearly has charismatic leanings, to put it no stronger. Very well. Many good people do. That is not what disturbs me here. Nor is it that an Evangelical – Harper – moved into Orthodoxy. Sadly, it is not unknown. But Eaton is clearly embarrassed by the fact that his mentor on the gift of prophecy has so defected. He is embarrassed, I say. And he is embarrassed enough to let us know it by his use of

---

[40] Even as I write, the move towards Rome is gathering pace. The vessel is not 'drifting' nowadays; it is rushing headlong, driven by turbine, wind and tide. Consider the articles by P.Andrew Sandlin ('The Importance of Being Catholic') and Clint LeBruyns ('The Evangelical Advantage: A New Engagement with the Petrine Ministry') in *Act 3 Review*, Vol.15, no.2, 2006, pp25-29,53-65. To fully appreciate the point I am making, I suggest, reader, that you read these articles in full – coupled with much else in that edition of the quarterly written in admiration of N.T.Wright and his work. See my *Infant* for extracts.

[41] Eaton p38. See 'Father Michael Harper' Obituary in *The Daily Telegraph* Feb. 5th 2010.

the '!'. *But this is woefully inadequate.* Harper had every right to defect to Orthodoxy. But Evangelicals who want to quote him, and are embarrassed by it, ought to recognise and deplore the fact that he did so – not simply use the '!' – rather like 'oops!'. It is simply not good enough! Moving into Orthodoxy is not a little slip, a *faux pas*, a minor indiscretion, a gaffe. 'Oops!'. Not at all. Orthodoxy and the gospel are chalk and cheese. And Evangelicals ought to be prepared to say so! Orthodoxy, and those who defect to it, must not be handled with kid gloves!

The trouble with this softly-softly approach is that, like a constant dripping, it wears away the stone. We are being softened up (unintentionally, I am prepared to accept – although in some cases, no doubt, I am naïve to say so), softened up to move *via* charismaticism back to Orthodoxy.[42]

I say it again, therefore. The drift – the drive! – to Rome and beyond is gathering pace – among the Evangelicals and the Reformed.[43]

So much for mass evangelism, the charismatic movement, the New Perspective and mysticism as drivers for sacramentalism. But that's

---

[42] I notice that Eaton is prepared to quote 'the Roman Catholic, Francis A.Sullivan [on] the "experiential aspect of New Testament 'baptism in the Spirit'"'. Eaton has questions about certain precise aspects of Sullivan's suggestions, but not a peep from him about what I consider to be the glaring issue. See Eaton p147.

[43] On the verge of going to press, Jan. 2011, I came across these advertisements which may be found on the websites of two prominent Evangelical colleges. From Wheaton: '"Orthodox-Evangelical Dialogue: What Have We to Learn from One Another?" A lecture by His Excellency, the Most Reverend Metropolitan Kallistos (Ware) of Diokleia' (wheaton.edu/Calendars/events.html). And this from Regent College, Vancouver: '"Heaven on Earth?" Theological interpretation of Scripture is becoming a common practice, both among Catholics and Evangelicals... This conference, hosted by Regent College in cooperation with the Centre for Catholic-Evangelical Dialogue (CCED), brings together numerous renowned Catholic and Evangelical scholars to ask the question: what are the implications if we read the historical, earthly text in the light of spiritual or heavenly realities? [Speakers are] Brian E.Daley, S.J. [the Society of Jesus; that is, Daley is a Jesuit] and Kevin J.Vanhoozer' (regent-college.edu/events/conferences/index.php).

not the end of the story. How could the ecumenical-liturgical-sacramentalist-Church come about? Infant baptism![44]
    Infant baptism a driver for *Baptists*? Baptists – Baptists – adopt infant baptism? Never!
    Read on!

Ecumenism, sacramentalism and infant baptism

It does not take any special prescience to see how easily all this could gel in the coming years. What the scholars teach today, the ministers will preach tomorrow, and the rank-and-file will believe the day after. Beasley-Murray, pessimistically, from his point of view, describing the situation in 1966, disagreed. He regretted that most Baptists 'still subscribe to [the] statement' that baptism is a symbol and not a sacrament, even though 'a majority of their theologians would repudiate it. The theologians, however, appear to exercise little influence on the preaching and administration of baptism in the churches'. If he was right in making this last statement in 1966, I have my doubts in the 21st century. Big doubts! He himself, a few paragraphs later, indicated the way things were going, even then: 'A considerable change of viewpoint has taken place in recent years among [Baptist] ministers as well as theological teachers'. And he explained why: 'The change is due, I believe, partly to a fresh examination of the teaching of the

---

[44] As Iain Murray has documented (Murray: *Evangelicalism* pp94,99-107,117,163-164,217), since the 1970s baptism (inevitably, infant baptism) has been the 'new theory' to defend and promote ecumenical unity between Evangelicals, Anglicans and Rome. In his admirable critique of this, Murray quoted William Beveridge: 'The church must needs be a congregation of faithful [believing – Murray] men, for until they be faithful [believing – DG agreeing with Murray] men, they cannot be of the church'. Beveridge was right, of course. But Murray showed the weakness of his own hand when he added: 'This is not to deny infant baptism, but the New Testament does not teach infant baptism as the norm. Baptism is to strengthen faith, not to create it'. Oh? If words mean anything, what Beveridge rightly said *does* deny infant baptism. And as for 'infant baptism' not being 'the norm' of the New Testament, Murray could say that again! Infant baptism is not only not the norm of the New Testament, it is not even in the New Testament!

Scriptures on baptism, and partly to participation in ecumenical discussion'.[45]

While I welcome – indeed, I demand! – an examination of the Scriptures on baptism and everything else, if this examination takes place wearing ecumenical glasses, the result will be a foregone conclusion.[46] As I have said, Baptist sacramentalists have little to fear – unless the non-sacramentalists wake up – and soon!

David Wright saw the current days, 'the dying days of Christendom', as he put it, as a good time to re-think baptism. As I have noted, he would have liked to have seen a higher status for infant baptism, a more sacramental approach. This, I am convinced is wrong and will lead to a new Christendom replacing the old, but still built on the old foundation – infant baptism. Satan is too wily to let such a powerful weapon slip through his fingers!

So, how will the new Christendom come about? Here is my suggestion: An increasing number of Baptists and Reformed infant-baptisers (theologians in the driving seat) will come together as sacramentalists (discussions between both parties have been going on since the late 1970s), adopt infant baptism in some form or another, and Rome will move just enough to bring them within range and so swallow them alive! That's my 'prediction'! After all, as Wright saw it:

Recent trends in ecumenical [that is, Romanist and Protestant] reflection on baptism must be regarded as favourable to Baptists' fundamental demand for baptism on profession of faith. Believer Baptists now have an unprecedented opportunity to promote a theology of baptism which confidently takes the full measure of the New Testament witness and no longer feeds on reaction against the distorting effects of the long reign of infant baptism.[47]

What a mixed bag! But the trend stands out a mile. It doesn't take a genius to work out where it will end up.

---

[45] Beasley-Murray: *Baptism Today and Tomorrow* pp14-15.
[46] What we bring to Scripture has an overriding effect on what we take away.
[47] Wright: *What...?* pp9,31; see also Wright: *What...?* p28; see earlier notes on the Romeward movement among Evangelicals, and Rome's changes, including Wright: *What...?* pp10,15-17,102; see also Jones pp105-129.

When Ross wondered whether or not the new approach will 'turn all Baptists into infant baptisers, or *vice versa*',[48] I have little doubt that some – and not a few, I fear – Baptists *will* end up as infant baptisers, with all that that entails for the individual and the church. It must be so if, as I fear, the present sacramentalist-ecumenical drive to Rome continues.

Sacramental Baptists are not at all embarrassed to acknowledge that they can see it coming. Fowler: 'Does genuine sacramentalism demand infant baptism?'[49] Quite a thought, is it not? Even though, at present, they clearly feel the need to fend off infant baptism,[50] sacramental Baptists have no illusions: 'The conclusion [of many contemporary infant baptisers] is that if Baptists are going to take seriously the divine action in baptism, then they will have to surrender their opposition to the baptism of infants'.[51]

Whatever else it is, that's clear enough. It is all very well for Fowler to say in reply that 'Baptist sacramentalists are neither unbiblical nor incoherent in their assertion that the grace which is active in baptism is the grace of applied redemption, a grace which has effects that cannot realistically be posited of any but confessing believers',[52] but this, I am sure, will come to be seen as whistling in the dark. Once sacramentalism is granted, comparison or contrast of 'prevenient' (in the baptism of infants) and 'applied' grace (in the baptism of believers) will fade away.

I have repeatedly made the point that sacramentalism is *the* issue. To re-use my illustration: If sacramentalism is the bushel, infant baptism is but a grain. Once sacramentalism is adopted, the difference between those who baptise infants and those who baptise believers will peter out, lose all relevance, and finally die and be forgotten. After all, both parties agree that it must be baptism and faith – or faith and baptism. What's the difference? In the case of infants, baptism precedes faith; in the case of believers, faith precedes baptism. To make a fuss about *that* – once sacramentalism rules the roost – will be dismissed as nit-picking. The call to find the

---

[48] Ross p112.
[49] Fowler: *More* p211.
[50] See Cross: 'The Evangelical sacrament' p196; Fowler: *More* pp211-219.
[51] Fowler: *More* p215.
[52] Fowler: *More* pp218-219.

biblical 'one baptism' will end up in only one unbiblical place – infant baptism. I go further. It will end up in indiscriminate infant baptism in this new (which is the old but new-fangled) Christendom.[53]

I am no prophet, of course, but I offer this suggestion as to how things might develop. The first step – and that's what I am concerned with here – will be for sacramental Baptists to accept infant baptism as valid; not quite right, of course, not quite as biblical as believer's baptism, but valid all the same. Indeed, it does not require any special insight to say as much! Substantial evidence for it has been in the public domain this past half century.[54] As long ago as 1965, the Baptist Neville Clark was making the opening moves: 'It would be arrogant, grievous and wholly unjustifiable for any [Baptist] to suggest that infant baptism is no baptism', he wrote. 'It is true baptism'. Fowler explained: In this change to a more tolerant climate, although infant baptism would be considered 'irregular', nevertheless 'Christians die and rise with Christ in [water] baptism... Those baptised as infants and those baptised as

---

[53] I have already noted Calvin's acceptance of Roman baptism. Note Fowler's talk of 'patristic teaching... apostolic succession' (Fowler: *More* p221). Such talk may well be just talk at present, but, reader, do not miss the less-than categorical: 'But even if such [apostolic] succession were granted, Baptists (and others) have rightly argued that the Acts... will not bear the weight of this doctrine of apostolic hands'. The New Testament *will not bear the notion* of apostolic succession? How weak! The New Testament never gives a hint if it! It's like saying the New Testament will not bear the notion of life on Mars! Apostolic succession? Nonsense! The very idea is abhorrent. The principle of the new covenant repudiates it.

[54] Indeed, Spurgeon warned about it in 1861. The report of the church meeting on April 8th 1861, stated: 'He [Spurgeon] would rather give up his pastorate than admit any man to the church who was not obedient to his Lord's command [in water baptism]; and such a course would certainly promote the downfall of any church that practiced it. The mixed Baptist churches were eating out the very vitals of the denomination'. Since, in the meeting, Spurgeon had been preceded by James Smith who had been speaking of the unbiblical nature of infant baptism, I think Tim Grass and Ian Randall were right to say that Spurgeon was talking about the wrongness of admitting members who had not been baptised as believers – even though they might have been baptised as infants (Spurgeon: *New* Vol.7 p260; Grass and Randall p61).

believers are not in totally different categories'.[55] As Fowler said: 'Clark argued emphatically against the re-baptism as believers of those who were baptised in infancy... Any such re-baptism is "a blow at the heart of the Christian faith"'.[56]

Clark spoke of 'the burning controversy within the church as to the rightful recipients of baptism'. He spelled out his own position. As he did so, he was prepared to make astonishing – incredible – concessions to the infant baptisers:

No immediately obvious or conclusive answer to this question is provided by an appeal to the practice of the New Testament age. To point out that the constant concern of the earliest Christians is with the

---

[55] Fowler: *More* pp111-112. In Fowler's reference (in 2006) to Clark (in 1965), we can trace the quickening of the Baptist pace towards infant baptism. It has not stopped. See the extended note on p320, where I sketch the details.

[56] Fowler: *More* p123. Here the sacramentalists are raking up old embers and fanning them into a flame. The question of re-baptism (and sins committed after baptism) was a hot potato for the Fathers. The Nicene-Constantinople Creed of 325 and 381 spoke of 'one baptism for the remission of sins'. But what did the Fathers mean by it? Some in the eastern Church did practice baby baptism at the time, but 'they seem to have believed that babies were not sinners or sinful, and hence, if baptised, were not baptised "for the remission of sins"'. The Greek Fathers such as John Chrysostom, Gregory Nazianzen and Cyril of Jerusalem, thought that a person could be baptised only once for the remission of sins. The baptism of babies, being without sin, did not come into that category. According to Cyril, heretics should be re-baptised since their baptism was not valid in the first place. In the western Church, Cyprian re-baptised heretics (Donatists in particular), and Donatists re-baptised Catholics, because, both sides argued, the first baptism in each case was invalid. This, however, lasted only for some 50 years in the west. When Augustine came up with the nonsense that original sin is removed in baptism, and, in addition, attempted to justify the validity of baptism performed (under certain conditions) by Catholics or Donatists, the normal western practice of not re-baptising was established. See Wright: 'One' pp328-332. See also my *Infant* for large extracts from Augustine, and for the way this was all played out with the Reformers – and is still being played out by the Reformed today. Would-be Baptist sacramentalists beware. Flirting with infant baptism will lead *you* into this minefield. May I suggest you read those extracts from Augustine before you finally decide? He is, after all, the great theologian of infant baptism, Calvin's (and all the others') mentor.

rite as applied to adult believers may be to advance an irrefutable claim; but in the end it is not clear that this is to do more than register the necessary conditions of every missionary situation, when the gospel is first proclaimed. In any event, evidence for the baptism of adult believers of the second generation is lacking. It has, indeed, been claimed that there are signs that within the New Testament period the practice of infant baptism was not unknown, and confirmation both of a direct and of an indirect nature has been adduced to support such a case.

I pause. Clark, as I have said, was here conceding massive ground to infant baptisers – in my opinion, without justification. I admit what he says about second generation believers, of course,[57] but talk of the baptism of infants is something utterly foreign to the New Testament, and for him so easily – so readily – to concede Reformed claims for the unbiblical practice was irresponsible to a high degree.[58] However, having noted Clark's incredible concession to infant baptisers, there can be little doubt as to what would follow:

The questioning of the legitimacy of infant baptism carries with it no necessarily absolute condemnation. Nor is there involved therein any simple, unqualified approval of the characteristic Baptist position. The practice of believer's baptism does not automatically authenticate any theology that may lie behind it... There is demanded of us some closer examination of infant baptism... It is clear that the problem of the theology of childhood cannot be evaded.

Clark examined the theology behind infant baptism: 'From the earliest times,[59] infant baptism has been a practice in search of a theology', he said. He was quite right![60] Clark briefly sketched the course taken by the Fathers in this quest, and again, quite rightly, did not like it. But – and – he had a sting in the tail – again, quite rightly – for Baptists:

History has repeated itself. Among the Baptists, in recent decades, there has grown up the practice of the blessing of infants. Again it arose in

---

[57] But note the baptismal silence in Eph. 6:1-4; Col. 3:20-21; 2 Tim. 3:14-15.

[58] See my earlier works for my exposure of the wrongness of Reformed arguments for infant baptism.

[59] That is, since its invention by the Fathers – it is unknown in the New Testament.

[60] See my Introduction above.

response to popular Christian demand. Again, it has been, more or less unsuccessfully, in search of a theology ever since.[61]

'The blessing of infants'. I can hear the old-covenant overtones in the phrase.[62] Why do those who want to invent rites for infants so often go back to the old covenant?[63] 'The blessing of infants', too, will come to be seen as a step along the road union with infant baptisers. Clark continued, inching ever closer to the infant-baptist position:

We must distinguish between believers (and their children) and unbelievers (and their children). The former belong to the sphere of the body of Christ; the latter belong to the world which is marked with the seal of redemption and the humanity which, by incarnation, the Son has brought into union with himself.[64] On the other hand, we must distinguish between believers and their infant children... The latter are those who, by the fact of their birth are specially related to the body of Christ.[65]

Clark came to the sacramental:

The... word and sacrament belong inseparably together... It is the response to the word which the Spirit empowers that makes baptism Christologically congruous and ethically meaningful. Existence in

---

[61] What a warning. Watch out for 'the little foxes' (Song 2:15). Little errors cast long shadows.

[62] It is not the only place where it can be found. It is objectionable – wrong – for ministers to use the aaronic priestly blessing as it stands (Num. 6:22-27) when closing a service; worse still is it, as I have witnessed, for a (Reformed Baptist) minister to raise his arms above the congregation, the palms of hands facing us, as he pronounces the words. It smacks of sacerdotalism; it is sacerdotalism. And the practice shows no signs of dying out. What are such Reformed Baptist ministers and churches about? Do they not fear they might be trespassing on Christ's prerogative (Luke 24:50)?

[63] I confess that I have not been guiltless myself in this regard – but never, may I hasten to add, being so foolish as to talk about 'blessing infants'.

[64] I simply cannot follow this. Christ became a man – but this does not mean that man has become 'Christian'.

[65] Oh? In what way? Biblically, I mean. Being children of believers, and all that that entails, while it is a tremendous advantage, is a far cry from being 'specially related to the body of Christ' by reason of birth. How such claims can be made in the light of John 1:11-13, and the like, is beyond me.

Christ is Churchly existence; that is to say, baptismal and eucharistic existence. Towards the pattern of Christian initiation which most fully, richly and completely declares this, we are called to move... The fullness of Christian initiation is to be found in the conjunction of baptism (whether or not accompanied by the laying on of hands) with first communion. This is the pattern of insertion[!] into the priestly body of Christ. Judged by this standard, both Baptist and infant-baptist practice may be found defective.

Clark spoke of the mode of baptism, rejecting the biblical (and traditional) Baptist claim for immersion only: 'We have no warrant for making any one mode obligatory'.[66] He was pleased with the growing tendency among infant baptisers to 'expound infant baptism and confirmation[67] as parts of a larger initiatory whole'. But he still thought that infant baptism was in a state of 'practical confusion'. He could say that again! See my *Infant* for the confusion which still persists among infant baptisers.

And what of his own constituency, the Baptists? Just this:

Nevertheless, such criticism carries with it no sweeping endorsement of Baptist practice. Here also, confusion reigns. The Baptist communion bids fair to become the only major branch of the... Church where baptism is not of universal observance – a somewhat curious basis from which to attempt to justify a separate denominational existence.

From this justified observation, Clark moved up a gear, deploring that, by Baptists:

The whole theological and sacramental progression proper to initiation is ignored and denied. Finally, the re-baptism as believers of those who have received baptism in infancy constitutes a blow at the heart of the Christian faith... For no baptism [that is, no baptism, not excluding the baptism of infants] can lack its proleptic [that is, its representative] element, and every baptism [not excluding infant baptism] points forward for its completion and fulfilment.[68]

---

[66] I profoundly disagree, as I have fully argued elsewhere.
[67] Confirmation is not confined to Anglicans. It is a Reformed practice, as I have already shown. It is, it goes without saying, foreign to Scripture. It is a hang-over from the medieval Church, Roman and Orthodox.
[68] Clark: 'The Theology' pp310-326.

To translate: According to Clark, it is wrong to treat those baptised as infants as unbaptised. They have been baptised, and should not be re-baptised! Their infant baptism was a true baptism, and represented spiritual realities as much as the baptism of a believer. To say otherwise, is to say that infant-baptiser churches are no churches at all.[69]

Or, as Alec Gilmore put it in 1966: 'It is better to acknowledge that infant baptism, though partial in its expression of the truth and though involving serious theological distortion, is nevertheless baptism, and cannot therefore be followed by believer's baptism being administered to the same person'.[70] Gilmore argued that the new covenant did away with circumcision, and this created a vacuum – this 'created the need[71] for something to bring home to a man his union with Christ and the realisation he was possessed by Christ's Spirit'. Gilmore went on to say that baptism filled this vacuum – which, as Fowler interpreted it, meant 'that baptism mediates the conscious experience of entrance into the sphere of redemption; in other words... a "seal"'.[72] Bearing in mind the way

---

[69] Fowler summarised Clark's position: 'The proleptic [representative] nature of every baptism (infant or believer), and the assumption that to reject the validity of infant baptism is to deny the validity of infant-baptiser churches' (Fowler: 'Oxymoron' p140). See above for Kevan's criticism of *Christian Baptism*, and especially Clark's contribution: 'Anything less Baptist would be hard to find' (Cross and Thompson: 'Introduction' p4). I can find no better words to express my view of Clark's work.

[70] Fowler: *More* p148

[71] The 'need'? What need? Something was needed to fill the vacuum left by the ending of circumcision? Why? What scripture speaks of this? I agree, of course, that the new covenant did away with circumcision, but where are we told that baptism has replaced it? Gilmore's talk was grist to the infant-baptiser's mill. He was conceding biblical ground. He must have realised what infant-baptism capital could be made out of this unbiblical concession. The alternative is naïvety of immense proportions.

[72] Gilmore p65; Fowler: 'Oxymoron' pp130-131. Beasley-Murray found 'it... impossible... to dismiss from [his] mind that in the Church from the 2nd century on, the term "seal" was used as a synonym for baptism'. He himself was persuaded of 'the probability that the "seal of the Spirit" is a synonym for the possession of the Spirit secured in baptism' (Beasley-Murray: *Baptism in the New Testament* pp171-177). Beasley-Murray might have been persuaded of it. I am not! In fact, I categorically deny it.

infant baptisers misuse circumcision and the seal, Gilmore's approach can lead to only one end. To return to my (by now, threadbare) illustration: the bushel of sacramentalism having been swallowed, the grain of infant baptism will hardly be noticed by Baptists – indeed, its so-called 'benefits' might well come to be praised – and how much more 'biblical' it sounds than 'dedication' – especially if all the blame for the 'excesses' of infant baptism can be relegated to the 3rd and 4th centuries and the medieval waste-paper basket.

Things don't stand still. The following extract sums up what this is all about, and what I deplore. In 1999, Porter and Cross said of White – one who, as I have explained, was influential in the rise of Baptist sacramentalism – that he:

Notes that infant baptism is a form of baptism prevalent in the modern Church that is very unlike that of the New Testament in form, content and theological significance, yet enshrining certain values and insights that in any final appraisal of the rite would have to be preserved and prized... [White and Beasley-Murray] revolutionised the Baptist understanding of the initiating sacrament. Both brought the sacrament of baptism out of Zwinglian shadows[!] and made us see that here was indeed a place of rendezvous between God and man, an integral part of that process[73] of conversion by which a man or woman is raised from death to life in Christ, is cleansed of sin, made a member of the body of Christ and endowed with the gift of the Spirit.[74]

Let the Baptist theologian Richard Kidd, as quoted by John H.Armstrong in 2007, speaking for himself, bring these extracts from sacramental Baptists, and those associated with them, to a close:

Elsewhere I have set out my reasons for denying that baptism is a seal. I draw attention, once again, to the part played by the Fathers in this.

[73] Note the word. I will return to it.

[74] Porter and Cross pp37-38. As long ago as 1927, Wheeler Robinson indicated the way the wind was blowing: 'There is... a growing minority of Baptists whose interpretation of the Lord's supper is Calvinistic rather than Zwinglian' (Wheeler Robinson: *The Life* p118) – which would, of course, have pleased Robinson, and which I deplore. The breeze of 1927, I am sorry to say, has turned into a gale in the early 21st century.

The world is already too racked with pain and conflict [said Kidd] to permit Christians the luxury of adding to its fragmentation by internal arguments about baptism... I can no longer work... with a stark and uncompromising contrast between believer's baptism, which is right, and infant baptism, which is wrong. Rather, I am discovering here two histories of the one sign we call baptism... These histories... cannot be mixed, nor should one be allowed to replace the other; for in both these ways, the proper integrity of each would be destroyed... But I would like to think I can participate in and celebrate the integrity of what is the other, without threat to what is profoundly my own.[75]

After such extracts, no Baptist can say he was not warned.

But all is not quite as it seems among sacramental Baptists, even those who are seemingly confident. Behind all the rhetoric, they are not as confident as they appear. Fowler exposed the muddle sacramental Baptists find themselves in over infant baptism. 'The failure to connect theory to practice on this point [on how to regard baptised infants] is the major deficiency of modern Baptist sacramentalism'.[76] Very well. So how did Fowler sort it out? On the one hand:

If God acts in baptism... then the human response may be relativised in a way that questions the traditional Baptist refusal to baptise infants. If the most fundamental reality in baptism is God's gracious action of uniting the individual to Christ (as some Baptist sacramentalists emphasise)... then there may well be a solid case for infant baptism. If baptism as a means of grace follows the contours of divine grace, then it may be that it should precede the individual's confession of faith. The argument for the priority of grace to the baptism of infants has become perhaps the most popularly cherished argument for infant baptism in the latter half of [the 20th] century, and its challenge needs to be considered... Does genuine sacramentalism demand infant baptism?

---

[75] Armstrong p21. A few moments ago, in an extended note, I referred to the report of the 1996 Baptist Union committee, *Believing and Being Baptised: Baptism, so-called re-baptism, and children in the church*, calling it a curate's egg; good in parts, but only in parts. Kidd was a member of that committee. Judging by the above, there is no doubt as to *his* position.

[76] Fowler: *More* p231. I draw attention to the tautological 'modern'. Baptist sacramentalism *is* modern. I will not keep repeating this comment, but it should be borne in mind.

Fowler went on to quote the infant baptiser, Cullmann, who, as I have already noted, argued, contrary to Scripture, for baptism before faith. 'But how', asked Fowler, 'does all this [Cullmann's claim] correlate with the New Testament passages which call for faith prior to baptism?' Quite. Fowler summarised Cullman's argument that black is white thus: 'What is demanded by baptism is *subsequent* faith'.[77] The New Testament – does it need saying yet again? – demands faith *before* baptism.

Fowler, I say, exposed the muddle the sacramentalists make for themselves, contradicting what he said before:

The one aspect of this [Baptist sacramental] theology which seems incoherent is the tendency of some to accept *de facto* infant baptism as valid baptism, which stands in opposition to historic Baptist theology, and does not seem to follow from the premises inherent in the sacramental theology of baptism.[78] If believer's baptism has the kind of significance which is affirmed in this theology, then it is difficult to see how infant baptism can be accepted as its equivalent without affirming either that there is power in the ritual apart from personal faith, or that baptism is purely declaratory-symbolic. The former alternative would make this theology something other than Baptist,[79] and the latter would make it something other than sacramental.[80] This tendency to affirm infant baptism after the fact appears to be inconsistent with the general theology being affirmed, but this calls into question only this one inference from the theology, not the theology itself.[81]

Oh?

Let me introduce a note of sanity. On the effort to fuse believer's baptism and infant baptism into one, Spurgeon's voice still resonates:

---

[77] Fowler: *More* pp211-212, emphasis his.

[78] Infant baptism not follow from sacramentalism? I couldn't disagree more! Chicken and egg, I agree, but that's what infant baptism and sacramentalism are – chicken and egg. Leaving the figure, I am convinced, as I have argued in my *Infant*, that sacramentalism came first and led to infant baptism. And infant baptism, as I have shown, itself produces and enforces the sacramentalism. Historically it has been so, and it is so today.

[79] Note Fowler's admission that 'sacramentalism' and 'Baptist' are mutually contradictory terms, as I have insisted all along.

[80] See the previous note.

[81] Fowler: *More* pp246-247.

We beg to say to all friends, that that point on which we differ – namely, believer's baptism – that we shall be very glad to see altered, because it is very wrong that there should be two or three baptisms, where there ought to be only one, and we believe we are certain that if you will find us a precept for the baptism of infants, we will follow it – a plain one, mark you. And as it is very clear to us, and we think to you, that believers were baptised, that is one baptism – that is plainly in Scripture, is it not? Very well, the other one – that is the other baptism.[82]

Again, addressing those who would combine the two baptisms:

They would form churches... in which Christ's ordinance of baptism would be left optional; some of them would even have a font and a baptistery in each place of worship, which, to our mind, is to form churches on the principle of despising the command of Christ, and counting it to be an utterly insignificant matter what the ordinance may be, and whether it be obeyed or not. 'Whichever you please, dear friends; pay your money and take your choice. Sprinkle the infant, or immerse the believer, our church does not care a farthing which'...[83]
We tell these gentlemen who are so set upon fusing the infant baptisers and the Baptists, that... we take liberty to say again that there is one Baptist at least who will never be absorbed into the projected unity... We have been open and above board in our expressions upon this business, and we wish others would be.[84]

My position precisely.

I leave this section on ecumenism, sacramentalism and infant baptism there. I now want to move on to look at the way in which this sacramental desire for a common baptism is spurred on by the growing tendency to re-define conversion.

Conversion re-defined as a process, and the emphasis upon corporate, not individual, salvation

The next sacramental driver I want to consider is the way in which conversion is being re-defined. What do I mean? There is a growing tendency to think that coming to faith, conversion, is a process and

---

[82] Spurgeon: *Speeches* pp185-186.
[83] A farthing being the lowest value coin in English currency at the time.
[84] Spurgeon: *Sword* pp326-328. See my earlier note on Spurgeon in 1861.

not a crisis,[85] an initiation (an admission into a society, especially with a ritual; see *The Concise*), and not a definite change. Connected with this is an emphasis upon corporate, not individual, salvation.[86]

Note my use of 're-defined'. I say that Baptist sacramentalists are *re-defining* conversion for Baptists, moving away from the New Testament definition of it, and moving ever closer to the Reformed-sacramentalist view of it.

Let me make my meaning clear. I do so in the words of John Baillie, one who, as he told us, was 'brought up in the very rigorous Calvinism of the Scottish Highlands at the turn of the present [that is, the end of the 19th and beginning of the 20th] century'.[87] Naturally, Baillie was no Baptist. But this is precisely why I use his testimony. He tackled the issue in hand in his aptly-titled *Baptism and Conversion*, and the fact that he was a non-Baptist – with no Baptist-axe to grind – lends considerable weight to his assessment of the traditional-Baptist view.

Let me establish his non-Baptist credentials. This is how he set out his own convictions:

[The] Christian life begins at [water] baptism... Baptism... is the rite of regeneration, of being born again into the newness of the Christian life... Our [baptised] children should be brought up from infancy as Christian children.[88]

---

[85] By 'crisis', I do not mean something necessarily dramatic. Rather, 'a time when something very important for the future happens or is decided' (*Encarta*). And by 'time', I do not mean 'process'. I am speaking of an occasion, an event, a juncture, a point in time.

[86] George: 'Regrettably, many Baptists and Evangelicals interpret their own conversion as a supreme act of individualism, a private response detached, if not divorced, from the corporate community of faith' (George p34). While I admit the speck of truth in this sack of error, that speck does not, I am afraid, make the sack good. Advocates of the corporate can end up in a very odd place. Holmes, for instance, arguing for the corporate as opposed to the individual, went so far as to say: 'Christian believers exist together or not at all, and so, necessarily, Christian believers minister together or not at all' (Holmes pp254-256). Really?

[87] Baillie p86.

[88] Baillie pp41,44.

Baillie was a sacramental infant-baptiser. Very well. So how did he describe the 'traditional' Baptist view of regeneration and baptism? Traditional Baptists, he said:

> Refuse to ascribe the regenerative efficacy to baptism itself, nor do they hold that baptism is necessary to regeneration, but only that it is the duty of all who believe themselves [to be] regenerate to submit themselves afterwards to baptism.[89]

A very fair summary, I should say.

As for 'conversion', that which Baillie attributed to Evangelicals in general, applies in particular to traditional Baptists:

> The definitive use of the term 'conversion' [for Evangelicals, in general, and traditional Baptists, in particular, is] to denote a single critical experience in which an individual becomes a Christian after years of discretion are reached... A man is not a Christian until he has passed through this experience.[90]

Surely this is right. This is the 'traditional' or 'conventional' Baptist view of conversion. Let me quote as traditional a Baptist as one could wish – John Gill – to verify it. In his *Body of Divinity*, Gill devoted ten closely-printed pages to explaining and developing what he saw as the biblical doctrine of conversion. The space he gave to it shows the importance he attached to the subject. I can give only the briefest digest.[91]

Gill distinguished regeneration and conversion thus:

> Regeneration is the sole act of God; conversion consists both of God's act upon men, in turning them, and acts done by men, under the influence of converting grace... Regeneration is the motion of God towards and upon the heart of a sinner; conversion is the motion of a sinner towards God. In regeneration, men are wholly passive, as they also are in the first moment of conversion; but by it [they] become active. It is therefore sometimes expressed passively: 'You are returned', or converted (1 Pet. 2:25); and sometimes actively: 'A great number believed, and turned to the Lord' (Acts 11:21).

Over several pages, he argued in detail that:

---

[89] Baillie p39.
[90] Baillie pp83,85.
[91] For Gill's statement in full, see the section marked 'Gill's Archive' at pbministries.org/books/gill/gills_archive.htm

Conversion... is a true, real, internal work of God upon the souls of men... The turn of the heart to God... a turn of the affections of the heart... Conversion is a turn of the mind from carnal things to spiritual ones, and from earthly things to heavenly ones... a turn of the will... They [the converted]... turn their feet to his testimonies... Conversion lies in a man's being turned from darkness to light... turning... from the power of Satan to God... turning men from idols to serve the living God... turning men from their own righteousness to the righteousness of Christ... Conversion lies in a man's turning to the Lord actively, under the influence of divine grace... Conversion is such an alteration in a man, as is not in his power to effect; it is like that of an Ethiopian changing his skin, and a leopard his spots... Conversion is the motion of the soul towards God.

'In redemption', said Gill, 'Christ turns away iniquities from his people, by bearing them, and making satisfaction for them; and in conversion, he by his Spirit and grace turns them from their iniquities'.[92]

This is the weight that traditional Baptists have attached to 'conversion'. Biblical weight, too.

To return to Baillie. He opened his examination of baptism and conversion by quoting Bishop Stephen Neill in his setting out of the two main views of conversion; namely, the traditional Baptist and the sacramental. This is what Neill said about the traditional Baptist view:

Conversion is the beginning of real Christian life. Christian nurture, education and worship may be valuable preparations.[93] But no one is, or should be called a Christian until he has personally encountered God in Jesus Christ, until he has personally repented, until he has personally

---

[92] Gill: *Body* Vol.2 pp292-302.

[93] But there is a risk. The notion of 'process' and 'nurture' is widespread. Those who use the 'Christianity Explored' course (or similar), or baptismal classes, should at the very least bear the danger in mind. I fear I have not always escaped falling into the trap of 'coaching' for the reply I am looking for. Colin Vincent recalled his own experience, many years ago (pre-dating such courses!): 'This brings back memories of the occasion when I asked for baptism in my young teens – I was taken into the deacons' vestry... and a young converted lady said to me as she passed through the vestry: *"Colin, don't let them convince you that something has happened to you when it has not"'* (e-mail to me Nov. 12th 2009, emphasis his). Colin rightly pointed out that while we grow *in* faith, we do not grow *into* faith.

accepted God's gift of salvation through faith in Christ, [having been] born again.[94] The reality of the Church in the world depends on there being enough people who have passed through this experience, and through whom it can be passed on to others.[95]

This is surely right. This *is* 'traditional' Baptist teaching.

But it is far more. It is the teaching of the New Testament.[96] So plainly is this written there, it would be almost superfluous to cite particular passages and examples of conversion. Let me come at it from the opposite direction. Where, in the New Testament, is there any record of any sinner coming to a saving knowledge of Christ *without* this 'crisis' experience? I freely admit that not all conversion experiences are so dramatic as that of Saul of Tarsus outside the gates of Damascus, but its principles are written large in every conversion experience recorded in the New Testament. And there is no believer in the New Testament whose experience contradicts it. Take the Acts. As I say, it is almost superfluous to cite individual incidents. But I will! See Acts 2:37-41; 4:4; 5:14; 6:7; 8:12-13,26-38; 9:1-19; 10:44-48; 11:15-21,24; 13:12,48; 14:1,21; 16:14-15,30-34; 17:4,12,30-34; 18:8; 22:1-16; 26:4-20; 28:24. Sinners heard the gospel; they were convicted of their sin; they were pointed to Christ; they repented and believed; they were baptised; they were counted as believers, Christians. And there is no exception. As for the letters of the New Testament, who can read, say, Romans 6:17; 10:9-17; 2 Corinthians 5:17; Galatians 1:11-16; 2:16; 3:2; Ephesians 1:13; 2:1-10; Colossians 1:6-7,13; 2:20 – 3:3; 1

---

[94] Neill had 'until by his faith he has individually been born again'. This would be the view of an Arminian Baptist, which I am not. Faith does not lead to regeneration. Regeneration leads to faith.

[95] Baillie p14.

[96] But what about Jesus' words to Peter: 'When you are converted' (Luke 22:32, AV)? Does this not lend credence to the notion of some sort of process? Not at all. Remember the context. Christ had just predicted Peter's denial, and the testing time he would have to go through – his grief, and so on. But not only that. He was assuring Peter that he would repent and be reinstated – restored to his former status. The words should be translated: 'When you have returned to me, when once you have turned again, when you have turned back' (NKJV, NASB, NIV respectively). This is not the 'conversion' at issue with sacramentalists, the conversion we are talking about here.

Thessalonians 1:2-10; 2:13-14; Philemon 10-16; Hebrews 10:26,32; 1 Peter 2:9-10 *etc.*, and fail to see that conversion, turning to Christ, is indeed a crisis? How can it be anything else? To be converted is to pass from death to life, to be taken from the realm of darkness and brought into the realm of light, to be brought from a state of damnation into a state of salvation, from ignorance of Christ to confession of him as Saviour and Lord, and so on.

Furthermore, take the biblical concept of 'calling'; that is, God's sovereign act in bringing sinners, by the preaching of the gospel, through the effective work of the Spirit, savingly to hear, know, believe and obey Christ as Saviour and Lord (Matt. 9:13; Acts 2:39; Rom. 1:6-7; 8:28-30; 1 Cor. 1:2,9,24-26; Gal. 1:6,15; Eph. 4:4; 2 Thess. 1:11; 2 Tim. 1:9; 2 Pet. 1:10, plus many more). Do such passages speak of a crisis or a process? Can there be any doubt?

John Murray distinguished the effectual call from the universal call of the gospel. The effectual call is, he said:

The call that ushers men into a state of salvation, and is therefore effectual. There is scarcely an instance where the terms are used to designate the indiscriminate overture of grace in the gospel of Christ... With scarcely an exception, the New Testament means by the words 'call', 'called', 'calling' nothing less than the call which is efficacious unto salvation... We often fail to grasp the rich meaning of biblical terms because in common usage the same words have suffered a great deal of attrition. This is true in respect of the word 'call'. If we are to understand the strength of this word, as used in this connection, we must use the word 'summons'. The action by which God makes his people the partakers of redemption is that of summons. And since it is God's summons, it is [an] efficacious summons... The summons is invested with the efficacy by which we are delivered to the destination intended – we are effectively ushered into the fellowship of Christ. There is something determinate about God's call; by his sovereign power and grace it cannot fail of accomplishment. God calls those things which do not exist as though they did (*cf.* Rom. 4:17)... When God calls men and women, it is not on the moment of haphazard, arbitrary, sudden decision. God's thought has been occupied with this event from times eternal. Hence the moment and all the circumstances are fixed by his own counsel and will... It is a calling that is represented in Scripture as that act of God by which we are *actually* united to Christ (*cf.* 1 Cor. 1:9)... [It is] the sovereign and efficacious summons by which the people of God [better, the unbelieving elect] are ushered into the fellowship of Christ and union with him to the end that they may become partakers of all the grace and virtue which reside in him as Redeemer, Saviour and Lord.[97]

In addition to the overall sense of Murray's words – he could only have been describing a crisis and not a process – note his proper use of 'summons', 'moment', 'event' and 'decision'. He was certainly not describing some drawn out process. He was speaking of a determinate act in a moment of time, an event. In short, a crisis.

'Crisis' must be the word. A sinner is either a natural or a spiritual man, spiritually dead or alive, under the wrath of God or not, in darkness or light, in one kingdom or another, in Adam or in Christ, submits to Christ as Lord or does not. The change, the calling from one state to another is, must be, a crisis. A process? Not at all. True, many experiences may or may not lead up to conversion,[98] but in a sinner's experience, there must come a crunch point *before* which he is *not* converted, and *after* which he *is* converted.[99] William James: 'Every man is at any given moment either in a state of sin or in a state of grace, and from this it follows that the transition from the one state to the other must accomplish itself in a single moment'.[100] A man is either a new creation (2 Cor. 5:17) or he is not. The sinner may not know the precise point in time when his conversion took place, but that there is such a point, who can deny?[101]

---

[97] John Murray pp88-94, emphasis his.

[98] But I am far from advocating preparationism (see my *Offer*).

[99] A man is born again or he is not. Without overstretching the analogy, a baby is either in its mother's womb or in the world. I realise there is a certain process involved in natural birth, but the principle holds. A man is either unregenerate or he is regenerate. Calvin did not see it this way. Allowing that he can be confusing, at least sometimes muddling regeneration, repentance, faith and sanctification (Calvin: *Institutes* Vol.1 pp508,515-517; Harrison p34), consider: 'By repentance, I understand regeneration... This renewal... is not accomplished in a moment, a day, or a year, but by interrupted, sometimes even by slow, progress' (Calvin: *Institutes* Vol.1 pp515-516. See Baillie p77). It does not take a genius to see where this kind of teaching might lead. Indeed, it is even now feeding directly into the sacramental driver of regarding conversion as a process.

[100] Baillie p92.

[101] Lest I be misunderstood, although I am stressing conversion as a crisis, I fully accept that the external proof of such an experience is the life lived

Sacramentalists! *They* deny it. For them, conversion – if they use the word – is a process, not a crisis. And when they do speak of 'conversion', they give it a much lower status than traditional Baptists (indeed, than Scripture). And they do this directly as a consequence of their practice of sacramental baptism. It is inevitable. After all, since they think grace is conveyed by baptism, conversion must be a process, baptism being a part of it. (In the case of infants, that process can be drawn out over several years). Thus sacramentalism corrupts the whole concept of conversion.[102]

Let me justify my claim that sacramentalists have long had this false view of conversion. In addition to what I have said in my *Infant*, consider first of all Rome.

Rome talks of 'conversion'. Oh yes! But what does Rome mean by it? One of two things. In the first place, when she talks of 'conversion', Rome is thinking of the decision by a Romanist to take up the monastic life; this is Rome's idea of 'conversion'! A second way in which Rome uses the word is to denote submission to the Papacy by those from other religions (principally Protestants) or schismatics (those whom Rome defines as former Romanists who had defected but now want to re-submit themselves to Rome). Such is the Roman notion of conversion.[103] And it is a nonsense from A to Z – if we are supposed to be talking about biblical conversion.

---

after professed conversion. John 13:35; 2 Cor. 5:17; Heb. 12:14; 1 John 3:14; 4:20, for instance, cannot be gainsaid. I have no desire to gainsay them! A ton of talk about a conversion-crisis experience will not carry the same weight as an ounce of Christ-likeness in the consequent life. And if there is none of the latter, no talk of the former carries any weight whatsoever. But this is not the issue here.

Conversion (justification) is a crisis; sanctification is a life-long process. Rome confuses the two. Consistent sacramentalists always do. And it is fatal.

[102] If I am asked why a Reformed infant-baptiser like John Murray could speak so admirably of 'calling', as I pointed out in my *Infant*, it is yet another illustration of how, when baptism is not in view, Reformed infant-baptisers speak scripturally – but when they come up against the word 'baptism', reason often seems to go out of the window.

[103] Baillie pp67-68. As I go to press, early 2011, the first candidates are entering the Pope's special section within the Roman pale for those Anglicans who want to 'convert' and yet 'keep their own traditions'.

Can anyone who takes the Bible seriously be in any doubt as to whether conversion means to be incarcerated in a monastery, or to turn to Christ? to submit to Rome, or to submit to Christ?

So much for Rome. What about Luther? Luther spoke often about conversion, but failed to define it, and 'is far from definite about the stage or event in the progress of the Christian life' he was talking about. Indeed, he thought that a sinner needs a repeated conversion every time he sins.[104] We need not spend any time on such a muddled, ill-defined, non-defined notion, except to say it is light-years away from the New Testament.

What about Calvin? What did he have to say on conversion? Judging by his *Institutes*,[105] precious little! I have been able to find the word 'conversion' on only four occasions in those two volumes. I do not fault the man merely for his lack of use of the word – but what about the concept?[106] The fact is, even on those rare occasions when Calvin used the word, he assumed its meaning, did not make an issue of it, and, even then, he spoke of it only to defend the principle that every aspect of conversion proceeds from the grace of God.[107] Quite right, of course – but woefully inadequate as a treatment of such an important biblical concept. As I say, he did not make an issue of it. But what else, in New Testament terms, is conversion – if not an issue? That is precisely what it is!

Let Baillie have his say:

---

[104] Baillie pp70-74.

[105] It must not be forgotten that Calvin made it clear that we should take his doctrine from the *Institutes*: 'I have endeavoured [here in the *Institutes*] to give such a summary of religion in all its parts... Having thus... paved the way, I shall not feel it necessary, in any Commentaries on Scripture which I may afterwards publish, to enter into long discussions of doctrine... In this way, the pious reader will be saved much trouble and weariness, provided he comes furnished with a knowledge of the [*Institutes*] as an essential prerequisite... seeing that I have in a manner deduced at length all the articles which pertain to Christianity' (*Institutes* Vol.1 pp21,23, in his prefixed explanations for the work dated 1539 and 1545).

[106] I admit that the word itself does not appear very often in Scripture – but the concept does! And that is what counts. Compare 'trinity', 'non-elect', 'total depravity', 'unconditional election', 'particular redemption', 'limited atonement', 'definite atonement', 'effectual calling' or 'irresistible grace'.

[107] Calvin: *Institutes* Vol.1 pp253-257.

How then does Calvin use the term 'conversion'? I find it even less of a key term for him than it is for Luther... In all his references to conversion in the *Institutes* he treats it as if it were for him a subsidiary term equivalent to repentance. 'Under the term "repentance"', he writes, 'is comprehended the whole of conversion to God'... It would seem to follow that infants are converted as well as regenerated at baptism, and that Calvin does not think of conversion as a distinctively later stage.[108]

And what about the men of Westminster? What did they have to say about 'conversion'? They continued driving down Calvin's road. Baillie again:

[In] the Westminster Confession, we note again that conversion is far from being one of the key terms with which it operates. It occurs only in the section on free will, where it is said that the natural man is not able to convert himself.

Why such a measly treatment of conversion? Infant baptism, of course! So what of infants baptised as babies? Do they need to be converted? What did Westminster say of them? How should they be addressed? Baillie again:

The answer according to the Larger Catechism is that they are expected to improve their baptism... This concept of 'improving our baptism', of making the remembrance of it determinative throughout the whole of later life, is true and original Reformation teaching, both Lutheran and Calvinist.[109]

Baillie was right. As I have made clear in my *Infant* and throughout this book, this is precisely the way sacramental infant-baptisers look at conversion and baptism. What they say on conversion falls far short of the New Testament. And what they do say is jumbled up with coping with the consequences of their infant baptism. And, as I have explained, there isn't an atom of Scripture to justify such talk. 'Improve their baptism', indeed!

Let me say it again. The sacramentalist Church may try to justify this approach to conversion – indeed, it has been attempting it ever since the start of Christendom – and has to go on with it when faced with the massive pool of unbelievers it produces by baptising them

---

[108] Baillie pp77-78. 'Sacraments lead [to]... daily conversion' (Beeke p134).
[109] Baillie pp78-79. Of course it is. See Westminster pp257-258.

as babies, but it cannot be argued from the New Testament. I wait to be shown one apostolic injunction: 'Remember and improve your baptism' – let alone: 'Remember and improve your baptism received as a baby'. Do those who base their practice on the Westminster documents address those they baptised as babies in terms of Acts 16:31; 17:30? Do they demand their conversion? Do they ever preach Isaiah 45:22; 55:1-7; Mark 1:15; and so on, to them? If not, why not? Or are they content to keep reminding them of their baptism?

Compare Gill and Calvin on the subject of conversion.[110] And it is not just a question of the quantity of ink. Conversion is of unspeakable importance to the traditional Baptist. It is of little importance to the consistent sacramentalist. Reader, which of these matches the New Testament?

Just now I cited Baillie quoting Neill to define the traditional Baptist view of baptism and conversion. Listen to Neill defining the sacramental infant-baptiser view:

Christian life begins at baptism, when by the grace of God operating through the Church, original sin is taken away, and the divine life is sown as a seed in the heart of man. Through Christian teaching, through life in the Church, and through the grace of the sacraments, this seed can grow. Though growth may be hindered by resistance on the part of the individual, nevertheless it is a continuous process. To demand any other decisive new beginning is to deny the reality of the grace of God. What the individual is called to do is to recognise the reality of what God has already done in him, and to take that seriously.[111]

Well, that's clear enough.

Here is the choice. Conversion is either a crisis or a process. The traditional Baptist regards it as the former; the sacramental infant-baptiser as the latter. In the former, the sinner has to be called to repentance and faith. As he is regenerated by the Spirit of God, he comes to repentance and faith in Christ, and confirms him by baptism. In the latter, a sinner becomes a Christian by being baptised as a baby, and by a process of church life and partaking of the sacraments, he is called upon to improve his baptism.

---

[110] See above. For Calvin's own experience, see Ganoczy pp9-10.
[111] Baillie p14.

The choice between these two has to be made. One is found in the New Testament; the other is not.

If infant baptisers object that the New Testament is concerned with the conversion of pagans, and the principles of conversion found in those pages apply only to the conversion of such – and not to those baptised as babies – my answer is simple – and stark. Very well, I say. Let's be honest about it. In that case, we have two gospels, two ways of salvation, two ways of preaching for two sorts of hearer. One hearer is pagan, a sinner, an unbeliever. The other is 'Christian', baptised as a baby, but whether or not to be regarded as an unbeliever, from my reading of infant baptisers, I cannot fathom. The two gospels are very different. Addressing the one sort of hearer, the preacher demands their repentance and faith. Addressing the other, he calls for their continued attendance at Church, especially the sacraments, and to remember and improve the infant baptism they unknowingly received as a baby.[112]

What is more, if the infant baptiser is right, and we have two different ways of addressing the two classes of hearer, where do we find the ground rules for these two sorts of preaching? When addressing pagans, we can turn to the New Testament to find our texts and deduce our principles. We do. We must. And we find abundant material. But where do those who believe that conversion is a process go when they want to address the huge numbers of these so-called 'Christians' they have produced? What texts do they choose? What New Testament examples do they draw on? Where do they go to find their principles? The Westminster documents? The material produced by the advocates of the Federal Vision?[113] Or what?

And as for two gospels – two gospels, indeed! – what now of:

You are turning away... to a different gospel... There are some who trouble you and want to pervert the gospel of Christ... If we, or an angel

---

[112] How do such preachers address a mixed congregation? See my *Offer* and *Septimus Sears* for the similarity between this and hyper-Calvinists with their view of sensible and non-sensible sinners. See my *Particular* for a similar problem for Amyraldians.

[113] A modern Reformed infant-baptiser approach to the sacraments – which, as I have shown in my *Infant*, its advocates cogently argue they find in Calvin *et al.*

from heaven, preach any other gospel to you than what [the apostles] have preached to you, let him be accursed... I say again, if anyone preaches any other gospel to you than what you have received, let him be accursed (Gal. 1:6-9).

My point in saying all this is twofold. *First,* I am drawing attention to the fact that treating conversion as a process is an ingredient in the contemporary drive towards sacramentalism. But, *secondly,* I cannot help spelling out to all would-be sacramentalists (especially Baptists) the consequences of adopting the notion that conversion is a process and not a crisis. This has long been the view (or, at least, the practice) of Roman, Lutheran, Calvinist and Anglican sacramentalists. Now it is becoming the view of Baptists; that is, *sacramental* Baptists. It is inevitable, of course – since they are rejecting the 'traditional' Baptist view of conversion and adopting the Reformed view. As a direct result of their re-definition of baptism, they have to re-define conversion. *And that is what they are doing.* Those who adopt sacramentalist views are bound to change the way they define conversion, and how they address sinners. Baptist sacramentalists are making their choice, and will have to live with the consequences. They know it – or ought to! History tells them that for at least 1500 years sacramentalists have been trying to cope with the consequences of sacramentalism. And the results are plain for all to see. Baptist sacramentalists, as I have shown, claim to put history high on the agenda in making their case. Very well. Let them remember the history of sacramentalism, and its disastrous baggage! If they adopt sacramentalism, they will have to pick up the baggage. It will have their name on the luggage label.

Traditional Baptists, in the past, would have been horrified to think of such a doctrine and practice raising its head among them. Now, however, we are living in a different climate, a very dangerous climate.

It is high time I proved that Baptist sacramentalists are abandoning the concept of conversion as found in the New Testament – abandoning the gospel as found in the New Testament – and going over to the idea of conversion in the 'gospel' invented by Christendom to cope with the consequences of sacramental baptism.

I start with Cross, setting out Beasley-Murray's position. This is the extract I was referring to in an earlier footnote when I was detailing the way in which Baptists have changed in their approach to infant baptism during the past fifty years (that is, quickened their approach to it; see the extended note on p320). A comparison of what Beasley-Murray said in the 1950s and 1960s (see that extended note), with what he said in the 1990s (see the following extract), makes this movement crystal clear:

The greatest surprise to Baptists is the modified position on infant baptism adopted by George Beasley-Murray. In his most recent work [1994] he explores the 'possibilities' of a rapprochement between believer's baptism and infant baptism when infant baptism is seen as attesting 'the commencement of the work of grace within the baptised with a view to its blossoming into fullness of life in Christ and his body the church as the individual's life progressively opens to Christ'. This could be supported... especially if focus was placed on 'initiation'; that is, the whole process of leading individuals to Christ and into the church. He asks 'that churches which practice believer's baptism should consider acknowledging the legitimacy of infant baptism, and allow members in infant-baptiser churches the right to interpret it according to their consciences'.[114] In practice, this would involve believer-Baptist churches refraining from 're-baptism'. Beasley-Murray's cautious optimism has received the support of David Wright... Beasley-Murray and Wright... seek to establish a *modus vivendi* in which there is mutual recognition of each other's convictions and a striving after the possibility of rapprochement. As such, this position is to be highly commended as a most fruitful way forward, and also, given the present state of the debate, quite probably the most realistic. The Church today desperately needs such a *modus vivendi*, and I applaud such work, which could well lead to an acceptable common theology of baptism.

This, I submit, shows the way the sacramental-Baptist wind is blowing. Worse is to come! Cross rightly saw that if it stopped there, it would lead to 'the continuation of [the] two baptisms'; consequently he appealed for 'baptismal reformation'.[115]

How might this come about? 'For too long, Christians, Evangelicals especially, have understood conversion to be

---

[114] Reader, I certainly allow infant baptisers to interpret Scripture as they will, according to their conscience – indeed, I think all professing believers should interpret Scripture according to their own judgement as they believe God has shown them – but I do not accept that I have to go along with their conclusions, nor refrain from criticising their arguments.

[115] Cross: 'One Baptism' pp205-206.

punctiliar...[116] Conversion is a process, a journey... When we recognise conversion as a process... such questions' – such as the order of repentance, believing, water baptism, forgiveness and the reception of the Spirit – 'such questions lose their relevance'.[117]

Thus, the misguided – unbiblical – notion that baptism and profession form a process will prove very helpful in this quest for a common baptism (and conversion). One group will practice infant dedication, followed by 'Christian' nurture, leading to profession of personal faith in baptism in the teens; the other group will practice infant baptism, followed by 'Christian' nurture, leading to some form of public profession of personal faith or 'confirmation' in the teens.[118] As long as both groups regard baptism as a sacrament, and conversion as a process, the difference between them will be trivial – and will soon wither to nothing.[119]

Fowler mused aloud on how 'progress' might be made:

Some Baptist sacramentalists have argued that although baptism ought not to be applied to infants, when in fact it has been done, this is a real baptism... But what factors might constitute the validity of such (irregular) baptisms?... Is it the fact that such baptism incorporates the infant into the Christian community for spiritual nurture? If so, would not the same thing be true of a service of infant blessing and dedication in a baptistic context?[120]

---

[116] Which I take to mean 'punctuated'; that is, at one moment a sinner is not converted, the next moment he is – a once-for-all crisis. See my *Infant*. See Wright: *What...?* p61 for an extract from those who – ridiculously – think *baptism* is not punctiliar. Whatever else baptism is, it is punctiliar. That is, a person is either baptised or he is not!

[117] Cross: 'The Evangelical sacrament' p206. See the earlier comment where I pointed out that once sacramentalism is granted, the differences between infant baptism and believer's baptism will soon lose all relevance and peter out. 'Nit-picking' was how I described it. People like me will be accused of 'nit-picking'. If so, thank God for such 'nit-pickers', say I.

[118] See Wheeler Robinson's assessment of the 'normal' practice in Baptist churches in 1927 – 'Christian home, the Sunday school... Cradle Roll... Dedication services' (Wheeler Robinson: *The Life* p89).

[119] See Lane pp143-146.

[120] Fowler: *More* pp228-232. Fowler also discussed whether simply using the term 'baptism' might be enough; whether or not water is absolutely necessary; whether the motion of sprinkling or dipping in itself might not do; what if God is not mentioned; what if infant baptism is treated simply

Nobody can say we were not warned.

'Process', I say, is the in-word. But it is nothing new. Over a hundred years have passed since Wheeler Robinson who, launching the rise of sacramentalism among the Baptists, put forward the idea that conversion should be thought of as a process. In 1905, he started cautiously:

In our determination to maintain the full significance of New Testament baptism, we may have looked too much for cataclysmic changes instead of the still, small voice, and have failed to welcome some whose conversion was as quiet and gradual as the coming of spring.[121]

By 1927, he had become far more dogmatic: 'We must, of course, put aside the idea that conversion necessarily means a startling and dramatic experience'. Very well. I agree about the 'startling' and 'dramatic'. Nevertheless, conversion is conversion. Biblical clarity was noticeably lacking in Robinson's way of addressing this vital topic: The 'awakening of human personality to the presence and power of the divine, however achieved, is of the greatest significance and importance. In this large sense of the term, there must always be conversion in Christian experience, and the baptism of believers, marking (among other things) this crucial re-adjustment, is emphasising that which deserves to be emphasised'.[122]

---

as a declaration – though this would destroy the sacramental point which is what this is all about! He raised what is being called 'baptismal repair' – the re[!]-baptism of those baptised as infants. Fowler realised that this muddle cannot be allowed to go on: 'The failure to connect theory to practice on this point [on how to regard baptised infants] is the major deficiency of modern Baptist sacramentalism'. Its advocates need not worry. The theologians are busy forging the necessary theology. Don't forget the part played by Augustine 1600 years ago. Cometh the need, cometh the man! See the Introduction.

[121] Cross: 'Pneumatological' p175.

[122] Wheeler Robinson: *The Life* p88. The 'awakening of human personality to the presence and power of the divine', is not the same as conviction of sin leading to repentance and faith. Not the same at all! A person who has had recent experience as a member in a Baptist Union church commented on the point I am making: 'This is absolutely *crucial*. In my experience, the first is what is now popularly preached – not the second' (emphasis original).

Cross observed that Payne:

Identified the work of Wheeler Robinson and his plea for the recovery of the New Testament emphasis on the Spirit, along with the introduction of a service of infant dedication/presentation, as being instrumental in this [sacramental] turnabout [in Baptist thinking]. His [Robinson's] discussion [in 1925] of conversion as 'a spiritual journey' was not really taken up until the 1970-80s, and was developed by Baptists in several important works in the mid-1990s.[123]

And not only among sacramental Baptists. Anglicans, too – not excluding Evangelical Anglicans – have been thinking along these lines. Colin Buchanan and Michael Vasey:

Baptism is part of the process of making people disciples – and, *along with repentance and faith*,[124] is the initial, or 'initiatory', part... Since 1979, new perspectives and approaches have emerged, not least through different sections of the Church wrestling with the reality of baptism... [The first of which is:] 'Faith as a Journey'... Coming to faith in Jesus Christ is not [now for some – it still is for me, DG] simply a single isolated transaction between an individual and God. Both coming to faith and the life of faith thereafter[125] are [now for some – not for me, DG] to be seen as an accompanied journey: the individual responds to God's once-and-for-all act in Jesus Christ (proclaimed in baptism) and enters a community of faith and service... Even within Evangelical circles – those most characteristically devoted to individualistic decision and discipleship – missions that centred on a public decision have been giving way to nurture or enquirer groups... The journey to faith [even among Evangelicals, concluded a certain report cited by Buchanan and Vasey] normally takes between one and four years.[126]

---

[123] Cross: 'Pneumatological' p175.

[124] Note the *along with*, extra emphasis mine. 'Making disciples'? In the context, Buchanan and Vasey would seem to be talking about 'being converted, being saved, coming to Christ'. In the New Testament, this is ascribed to faith and repentance. Baptism then follows – after a person has been 'made a disciple' in the sense of 'being converted'. In this connection, it is utterly wrong to put baptism on the same level as faith and repentance. Baptism *along with* faith and repentance? See the following chapter for my comments on Matt. 28:19.

[125] I have no quarrel, of course, with this latter aspect. It is the first part I disagree with.

[126] The same person I mentioned in the note just above (that is, the one who has recent experience as a member of a Baptist Union church) also informs

Buchanan and Vasey quoted another author who argued:

What is needed in... evangelism is a wholesale adaptation of approach in the light of the *process* norm as opposed to the *crisis* norm... Alpha groups also reflect the same shift. Central to this rethinking of the practice of baptism has been the Roman Catholic... [and] the Church of England [initiatives. The latter state:] Baptism must be the gateway to nurture and a real participation in the Christian community.[127]

This is the way the tide flows, and it explains why I write. Consider this:

A report put before the Church of England general Synod at its February [2006] meeting describes conversations between Anglicans and Baptists. The question is raised about the Baptist Union being ready to recognise 'a place for the baptism of infants within the whole journey which marks the beginning of the Christian Life'. It also looks at the matter of parishes being prepared to accept those who have had a 'second baptism'. The report is called *Pushing the Boundaries of Unity* and is described as exploring [experiencing?] 'unexpected convergence'.[128]

---

me that 'this idea is now more often heard than the "simple isolated transaction". For this reason, "conversion" and "born again" are seldom used'.

[127] Buchanan and Vasey pp4,14-18, emphasis original, except where specified.

[128] *Protestant Truth*, March-April 2006, p32. The person I mentioned in two notes just above, also told me: 'I raised the issue within our [Baptist Union] circles about the same time [February 2006] when, at an "infant-dedication", in the prayer, the elder said: "Thank you, Lord, that —'s name is written on the palm of your hands". I was told this is a Baptist Union prayer. I asked exactly what was meant by it'. No real answer was given. Apparently, the fact that it was a Baptist Union prayer was reason enough to say the words!

This step is only the latest in the long-standing drive for union between Baptists and Anglicans. Remember, Anglicans held (and still hold) to baptismal regeneration. The 19th century Tractarian movement had set alarm bells ringing, but nothing Anglican Evangelicals could do could alter the fact that the Church of England in its *Book of Common Prayer* taught and practiced baptismal regeneration. Towards the end of the 19th century, efforts were set in train to reconcile Anglicans and Baptists. These have continued. See the extended note on p324, where I point out some of the

Convergence on baptism will bring convergence on a great many other things. Jane Shaw:

For Christians, the rite of baptism brings us into the body of Christ. It is about sharing a radical equality as children of God. Paul made this clear in [Gal. 3:26-28][129]... That bond of baptism... we call... a baptismal covenant. The Gospels relate that when John the Baptist baptised Jesus, God's voice boomed from the heavens: 'This is my son [*sic*], the Beloved, with whom I am well pleased'. And the heavens echo with that phrase [*sic*] every time a child or adult enters the waters of baptism: 'This is my daughter, my son, the Beloved, with whom I am well pleased... In the baptismal covenant, there are rightly no distinctions between persons. We are all the beloved children of God... Baptism is therefore the foundation of our identity as Christians... [As] to the Anglican crisis [disagreements about homosexuality]... all we really have to do in the midst of this crazy Church dispute is be awake to our relationship with a loving God. And to do that, warring Anglicans simply have to recall their baptism: that moment when the waters washed over us, and the heavens echoed with God's declaration about each of us – you are my beloved son, my beloved daughter, with you I am well pleased.[130]

Baptists awake!

And such discussions are taking place not only between Baptists and Anglicans. Certainly not! The net is being cast far wider than that! Fowler:

In the years since [Baptist Sacramentalism has been promoted] various groups of Baptists have engaged in formal dialogue about baptism with other traditions, and in some cases entire issues of Baptist journals have been devoted to the topic. Baptist-Roman Catholic dialogues are displayed in... [Fowler cited examples]. Baptist-Lutheran dialogue can be found in... Unfortunately, these dialogues post-date the British [Baptist sacramentalism Fowler had written about], and most of the Baptists involved are not strongly sacramental in orientation... Although [Baptist sacramentalism] is similar in various ways to the baptismal theologies affirmed by Roman Catholics, Lutherans, Calvinists and Disciples [of Christ] in their explanations of the baptism of confessing

---

milestones already passed along the way (until the 1950s). They tell their own tale.

[129] See the following chapter for my comments on this passage.

[130] Shaw. What a phenomenal muddling of Scripture!

believers, it cannot be identified completely with any of those constructions of baptismal theology.[131]

Just so. But give it time! Fowler again:

Even the Roman Catholic Church in the post-Vatican II era has re-focused its baptismal theology in the direction of an adult paradigm with the publication of its revised *Rite for the Christian Initiation of Adults* (1972), and some Roman Catholics have argued that infant baptism ought to be terminated.[132]

So... summarising all this, we can see that, as I have shown elsewhere, Reformed sacramentalists want a higher status for baptism of infants, while some Romanists are suggesting infant baptism be stopped![133] And, as I have already noted, the sacramental Baptists, moving ever closer to the practice, are, above all, congratulating themselves that they will be able to bring it all together; indeed, to bring all together under one ecumenical banner. Fowler: 'Perhaps Baptist sacramentalism would offer a more compelling alternative'[134] to all the other solutions of the 'problem'.

---

[131] Fowler: *More* pp235,246.

[132] Fowler: *More* pp249-250. They will argue in vain. Satan won't let such a powerful tool of delusion slip through his fingers.

[133] And not only Romanists. Bridge and Phypers recorded the baptism of an infant in an Anglican church in the 1970s. After the service, and after congratulating the people on it, came the reply: 'Yes, it's an improvement – but just wait until we get rid of infant baptism altogether!' (Bridge and Phypers p189). We will have a long wait! Forty years have passed already.

[134] Fowler: *More* p250. In addition to the extracts I have already included on this, consider Beasley-Murray's citation of Wheeler Robinson who claimed that sacramental Baptist 'teaching, far from being alien to Baptist tradition, could be held with a good conscience *alone* by Baptists'. Wheeler Robinson: 'Those who follow the practice of the New Testament of administering baptism to believers only, ought also to follow it by more closely associating it with the baptism of the Holy Spirit; they are the only people who can do this without risk of "sacramentarianism" [sacerdotalism], since they alone require those moral and spiritual conditions in the recipient of baptism which rule out a materialistic mediation' (Beasley-Murray: *Baptism in the New Testament* p277, emphasis original; see also *Baptism Today and Tomorrow* pp82-85). Wheeler Robinson again: 'Here, then, is the present Baptist opportunity, and it is a great one. No other Church has been loyal to the New Testament

What a thought! After all the years of struggle, when Baptists have rightly been the off-scouring of Christendom, at last – at long last – these sacramental Baptists have found the clue to the maze. Through their adoption and promotion of sacramentalism, Baptists will not only be accepted by other Churches – they will be the keystone in the ecumenical arch. Mixing my metaphors, all the other stones, chipped and cracked, will look up to these new-comers to the debate, grateful to them for the way they have cracked the problem which has bedevilled Christendom for the last 500 years at least.

Remarkable! What a dream!

What are we to make of all this? Is it a passing shower in a tea cup? Are things so muddled that I am foolish to take it as seriously as I do? Indeed, in all this confusion, are there not some hopeful signs?

No! A resounding, No! Of course things are muddled. Of course all sorts of things are being said. But one strand keeps running through it all. Sacramentalism! *This* is the issue. Sacramentalism. As long as sacramentalism holds sway, I am sure that all sorts of compromises and adjustments will occur. Sacramentalism once adopted, the gate will have been swung wide open to let in all manner of error and nonsense. For the Evangelical, Reformed, Baptist, Anglican and Romanist – all and sundry – as long as there is agreement over sacramentalism, all the rest will fall in place. I have said where I think it will end up. Infant baptism! Sacramental infant-baptism will become the norm, must become the norm.

The logic is remorseless, unanswerable. If I believed that water baptism conveyed grace, I would baptise infants as soon as possible. Of course I would! As their parents, my wife and I wanted our children to be (regenerated) and converted. We longed for it, prayed and worked constantly to that end. If we had thought that sprinkling them, when new-born, would have conveyed the necessary grace to

---

connection of baptism with personal faith. No other Church, therefore, could give so forcible a testimony to the work of the Spirit on the believer, which is not less [that is, which is equally, at the same time?] emphatically linked with baptism in the New Testament. If any Baptist reader is afraid that this may mean a sacramentalism of the lower kind... let it be said quite distinctly...' (Wheeler Robinson: *The Life* p178). Robinson went on to try to fend off criticism of sacramentalism.

them, it would have been daft – criminal – not to baptise them at once. The logic, I say, is inexorable.

H.M.Carson thought, in the 1960s, that Reformed Baptists and others would stay clear of this. I hope this remains the case.[135] The point of my book, however, is to show how, in the early 21st century, a growing number of Baptist (and Reformed) scholars are increasingly adopting a sacramental approach to baptism;[136] conversion (which itself is radically re-defined) is being thought of as a process, begun with baptism; water baptism and the gift of the Spirit are said to form one experience, incorporating the believer into Christ; justification is thought of as a corporate, rather than an individual, experience; and so on.

We must be clear about this. In the medieval Church, a sinner was 'saved' in a corporate way. As I explained in my Introduction, this is what sacralism leads to, this is what sacralism means. In the Dark Ages, therefore, 'salvation' was mediated through the Church by its sacraments. A sinner was 'saved' by submitting to those

---

[135] H.M.Carson: *Farewell* pp136-137. But as E.J.Wood noted – in 1968: 'In these days of false ecumenism and widespread desire for unity at almost any price, it is not surprising that many Baptists are wondering whether it is really necessary to insist on the principle of believer's baptism, and to reject other forms of baptism as practiced by other believers. Many Baptist leaders have in fact expressed their readiness to recognise infant sprinkling as valid as an initiatory ordinance in the much-longed-for united Church. Others see infant baptism as not without value and therefore to be tolerated, if not welcomed, for the sake of a common denominator among the Christian denominations. Even some Strict Baptists are questioning the rightness of the principle of restricted communion, and therefore a consideration of these two ordinances seems to be essential and timely' (Wood, unnumbered pages, but taken from the opening page of the text). Wood was giving the 'Presidential address... at the 22nd Annual Assembly of the National Strict Baptist Federation at "Zoar" Ipswich – Oct. 30th 1968'. As for the point about Strict Baptist and closed communion, with the passing of 40 years, it is becoming increasingly rare to find a Strict Baptist church these days. And for how long, I wonder, will closed communion continue to exist in Grace Baptist churches?

[136] The increasing acceptance of Calvin's views on the Lord's supper comes into this. As does the resurgence of the Fathers – among the Reformed, I mean! See the earlier extended note on this.

sacraments. There was no emphasis upon individual trust in Christ, individual repentance and turning to God for oneself. A sinner was 'saved' through a priest administering the sacraments over him and to him. And he was 'saved' in a corporate way, by belonging to the system, and adhering to its rules.

It was a nonsense from start to finish. That is why I put 'saved' in quotation marks. While a few had a measure of biblical light, it was Luther who, with his re-discovery of the biblical doctrine of justification by faith, and his open promulgation of it, blew this lethal mumbo-jumbo right out of the water. Although, as I have shown, he (sticking to the sacramental infant-baptism he inherited from Rome) failed to work out the proper consequences, from his time on, many preachers recovered the biblical way of addressing unbelievers. The sinner was commanded to repent and believe and call upon the name of the Lord – for himself. And if he so came to Christ, he was promised salvation by grace through faith – not through sacraments. And he was saved by himself, for himself, as an individual sinner. As he would have to die for himself, and appear before God's judgement for himself, so he was saved – as an individual. And he was saved directly by calling upon Christ.

Sacramentalism was the arch-enemy of this individual conversion experience. And it still is. With the coming of the Reformation, Rome not only refused to give up its medieval practice, it tightened it. The Reformers tinkered with it. The Anabaptists rejected it. Now sacramental Baptists are going back to it. Under this drive towards sacramentalism, conversion will increasingly come to be regarded, not as an individual crisis, but as a process and a corporate matter.[137]

In 2006, Cross was saddened, from his point of view, that 'while a great many British Baptists accept the use of sacramental terminology for baptism, this has not been accompanied by a truly sacramental theology or practice of baptism'.[138] In other words, the language has been adopted, but the theology and practice, lagging behind, has not.

Not yet, that is! The sacramentalists need lose no sleep over it. A growing number of Baptists are certainly prepared to use

---

[137] See McGrath: *Twilight* p199.
[138] Cross: 'Pneumatological' p176.

sacramental language;[139] the theology, as always, will follow.[140] The tide is running strongly the sacramentalist way. If things go unchecked, not only the language but the practice and the theology of sacramentalism will triumph. Roman errors will sweep the field. Rome will be top-dog once again. And we shall be plunged into another Dark Ages.

As an indication of the ways things are going, it is instructive to observe the changes which have come about this past twenty-five years in Evangelical and Reformed reaction to the 1982 Lima declaration issued by the World Council of (Romanist, Orthodox, Lutheran, Anglican, Baptist and other) Churches: 'Baptism, Eucharist and Ministry'. Paradigm shifts have been taking place among the Reformed and Evangelicals.

Let us have a look at them.

Recent paradigm shifts – as shown by Evangelical and Reformed reaction to Lima 1982

Let David Wright explain what we are talking about – the Lima document itself:

The... Lima report... is a product of the Faith and Order Commission within the World Council of Churches, and reached its final form at a conference in Lima in which Catholics and Eastern Orthodox were full

---

[139] Take hymn books used by Reformed (Strict or Grace) Baptists this past hundred years. The changes in baptismal hymns when moving from *Gospel Hymns* (1915-1950) to *Grace* (1975) to *Praise!* (2000) is instructive. Allowing that when the writers spoke of being baptised into the death of Christ, they meant it symbolically, and not sacramentally (even though I am not always sure of this in the modern hymns), of the fourteen hymns in *Gospel Hymns*, not one is definitely sacramental; and in the possible exception, number 984, it is quite possible (likely?) that the sealing mentioned is the sealing of the Spirit, and nothing to do with baptism. Of the twelve hymns in *Grace*, not one is definitely sacramental. But of the six hymns in *Praise!*, four are definitely sacramental.

[140] See under 'Baptists and Other Sacramental Traditions' (Fowler: *More* pp234-247).

participants along with Lutherans, Reformed, Baptists, Anglicans and others.[141]

Very well. What did Evangelicals make of it at the time? In 1989, Paul Schrotenboer edited the World Evangelical Fellowship response to the Lima declaration:

We find we cannot approve the sacramentalist language of the entire section [on baptism] (baptism unites, initiates, gives participation, effects). To be sure, many in the WEF constituency [Reformed infant-baptisers, in particular] would not feel that the problem lies in the language itself since Reformed theologians have often used similar language... The problem, they would argue, is that sacramental language [in Lima] is not accompanied by an equally firm emphasis on the need for faith, repentance and conversion, as presuppositions of baptism.

I pause.[142] These 'presuppositions for baptism' are, of course, biblical requirements, pre-conditions, for baptism. To insist upon them is to destroy sacramentalism. Lima, therefore, could not possibly argue for sacramentalism *and* the biblical requirements for baptism. The two cannot co-exist.[143] For WEF to demand both showed either naïvety or a woeful ignorance of the deep-seated consequences of sacramentalism. Using sacramental language leads, in the end, to sacramentalism itself. And this, in turn, leads to the destruction of salvation.

But let Schrotenboer continue, albeit weakly:

---

[141] Wright: 'One' p334.

[142] In addition to what I say in the main text above, notice the admission that the Reformed use the same sacramental language as Rome and the Orthodox. Notice further that the Reformed think they get off the hook by their use of qualifiers. Note, in particular, their talk of the need for faith, repentance and conversion *before* baptism. Before? Yes, indeed. A 'presupposition', after all, is something required as a prior condition. But if faith, repentance and conversion *are* required *before* baptism – as they are, biblically speaking – why do the Reformed continue to baptise infants? Which of the two sets of language do they *really* believe? Is it the sacramental language of Rome and the Orthodox, or the biblical language of faith, repentance and conversion before baptism?

[143] As I have said, Baptist sacramentalism is an oxymoron. Now I am going further. 'Baptist sacramentalism' is not only a contradiction 'in terms'. It is – or ought to be – utterly self-destructive.

Many WEF constituents would go farther and insist that the clearly sacramentalist language of the Lima document depends far too heavily on Church tradition that cannot be traced back to the New Testament itself. Even when conversion and faith properly receive some stress, the clause in question is weakened by being subsumed under an introductory sentence which claims that baptism makes us partaker of the mystery of the death and resurrection of Christ. The same paragraph goes so far as to say: 'Thus those baptised are pardoned, cleansed and sanctified by Christ...'. Again, 'signifies and effects' implies a sacramentalist causation that few Evangelicals could support... In short, most Evangelicals will regret the persistently sacramentalist thrust of the entire document.[144]

On the 'use of Scripture', Schrotenboer observed:

Many of WEF's constituents would question the baptismal exegesis of [Lima]... Among the passages quoted are many that do not refer to water baptism (1 Cor. 12:13 of paramount importance). Most would find considerable difficulty with the appeal [Lima] makes to John 3:5; 1 Cor. 6:11; Tit. 3:5; Heb. 10:22, to cite but a few examples.

And what of that which I would call 'the sacramental sleight of hand' – that is, the standard way of finding a fudging-formula; namely, by suitable silence or ambiguous language, give a mere appearance of agreement? Schrotenboer, once again far too weakly, I am afraid:

It appears to us [WEF] that the framers of [Lima] too frequently use language that is patient [tolerant] of mutually exclusive interpretations. If we are not mistaken in this impression, we must ask whether genuine unity is achieved when each party reads [Lima] in such a way that the presence of mutually unacceptable opinions is actually hidden... Further, silence on some issues may (doubtless unwittingly[!]) convey a greater impression of agreement than is in fact the case.[145] For instance,

---

[144] In calling Schrotenboer's (WEF's) response to Lima 'weak', I was being 'weak'. I should have used 'deplorable' or some such word. I refer to his use of expressions such as 'far too heavily', 'weakened', 'few Evangelicals could support' and 'regret'. Those who claim Scripture to be their sole authority, should not use sacramental language. Sacramentalism actually destroys salvation – it does not merely weaken it. No Evangelical should support sacramental language – Evangelicals should *abhor* it, not *regret* it.

[145] If the omission is 'unwitting', it calls the discernment of the men of Lima in question; if it is 'witting', it questions their integrity.

although the Lima document makes it clear that faith is the required condition for fruitful reception of baptism,[146] and although the Commentary gently takes to task those Churches that practice infant baptism 'in an apparently indiscriminate way', neither makes clear what faith is required. [Lima] does not rule out the Roman Catholic view that the absence of conscious objection is a sufficient condition for infant regeneration [in baptism]. Most Evangelicals, regardless of their views of infant baptism, would judge such an uncertainty to be a serious liability.

The Roman Catholic view of infant baptism a serious liability to Evangelicals? Is that all? A serious liability? It is an abomination!

And what of Lima's 'grounding [of Church] unity in baptism'? Schrotenboer: 'To base unity in the rite of baptism is entirely foreign to Scripture, since 1 Corinthians 12:13 does not refer to water baptism'. As I will show, he was right in that at least!

But what about the 'rc-baptism' of those 'baptised' as infants? Is it right or wrong to treat infant baptism as no baptism at all?[147] Grievously (or foolishly), Schrotenboer played right into the hands of those who are striving for unity on the basis of sacramental baptism – both infant and otherwise:

Most believer Baptists among WEF constituents would question[!] the likelihood 'that infant baptism was also practiced in the apostolic age'... The distinction 'between those who baptise people at any age and those who baptise only those able to make a confession of faith for themselves' holds interest[!], but the real distinction, as we see it, is between those who baptise only those who do make a confession of faith for themselves, whatever their age[!], and those who do not. Both positions require similar attitudes to Christian nurture; this point is well taken. Nevertheless, historic [biblical!] believer-Baptist conviction cannot accept the two positions as 'equivalent alternatives', for the simple reason that believer Baptists, to be consistent, normally consider infant baptism to be no baptism at all. In [Lima], essential disagreements between infant baptisers and believer Baptists are treated

---

[146] It is not! Faith is *not* the required condition for fruitful reception of baptism! Fruitful reception, indeed! Faith is the required condition for one to be baptised, full stop. Anything else is rank disobedience to Christ, and a criminal twisting of his ordinance.

[147] In addition to what I have said here, see my earlier works for the long history of the struggle over this question from the Fathers through to Calvin and beyond.

as if they were differences in emphasis only. In reality, the differences are historic and profound [and biblical!]

In conclusion: 'Virtually all [WEF constituency] would find difficulty subscribing to the whole [of Lima], primarily because of the emphasis on sacramentalism which most of us find unwarranted by Scripture'.[148]

A 'fittingly' weak conclusion to an article by an Evangelical showing a consistently weak reaction to Lima. It reminds me of the way Neville Chamberlain waged war against Nazi Germany in 1939-1940. Afraid to drop bombs or sow mines, lest such blatant belligerency should offend that nice Mr Hitler, and force him to retaliate, he contented himself with asking the RAF to drop leaflets. Even this, however, backfired in at least one case. A packet of these leaflets, the parachute failing to open, scored a direct hit and killed someone on the ground.

But, at the time of Lima and just after, not all the Reformed and Evangelical reacted so feebly. Oh no! Take Wright himself. What did he, speaking twenty years ago, make of Lima's declaration? In contrast to the weak, but over-tolerant WEF response, Wright was warmer, much warmer:

This is a report of enormous importance. It has already [in 1988/1989] become, within most of the Churches, the standard starting-point for ecumenical reflection on baptism, eucharist and ministry. In a nutshell, its approach to the divergence in baptismal practice suggests that there may not be much difference between infant baptism followed by Christian nurture within the believing community issuing in personal confession of faith, and the nurture of a child within the congregation, perhaps after thanksgiving for its birth and the parents' commitment to their Christian responsibility, leading to baptism on personal confession of faith. Two key sentences which appear in the [Lima] Commentary are these: 'The differences between infant and believer's baptism become less sharp when it is recognised that both forms of baptism embody God's own initiative in Christ and express a response of faith made within the believing community... A discovery of the continuing character of Christian nurture may facilitate the mutual acceptance of different initiation practices'.

---

[148] Schrotenboer pp291-313.

Embrace it all! Wright pointed out there was 'nothing breathtakingly new' in this, 'except that, on the basis of agreement among official representatives of Baptists, as well as the majority of infant-baptiser churches, it claims to offer a path to inter-baptism – the mutual recognition of the two dominant forms of baptism'. Wright commended the report for study by the students of the London Bible College (whom he was addressing at the time),[149] as 'a text we dare not ignore'. He spelled out a possible way forward: 'What the Lima report proposes... is already a reality in some churches; namely, the observance of both infant and believer's baptism as "equivalent alternatives"'. He spoke of 'double-practice' churches. He noted some of the reasons for this mutual accommodation: 'Recognition of the greater reluctance of even some Christian parents today to decide for their children; accommodation to the unceasing and perhaps increasing questioning of infant baptism on both historical and theological grounds... respect for a new atmosphere of ecumenical baptismal debate; even perhaps an attempt to come to terms with the difficulties of administering a consistent infant-baptiser discipline as the age of Christendom and the Christian society no longer provides viable models for remnant or gathered churches'.[150]

But, supportive as he was for Lima, Wright was not (in 1988/1989) starry-eyed about the prospects:

The [Lima] approach, exemplified in the fully-fledged 'double-practice' churches, appears to accept that there is no realistic hope of reaching agreement on one form of baptism... One short-term or medium-term result of ecumenical encounter on baptism has in fact been increased

---

[149] Kevan's old college, remember. 'How the gold has become dim! How changed the fine gold!' (Lam. 4:1).

[150] Wright showed a deplorable failure to grasp the point here, especially bearing in mind his encyclopaedic historical-awareness. It is not simply Christendom which makes it impossible for infant baptisers to have gathered churches. Even when society wants gathered churches – witness 17th century New England (as I have shown elsewhere) – history proves that infant baptism itself makes the very notion of a gathered church unworkable. And not only unworkable. A gathered church is a church formed only of regenerate members. Infant baptism, by its very nature, destroys the principle. Indeed, infant baptism is one of the main pillars of Christendom!

polarisation... Baptists have rightly challenged infant baptisers whether they really regard infant baptism as full, complete baptism. If they do, why do they place so much stress on confirmation or admission to communicant membership? Are we not members of Christ's body by virtue of baptism, and ought not baptism to admit to the Lord's table?... It is an index of the unbiblical imbalance some of our Evangelical [infant-baptiser] churches have fallen into on baptism, that this later ceremony is accorded greater significance than baptism itself. It is not unknown, even in our blue-riband Evangelical [infant-baptiser] congregations, to have a teenage convert baptised prior to a service, in the presence of the elders alone, before he or she proceeds into the congregation to be admitted to communicant status on a par with others who had the good fortune[!] to have been baptised in infancy. If we administer baptism to babies, we have no warrant to treat it less than the full dominical ordinance [that is, ordained by Christ(!)] or sacrament.[151]

Note the words 'or sacrament'. Note the subtle move from 'ordinance' to 'sacrament'; that is, by Wright's use of 'or' he equated the two. As I have shown, of course, there is a fundamental clash between the two words 'ordinance' and 'sacrament'. As for 'sacrament', this, I think, has proved – and is proving – in the twenty years since Wright penned those words, the way the impasse will be broken. Sacramentalism is the key. As I have said, once sacramentalism is adopted, differences about the time and mode of baptism will wither. And as night follows day, attendance at the supper will have to follow; the one sacrament must lead to the other

---

[151] Wright: 'One' pp334-337. Wright deplored the prospect of a coming to terms between infant baptisers and Baptists on the basis of 'infant baptisers' accepting 'that baby baptism is incomplete until something like confirmation... has taken place. Baptists might be readier to "buy" infant baptism on these terms – baptism by instalments, as it were. I very much hope that this will not be the case', said Wright. 'It is surely far healthier to acknowledge that we have inherited two different patterns of baptism, and to accept the other's practice without being able to endorse it, than to fudge the issue in this way'. This, it seems to me, is just replacing one fudge by another! The most healthy way – the only way – it to get back to Scripture, determine what Scripture says, and obey that. If we cannot agree, let us separate and be consistent with ourselves, at least – regretting, no doubt, that we cannot see eye-to-eye on the matter, but looking to that day when all will revealed, and all who are in Christ shall be truly one in everything.

with no delay. And, hey presto, the deal will be done. Rome is waiting.

During the quarter of a century which followed Lima, Wright worked hard for unity on sacramental baptism. In 2005, he was more hopeful than he had been in 1988/1989. Looking back over those intervening years, he described Lima as 'perhaps the most widely studied ecumenical texts of the 20th century', and spoke of it as one of the 'signs of hope', 'in the third millennium', along with 'the growing evidence of sacramental thinking among Baptist theologians, and the increasing adoption of dual-practice church polities [on baptism], to the highly significant developments in the Catholic Church since Vatican II'.[152]

So much for Wright. Now for even stronger Evangelical support for Lima.

In 2006, Clint LeBruyns described the Lima document as being 'widely regarded as the most significant theological achievement of the ecumenical movement... became the most widely distributed, translated and discussed ecumenical text in modern times'. There was one 'unfortunate omission' in the text, he said; namely, 'the ministry of the bishop of Rome'. Nevertheless, overall, said LeBruyns, the document 'is perhaps reflective of the most methodological paradigm shift in the Evangelical mind'.[153]

LeBruyns summarised the history of sacramentalism since the middle of the 20th century:

Various Protestant Churches have engaged in ecumenical conversations with Roman Catholicism from as early as the 1950s. Most visible in their participation are the Lutherans and Anglicans, followed by the Methodist and Reformed traditions. These consultations owe their origin primarily to the influence of Vatican II. Evangelicals, on the other hand, have generally maintained a silence when it comes to the Vatican. In the past decade [written 2006], however, they have started to join the discussions. A most notable evidence of this renewed interest is the 'Evangelicals and Catholics Together Project'. See Charles Colson and Richard John Neuhaus (eds.): *Evangelicals and Catholics Together...* (1995). Their most recent work is *Your Word is Truth: A*

---

[152] Wright: *What...?* pp10,14.
[153] LeBruyns pp58-59.

Project of Evangelicals and Catholics Together (2002)... which explores anew the relationship between Scripture and tradition.[154]

And, of course, it is not only Lima. We seem to be getting a steady stream of striking illustrations of what I am trying to say.

Take the paper written by the Principal of Bristol Baptist College, Christopher Ellis: 'A View from the Pool. Baptists, sacraments and the basis of unity', being a consultation paper on 'The Sacramental Dimension of Baptism' convened by the Faith and Order Commission of the World Council of Churches in Prague, June 2000. In this paper, Ellis dealt with the ecumenical drive, sacramental baptism, the place of infants and children within church, the definition of a believer, conversion, liturgy, church membership, infant baptism, and so on. He raised such questions as: 'Does baptism *effect* a change in the relationship between God and the person baptised, or does it *express* a gospel reality? If you believe it does both, then what is the effective nature of proclamation in relation to those who cannot answer for themselves [principally, infants]?... Is baptism a *means* to salvation, or an *expression* of salvation already effected?' Drawing near the end of his paper, Ellis stated: 'I have tried to argue for a vision of unity which can be described as "reconciled diversity", and a plurality of baptismal practices which such a view might imply'. Just before this admission, he had issued a 'caution': 'We should avoid using the word "baptism" to denote this initiatory process of proclamation/nurture, baptism and communion. The attractions of calling the whole process "baptism" are considerable, but the waters are likely then to be muddied and the process muddled'.[155]

Oh dear! My conclusion, and my caution, would have been somewhat more stark!

And, reader, remember Ellis was writing as the Principal of Bristol Baptist College. I draw attention to the words 'Principal', 'Baptist' and 'College'. We are not talking about an inexperienced private individual who happens to hold to infant baptism. We are talking about an experienced public figure who is a Baptist teacher.

---

[154] LeBruyns p64. See my *Infant* for a fuller extract from LeBruyns, and my comments on this and other, connected, matters.

[155] Ellis pp107-120, emphasis his.

Think of the generation of students who will pass through the hands of such a man with such views, students who will be trained as ministers, who will stand in countless pulpits, and publish who knows how many books, pamphlets and tracts upon the subject. The damage to the churches and individuals, under the responsibility of such a man, could be immense. And what about the other Baptist Colleges?

And take the experience of Francis J.Beckwith, set out in his book *Return to Rome: Confessions of an Evangelical Catholic.* Beckwith, baptised a Roman Catholic as an infant, defected from Rome to become an Evangelical – then became a leading Evangelical – and in 2007 returned to Rome, now calling himself an Evangelical Catholic. His book clearly sets out the link, the fluidity, between Rome and Evangelicals, Reformed, Baptists and charismatics, in many fields – the Fathers (Augustine, in particular), justification, saving faith, baptism, conversion, mysticism and medievalism. The following extract will give you, reader, a sense of what I am talking about:

Justification refers not only to the Christian's initial entrance into the family of God at baptism – which is administered for the remission of sins – but to the intrinsic work of both the infusion of that grace at baptism and all the subsequent graces that work in concert to transform the Christian from the inside out. It is in and through this ongoing transformation that one is made justified... and thus gifted to share in the divine life of Christ... 'Sanctification' is the ongoing intrinsic work of justifying... the Christian by means of God's grace, the same grace that intrinsically changed the believer at the moment of [his] initial 'justification' (that is, at baptism) into an adopted child of the Father... The chief distinction between the Protestant view of justification on the one hand, and the Catholic and Church Fathers' view on the other, rests on whether Christ's grace is infused or merely imputed at the moment one becomes a Christian at baptism and/or conversion... The Council of Orange (AD529)... argued that Adam's original sin is inherited by his progeny, and can be removed only by the sacrament of baptism. By the means of baptism, God's unmerited grace is infused for the remission of sins... [Quoting from the *Catechism of the Catholic Church*:] 'Justification is conferred in baptism, the sacrament of faith'... For my [Reformed] friend [Gregory Koukl] as well as many others, the 'grace' the Christian acquires at his initial conversion (and/or baptism) is just the name the Bible attributes to the legal declaration that we are no longer considered guilty in the eyes of God for our sins, because Christ took our punishment on the cross. Catholics, of course, do not deny that Christ died for all our sins, or that he 'offered his life to his Father through the Holy Spirit in reparation for our disobedience' [*Catechism of the Catholic Church*], or that 'by one man's disobedience many were made sinners, so by one man's obedience many will be made righteous'[156] [*Catechism of the Catholic Church*, quoting Rom. 5:19]. But, again, for Catholics, the gift of grace is far more than a legal declaration. 'It', in the words of the [*Catholic*] Catechism, 'conforms us to the righteousness of God, who makes us inwardly just [righteous] by the power of his mercy'... Justification is about our being part of a communion of saints, the body of Christ, with whom we can receive and share the unearned and totally gratuitous wonders of God's grace, through baptism, the eucharist, confession and all the sacraments... In the eastern Church... the Christian life is a process of intrinsic change towards godliness that begins at baptism... After all, if I return to the [Catholic] Church and participate in the sacraments, I lose nothing, since I would still be a follower of Jesus and believe everything that the Catholic creeds [Nicene, Athanasian *etc.*, which the Reformed accept] teach, as I have always believed [both as a Catholic and an Evangelical]. But if the [Catholic] Church is right about itself and the sacraments, I acquire graces I would have not otherwise received.[157]

---

[156] 'Made', καθιστημι, should be translated 'constituted, declared'. This is the crux of the matter. Justification does not change the sinner; it constitutes or declares him right in the sight of God. The Bible teaches the *imputed* righteousness of Christ by faith, not *imparted*. See my *Particular*.

[157] Beckwith pp85-86,91-92,108,110,113,116. While I agree with the writer of the following review, much more needs to be said. 'Many of the Evangelical Protestants who are going to Rome are those who originally came from Rome, and who, it could easily be argued, were converted to a theologically weak, emotionally hyped and historically dubious Evangelicalism, which never required them to entirely leave Rome behind. Also, most Evangelical protestants who are currently converting to Rome are those whose experience of Evangelicalism has been less than desirable. What Rome lacks in orthodoxy, it tries hard to make up for in the areas of history, tradition, ceremony and the like. Even its theology is impressive to many modern Evangelicals, if only because their own theology is often practically non-existent. It must surely be one of the tragedies of modern Evangelicalism that we would leave our [constituents] so vulnerable to the attractions of Rome. Yes, Beckwith had to wrestle long and hard with Rome's teaching on subjects such as the real presence of Christ in the eucharist, the authority of the Church, the primacy of the Papacy, penance,

Reader, I have not been spending my time – and yours – in word-spinning about mere theory. Here it is in black and white – and see Beckwith's book as a whole – here is a real-life illustration of, as I said, today's fluidity between Rome, the Reformed, Baptists and Evangelicals. And sacramentalism is at the root of it all. Ignorant of the fact most believers seem to be, and lack of discernment blinds many, I am afraid, but this is what is going on behind the scenes. And not so far behind the scenes, at that![158]

Finally, after I had 'finished' what I thought I had to say on the subject, I came across the publishers' blurb for George Hunsinger: *Let us Keep the Feast*, Cambridge University Press, Cambridge, 2008:

The theology of the eucharist has long been the subject of heated debate, particularly since the Reformation. George Hunsinger's book explores ways in which Christians might resolve their differences in this area. With the aim of fostering ecumenical convergence, he tackles three key issues dividing the Churches about the eucharist: real presence, eucharistic sacrifice, and ordained ministry. Hunsinger, a Protestant theologian in the Reformed tradition, brings Eastern

---

and so on, but the reality is that his experience of a diluted Evangelicalism made his move far easier than it would otherwise have been' ('Rome sweet home?' p76). What more needs to be said? 'Diluted Evangelicalism', yes. It is the very weakness of Evangelicalism which makes the move to Rome easier. Yes. But it is not just Evangelical *weakness*. Reformed theology, itself, is highly sacramental. As I have shown (above and in my *Infant*), it is those who are taking Calvin and Westminster seriously who are leading the drive today – yes, the drive today – to Rome. Let us call a spade a spade here! Some supporters of the *Protestant Truth* – the strongly Reformed – by holding to Calvin and Westminster on infant baptism, unavoidably hold to sacramentalism. And this is the basic driver towards Rome. They may not recognise it. They may deny it. But the evidence is incontrovertible, as I have shown. Jane Dempsey Douglass: 'Many heirs to [Calvin's] thought have been active leaders and participants in the modern ecumenical movement, believing that Calvin's theology supported their work'. She herself claimed to have identified 'elements of Calvin's own thought and work which laid a foundation for ecumenical work', and this in justification of her opening remark: 'John Calvin can be seen in an ecumenical context from the 16th century right into the 21st' (Douglass pp305-316).

[158] See Soper pp253-255 for his 2009 article 'More Downgrade in the FIEC'.

Orthodox views more systematically into the discussion than has been common in the west. He also discusses the social significance of the eucharist. His detailed conclusion summarises and clarifies the argument as a whole with an eye to explaining how the views proposed in the book could lead the Churches, beginning with the Reformed Church, closer to the day when obstacles to eucharistic sharing are overcome... A groundbreaking discussion of the three most divisive eucharistic issues: real presence, eucharistic sacrifice, episcopal succession. [He] addresses the main points of impasse in current ecumenical discussion and suggests how they can be overcome. [He] relates the eucharist to contemporary concerns about justice and peace.

Then came extracts from Reviews:

This volume is an ambitious project which makes a major contribution to theological and ecumenical exploration of the eucharistic tradition (*Worship*).

Hunsinger is amazing... Not only is he a top-notch theologian who finds significant common ground between the Reformed, Roman Catholics, and Eastern Orthodoxy, but he also manages to argue for women's and gay ordination in a logical and level-headed way... He is a model for peaceful discussion (*Books, Catholicity, Sacraments, Theology*).

Sympathetically explored... fascinating (*Church Times*).

So thank God for George Hunsinger. He refuses to let past polemics die. In this elegantly written and well-argued book he addresses each of the areas of contention with clarity and generosity in the hope that we can rediscover the unity that is ours (*Christian History*).

Comprehensive in its coverage and challenging in its conclusions (*Journal of Theological Studies*).

It is not only George Hunsinger who 'refuses to let past polemics die'. Reader, you have in your hands my contribution to the battle!

And what of my contribution? Just now I spoke of a steady stream of sacramental material. Perhaps I should re-phrase it, and say there seems to be a flood of new material, appearing daily, to demonstrate the rise and unceasing spread of sacramentalism. What is my reaction?

I will tell you. If I may be allowed to accommodate the words of the 17th century Leveller, John Lilburne:

I scorned to be so base as to sit down in a whole skin... while the liberties and freedom of the [gospel] were in danger.[159]

With this thought coursing through my brain, what have I done about it?

I... with my poor one talent... have used my best endeavours... to show the maladies and remedies of this sick, swooning, bleeding and dying [cause of Christ in this land].[160]

* * *

So I bring this long chapter to a close, a chapter in which we have looked at the drivers of Baptist sacramentalism. As we have seen, they are various. But whatever the drivers, let us not forget the issue. Which is? Sacramentalism! Sacramentalism is *the* issue. For at least 1700 years it has played a fundamental role in Romanism, and for nearly 500 years among the Reformed. Now it has risen and is growing among the Baptists.

Sacramentalism. We have looked at history – since, as I have shown, that is where Baptist sacramentalists want to start – and we have looked at their theological statements, and the principles and practices which have been driving them Romeward. But Scripture, not history, not theology or current practice, is the touchstone. Scripture! It is high time we looked at it. Indeed, we should have started there. Especially do we need to examine what Baptist sacramentalists say upon the relevant biblical passages. And when I say 'examine', I mean 'test' – test by Scripture. Let us probe these sacramental-Baptist statements. Let us take a hard-nosed look at their exegesis. Let us do so with an open Bible before us. This is the ultimate test. 'To the law and to the testimony! If they do not speak according to this word, it is because there is no light in them' (Isa. 8:20).

---

[159] Lilburne spoke of the 'liberties and freedoms of the *kingdom*' in *A Whip for the Present House of Lords* (Feb. 27th 1648).

[160] Lilburne spoke of the 'sick... dying *nation*' in his *England's Birthright Justified* (Oct. 10th 1645). For both extracts, see Gregg pp99,126,401,402. See Pauline Gregg's note on her p401.

Scripture Passages Used by
Baptist Sacramentalists

As I warned right at the start, the tone of my book has been largely negative. It could not have been otherwise, since I have been trying to show what is wrong with the sacramentalist view being put forward by a growing number of Baptist scholars. Not only that. I have been sounding a warning about it. Negative, therefore, the tone has had to be.

In particular, this chapter we now come to, and the one which follows, will follow the same path; not entirely, but largely so. I cannot avoid it – if I am to examine sacramental-Baptist statements on all the relevant passages of Scripture. And this I must do. Scripture is the supreme authority in formulating any doctrine or practice. We must 'search the Scriptures' (John 5:39, AV). We must search the Scriptures for ourselves, and come to our own judgement about what they teach. Acts 17:11 is the principle. We must submit the claims of others to the touchstone of Scripture. Let us fall in line with the Bereans and search 'the Scriptures... to find out whether these things [are] so'.

That is what I now intend to do with regard to Baptist-sacramentalist interpretations of the relevant scriptural passages, and the deductions they draw from them. I will be pointing out what I see is wrong with their arguments. I think they read far too much into these passages, and, as a consequence, read far too much out of them.

Disapproving, then, must be the tenor of what is to come. But I do not apologise for it. A physician cannot be blamed if he looks for disease. For it is only by discovering it, and getting to its cause, that he can really set about the cure.

Having said all that, the next two chapters will not be entirely negative. I will also be setting out what I consider to be the right deductions from the passages in question.

As is only to be expected, many of the passages used by Baptist sacramentalists to make their case are the very same as those used by their Reformed counterparts. I have, of course, already looked at

155

these in my *Infant* – and I refer you, reader, to that volume. However, to enable this present work to stand on its own, I will include the most relevant parts of those comments – relevant to answering Baptist sacramentalists, that is.

But before I start, I must clear the ground, and in three particulars. Otherwise, when we come to individual passages we might well be talking at cross-purposes. That, of course, would be pointless. And worse.

Three questions to be decided

1. 'Baptism with/in/by the Spirit'

This biblical phrase comes up time and again in this debate, and if I do not stop to say what I mean by it, the danger is we will be referring to different things, and therefore have no chance whatsoever of coming to an agreement – or properly defining our real disagreement. And that would be grievous. I am afraid I have to plead guilty to having used the phrase, or its equivalent, in this book so far, without careful definition. Let me put the matter right, and say what I understand by the phrase.

And there is need. For there is a spectrum of meanings which various teachers attach to it.[1] That fact, on its own, tells us that it is foolish to be dogmatic.

Let me quote all the passages where the phrase is used:

[Christ] will baptise you with the Holy Spirit and fire (Matt. 3:11).
He will baptise you with the Holy Spirit (Mark 1:8).
He will baptise you with the Holy Spirit and fire (Luke 3:16).
This is he who baptises with the Holy Spirit (John 1:33).
John truly baptised with water, but you shall be baptised with the Holy Spirit not many days from now... You shall receive power when the Holy Spirit has come upon you (Acts 1:5,8).
Then I remembered the word of the Lord, how he said: 'John indeed baptised with water, but you shall be baptised with the Holy Spirit' (Acts 11:16).

---

[1] Nigel Pibworth has listed seventeen different ways various teachers interpret the phrase! Yes, seventeen.

For by one Spirit we were all baptised into one body... and have all been made to drink into ['into' is omitted in some texts] one Spirit (1 Cor. 12:13).

Many would add a considerable number of other passages to this list – passages, though they do not contain the phrase in question, nevertheless seem to speak in similar terms. Whether this is right, is open to question. But confining ourselves to the direct, unambiguous New Testament use of the phrase, what do we make of these seven passages?

Leaving 1 Corinthians 12:13 aside for the moment, let me say something about the Acts passages.

Acts 2 records the immediate fulfilment of Christ's promise to his disciples in Acts 1. And Acts 11 is Peter's explanation of the events of Acts 10. And the two sets of passages are linked, as I will explain.

On the day of Pentecost (Acts 2), Peter, quoting Joel 2:28-32, explained that what was going on was the fulfilment of Christ's promise (Acts 2:14-21,32-33). Acts 2, as I said, records the immediate fulfilment of Christ's promise in Acts 1.

What about Acts 10 and 11? As a result of the events of Acts 10, Peter was hauled before 'the apostles and brethren who were in Judea', and was challenged about his breaking of Jewish laws by going into the house of a Gentile and eating with him and his friends. 'The circumcised believers' in Jerusalem 'criticised him' for it (Acts 11:2, NIV). Peter had his defence. God had spoken to him in a vision at Joppa. At God's command, he and six friends had gone with the three men sent by Cornelius. As he was preaching in Cornelius' house, he said, the Holy Spirit fell upon the Gentiles gathered to hear him. Peter further explained that he then recalled the promise which Christ gave the believers after the resurrection (Acts 1). Referring his interrogators back to that promise, and to the experience of Acts 2, he drew the proper conclusion: The fact that God had given the Gentiles 'the same gift as he gave us when we believed the Lord Jesus Christ' – indeed, as Peter was able to testify, he himself had been a witness of the Gentiles having the same experience as they (the Jews at Pentecost) had had 'at the beginning' – 'who was I that could withstand God?' (Acts 11:1-18). 'Then I remembered the word of the Lord, how he said: "John indeed baptised with water, but you shall be baptised with the Holy Spirit"' (Acts 11:16). See Acts 1:5,8.

I draw your attention to Peter's words in Acts 11:15. Reader, what do you make of them? 'The Holy Spirit fell upon them [the Gentiles] *as upon us at the beginning*'? Let me stress the words again: '*as upon us at the beginning*'.[2] Why did he refer back to Pentecost? Thousands had been converted since Pentecost (Acts 4:4; 6:1,7; 8:6-8,12,37-38; 9:1-19). Why did Peter not refer to *those* events? And why did he not say: 'The Holy Spirit fell upon them [the Gentiles] *as he always does when anybody is converted*'?

The only 'solution', it seems to me, is that Acts 2 and 10 (I would put Acts 8:14-17 in the same category)[3] record unique experiences,[4] epoch-making events, in direct fulfilment of Christ's promise: 'You shall be witnesses to me in Jerusalem, and in all Judea and Samaria, and to the end of the earth' (Acts 1:8). At each of these explosive events – Pentecost, Samaria and Cornelius (Acts 2, 8 and 10) – when God, in his sovereignty, catapulted the gospel into its next phase in its world-wide spread, Christ marked the significance of the occasion by pouring out his Spirit in a signal demonstration of his power. And that is why Peter referred back to the beginning. Pentecost, Acts 2, would always mark the great precedent for these things.

In short, Peter, in his reference to the gift of the Spirit (Acts 11:15-17), was not talking about a common, everyday experience. This outpouring, and the other outpourings of the Spirit we are talking about, comprised a unique series of events marking the step-changes as the gospel moved from Jerusalem to the ends of the earth. And these outpourings are called 'baptism with the Holy Spirit'.

This is not to say that there were not repeated *fillings* of the Holy Spirit throughout Acts (Acts 2:4; 4:8,31; 6:3,5; 7:55; 9:17; 11:24;

---

[2] See also Acts 15:7-9.

[3] And what about Acts 19:1-7? I find the passage difficult to fit into the scheme of things. I am not alone. It seems to record an event even more unique (with apologies for my linguistic solecism). I will come back to this passage.

[4] I am at a loss to find the right word. How can two or three events each be unique? 'Special' seems inadequate. But I think my meaning is clear.

13:52), but were not some of these fillings something different to the baptism with the Spirit? It certainly appears so – to me, at least.

Again: Is there any example of an *individual* being baptised with the Spirit? Was it not a *corporate* phenomenon in Acts 2, 8 and 10, a *community* experience?

Following on from that, if it is granted that the baptism with the Spirit, accompanied by these remarkable signs and wonders, marked these epoch-making events, does it mean that 'the baptism with the Spirit' has now ceased – that it ceased when the gospel reached the Gentiles in Acts 10? Is there any other occurrence of it mentioned in Acts? Or in the rest of the New Testament – apart from 1 Corinthians 12:13? If it were not for 1 Corinthians 12:13, this, for me, would seem to be the case; namely, that the baptism with the Spirit marked these step changes in the spread of the gospel, and referred to a corporate, not an individual, experience.

But there stands 1 Corinthians 12:13. And, to my mind, 1 Corinthians 12:13 destroys that interpretation, that conclusion; namely, that the baptism with the Spirit recorded in Acts 2, 8 and 10 never occurred again. *That* cannot be the explanation.[5]

Nor can I limit 1 Corinthians 12:13 to a corporate experience. By that, I mean it must be speaking of an individual experience. Why? For this reason: If Paul was saying that all the Corinthians had been baptised by the Spirit into one body – and this had happened as a unique corporate experience on the initial occasion – then anyone who joined them from that time on would not be so baptised. This I regard as untenable. The Corinthian believers had not all been converted on the same occasion, surely? No, I can only deduce that, when Paul wrote, every believer at Corinth had been individually baptised with or by the Spirit. And, as a consequence, every believer who has ever lived, has been so baptised.

My 'solution' to the question, therefore, runs something like this. Every believer is baptised with the Spirit. But at certain unique times – three times in Acts (Acts 2, 8 and 10)[6] – God accompanied

---

[5] J.Wallis wrote (in 1824) against the views of Joseph Irons. Wallis thought that 'the baptism with the Spirit' was apostolic, ceased after their death, and is no longer available today (Wallis pp11-12,23). It is hard to take Wallis seriously on this point since he failed even to mention 1 Cor. 12:13.

[6] See my earlier note on Acts 19:1-7.

this baptism with remarkable signs and wonders. The baptism with/in/by the Spirit is repeated in every sinner coming to Christ, but the signs and wonders which accompanied it ceased when those epoch-making events were complete.

So let me state the way in which I will use the phrase 'baptism with/in/by the Spirit' in what follows. By 'baptism with/in/by the Spirit', I mean that sovereign act of God the Holy Spirit whereby he translates the sinner out of Adam into Christ, delivers him from the power, domain, realm and authority of darkness, and transfers him into the kingdom of Christ (John 3:3-8; Rom. 5:12-21; 6:1-23; 7:1-6; 1 Cor. 2:12-16; Eph. 4:17-24; Col. 1:13; 2:10-15; 3:1-4 *etc.*). This, to my mind, is the fundamental meaning, the heart of being 'baptised with the Spirit'. This is what I understand by spiritual baptism. It is an experience which all believers have. They could not be believers without it:

Unless one is born again, he cannot see the kingdom of God... Unless one is born of water and the Spirit, he cannot enter the kingdom of God. That which is born of the flesh is flesh, and that which is born of the Spirit is spirit... You must be born again... born of the Spirit (John 3:3-8).[7]

Spiritual baptism, then, is regeneration, that work of God's Spirit by which he turns unbelievers into believers.

Of course, God, with this gift of regeneration, grants not only saving faith and repentance to the sinner, but, as the sinner trusts Christ, he grants the whole panoply of grace by the Spirit – which includes anointing, the sense of sonship, adoption, a deposit, foretaste and guarantee of future glory, the inner witness, the seal of the Spirit, liberty in access to God, and so on (John 1:12-13; 4:10,14; 6:63; 7:38-39; 14:16-17; 16:14,26; Acts 2:38; 10:47; Rom. 8:9-17; 1 Cor. 2:12; 3:16; 6:19; 12:3; 2 Cor. 1:20-22; 5:5; 6:16; 11:4; Gal. 3:2,14; 4:4-7; 5:5,16-26; 6:8; Eph. 1:13-14; 2:18,22; 3:14-21; 4:30; 1 Thess. 4:7-8; 1 John 2:20,27; 4:13; 5:6-11,14-15 *etc.*). And, of course, there is the repeated record of people 'full of the Spirit' or 'being filled with the Spirit' (Luke 1:15,41,67; 4:1; Acts 2:4; 4:8,31; 6:3,5; 7:55; 9:17; 11:24; 13:52; Eph. 5:18).

---

[7] I will return to these verses.

Now, whether or not the bestowal of all of these gifts and graces should be included in 'the baptism with the Spirit', is open to question. If it does, then the question has to be faced: If a professing believer lacks any one of these gifts or graces, does it mean that his profession is false? Or does every believer have these gifts but in many cases the believer grieves or quenches the Spirit (Eph. 4:30; 1 Thess. 5:19)?[8]

My own view is that which I have already stated. Fundamentally, 'the baptism with the Spirit' is regeneration, but regeneration never comes alone. Packer:

Can it be convincingly denied that 1 Corinthians 12:13... refers to one aspect of what we may call the 'conversion-initiation complex' with which the Christian life starts, so that according to Paul every Christian as such is Spirit baptised? Surely not.[9]

Note the 'one aspect'. This is my view, except that I would put it even stronger. The *leading* aspect of 'the baptism of the Spirit' is regeneration, but it also includes all those other things in what Packer calls the 'conversion-initiation complex'. As he pointed out, if this is not so, and if 'the baptism with the Spirit' refers to some kind of further, special, second blessing, then, whereas all the believers of Paul's day (at least Paul and the Corinthians) had this experience, many today do not. What is more, if the Corinthians had received this so-called 'second blessing' (which, presumably, made them into outstandingly spiritual believers), it is passing strange that Paul had to write such things as 1 Corinthians 3:1-3 to them; indeed, see his entire first letter, where the low spiritual state of the Corinthians is written plain for all to see.

Perhaps there is another approach which might yield satisfactory results. Is it possible to try to distinguish between 'the baptism *with* or *in* or *by* the Spirit'? No! Trying to distinguish between 'the baptism *with* or *in* or *by* the Spirit' fails because in Matthew 3:11, Mark 1:8, Luke 3:16, John 1:33, Acts 1:5, 11:16 and 1 Corinthians 12:13 'the same preposition εν is used, making the Spirit the "element" in which Christ baptises, so that the distinction is

---

[8] See Eaton pp145-147.
[9] Packer: *Step* pp202-203.

linguistically baseless'.[10] Whatever the meaning of 'the baptism *with* or *in* or *by* the Spirit', in each case, '*with* or *in* or *by*', it speaks of the same experience.

So, there it is. For my purposes, when I speak of 'the baptism with the Spirit', I am thinking primarily of that sovereign act, that regenerating act of God the Holy Spirit, by which he translates the sinner out of Adam and unites him to Christ, and delivers him from the power, domain, realm and authority of darkness, and transfers him into the kingdom of Christ. This is what I understand by the phrase 'the baptism with/in/by the Spirit'.

That this little discussion has solved all the problems connected with this subject, I am not so stupid or arrogant as to suppose. Nevertheless, for the purpose of my book, the precise meaning of 'the baptism with the Spirit' is not really a bone of contention. The real issue is not, precisely, what the baptism of the Spirit comprises, but whether or not that baptism is conveyed or produced by water baptism. And on that issue, above all it is not what the professional theologians and scholars think, but what the many thousands of 'ordinary' believers think about baptism in water and its connection or otherwise with the baptism with the Spirit. The scholar may write and the preacher may preach – but what do the people in the pew take away with them? And when their theologians and ministers start to talk in highfaluting terms about water baptism, linking it with the baptism of the Spirit, what *do* those 'average' believers think? I suggest that although they may well have no distinct understanding of the phrase, 'the baptism of the Spirit', they think it must be important, it sounds important, whatever it is. And that 'something', whatever it is, takes place in and through water baptism.

And herein lies the danger!

Now for the *second* matter I spoke of.

2. The distinction between water baptism and Spirit baptism
We must distinguish between water baptism and spiritual baptism.[11] The New Testament does, and does it in no uncertain terms. 'John

---

[10] Packer: *Step* pp202-203.
[11] For more on this, see my earlier books.

truly baptised with water, but you shall be baptised with the Holy Spirit not many days from now' (Acts 1:5). Not only are the two baptisms different, they have no cause-effect connection with each other – none whatsoever. It is true that water or washing is mentioned in John 3:5, 1 Corinthians 6:11, Ephesians 5:26, Titus 3:4-7 and Hebrews 10:22, for instance, but this is figurative,[12] in exactly the same way as the fire in Matthew 3:11 is figurative – 'he will baptise you with the Holy Spirit and fire'. Those who think the water is literal, must be consistent and in addition to dipping them in water, they should roast those they baptise! But the water and the fire are both figurative; they symbolise the purifying, cleansing, renewing power of the Spirit of God in regeneration,[13] in which he gives a new, clean heart (Ps. 51:10; Ezek. 18:31; 36:25-27; Mal. 3:1-3; Heb. 10:22).

Peter, when he dealt with Cornelius, distinguished the two baptisms – by the Spirit and by water; he only thought of water baptism *after* the people had been spiritually baptised and the evidences of it were clearly visible (Acts 10:44-48). Peter later explained that when he saw these evidences which demonstrated that his hearers had been spiritually baptised, then he 'remembered the word of the Lord' that 'John indeed baptised with water, but you shall be baptised with the Holy Spirit' (Acts 11:15-16). As Peter said: 'God gave them the same gift' (Acts 11:17). Notice that – God gave the gift. They were spiritually baptised by God *directly*; it did

---

[12] Contrary to Fowler (*More* pp156-195), and to Beasley-Murray – who, on Tit. 3:5-7, started in a way which I find utterly incomprehensible: 'The meaning of Tit. 3:5-7 depends in part on the background assumed for it. It is most usually regarded as moving towards the later theology of the Catholic Church. This may be so, but we cannot be sure'. Leaving that nonsensical speculation aside, Beasley-Murray was definite on the passage: 'Its central conception is that in [water] baptism the corresponding event occurs in the life of the individual as happened to the church at Pentecost... The saying implies a realistic, rather than a symbolic understanding of baptism, but that applies to most of the Pauline utterances on baptism' (Beasley-Murray: 'Baptism in the Epistles of Paul' pp143-144). I vigorously dispute this. I will give my reasons when looking at the passages in question.

[13] Not excluding, of course, those repeated cleansings necessary in all our approaches to God. See below on Heb. 10:22.

not involve water at the hands of a minister. God baptised the people with the Spirit, he gave them the gift of the Spirit – and he did so directly, without water. Likewise it was Christ, said Peter, who had poured out the Holy Spirit at Pentecost (Acts 2:33) with no reference to water baptism.

What is more, the concept of washing, cleansing and sprinkling is common in the New Testament (John 13:8; 15:3; Acts 18:6;[14] 2 Cor. 7:1; Heb. 12:24; Jas. 4:8; 1 Pet. 1:2; 1 John 1:7,9; Rev 1:5; 7:14), without any suggestion of baptism. All these references are figurative. All![15]

In short, water baptism is a symbol of spiritual baptism, yes, but, I repeat, the two are clearly differentiated in Scripture. We know that water baptism is a baptism which is to take place at or after conversion; in other words, leaving aside the extraordinary circumstances of Pentecost, in New Testament terms water baptism takes place only and always after a person has been baptised with the Holy Spirit. It is true that in one or two verses spiritual and water baptism appear to be telescoped together – as in Acts 2:38 and 22:16 – but even in those verses there is no warrant to think that the water baptism produced the spiritual baptism, or that the two were identical. As I say, the New Testament makes a clear distinction between the two. This distinction must not be blurred. To do so is to make a great mistake, and to make a great mistake with massive consequences.[16]

So much for the second matter to be decided. Now for the *third* question I spoke of.

---

[14] 'Pure' – καθαρος – 'clean, pure, free from the admixture or adhesion of anything that soils, adulterates, corrupts' (Thayer).

[15] Of course, in John 13, Jesus did literally wash the disciples' feet. My reference, however, is to his remark to Peter: 'He who is bathed needs only to wash his feet, but is completely clean [καθαρος]; and you are clean [καθαροι], but not all of you' (John 13:10). 'You are καθαροι', it goes without saying, has nothing to do with water. If anybody disputes this, perhaps they could write to me and explain why Judas (of whom Jesus was obviously speaking) was not 'clean' when, clearly, he had been as much washed as any other disciple.

[16] I will have more to say on this when looking at John's baptism.

3. Which glasses will you wear?

As I said, in this and the following chapter, I am going to look at every passage in the New Testament which has any relevance to the claim that baptism is a sacrament. In some of these passages (principally Rom. 6:1-11; 1 Cor. 12:13; Gal. 3:27; Col. 2:11-12; 1 Pet. 3:21), the apostles make huge claims for the power and efficacy of the baptism in question. We dare not minimise or water down (no pun intended!) those claims. That must be the golden rule here. Let the apostles state their case and make their claims. And let us accept them – hook, line and sinker.

Now, whether we like it or not, whether we admit it or not, we all put on a pair of glasses[17] as we come to these passages. And those glasses will determine what conclusions we draw. In saying this, I am simply recognising facts – and trying to make sure, reader, that you understand that this is what is happening to you, even though you may not realise it or like to admit it.

What am I talking about?

Just this. There are three ways in which all of us approach these verses. We all put on one of three pairs of glasses.[18] I do. You do. We all do. Which pair will you be wearing?

There is always a danger with illustrations. In case mine should be mis-read, let me explain. Of course, in approaching Scripture, we can be prejudiced. We can deliberately – defiantly, obstinately, stubbornly – read the text in the way we have blindly pre-determined. I am not accusing anybody of that; although, I realise, it is not unknown! No! I am talking about the wearing of prescription glasses after a proper optometrist's test. In other words, I am thinking of the way we read Scripture *after a proper examination of all the evidence*. I am thinking of the way this governs our view of particular passages. This is what I mean by wearing glasses. I am not being pejorative.

So, reader, I say again, we all put on one of three pairs of glasses. I do. You do. We all do. Which pair will you be wearing?

---

[17] That is, we all adopt a frame of reference.

[18] I am oversimplifying. No doubt there are other ways of reading the passages. But these are the main ways I have met and with which I am concerned.

Glasses number 1. When most non-sacramental Baptists – that is traditional Baptists, conventional Baptists – read the passages in question, when they see 'baptism' they read 'water baptism'. Indeed, they often seem to assume 'baptism' means 'water baptism', and do not pause to consider that it might be something else. They simply take it as water baptism. To avoid the sacramental implications this inevitably entails, they nearly always quickly go on to speak of this water baptism as a *representation* of the spiritual experience being spoken of – union with Christ, washing from sin, regeneration, salvation or whatever.[19]

Glasses number 2. When sacramentalists read 'baptism' the passages in question, they, too, see water baptism. Indeed, they, too, often simply assume it. They then argue that water baptism *produces* the grace spoken of – or, at least, that God *conveys* that grace through water baptism. Some sacramentalists state this baldly and add no qualifiers whatsoever; all who are baptised are regenerate, united to Christ, and so on. Others introduce various qualifiers of one sort or another to get them off the hook. I have spoken of these in my *Infant* and throughout this present work. In particular, Baptist sacramentalists seem to be fond of the notion that water baptism is *a* means of conveying the grace. This is one way in which they try to qualify the passages in question.

Glasses number 3. Let me admit it at once; these are my glasses. I do not say I am the only one to wear them. Not at all. They are worn by those non-sacramental Baptists who refuse the first pair. That is, they do not use the notion of 'representation'. But since I cannot speak absolutely for anybody else – although I think most in this group would agree with me – I will use the first person. I am not, however, implying that I am unique! With that understood, let me go on.

When I read the baptism passages, I always ask a question: Which baptism is this passage speaking about? I do this because of

---

[19] One exception seems to be Gal. 3:27, where they often take 'the putting on of Christ' to mean an open profession of Christ. If so, they are, at that point, virtually wearing the third glasses – they are not using the notion of 'representation'. I will explain further when talking about the third pair of glasses.

Matthew 3:11, Mark 1:8, Luke 3:16 and John 1:33. John the Baptist made it as plain as day that there are two baptisms, water and Spirit. Therefore, every time I come across 'baptism', I know I have to decide which of the two baptisms the passage is referring to. I dare not assume it is water baptism. I have to make a deliberate decision. How do I make that decision? Principally by the context, and by weighing the consequences of my choice against the rest of the New Testament. Having decided which baptism is being spoken about, I stick with the consequences, and I add no qualifiers. In the passages at issue (Rom. 6:1-11; 1 Cor. 12:13; Gal. 3:27; Col. 2:11-12; 1 Pet. 3:21), I am convinced the baptism in question is baptism with the Spirit.[20] And I am further convinced that this baptism does not *represent* the grace spoken of; it *conveys* it, it *produces* the grace spoken of. And all who have received the baptism with the Spirit, without exception receive the grace spoken of.

One of these three glasses, reader, you will be wearing. My pair, as I have said, is the third. Which is yours?

Let me offer an assessment of the three. To my mind, the least 'worthy' is the first. Indeed, the representational view, it seems to me, has nothing to commend it. Overwhelmingly popular among traditional Baptists it may be, and unpopular it may make me for saying it, but it is, to me, a fudge, a handy tool to let the non-sacramentalist Baptist get himself off the sacramental hook. But it fails – because it fails to take the text seriously enough. What do I mean? I can see no hint of a suggestion of representation in the text in the passages concerned. In fact, 'representation' introduces the reddest of red-herrings, and in the worst of places! The notion is forced into the text, as I say, to avoid sacramental overtones and consequences.

Of course, I fully accept that water baptism does represent the experience of saving grace, but representation of saving grace by water baptism is not what the apostles are writing about in these passages. No, not even in 1 Peter 3:21! I say it again: The context and argument of the passages in question will not allow the notion

---

[20] See the previous note. Some who would otherwise agree with me – and wear the third glasses – take Gal. 3:27 to refer to the profession of Christ.

of representation. As I will contend when looking at those individual passages which come into this debate, if we say that the apostle inserts the notion of representation at that stage in his argument – and, therefore, introduces such an anti-climax, for no significant purpose that I can see, and without any hint that he is doing it – then we have to accept that he breaks the flow and the thrust of the case he is making, and grievously distracts from his progress to a climax. And this, to my mind, is ridiculous; indeed, it is fatal to the original supposition. As I said, it is the worst of places in which to introduce the notion of 'representation'. For this reason, I cannot wear the first glasses.

I have more respect for the second pair. Those who wear them do take the text seriously. They do not fudge it by the idea of 'representation'. The baptism in question is effective and produces or conveys the grace spoken of. Sadly, from what I have read, it seems that most who wear these glasses do not stop to ask the inevitable question raised by Matthew 3:11, Mark 1:8, Luke 3:16 and John 1:33. They seem simply to assume the baptism in question is water baptism. Having done that, however, a number of teachers – namely, Papist, some Reformed and some sacramental-Baptist – refusing to qualify the consequences, are consistent, and accept – indeed, glory in – the sacramental consequences. And I respect them. I say that without the slightest suggestion of patronisation. I respect consistent sacramentalists. Their view I find abhorrent, because it contradicts the overwhelming evidence of the New Testament, and leads to consequences repugnant to it. But at least those sacramentalists are consistent; consistently wrong, but consistent. Other sacramentalists, however, both Reformed and Baptist, though wearing the second glasses, qualify the text to get themselves off the sacramental hook. For this, I am afraid they do *not* earn my respect.

As for the third pair of glasses – as I have said, they are mine – when faced with any of these passages, the question always asked is: Which baptism are we talking about? The answer cannot be assumed. As I explained, to my mind, this question is not only justified but essential in light of Matthew 3:11, Mark 1:8, Luke 3:16 and John 1:33. I am convinced that John's statements warrant us – force us – to answer this question before we go on to expound the passages. Having asked that question, and decided (by context and consequences – see above) which baptism any particular passage is talking about, I stick with it, accept all the consequences, and apply no qualifying fudge. And the conclusion I come to is that the baptism in the passages in question is spiritual baptism. Spiritual baptism always produces or conveys the grace spoken of, and it does it for all who have been so baptised, no 'if' or 'but' or 'maybe'. Above all – above all, I say – it is the only approach to the passages which does not introduce a red-herring or an anti-climax (water baptism, whether representative or qualified) into the apostolic argument. Indeed, not only does it not in any way interrupt the apostle's line of reasoning, it enhances it. And of the three approaches to the passages in question, it is the only one of which this can be said. In itself, this, to me, clinches the argument.

So much for the third matter I spoke of.

* * *

Having cleared the ground by answering those three questions, we can now move on to look at the passages used by Baptist sacramentalists to make their case, weigh the comments they make, and probe the conclusions they draw.

Let me start with Fowler's general conclusions on the various Scriptures in question:

The New Testament consistently views baptism as a[21] means of entrance into eschatological salvation wrought by Jesus Christ. Although the crucial factor from the human side is penitent faith in Christ, this faith is not normally thought of as fully formed apart from baptism... The New Testament evidence seems to point consistently to baptism as the locus [point, place] for the actual, personal experience of Messianic salvation.[22]

---

[21] Why this reticence? It cannot be *a* means. If it is 'means' at all, it must be *the* means.

[22] Fowler: *More* pp164,216.

Quite a claim for water baptism, is it not? Let us see. Let us see if the New Testament really does warrant such a far-reaching sacramentalist claim. Let us look at the passages.[23]

Matthew 3:1-12 and Mark 1:4-8

John the Baptist came preaching... saying: 'Repent...'... [They] were baptised... confessing their sins (NKJV). John the Baptist came, preaching... saying: 'Repent...'... They were being baptised... as they confessed their sins (NASB). John the Baptist came, preaching... saying: 'Repent...'... Confessing their sins, they were baptised (NIV).

John came baptising... and preaching a baptism of repentance for the remission of sins... [They] were... baptised by him... confessing their sins (NKJV). John the Baptist appeared... preaching a baptism of repentance for the forgiveness of sins... They were being baptised... confessing their sins (NASB). John came, baptising... and preaching a baptism of repentance for the forgiveness of sins... Confessing their sins, they were baptised (NIV).

Clearly, we are speaking about water baptism. On that, surely, we must all be agreed. Water baptism is the issue here. Consequently, if the passages are sacramental, then water baptism is a sacrament. There is no escaping it. But are the passages sacramental? Let us see.

Fowler set out the traditional view: 'John demanded repentance as a prerequisite for his baptism' – this interpretation meaning that 'one could not undergo John's baptism without first showing evidence of repentance'. Fowler did not agree. He set out his reasons:

This reading of John's words would demand that he personally examine the life of every person coming to him for baptism...[24] Those coming to

---

[23] In what follows, to avoid repeating cumbersome explanations, when there is no argument that we are speaking about water baptism, I will use 'the traditional view' for the view taken (and for centuries, taken) by the overwhelming majority of Baptists (that which I am convinced is the biblical view).

[24] Why? This argument is, I think, foolish. If it is right, the same stricture must be applied to all preaching of repentance (and faith) before baptism – both in Scripture and since. But are we really to believe, for instance, that

him for baptism were not declaring the evidence of their moral transformation, but were instead 'confessing their sins', the intent of which is surely to experience forgiveness. It seems, then, that the demand placed on the religious leaders is not to prove moral transformation prior to baptism, but to be aware that their baptism will demand that they live differently afterward.[25]

I agree, of course, that those being baptised by John were thereby saying they recognised they would have to live differently from then on. But that's not all they were saying. If they recognised that their life had to change, they were surely declaring that their present (former) way of life was wrong – sinful – and they knew it; they were admitting they were sinners. What is more, not only were they acknowledging that they were sinners, and had to change, they were saying they intended to change. In other words, they were repentant. John commanded them to repent; they repented. It was after their repentance that they were baptised.[26] After all, John was a preacher before he was a baptiser! It was by his preaching that the people were convicted of their sin. By being baptised, they confessed they had repented, and were determined to live a new life. They were not saying that although they had known they were sinners, they had waited until John's baptism to confess it and repent! To know I am a sinner, in the biblical sense, is to feel it, to confess it, to repent of it

---

Peter individually tested and verified every person who 'responded' on the day of Pentecost? Surely, as in Acts 8:37 (whether a gloss or not it shows the biblical approach), the burden is placed squarely upon the one being baptised: 'If you believe'; not: 'Since I have examined you and can vouch for the sincerity of your repentance and faith'. Speaking personally, while I would try to make sure as far as possible that those I baptise are genuine believers, ultimate responsibility rests on those baptised. I make this clear to them. I baptise you, I tell them, on profession of your faith. Not because I can guarantee you are a believer, and certainly not to make you a believer. Calvin: 'Christ enjoins that those who have submitted to the gospel, and professed to be his disciples, shall be baptised' (Calvin: *Commentaries* Vol.17 Part 1 p385). Just so; those who have 'professed to be his disciples'. I would add, 'and give credible evidence of it'.

[25] Fowler: *More* p168.

[26] As Peter: 'Repent, and... be baptised' (Acts 2:38). Beasley-Murray: 'Baptism in the New Testament is wedded to repentance... What God has so joined no man should put asunder' (Beasley-Murray: *Baptism Today and Tomorrow* p70).

and be determined to change. John's baptism marked all this, but it was not the occasion of their repentance, nor did it produce it! They were being baptised because they were repentant.

But at what point – and on what basis – did they experience forgiveness? The important word in the extract from Fowler is 'experience'. 'The intent of' their baptism, according to Fowler, was that they should '*experience* forgiveness'. This is a large claim. Is it right? Were they being baptised in order to obtain, to experience, forgiveness? Were they being told – and did they believe – that their baptism would bring them forgiveness? Did it? If so, then John's baptism was indeed sacramental.

But that is not why they were being baptised.

John commanded the people to repent; he preached a baptism of repentance for the forgiveness of their sins. What was the connection? Why were the people coming to John to be baptised? They were not being baptised in order to repent. Certainly not! As I have argued, they were baptised because they *had* repented and were repentant. In other words, the 'baptism of repentance' meant 'baptism *because* they had repented'.[27] Their baptism was a mark of

---

[27] Beasley-Murray: 'It is not feasible that either Jesus or John meant... "Come to baptism that God may turn you"' (Beasley-Murray: *Baptism in the New Testament* p35). Paul told the congregation in the synagogue at Antioch in Pisidia: 'John... preached... the baptism of repentance to all the people of Israel' (Acts 13:24). If he meant John's baptism *produced* repentance, if baptism was the nub of the question, why did the apostle not preach the same at Athens? When he told the Athenians: 'God... commands all men everywhere to repent' (Acts 17:30), why did he not mention baptism, or, rather, insist on baptism, or actually baptise at that very point? Indeed, how on earth could he pen 1 Cor. 1:13-17? It could not be made more clear – repentance, not baptism, is the heart of the matter. I will return to 1 Cor. 1:13-17. Notice also that when, in Matt. 21:32, Christ rebuked the chief priests and the elders, and spoke of John, he could say: 'John came to you in the way of righteousness, and you did not believe him; but tax collectors and harlots believed him; and when you saw it, you did not afterwards relent and believe him'. The word used, μεταμελομαι, carries the idea of 'regret' (verse 29) or 'relent' (verse 32). See Matt. 27:3; 2 Cor. 7.8; Heb. 7:21. The point is, the religious leaders did not relent, repent, and so believe John. Of course, Christ was saying they should have been baptised, but his emphasis was upon their lack of repentance and faith – not

their repentance; it showed, it demonstrated, it illustrated their repentance. Likewise, their 'baptism of repentance for the forgiveness of sins' meant 'baptism to mark their experience of repentance and, through repentance, their forgiveness of sins'. Their baptism illustrated that they had repented, believed, been forgiven and washed from sin, and had started a new life. This is borne out by the many scriptures which teach that repentance – with no mention of baptism – leads to forgiveness, and that sinners are commanded to repent (with the promise, implied or stated, of forgiveness) (Matt. 9:13; Mark 1:15; 2:17; 6:12; Luke 5:32; 13:3,5; 15:7; 24:47; Acts 3:19; 8:22; 11:18; 17:30; 26:20; Rom. 2:4; 2 Tim. 2:25; 2 Pet. 3:9).[28]

In short, the people came to John to be baptised because, under his preaching, they knew they were sinners, and, having been convicted, were repentant, knew they were forgiven, knew further that they had to change their life in light of it (after all, this is a vital aspect of true repentance), and were determined to change, and wished to confess all this by baptism.

Calvin, though confusing, got the central point right:

This confession was a testimony of repentance...[29] In baptism, [John] declares[30] that our sins are forgiven, and calls us to repentance.[31] That men may come forward, in a right manner, to be baptised, confession of

---

baptism. They should have repented – and been baptised as a mark of their repentance.

[28] If forgiveness of sins comes through, by or in water baptism, none of these Scriptures could have been written. None of them. This, I suspect, is why the sacramentalists claim that baptism is *a* means of salvation; it helps them evade the fact that, in Scripture, forgiveness of sins is unequivocally and repeatedly ascribed to faith and repentance with no mention of water. Are we to believe, then, that some are saved through (because of) water baptism, and others are not?

[29] Quite! Baptism is a 'testimony of repentance'; it does not produce it.

[30] Quite! Baptism 'declares' the forgiveness of sins; it does not produce it.

[31] Calvin lacked precision here. How can anybody have their sins forgiven, and then be called to repentance? I don't think Calvin meant that. Nor do I think Calvin meant that by baptism they would obtain deliverance from sin. Rather, John, in his preaching-baptising ministry, *declared the way of forgiveness*, and called for repentance. The alternative is to think that Calvin was guilty of glaring self-contradiction in a very short space.

sins is demanded from them; otherwise, the whole performance would be nothing but an idle mockery.[32]

William Hendriksen:

Without confession of sins no baptism! For those who truthfully repented of their evil state and wicked conduct, baptism... was a visible sign... of invisible grace... the grace of the forgiveness of sins and adoption into God's own family... To be sure, a man must already be converted before he can properly receive baptism.[33]

Gill:

They were called to repentance by John's ministry, and had the grace of it bestowed upon them; being thoroughly convinced of sin, and truly sorry for it, they were ready to acknowledge and confess it to God and men... Now this is the character given of the very first persons that were baptised by John, and ought surely to be attended to by us; and as much care as possible should be taken, that none but such as have a true sense of sin, and are brought to a humble and hearty acknowledgement of it, be admitted to this ordinance... John required repentance antecedent to it, and administered it upon profession of repentance, as an open testimony of it... not for the obtaining the remission of sins, as if either repentance or baptism were the causes of pardon of sin,[34] but the sense is, that John preached that men should repent of their sins... and upon their repentance... be baptised; in which ordinance, they might be led to a fresh view of the free and full forgiveness of their sins.[35]

---

[32] Calvin: *Commentaries* Vol.16 Part 1 p184.

[33] Hendriksen: *Matthew* p200; *Mark* p37. But, as with Calvin, Hendriksen lacked precision. Was baptism a sign of grace *already* given or *to be* given in the baptism? To my mind, judging by Hendriksen's comment on Mark, he meant that baptism follows conversion – it does not produce it: 'A man must already be converted before he can properly receive baptism'. But what did Hendriksen mean when he said: 'By means of baptism, conversion is powerfully stimulated'? The alternative to saying that Hendriksen was muddled is to say he contradicted himself.

[34] Gill, too, should have been more precise. Although he was right to deny that (faith,) repentance or baptism is the *cause* of pardon – the cause of pardon is the grace of God – the truth is, faith and repentance are the *means* of pardon. But *baptism* is neither the cause nor the means of pardon. Gill, of course, did not lack precision on the baptism question.

[35] Gill: *Commentary* Vol.5 pp17-18,307.

This is my view of the verses. Baptism follows repentance and forgiveness of sins, and marks and illustrates both. But if the sacramentalists are right, and John, by baptism, brought the people into the experience of forgiveness, then baptism is a sacrament. The choice has to be made. There is no halfway house. If baptism is a sacrament, all who are baptised are forgiven. Seeing this goes against so much plain text of the New Testament, the sacramentalist claim must be wrong.

Before I move on, note John's words: 'I indeed baptise you with water unto repentance, but he who is coming after me is mightier than I... He will baptise you with the Holy Spirit and fire' (Matt. 3:11); 'I indeed baptised you with water, but he will baptise you with the Holy Spirit' (Mark 1:8). Now, allowing for the transition period in which John was baptising, whatever else was going on, John made it as plain as day that the people he was baptising were not receiving the baptism of the Spirit in and through their water baptism. Indeed, as I have already explained, he clearly distinguished the two baptisms. But how could this be if the sacramentalists are right? They argue that baptism in water and baptism by the Spirit are one and the same. John's explanation flatly contradicts this.

In Matthew 3:11, Mark 1:8, Luke 3:16 and John 1:33, a clear distinction is drawn between these two baptisms.[36] John baptised with water; Jesus baptises with the Holy Spirit. Both men were baptisers, but they baptised in different realms. Furthermore, Jesus is still baptising to this very day, something which is not always appreciated. A comparison – even a contrast – is drawn between John the Baptist and Jesus Christ as to their persons (John 1:19-28;

---

[36] Contrary to Calvin: 'John... did not mean to distinguish the one baptism from the other'. But he did. As Calvin immediately went on: 'But [John] contrasted his own person with the person of Christ, saying, that while he was a minister of water, Christ was the giver of the Holy Spirit... The apostles... and... those who baptise in the present day... are only ministers of the external sign, whereas Christ is the author of internal grace' (Calvin: *Institutes* Vol.2 p517). In other words, John *did* contrast the two baptisms. If Calvin's words here are not self-contradictory, I don't know what is. Whenever John's words are quoted in the New Testament, the *contrast* between the two baptisms is always made (Matt. 3:11; Mark 1:8; Luke 3:16; Acts 1:5; 11:16; see also John 1:26).

3:26-36; 5:31-37). One was a great prophet; the other is the Son of God. And there is a corresponding contrast drawn between their baptisms. This contrast is not between two water baptisms, but between two baptisms in two totally different realms – baptism in water and baptism in the Spirit. 'John truly baptised with water, but you shall be baptised with the Holy Spirit not many days from now' (Acts 1:5). I repeat, these two baptisms (water baptism and Spirit baptism) must be carefully distinguished.

Finally, let us bear in mind John's own testimony about his ministry. 'That he [Christ] should be revealed to Israel, therefore I came baptising with water' (John 1:31). John looked upon his baptismal ministry, not as that which would *convey* grace to Israel, but as that which would *display* Christ to Israel. Baptism, for John, was not a rite which *conveyed* repentance and forgiveness to the people, but an ordinance to *illustrate the gospel* to them, and *teach* them more about it. John baptised repentant believers. He was no Baptist sacramentalist.

Matthew 28:19-20

Go... and make disciples of all the nations, baptising them... teaching them to observe all things that I have commanded you.

An unlikely or strange choice this passage, it might be thought, for any sacramentalist (Baptist or Reformed) to build his case. It would seem a forlorn task. And, as Fowler admitted, the sacramental Baptists he had referred to 'did not emphasise this text as a support for the sacramental sense of baptism'. Just so! But that was not the end of his sentence. He went on: 'But it may in fact be useful in that regard'.[37] Oh? Let us see.

Fowler raised the traditional view of the passage, only to dismiss it:

Although many Baptists have assumed a chronological relationship (make disciples, then baptise the disciples, then continue to teach them), this is not a self-evident interpretation. It may well be... that baptism

---

[37] Fowler: *More* p158.

makes one a disciple of Christ rather than testifying that one has already become a disciple.[38]

Really? The time sequence, the order of the events, not 'self-evident'? To my mind, 'self-evident' is precisely what it is!

Once again, however, note the choice. Baptism either makes a sinner into a disciple, or testifies that the sinner has become a disciple. Which is it?

Fowler again set out the traditional view:

A dominant stream of Baptist thought has interpreted [the passage] along these lines: 'Go (to all the world) and make disciples of all the nations, then baptise (these who have become disciples) as a sign of their (previous) entrance into union with the triune God, and then go on teaching them how to live in obedience to the commands of Christ'.

Not at all, said Fowler; it is 'very unlikely that the statement means: "Make disciples, then baptise them, and then teach them"'. That is, if I may translate, according to Fowler, it is very unlikely that the passage means 'preach, see conversions, baptise the converted, then teach them'.

The actions of baptising and teaching are subordinate to that of discipling, and the natural conclusion is that in terms of this text, a Christian disciple is one who has signified faith in Christ by baptism and entered into the process of learning how to live out this baptismal commitment. But this implies that baptism is instrumental in the entrance into discipleship, not that it bears witness to a previous entrance into discipleship.[39]

'This implies that baptism is instrumental in entrance into discipleship'. Really? In light of the meaning Fowler has attached to 'discipleship', is *this* the right implication of what he called the 'natural conclusion'?

Let's get down to the text. First of all, let me deal with the 'baptism'. There is no doubt whatsoever. Christ was speaking about water baptism. Nobody, surely, questions it. So far so good.

Now for matters more controversial. First, the passage speaks of discipleship. What is this discipleship? 'Make disciples' – what is

---

[38] Fowler: *More* pp158-159.
[39] Fowler: *More* pp165-166.

this? One of two things. It means either the outward profession of faith, or the internal regenerating work of the Spirit.

If the former, it means 'bring to an open profession of faith',[40] and thus Christ commands us[41] to preach for saving faith, following which we are to baptise those who make profession of faith, and to baptise them as part of their confession before the world (Mark 16:15-16; Rom. 10:9-10), marking the start of their open discipleship.[42]

But if discipleship is taken to mean regeneration, and this is accomplished by baptism, then Christ commands us to regenerate sinners by baptising them in water; that is, to 'make disciples' means to 'regenerate them by water baptism'.

This is the choice.

The second suggestion strikes me as novel in Christ's ministry; startlingly so. Where did Christ ever do such a thing himself? What is more, if water baptism produces regeneration, it certainly brings

---

[40] Clearly, not that the preacher-baptiser knows with absolute certainty the genuineness of the profession. Indeed, mere profession is no guarantee. In his own day, many followers of Christ were called disciples, or believers, or were said to have believed on him, even though they eventually proved they did not belong to him (John 2:23-25; 6:2,26,60-66; 7:31-53; 8:30-59). And still it goes on. Some who call Christ, 'Lord, Lord', will be told by him that he never knew them (Matt. 7:21-23). Some who 'honour' Christ 'with their lips' have 'their heart... far from' him (Matt. 15:8). Simon (the sorcerer), though he 'believed... and... was baptised', proved his heart was 'not right in the sight of God', that he was 'poisoned by bitterness and bound by iniquity' (Acts 8:9-23). All these, however, before being unmasked, would have looked like true believers, would have been treated as such by others – including, where relevant, being baptised.

[41] I am taking it for granted that Christ's words did not apply merely to the apostles. Nor do I think they apply to Jewish preachers in some supposed age to come. I am convinced Christ's words constitute the manifesto for believers throughout this gospel age. As far as I can tell, Baptist sacramentalists are of the same opinion. The point, therefore, does not affect the argument.

[42] 'To disciple a person to Christ is to bring him into the relation of pupil to teacher, "taking his yoke" of authoritative instruction ([Matt.] 11:29), accepting what he says as true because he says it, and submitting to his requirements as right because he makes them' (Broadus quoted by D.A.Carson pp595-596, who cited Matt. 12:46-50).

178

forgiveness of sins. If water baptism brings regeneration which leads to forgiveness of sins, why did Christ command sinners to repent and believe – with no hint of a suggestion that they should be baptised? As he did repeatedly (Matt. 9:13; 11:28; Mark 1:15; 2:17; Luke 5:32; 13:3,5; 15:7; 24:47; John 6:29; 7:37-38; 12:36). And when he did command them to be baptised, why did he command repentance and faith before baptism (Mark 16:15-16 – leaving aside Matt. 28:19)? Where did he ever suggest that the disciples should regenerate sinners by baptism? Where had he himself ever regenerated by baptism? The notion is completely out-of-keeping with his ministry. And because of this, I find it more than passing strange that Christ, at this point having introduced the startling idea, did not stop, explain it further, develop it – and all in precise detail; or, at least say that very soon the Holy Spirit would make it all clear to them.[43] Surely this would have been necessary since he (Christ) himself had never given any indication of acting in that way, and never afforded baptism such a high status.

Leaving to one side this passage, where is there any other passage (granting for sake of argument that *this* passage fits the bill – which I do not accept; see below), where is there any other scriptural suggestion that the apostles knew that they had – or would be given – the power and right to regenerate by baptism? And what evidence is there to suggest that from this point they now knew and taught that they possessed the power to regenerate by baptism? And what evidence is there for saying that they so used this power? Where do they claim to have the right or power to regenerate? They had the right and duty to preach; which they did. They had the right and duty to baptise; which they did. Where is the corresponding commission to regenerate, let alone regenerate by baptism? Where did they claim it?[44]

---

[43] And not only for the apostles. If the apostles were to regenerate by baptism, this must be the way to advance the gospel for all time – for us as much as them. And if Christ was saying that we, today, are to regenerate by baptism, we need to be clear about all the conditions. Where, in Scripture, do we find such detailed instruction? In literature subsequent to the Fathers, yes, we find it in abundance – but where in Scripture?

[44] Let me list the relevant passages: 'Go into all the world and preach the gospel to every creature. He who believes and is baptised will be saved; but

But, as always, we are faced with the familiar choice. Either we are to baptise those who profess faith, or baptise in order to regenerate. Which is it? My own view, repeating what I said a few moments ago is that Christ commands us to preach for saving faith, following which we are to baptise those who make profession of faith, and to baptise them as part of their confession before the world (Mark 16:15-16; Rom. 10:9-10), marking the start of their open discipleship.

Next, everybody inserts a word in the passage – and this takes us back over the ground just covered. Some insert 'and': 'Go... and make disciples of all the nations, *and* baptising them... teaching them'; others, however, insert 'by': 'Go... and make disciples of all the nations, *by* baptising them... teaching them'. Clearly, the consequences of these two alternatives are very different. Those who take the former route, inserting 'and', end up with the traditional view of the passage; those who take the latter, 'by', end up with the sacramental view. Under the traditional view, our task is to preach the gospel so that sinners are brought to a credible profession of faith, and once that has occurred, *then* to baptise them. Under the sacramental view, our task is to preach to and baptise sinners to make – *in order to make* – them disciples. On this view, saving faith is not necessary. As long as 'all nations' are preached to and baptised, they will become 'disciples'.[45]

---

he who does not believe will be condemned' (Mark 16:15-16). 'Repentance and remission of sins should be preached in [Christ's] name to all nations, beginning at Jerusalem. You are witnesses' (Luke 24:46-48). 'You shall receive power when the Holy Spirit has come upon you; and you shall be witnesses to me in Jerusalem, and in all Judea and Samaria, and to the end of the earth' (Acts 1:8). 'Christ did not send me to baptise, but to preach the gospel' (1 Cor. 1:17). In all of this, I fail to see the slightest suggestion of any power, command or right to regenerate. And certainly not by baptism! Incidentally, why is there no mention of baptism in Luke 24:47? Beasley-Murray: 'Certainly the omission is strange' (Beasley-Murray: *Baptism in the New Testament* p79). If the sacramentalists are right, it is more than 'strange'; it is inexplicable. As is 1 Cor. 1:17.

[45] Infant baptisers reverse Christ's order when baptising infants. They baptise and *then* teach. *If* this is the right thing to do – *if*, I say, then promiscuous baptism for infants – as early as possible – would seem the best way to fulfil Christ's command.

This is the choice. Preach so that sinners will be convicted and converted – brought to faith and repentance – and then baptise them as a mark of this conversion. Or preach and baptise as many as possible – to make them disciples, with *no* mention of repentance and faith.

The latter alternative is clearly nonsensical. Where in the New Testament are we given the impression that the great work of 'evangelising' is to address as many as possible and then baptise them all – irrespective of any response? I will return to the following passage in the next chapter, but if the sacramentalists are right, how could Paul declare this:

I thank God that I baptised none of you except Crispus and Gaius, lest anyone should say that I had baptised in my own name. Yes, I also baptised the household of Stephanas. Besides, I do not know whether I baptised any other. For Christ did not send me to baptise, but to preach the gospel, not with wisdom of words, lest the cross of Christ should be made of no effect (1 Cor. 1:14-17).

If sacramentalists are right, Paul could never had said such thing.

But we have got ahead of ourselves. What scriptural help can we find for deciding whether to insert 'and' or 'by' in Matthew 28:19-20? One of the two (or their equivalents) must be inserted! Which is it? What scriptural precedent can we follow? Certainly, 'by' is perfectly proper – at times. For example: 'He spoke, saying', obviously means he spoke *by* saying. But there are passages where 'by' will not do; it must be 'and'. Take for example 'Men marvelled, saying (Matt. 8:27).[46] 'A man came to him, kneeling' (Matt. 17:14).[47] 'Pharisees... came to him, testing him' (Matt. 19:3) ('and saying to him'; 'and' is in the Greek). 'He answered *and* said' (Matt. 19:4 – there is no 'and' in the Greek).[48] And so on and on.

Consequently, the significance of 'and' – which, in the following verses, is in the original – stands out. 'Repent, *and*... be baptised... Those who gladly received his word were baptised' (Acts 2:38,41). 'When they believed... men and women were baptised... Simon... believed; *and*... was baptised' (Acts 8:12-13). In particular: 'Jesus

---

[46] 'Men marvelled' – not '*by* saying', but '*and* saying'.

[47] 'A man came to him' – not '*by* kneeling', but '*and* kneeling'.

[48] 'He answered *and* [he] said' – not 'he answered *by* [he] said' (ειπεν).

made *and* baptised more disciples than John' (John 4:1). Note the 'and' and not 'by'. 'Jesus made *and* baptised... disciples'. He 'made' the disciples, *and* then baptised them. He did not make the disciples by baptising them. As Arthur W.Pink observed:

It is important to observe the order of the two verbs here, for they tell us who, alone, are eligible for baptism... The fact that 'baptising' here comes after, and not before, the verb 'made', proves that they were disciples first, and were baptised subsequently. It is one of many passages in the New Testament which, uniformly, teaches that only one who is already a believer in Christ is qualified for baptism.[49]

If, however, in John 4:1, it is thought the 'baptised' qualifies the 'made', then, as Pink put it, 'the ["made"] denotes the action, and the ["baptised"] how the action was performed';[50] that is, the disciples were made so by baptism. In which case, the 'being made disciples' means being recognised as professed believers before men. In other words, the verse speaks of those who, having come to faith, were acknowledged as, and proclaimed to be, professing believers by baptism. As Spurgeon said:

We are planted in God's house in two respects. First, in regeneration, when we are born into the house; and secondly, at our profession of faith, which should be by baptism, when we are publicly brought into the house and planted in the likeness of Christ's death by being buried, after his commandment, in the water.[51]

What about Gill? Linking John 4 and Matthew 28, Gill declared:

The method Christ took [in John 4] was, he first made men disciples, and then baptised them; and the same he directed his disciples to [in Matt. 28], saying: 'Go and teach, or disciple, all nations, baptising them *etc.*' And this should be a rule of conduct to us, to baptise only such who appear to have been made the disciples of Christ. Now a disciple of Christ is one that has learned of Christ, and has learned Christ; the way of life, righteousness and salvation by him; who is a believer in him, who has seen a beauty, glory, fullness and suitableness in him as a Saviour; and is come to him, and has ventured on him, and trusted in him... and such who are Christ's disciples in this sense, are the only

---

[49] Pink Part 1 p157.
[50] Pink Part 1 p157.
[51] Spurgeon: *Metropolitan* Vol.23 p410.

proper persons to be baptised; these are they that ought to put on this badge and wear Christ's livery. Nor can [water] baptism be of any use to any others; for such only are [already spiritually] baptised into him, and into his death, and partake of the saving benefits of it; for whatsoever is not of faith is sin; and without it also it is impossible to please God.[52]

D.A.Carson:

Baptising and teaching are not the *means* of making disciples, but they characterise it. Envisaged is that proclamation of the gospel that will result in repentance and faith, for μαθητευω... entails both preaching and response. The response of discipleship is baptism and instruction. Therefore baptism and teaching are not coordinate – either grammatically or conceptually – with the action of making disciples.[53]

Charles Hodge (certainly no Baptist!):

The commission was: 'Go into all the world, and preach the gospel to every creature'. This does not mean that baptism was not included, but it does mean that baptising was very inferior to preaching. It is subordinated in the very form of the commission: 'Go therefore, make disciples of all nations, baptising them' *etc.* The main thing was to make disciples; recognising them as such by baptism was subordinate, though commanded.[54]

Calvin got it nearly[55] right:

The meaning amounts to this, that by proclaiming the gospel everywhere, they should bring all nations to the obedience of the faith,

---

[52] Gill: *Commentary* Vol.5 p627.

[53] Carson noted 'a close syntactic [correctly formed according to the ordering of words *etc.* and their relationship – see *Encarta*] parallel' with: 'And lend to them without expecting to get anything back' (Luke 6:35). 'Not expecting anything in return is certainly not the *means* of the lending, but it... characterises the lending' (D.A.Carson p597, both emphases his).

[54] Hodge: *1 Corinthians* p17.

[55] Unfortunately, Calvin also talked about baptism as a seal. In addition, he was not precise enough. And after making an excellent case from the passage, he spoiled it by a ridiculous *non-sequitur* of a conclusion, arguing for the baptism of infants.

and next, that they should... ratify their doctrine by the sign[56] of the gospel. In Matthew, they are first taught simply to teach; but Mark [16:15] expresses... that they should preach the gospel... Christ enjoins that those who have submitted to the gospel, and professed to be his disciples, shall be baptised; partly that their baptism may be a pledge of eternal life before God, and partly that it may be an outward sign of faith before men. For we know that God testifies[57] to us the grace of adoption by this sign, because he engrafts us into the body of his Son, so as to reckon us among his flock;[58] and, therefore, not only our spiritual washing, by which he reconciles us to himself, but likewise our new righteousness, are represented by it...[59] All who present themselves for baptism do, as it were, by their own signature, ratify their faith... But as Christ enjoins them [the apostles – and us] to teach before baptising, and desires that none but believers shall be admitted to baptism,[60] it would appear [it most definitely is the fact!] that baptism is not properly administered unless... it is preceded by faith... Baptism is joined to the faith of the gospel, in order to inform us that the mark of our salvation is engraven on it; for had it not served to testify[61] the grace of God, it

---

[56] In this extract, note Calvin's use of 'sign' (that is, 'symbol'), not 'effective sacrament'. The sign, according to Calvin, represents what has already happened. Excellent!

[57] Note Calvin's use of 'testifies'. Excellent! Not 'grant' to us, or 'produce in' us, or 'guarantee'. God does not by baptism guarantee that the one baptised is truly adopted. Baptism, therefore, cannot be a seal.

[58] 'God testifies to us the grace of adoption by this sign, because he engrafts us into the body of his Son, so as to reckon us among his flock; and, therefore, not only our spiritual washing, by which he reconciles us to himself, but likewise our new righteousness, are represented by it'. Calvin left himself open to ambiguity here. I am sure he meant that God 'engrafts us [by the grace of adoption, by spiritual baptism, not water baptism] into the body of his Son, so as to reckon us among his flock; and, therefore, not only our spiritual washing, by which he reconciles us to himself, but likewise our new righteousness, are represented by it [water baptism]'. And he was spot on!

[59] God does not adopt us, engraft us into Christ, wash us from our sins, reconcile us or justify us by water baptism. Baptism, according to Calvin, *represents*, as a 'sign', these things, things which have already happened to us. Excellent! If only he had stuck to it! And stuck also to the general point about faith *before* baptism.

[60] This is worth underlining: 'None but believers shall be admitted to baptism'.

[61] 'Testify' once again – not convey!

would have been improper for Christ to have said that they who shall believe and be baptised shall be saved [Mark 16:16].[62]

Matthew Poole, likewise:

I cannot be of their mind who think that persons may be baptised before they are taught. We want [lack] precedents of any such baptism in Scripture, though indeed we find precedents of persons baptised who had but a small degree of the knowledge of the gospel; but it should seem that they were all first taught that Jesus Christ was the Son of God, and were not baptised until they professed such belief (Acts 8:37).[63]

Andrew Fuller:

Is it not plainly the order of things as stated by our Lord Jesus Christ... that we are first to teach men, by imparting to them the gospel; then, on their believing it, to baptise them; and then to go on to instruct them in all the ordinances and commandments which are left by Christ for our direction... [This] must, I think, be approved by every Baptist... The ordinary way in which the mind of Christ is enjoined in the New Testament, is by simply stating things in the order in which they were appointed and are to be practiced; and that this is no less binding on us than if the connection had been more fully expressed. It is as clear... as if it had been said: 'Go, first teach them the gospel; and when they have [savingly] received it, baptise them; and, after this, lead them on in a course of evangelical obedience'.[64]

And, of course, Gill, although I would not endorse all his supporting arguments:[65]

---

[62] Calvin: *Commentaries* Vol.17 Part 1 pp383-388.

[63] Poole Vol.3 p146. Excellent! Sadly, like Calvin, Poole went on ridiculously to argue for the baptism of infants.

[64] Fuller: *Essays* p857. Meanwhile, he had moved to 1 Cor. 11:23-26, concerning the Lord's supper. In this passage, Christ's institution and ordering of his supper is clearly and precisely laid out, and should not be tampered with. Fuller challenged Rome for not allowing the cup to the laity. Ignoring the unbiblical notion of 'laity', Fuller was quite right to draw attention to the fact that Christ joined the bread and the cup for all who partake – and no man has any right to ignore or tinker with his institution. Similarly for baptism.

[65] Based on the gender changes in the Greek. I accept Fowler's conclusion: 'Restricting baptism to those who respond positively to the gospel is

They are such who have learned to know themselves, their sin, and lost estate by nature... and who are taught and enabled to part with all for Christ... and to believe in him, and give up themselves to him... such as are taught, and made disciples by teaching, or under the ministry of the word by the Spirit of God: Christ's orders are to baptise... dip them... that is, in water.[66]

If this is not the meaning of Christ's commission, then I fail to see how anything other than indiscriminate baptism can be the inevitable result – which, in the end, will lead to indiscriminate *infant* baptism. After all, if, as sacramentalists argue, baptising regenerates, conveys grace, or whatever, why not repeat the inexorable logic of the Fathers,[67] and come to the inevitable conclusion; namely, to baptise as early as possible, even as new-born?[68] Coupled with the modern tendency among sacramental Baptists to tolerate infant baptism, this move to indiscriminate infant baptism cannot long be delayed; that is, if sacramentalism wins the day.[69] If the sacramentalists are right, indiscriminate baptism ought to follow – at least for those adults who want it, or are willing to undergo it – and for all babies, where a parent requires or accepts it. Indeed, as has happened, it might even lead to enforced baptism – the end, it might be thought, justifying the violent action. After all, since, as the sacramentalists claim, it is the baptising itself which accomplishes salvation – irrespective of the willingness or otherwise of the one baptised – promiscuous baptism at the earliest possible opportunity must be the norm. Indeed, the baptising of *infants*

---

biblically defensible, but not on the basis of gender shifts in Matt. 28:19' (Fowler: *More* p165).

[66] Gill: *Commentary* Vol.5 p305.

[67] Telescoping their debates about sin before and after baptism – while still coming to their final opinion.

[68] Unless, of course, people want to go back to those Fathers who thought that baptism should take place as late as possible to remove as much sin as possible – as, for instance, with Constantine. This would be felt even more strongly by any who agreed with those Fathers who thought that sin after baptism is fatal. The debate for the sacramentalist hinges, I suppose, on whether he thinks baptism removes all previous sin, or all sin, full stop.

[69] As I have argued in my *Infant*, sacramentalism was the key factor in the rise of infant baptism among the Fathers.

should not be delayed at all. If the sacramentalists are right, Christ has commanded us to make Christians by baptising. If so, let's do it! What is more, if this is the case, what need is there for teachers in the first place?

All this, of course, is diabolical nonsense. It can only come from a wrong interpretation of Christ's commission.

In concluding this glance at Matthew 28:19-20, I note Beasley-Murray's comments:

'Make disciples of all nations', runs the command. How is this brought about? It might be considered as self-evident that disciples are made by the preaching of the gospel; that such as have become disciples are then baptised, and the baptised proceed to instruction; the two participles baptising... teaching... successively follow the action of the main verb.

I pause. Excellent – apart from the 'it might be considered as self-evident'. 'Might be'? It *is* self-evident! But Beasley-Murray was preparing the ground for what he wanted to say:

Objection has been taken to this interpretation, however, for since the New Testament letters do not appear to reckon with the phenomenon of an unbaptised disciple,[70] how can one become a disciple and then be baptised?

The objection is puerile. I grant the obvious time-lag between a sinner being regenerated and coming to saving faith, and being baptised. The sinner is converted by an inward secret work of the Spirit. His baptism marks his discipleship before the world. There is clearly a gap, however small, between the two. Indeed, for all I know, or anybody else knows, there might well be a secret gap between the sinner's regeneration and his repentance and faith. Getting back to the inevitable (brief) interval between coming to faith and being baptised – this does not turn the man into an 'unbaptised disciple'! The suggestion is ridiculous. What the New Testament does not recognise is a professing believer who, for no good reason, refuses or neglects to be baptised. *Such* a man or woman is the real 'unbaptised disciple'.

---

[70] Weak! The New Testament knows *nothing* of an unbaptised believer – apart from the thief on the cross.

But serious consequences come from the objection Beasley-Murray raised. He himself drew attention to the devastating claim which follows from it:

Accordingly it is proposed that the participles describe the manner in which a disciple is made: the Church is commissioned to make disciples *by* baptising men [and women] and putting them under instruction.

I pause. As I have explained, if 'making disciples' means marking the start of the outward profession of Christ before the world, excellent. But this is not what is intended by the suggestion. Far from it! The idea behind it is that men and women are regenerated, converted, joined to Christ, and all by baptism. Beasley-Murray rightly[71] gave this short shrift, though he started weakly: 'The exegesis itself is dubious'. It is worse than 'dubious'. He got stronger however:

The situation envisaged in the commission [is] that proclamation of the redemption of Christ should be made and those responding in repentance and faith should be baptised and come under instruction. Baptism and instruction do not stand in the same relation to the action of making disciples. The chief action in the main verb is preaching, the plain commonsense of which is doubtless the reason for its lack of mention; but the preaching must be received if a hearer is to become a disciple, so the reception of faith is also presupposed in the verb 'make disciples'. It is when a hearer believes and is baptised that he becomes a full disciple...[72] The relationship denoted by the participle 'baptising' to the verb 'make disciples', therefore, cannot baldly be stated as instrumental... [The fact is,] κηρυγμα [preaching] precedes the διδαχη [teaching], the offer of grace [in preaching] before the ethics of discipleship [in teaching and obedience]; and it is when the gospel of grace is received that the ethics of gratitude may be learned and applied.[73]

In short: Baptism follows conversion; it does not produce it. I agree. Matthew 28:19-20 does not support the Baptist sacramentalist's case. There is no sacramentalism in the passage.

---

[71] Even though Baptist sacramentalism – which Beasley-Murray advocated – will itself lead to this very thing.

[72] I would say 'open', 'professed', disciple.

[73] Beasley-Murray: *Baptism in the New Testament* pp88-90, emphasis his.

John 3:5

Christ was dogmatic:

Most assuredly, I say to you, unless one is born of water and the Spirit, he cannot enter the kingdom of God.

In a somewhat self-contradicting passage, Fowler argued:

Interpreters of the Gospel of John hold widely varying views of the Johannine attitude towards sacraments,[74] some seeing in the Gospel a pronounced sacramentalism couched in references to water, flesh and blood, while others see in it a corrective to excessive sacramentalism.[75] Baptist sacramentalists have been generally reluctant to base their theology on any of these general schemes, given the uncertainty of their assumptions...[76] Christian interpreters have traditionally understood this 'water' [in John 3:5] as a reference to baptism,[77] and Baptist sacramentalists normally have shared this opinion... Some [however] have suggested that 'water' here is purely figurative, denoting the spiritual cleansing and transformation wrought by the Spirit, as promised by the prophets (Ezek. 36:25-27). Although this is possible, it is difficult to read John 3:5 in its context without thinking of baptism (*cf.* [John] 1:24-34; 3:22-23; 4:1-2)... In a real (though secondary) sense water (baptism) is a vehicle[78] of spiritual rebirth; which is to say that baptism is sacramental in character.[79]

I dispute Fowler's conclusion on the verse. Nevertheless, he was right to bring in other passages which deal with the question of water at the point of regeneration.

But before we get carried away, let us pause and ask ourselves whether or not we should be talking about water baptism at all when thinking about this verse, John 3:5. We must not just assume 'water'

---

[74] Fowler was begging the question, and introducing a subtle gloss. John had no 'attitude towards sacraments'. They didn't exist.

[75] Another subtle gloss. In such references, I see no suggestion of any sacramentalism whatsoever.

[76] The assumptions of the 'interpreters' and their 'general schemes', or of Baptist sacramentalists?

[77] I dispute this sweeping generalisation. Many have not so understood the passage.

[78] Once again, I ask: Why this reticence? Baptism either is, or it is not, *the* vehicle of spiritual rebirth. How can it be *a* vehicle?

[79] Fowler: *More* pp162-163.

means water baptism. Nor must we be steamrollered into taking it for granted. After all, if Christ had meant 'baptism', why did he talk about 'water', and not use the word itself? While this may not be conclusive, it is not without significance.

Let us go back a bit. Let us pick our way through the verse – indeed, the passage – with care, starting with what is beyond dispute. Christ was speaking of regeneration, was he not? His subject was the new birth: 'Unless one is born again... Unless one is born of... the Spirit... You must be born again' (John 3:3,5,7). The thrust of Christ's words to Nicodemus are unmistakable. Christ spoke of the new birth, the necessity of the new birth, and he contrasted it with natural birth: 'That which is born of the flesh is flesh, and that which is born of the Spirit is spirit' (John 3:6).

Just a minute! There's a word missing! And a very important word at that. In terms of this debate, perhaps the most important word of all.

I admit it. I left out the word 'water'. I did it deliberately and knowingly – but without the slightest intention of pulling the wool over anybody's eyes. The fact is, by missing out the word 'water', the thrust of Christ's words stand out clearly. He was speaking about the new birth was he not? The 'new birth' is the vital point in this passage. Surely, that much must be beyond dispute.

But, of course, Christ did bring 'water' into the discussion. And he not only brought it into the discussion. Whatever the water speaks of, unless a sinner has been born of that water, he will not enter the kingdom; he will not – he cannot – be saved. Jesus expressly said so: 'Unless one is born again, he cannot see the kingdom of God... Unless one is born of water and the Spirit, he cannot enter the kingdom of God' (John 3:3,5).

Let me understate the case: Large consequences, therefore, depend on getting this 'water' right, and large consequences follow if we get it wrong! Large consequences? Without this 'water', nobody can be born again. And all who experience this 'water' *are* born again. So, what is the 'water'?

The sacramentalists – or, at least, many of them – think this 'water' is water baptism. Very well. Let us weigh the consequences. If the water refers to water baptism, then no unbaptised person will be, or can be, regenerated and saved. 'Unless one is born of water and the Spirit, he cannot enter the kingdom of God' (John 3:5). Now who will say that no one can be saved without water baptism?[80] Will the sacramentalist? Some will, no doubt, but many will recoil from going that far. Why? I draw attention, once again, to the evident reticence among sacramental Baptists. They seem to lack the courage of their convictions. Why? The sacramentalist view of John 3:5 makes baptismal regeneration by water unavoidable. Whatever the water speaks of, Christ declares it to be absolutely indispensable for regeneration. If this water is water baptism, then no amount of wriggling will get round it – without water baptism, there can be no regeneration, no salvation. For this reason alone, the 'water' cannot be water baptism. Whatever the 'water' is in John 3:5, it is *not* water baptism!

Moreover, as Robert Anderson observed, Christ did not say a man has to be born of water *and* be born of the Spirit; he said born of water and the Spirit – not the same thing at all. Christ was not speaking of two births. And he was not speaking of two baptisms, baptism by water *and* baptism by the Spirit.

That being the case, the truths I set out earlier – concerning the two baptisms, baptism with water and baptism with the Spirit – have no relevance in John 3:5, since we are not talking about water baptism in the first place!

Since I have already argued that 'baptism with/in/by the Spirit' is the same as regeneration, it is my conviction that Christ was here speaking of one baptism – baptism by the Spirit – and one birth – new birth by the Spirit, contrasting it with the old birth by the flesh,[81] baptism by the Spirit and regeneration being one and the same thing. 'Unless one is born again... unless one is born of water and the Spirit... you must be born again' (John 3:3,5,7). Although water is in the passage, *water baptism is not*. Consequently, John

---

[80] What about the thief on the cross? Rome ridiculously argues that he was baptised – by the spurting blood of Christ! Such an argument proves the paucity of the case. In asking this, I am not minimising baptism, but I am certainly saying that baptism is not a saving ordinance. Scripture does not warrant us saying that it is. Furthermore, circumstances can easily be envisaged where someone is converted, and baptism is simply not possible. See the Appendix for Helwys on the point.

[81] See Anderson p222.

3:5 fails to establish sacramental water baptism, simply because the verse does not speak of water baptism in the first place.

But D.R.Griffiths was one sacramentalist who had no doubts: 'The positive teaching of [John] 3:5 is... that entrance into the kingdom of God is impossible except by means of the rebirth in baptism which is both a water baptism and a bestowal of the Spirit'.[82]

This is clear enough; but clearly wrong. If Griffiths was right, the thief on the cross, as I have already mentioned, could not have been saved. Nor could Paul had told the jailer that if he believed he would be saved. And that's just two examples. And there's plenty more where they came from!

The water in John 3:5 does *not* speak of baptism. If it does, as Calvin said:

Then... by baptism we enter into the kingdom of God, because in baptism we are regenerated by the Spirit of God. Hence arose the belief of the absolute necessity of baptism, in order to the hope of eternal life... But it is absurd to speak of the hope of salvation as confined to the sign. So far as relates to this passage, I cannot bring myself to believe that Christ speaks of baptism.

Excellent.

So why does Christ introduce 'water'? As I have explained – see above – the water and the fire are illustrations – they are figures – of the cleansing power of the Holy Spirit in uniting a sinner to Christ. Let Calvin continue his comments in the above:

'Water' or 'fire' [express the Spirit's] power... By 'water'... is meant nothing more that the inward purification and invigoration which is produced by the Holy Spirit.[83]

Excellent.

Some would make the figure even more dominant, and translate the και – 'of water και of Spirit' – as 'even': 'Most assuredly, I say to you, unless one is born of water *even* the Spirit, he cannot enter the kingdom of God'. There is ample scriptural warrant for such a translation of και. Compare: 'What did you go out to see? A

---

[82] Griffiths p158.
[83] Calvin: *Commentaries* Vol.17 Part 2 pp110-111. See Newton p27.

prophet? Yes, I say to you, and [that is, even, καὶ] more than a prophet' (Matt. 11:9). 'He who believes in me, the works that I do he will do also; and [that is, even, καὶ] greater works than these he will do' (John 14:12). 'Even [καὶ] those who have wives' (1 Cor. 7:29). 'It is shameful even [καὶ] to speak of those things which are done by them in secret' (Eph. 5:12). And so on.

In other words, getting back to John 3:5, Christ made his point by stating it and then illustrating it. Regeneration is by the Spirit – that is the statement; regeneration is by water – that is the illustration. To be 'born of water and the Spirit', therefore, is one act, one event. It is to be regenerated, born again. Colin Kruse commented on this, saying that 'spiritual regeneration alone is depicted with a double metaphor':

In support of this view is the fact that elsewhere in [John's] Gospel, water functions as a metaphor for the Spirit (John 4:10,13-15; 7:38) as it also does in places in the Old Testament (*e.g.*, Ezek. 36:25-27). The expression 'water and the Spirit' is a hendiadys, a figure of speech using two different words to denote one thing, something suggested by the fact that both 'water' and 'Spirit' are... without the article ['the'] and governed by the one preposition (literally, 'of water and spirit').[84] Jesus is saying that to enter the kingdom one must be born of water; that is, of the Spirit. This view is also supported by the fact that in this passage, Jesus uses a number of parallel expressions that are all related to seeing and entering the kingdom: 'born again/from above'; 'born of water and the Spirit'; 'born again/from above'; 'born of the Spirit'.[85] If all these expressions are in fact parallel and synonymous, then to be 'born again/from above' and to be 'born of water and the Spirit' mean the same as to be 'born of the Spirit'.[86]

Just so.

But still many sacramentalists argue that John 3:5 *does* speak of water baptism, and that water baptism regenerates.

In which case, those who argue in that way, have to face some practical questions. When an adult is baptised (to regenerate him), is he willing or unwilling? If he is willing, how does he (an

---

[84] Kruse noted that Tit. 3:5 ('the washing of rebirth and renewal by the Holy Spirit') is also a hendiadys.
[85] John 3:3,5,7,8.
[86] Kruse p109.

unregenerate man) have the will to be baptised in order to be regenerated? Surely, a spiritual will can be found only in one who is regenerate (Rom. 8:5-8; 1 Cor. 2:14).

Again: If water baptism does regenerate, how can Baptist sacramentalists argue (rightly, of course) that only believers should be baptised? As they do.[87] They should, of course. I have no quarrel with *that*. As I say, according to Scripture, only believers can be baptised. My point is: How can sacramentalists maintain it?

What do I mean? Regeneration precedes faith (John 1:11-13; 3:3-8,14-21; 1 Pet. 1:22-23). It must. A dead sinner cannot exercise living faith. A believer, therefore, is one who has been regenerated; until he is regenerate, he cannot believe. Consequently, to baptise a believer, is to baptise someone who is regenerate – so how can baptism (of a believer who, by definition, must be regenerate) *produce* regeneration? Baptise someone who is already regenerate in order to regenerate him? The thing is patent nonsense. *Baptist* sacramentalism is clearly self-destructive.

Further, as before, if John 3:5 does speak of regeneration by water baptism, indiscriminate infant baptism is the only logical outcome. For if water baptism does regenerate, why delay it? Baptise babies on leaving the womb!

Moreover, let us go back for a moment to the link between John 3 with the other 'water' passages I listed earlier – John 3:5, 1 Corinthians 6:11, Ephesians 5:26, Titus 3:4-7 and Hebrews 10:22, for instance. We can broaden the point. Look at all the texts, reader, which are cited by the sacramentalists. They say they want to take these passages as they stand; that is, as *they* say they stand. Very well. Let's do it. If sacramentalists are right, and these verses speak of water baptism, then it is by water baptism that a sinner is regenerated; by water baptism that a sinner will see or enter the kingdom; by water baptism that a sinner is united to Christ; by water baptism that a sinner receives the Spirit; and so on. *And it is **only** by water baptism.* That is what those passages teach. In other words,

---

[87] See, for instance, Wheeler Robinson: *The Life* pp176-177; Underwood p270; Beasley-Murray: *Baptism Today and Tomorrow* p37; White p274; Fowler: *More*; and many others. Wright spoke of the 'Baptists' fundamental demand for baptism on profession of faith' (Wright: *What...?* p31).

the New Testament does teach baptismal regeneration by water. That is, if the sacramentalists are right.

Sacramentalists must face the issue. They can't have it both ways. Either the passages speak of water baptism, or they do not; either we take the passages as the sacramentalists say we should, or we do not. If the passages do assert what sacramentalists say they do, they do not describe an 'ideal baptism'; they describe that essential baptism which is indispensable for anybody and everybody who would be a Christian.[88] Do the sacramentalists believe their own arguments? If so, will they stop talking about baptism being *a* means of regeneration? How can it be *a* vehicle of regeneration? It is *the* means, *the* vehicle of regeneration, or no means at all. If sacramentalists are not prepared to stand by what they assert, let them drop all their claims for baptismal sacramentalism.

There are only two stable positions – baptismal regeneration by water, or the baptism of believers as a symbol of their regeneration. The choice has to be made.

In my view, John 3:5 certainly does not teach that water baptism regenerates. In other words, it cannot be adduced in support of Baptist sacramentalism.

The book of Acts

Before looking at individual passages, a word or two on Acts in general.

Not every detail in Acts (or the Gospels) should be taken as normative for church practice; the letters are designed for that purpose. Acts records a transition period, a time of explosive spiritual power when extraordinary things were going on – some unique in the history of the church. And I mean unique, never (whatever some may claim) to be repeated. That being the case, just as hard cases make bad law, so to use extraordinary – unique – events as normative for the church today, is far from sensible.[89]

Coming to the question in hand, Fowler was dogmatic:

---

[88] I deliberately commit a tautology – using 'essential' and 'indispensable' in the same sentence – to make the point.

[89] See my earlier extended note on baptism and local church membership, where I raise the immediacy of New Testament baptism.

The book of Acts is a source of sacramental teaching about baptism...
When the text gives an account of what might be called didactic
[instructional, teaching] baptismal language, the sacramental sense is
strong... The result of... baptism being... forgiveness by God, and the
bestowal of the Holy Spirit.[90]

This cannot go unchallenged. Let me grasp the nettle.

Consider every reference to water baptism in Acts; 'divergent' is
the word. Baptism is linked with the forgiveness of sins and the gift
of the Spirit in Acts 2:38; with the forgiveness of sins, but no
mention of the Spirit, in Acts 22:16;[91] with neither forgiveness nor
the Spirit in Acts 8:12-17,38; 9:18; 16:15,33; 18:8; it follows the
(independent) gift of the Spirit, and is clearly distinguished from it,
in Acts 10:44-48; 11:15-17; it precedes the (independent) gift of the
Spirit, and is clearly distinguished from it – coming, as it does, with
the laying on of hands, not baptism – in Acts 8:12-17; 19:5-6; and
Paul's baptism is described in different terms in Acts 9:18; 22:16.
Note also, baptism is linked with the gift of the Spirit only in Acts
2:38, and with the forgiveness of sins only in Acts 2:38; 22:16, and
this last is Paul's testimony about his experience in Acts 9. The gift
of the Spirit is linked with faith with no mention of baptism in Acts
11:17, and even when it is remotely connected with baptism in Acts,
the gift of the Spirit refers to the extraordinary (Acts 2:1-33; 10:45-
46; 11:15-17; 19:6; and, so I think, Acts 2:38; 8:15-17; 9:17), not to
be repeated in these days. In the 'extraordinary', I include events,
circumstances (take Acts 19:3-5, for instance; who else was re-
baptised following John's baptism?)[92] and gifts. Indeed, the

---

[90] Fowler: *More* p159.

[91] H.B.Swete: 'In the case of Saul... it is not clear whether the gift of the
Spirit preceded, accompanied or followed baptism' (Porter p123).

[92] Porter recognised that this 'episode is certainly one of the most complex
in exegesis of the book of Acts... Major problems... Six views... There is no
set of arguments with overwhelming force'. Even so, this did not stop him
declaring: 'In many ways, this passage is a very strong one for establishing
the sacramental value of baptism as presented in the book of Acts... It
appears that baptism in this instance, since it is "repeated", indicates more
than a symbolic value, but one that sacramentally mirrors the receipt of the
Holy Spirit' (Porter pp126-127). Why? I simply cannot follow the
argument. According to sacramentalists, baptism is supposed to accomplish
something. But Paul re-baptised these people, and yet, according to these

extraordinary is characteristic of most of the history of Acts, as I have already noted. As for the 'extraordinary' baptisms, they occurred at specific and significant times for the gospel advance – Pentecost, Samaria, Cornelius and the Ephesian disciples – Acts 1:4-8 having set the scene for the entire book.[93] These events, therefore, (for the moment adopting James Packer's illustration) are to be seen as 'milestones' in the history of the church, not 'models' of church practice to be copied today; so much so, 'I guess Luke would have been both startled and distressed had he foreseen how some of his latter-day readers would misconstrue him in these matters'.[94]

But Packer's milestone-illustration is too placid, conjuring up, as it does, the present-day church (at least for many of us in the UK), plodding on its weary way. Acts reads very differently. Far from being a 'normal' history, some events are given much space, while several months or even years are telescoped into a few words, according to their importance in Luke's overall scheme. Note, perhaps in particular, the way the history tails off with Paul in Rome. Luke, it is clear, did not intend to give a sedate history, a measured account, rounded and nicely balanced – as editors and publishers would demand today. Rather, recording volcanic events, he did not concern himself with the precise order within each eruption, nor did he stand back and formulate a theology for church

---

sacramentalists, the very act of repetition is supposed to prove the sacramental view of baptism! If so, why not baptise again and again and again? Moreover, if John's baptism was sacramental – as Baptist sacramentalists claim – see above – why did the first baptism fail to give what the sacramentalists claim for it? Why was it necessary to repeat it? What *exactly* did John's baptism fail to do? Do the sacramentalists read their own claims for John's baptism? As I have already shown, 'the intent of' their baptism by John, according to Fowler, was that they should '*experience* forgiveness'. See above and Fowler: *More* p168. If these Ephesians did experience forgiveness by John's baptism, why were they now being re-baptised? Does this kind of talk not open the door, at least a crack, for those who might want to argue for re-baptism after every sin? And what is Porter's 'sacramentally mirrors'? Does baptism convey grace or illustrate it? If the latter, why are we having this discussion? As for repetition proving the inadequacy of a procedure, compare Heb. 10:1-18.

[93] See Macleod pp11-18,29-38.
[94] Packer: *Keep* p205.

practice, but left that for others (for example, Acts 6:1-6 is probably best expounded in 1 Tim. 3:8-16, while Acts 1:15-26; 14:23 are best expounded in Eph. 4:7-16; 1 Thess. 5:12-13; 1 Tim. 3:1-7,14-16; 5:17-20; 2 Tim. 2:2; Tit. 1:5-9; and so on). The baptismal passages in question, therefore, are not germane to the regular and ordinary practice of baptism – which is what I am concerned with in this book.

Putting all this together, it is not wise to erect a massive building on so fragmented and varied a foundation, and to extrapolate from these (obviously) special and isolated events to set up a norm of such importance for the rest of the history of the church. In any case, the evidence, *even in Acts*, is that water baptism in general had no link with the gift of the Spirit and/or forgiveness of sins.

In other words, I agree with the Baptist sacramentalist, Cross, who questioned the idea of what might be called 'the normative order in the book of Acts'. As he said: 'The probable[95] explanation [of the diversity of Acts is] that Luke is not concerned with providing a pattern of conversion-initiation'.[96] Just so.

Another sacramental Baptist, S.I.Buse:

Many of our problems about baptism in New Testament times are posed by the narratives of Acts... Baptism may have been the normal rite of admission to the Christian community in the Acts... but it can hardly be described as... necessary for salvation...[97] [Some] have insisted that baptism with water and the gift of the Spirit are bound together in Acts... [but] such an assertion goes far beyond the evidence; for [Acts 2:38] is the only verse in Acts that explicitly links together baptism and the bestowal of the Spirit. Many scholars have denied the close connection even here... Thus [Acts] 2:38 should neither be explained away nor treated as determinative for the whole of the Acts... To assert that baptism and the gift of the Spirit always go together in Acts is to go beyond the evidence... Our examination of the evidence of the Acts on baptism has presented us with a most varied picture, but some features

---

[95] I would say it is almost certain.

[96] Cross: 'The Evangelical sacrament' p206.

[97] I agree. In quoting this, once again I am not minimising baptism. I simply wish to point out that Baptist sacramentalists admit that baptism is not essential to salvation. So I fail to see how they can make such claims as they do for its efficacy. If baptism conveys the Spirit and forgiveness of sins, who could be without it? What else can it be but essential?

stand out clearly. Baptism is regarded as important, but not as absolutely essential.[98] It is not necessarily bound up with the gift of the Holy Spirit.[99]

This testimony by a sacramental Baptist should not be forgotten.

Nor should this from Beasley-Murray:

To account for these divergences of practice [in Acts], and harmonise the theology (or theologies) presumed by them, gives fair room for the exercise of ingenuity, and it cannot be said that it has been wanting in the explanations provided. Some of the difficulties are attributable to the meagreness of the descriptions; the needful information for their satisfactory solution has not been provided.[100]

Why, even Fowler himself:

The book of Acts... the evidence [for sacramental teaching] is not as consistent as one might like[!]... There is no simple cause-effect relation between baptism and the gift of the Spirit... It would be unwarranted to construct a baptismal paradigm from such an exceptional case [as the Samaritans in Acts 8]...[101] The evidence of Acts does not allow for easy

---

[98] See the previous note.

[99] Buse: 'Baptism in the Acts' pp115-118,122,127-128; Fowler: *More* pp115-117. Fowler: 'Buse recognised that there is no standard description of [the relation between baptism and the gift of the Spirit] in Acts... To assert that baptism and the gift of the Spirit always go together in Acts is to go beyond the evidence... [Buse] saw too much diversity of experience represented in Acts to draw any firm conclusions about the exact relation between baptism and the benefits signified by it' (Fowler: 'Oxymoron' pp132-133). Quite! So... will sacramentalists now drop their claims for sacramentalism based on Acts?

[100] Beasley-Murray: *Baptism in the New Testament* pp104-122. I repeat my question in the previous note. Will sacramentalists now drop their claims for sacramentalism based on Acts?

[101] Fowler, as was his wont, argued that 'although this narrative [in Acts 8] clearly implies that there is no power inherent in baptism such that baptism automatically conveys the Spirit, it would be unwarranted to construct a baptismal paradigm from such an exceptional case' (Fowler: *More* p160). This is a remarkable argument. What is more, it is a subtle (if not clever) argument, subtle enough to mislead the unwary. Let me state the facts. Acts 8 demonstrates, as Fowler said, that, even in Acts, people could be baptised and not receive the Spirit (that is, what I believe to be the extraordinary gift of the Spirit, but most sacramentalists, I presume, would believe to be the

harmonisation... The initial movement of the gospel into the Gentile world can hardly be a timeless paradigm; its revolutionary character is the reason for its unusual form... If there is a normative understanding of the relation between baptism and the Spirit in Acts... Acts 2:38 would then acquire special significance... The evidence of the narratives of Acts may be ambiguous.[102]

Again:

Relating this systematic perspective [of the assumed encounter with Christ and his Spirit in baptism] to the narratives of Acts is admittedly problematic, but this is true for every systematic perspective, given the obvious diversity of the narratives.[103]

So much for Acts in general.[104] As sacramental Baptists themselves admit, no sacramental case can be built upon the book as a whole.

---

ordinary, regenerating, gift of the Spirit). It actually does more. It demonstrates that a man could be baptised and still not be saved. Furthermore, since the case is clearly exceptional, let us agree – as is true so often in Acts – that no normative model can be drawn up. Except... except to say, as Fowler, it is clear that the gift of the Spirit does not always accompany baptism. The right conclusion from all this, therefore, is the following: Whatever paradigm is constructed for baptism, baptism cannot be the means for the (extraordinary or ordinary) bestowal of the Spirit. This example in Acts proves it. Finally, I agree with Fowler – exceptional events should not be used to formulate a norm. Therefore, I repeat the question I asked in previous notes: Will sacramentalists now drop their claims for sacramentalism based on Acts, since it is a record of the extraordinary events of apostolic times?

I note Fowler's rejection of 'automatically conveys'. This, of course, harks back to earlier discussions about *ex opere operato*.

[102] Fowler: *More* pp159-161.

[103] Fowler: *More* p220.

[104] And so much for Fowler's dogmatic assertion, with its far-reaching claim, with which I opened this section: 'The book of Acts is a source of sacramental teaching about baptism... When the text gives an account of what might be called didactic [instructional, teaching] baptismal language, the sacramental sense is strong... The result of... baptism being... forgiveness by God, and the bestowal of the Holy Spirit' (Fowler: *More* p159). I fail to see how this can stand up when placed alongside his other statements which I have quoted.

This fact, in itself, is highly significant. No sacramentalism in the Acts of the apostles![105]

But what, in particular, of Acts 2:38?

Acts 2:38

Repent, and let everyone of you be baptised in the name of Jesus Christ for the remission of sins; and you shall receive the gift of the Holy Spirit.

Not forgetting what we have deduced in general from Acts, what of this verse in particular?[106]

Clearly, we are talking about water baptism.

Here we have the record of Peter's response to the people who were 'cut to the heart' under his preaching and asked: 'What shall we do?' (Acts 2:37). Peter replied: 'Repent, and let everyone of you be baptised in the name of Jesus Christ for the remission of sins; and you shall receive the gift of the Holy Spirit' (Acts 2:38). These words, therefore, were addressed to sinners who had come under conviction of sin. And the first thing Peter told them to do was to repent; not, it is to be noted, to be baptised. They must first repent. Then they must be baptised. They must repent and be baptised. That was their duty. Peter further promised that if they obeyed, they would receive the gift of the Holy Spirit; that is, I believe, the extraordinary gift of the Spirit, manifested in clear extraordinary signs.

Baptist sacramentalists, however, draw far too much from the verse. Fowler:

On the surface, it would seem that Peter's exhortation recorded here plainly indicates that baptism is done for the purpose of personal salvation... The forgiveness of sins here is something experienced through baptism rather than a condition of baptism... Baptist sacramentalists assert that the natural and obvious sense of Acts 2:38 is that one submits to baptism as a repentant sinner seeking salvation, but they do not take that to imply that one who has come to repentance and

---

[105] I therefore repeat the question I asked in previous notes: Will sacramentalists now drop their claims for sacramentalism based on Acts?

[106] In addition to what I say here, see my *Battle*; *Infant*.

faith in Jesus as Lord but that for some reason has not been baptised is therefore damned.[107]

Putting to one side the extraordinary aspect – since it should not be used to establish the norm for our practice today (see above) – let me first get the red herring, at the close of the extract from Fowler, out of the way. There may be some non-sacramentalists who assert that an unbaptised person is lost, yes. But if they do, they fly in the face of Scripture. Damnation is never ascribed to lack of baptism, but always to lack of faith (Mark 16:15-16; John 3:18-19,36; 8:24; 16:8-9; 2 Thess. 2:10-12). In saying this, I do not minimise baptism but, once again, simply assert that baptism is not a saving ordinance. Nobody is saved by being water baptised; no one is damned for not being water baptised. So much for Fowler's red herring.

But let me turn Fowler's words back on himself. Having spoken so highly of baptism in the first part of the extract, why could he not assert that without baptism a sinner *will* be damned? Let me remind you of his words: 'Baptism is done for the purpose of personal salvation... The forgiveness of sins... is something experienced through baptism rather than a condition of baptism'. Very well. If Baptist sacramentalists are right, and water baptism does regenerate, convey saving grace, remove sins, or whatever, then that baptism is essential – however much they might squirm.

But why would they want to squirm? Let them shout it from the roof tops! Without water baptism which conveys saving grace, no one can be saved. They will be damned. In particular, if Acts 2:38 *is* saying what sacramentalists claim, there can be no 'if' or 'but' about it – water baptism saves. No water baptism? No salvation! Is that what their 'baptismal theology' comes to? Is that a conclusion the Baptist sacramentalists can live with? Clearly not. But why not – since they believe baptism is effective?

Let us come to Acts 2:38. Consider Mark (1:4); 16:16; Acts 2:38; 22:16, putting them together:

He who believes and is baptised will be saved... Repent, and let every one of you be baptised in the name of Jesus Christ for the remission of sins; and you shall receive the gift of the Holy Spirit... Arise and be baptised, and wash away your sins, calling on the name of the Lord.

---

[107] Fowler: *More* pp166-170.

Water baptism is definitely in view in these verses. What, then, do they teach? Do they teach that salvation comes through baptism? that baptism is, after all, a means of saving grace? that it is a sacrament? indeed, that it is *the* sacrament?

Not in my opinion.

I first note that in all three passages, faith (Mark 16:16), repentance and faith (Acts 2:38,41) or other evidence of regeneration (Acts 9:5-6,11,18; 22:8,10; 26:15), precedes baptism, and in Mark 16:16 damnation is expressly ascribed to unbelief, not lack of baptism. All this dovetails perfectly with the rest of the New Testament. Baptism does not convey the grace of regeneration, or the gift of faith and repentance. So much for the negative – what the verses do *not* teach.

What about the positive? What *do* the verses teach? Baptism exhibits, symbolises, pictures, represents, illustrates the salvation wrought in believers, and it is administered for their instruction and encouragement, and as a testimony to unbelievers. Supremely, of course, baptism is obedience to Christ. The one being baptised is stating (preaching) to fellow-believers, and to the world, that he has come to saving repentant-faith in Christ. He is declaring to all and sundry that he has quit his former way of life and, as a new man in Christ, he will henceforth be a follower of the Lord Jesus Christ (2 Cor. 5:17; 1 Thess. 1:9-10, for instance).

The alternative boils down to Luther's conclusion:

To put it most simply, the power, effect, benefit, fruit and purpose of baptism is to save... To be saved... is nothing else than to be delivered from sin, death and the devil, and to enter into the kingdom of Christ and live with him for ever.[108]

I do not see any half-way house between these two positions. Baptism cannot be *a* means of conveying saving grace. It is either *the* means of conveying saving grace, or it is a symbol of the saving grace *which has already been conveyed* by the Spirit. As always, the choice has to be made. Huge consequences inevitably follow. It would seem sensible, to say the least, to test any conclusion, drawn on these verses, by the doctrine and practice throughout the rest of the New Testament. And this, I submit, is unequivocal. Faith is the

---

[108] Wright: *What...?* pp96-97.

means of salvation, and grace is the cause (Acts 15:11; Rom. 3:21-31; 4:1-25; 5:1-11; Eph. 2:5,8). Baptism is neither the means or the cause of salvation.

Gill on Acts 2:38:

Not that forgiveness of sin could be procured either by repentance or baptism; for this is only obtained by the blood of Christ; but the apostle advises [weak! – he commands!] these awakened, sensible, repenting and believing souls to submit to baptism, that by it their faith might be led to Christ...[109] represented in the ordinance of baptism by immersion. The encouragement to it follows, 'and you shall receive the gift of the Holy Ghost'; not the grace of the Spirit as regenerator and sanctifier – for that they had already, and is necessary, as previous to baptism; unless it should mean [the] confirmation of that grace... but rather the extraordinary gifts of the Spirit.[110]

In short, Acts 2:38, I submit, does not teach sacramental baptism. If I am wrong, and it does, then sacramental Baptists are right. And this means that water baptism saves. The choice has to be made. You, reader, have to make yours.

Leaving the history of baptism as recorded in Acts, what of the rest of the New Testament? Not intending in the slightest to belittle the Acts, but the epistolary passages must be of fundamental importance – recording as they do, apostolic (Paul's, in particular) teaching on the subject. So let us now turn from the *narrative* record of the (extraordinary) apostolic *practice* of baptism to their (settled) *reasoned argument* on the subject.

It is at this point that we need to make sure we are wearing the right glasses. Let me remind you of the three pairs. *First*, some take

---

[109] I cannot work out what Gill meant by this. Did he mean they would be further instructed concerning Christ by their baptism? Since, as he said, they were already repentant believers, he could not have meant they would come to saving faith by their baptism. Nor could he have meant that by baptism they would be led savingly to trust Christ for forgiveness, since he had already denied that 'forgiveness of sin could be procured by... baptism'. Nor did he mean that baptism would confirm them – he said the Spirit would do that.

[110] Gill: *Commentary* Vol.5 p817. On Acts 22:16, Gill: 'Nor is there any such efficacy in baptism as to remove the filth of sin' (Gill: *Commentary* Vol.5 p976).

the baptism to be water baptism, but introduce the notion of representation. *Secondly,* some take the baptism to be water baptism, and say that water baptism really does accomplish all that is ascribed to baptism in the passage. *Thirdly,* some take the baptism to be spiritual baptism, and say that spiritual baptism really does accomplish all that is ascribed to baptism in the passage.

Romans 6:1-11

Do you not know[111] that as many of us as were baptised into Christ Jesus were baptised into his death? Therefore we were buried with him

---

[111] What was it that the Romans knew beforehand? Did they know what Paul was speaking about here? It seems as though they did. William B.Badke examined all the Pauline references to baptism in the apostle's letters written before Romans; namely, 1 Cor. 1:13-17; 10:2; 12:13; 15:29; Gal. 3:27. In other words, Badke was trying to unearth this 'common knowledge', this prior knowledge. Further, he said 'from Romans on, there are only four references to baptism: Rom. 6:3,4; Eph. 4:5; Col. 2:12. The pre-Romans references have no clear association stated between baptism and death-resurrection with Christ, while two of the three Romans or later passages state such an association'. Badke, I repeat, was trying to prise out what it was that the Romans 'knew'. Was it the link between baptism and the death-resurrection of Christ? Or...? Raising a caution, he went on: 'An argument from silence alone is always tenuous, especially when the total number of passages is so small. We could argue as easily that the pre-Romans lack of dying-rising terminology linked to baptism is simply due to the fact that the circumstances did not demand that Paul bring out this aspect of the rite'. Let me pause for a moment. We must bear in mind that the Romans could not consult the letters to Corinth and Galatia. But it was reasonable of Badke to look at those letters to see if he could unearth any 'common knowledge', any prior knowledge. To let Badke continue. Having sounded his cautionary note about silence, he went on to bring out 'two arguments from silence. *First,* a link between baptism and crucifixion-resurrection is not made explicit in Paul before the writing of Romans. *Secondly,* pre-Romans contexts in which a death-resurrection connection to baptism would have aided the argument do not contain such a connection'. Badke argued cogently, concluding: 'Even in... Rom. 6:3 – the foundational theme is allegiance... Thus we must argue strongly that baptism was never seen by Paul as demonstrating a change in the life of the believer without regard to a change in allegiance. The foundational meaning of baptism in Paul is a declaration of the acceptance of Christ's Lordship. The dying-

through baptism into death, that just as Christ was raised from the dead by the glory of the Father, even so we also should[112] walk in newness of life. For if we have been united together in the likeness of his death, certainly we also shall be in the likeness of his resurrection.

Make no mistake. This is the principal passage for baptismal regeneration. For, have no doubt, reader, that is what Paul teaches here – baptismal regeneration, baptismal union to Christ in his death and resurrection. The question is, of course, *which baptism is the apostle talking about?* Sinners, by baptism are united to Christ in his death and resurrection. This is a fact. There is no doubt about it. The question is, I say again: Which baptism are we talking about? In other words, referring to my opening remarks to this chapter and this immediate section, which pair of glasses should we wear?

Fowler, assuming the baptism in question is water baptism, plainly stated the sacramentalist position:

The references to baptism in the Pauline letters seem to give clear support for a sacramental sense of baptism. The *locus classicus* [the principal place where it is stated, the best statement of it] is... Romans 6:3-4... The text... seems to assert much more than a pictorial

---

rising theme, which was added later, certainly after the writing of 1 Corinthians, gave deeper meaning to that allegiance; namely, that the believer is connected to Christ because the believer has died with his Saviour, and has received Christ's life in place of his own' (Badke pp23-29). I will come back to this in the following chapter.

[112] At this point, Paul was not telling believers how they ought to live. The 'should' does not imply this. Rather, he was working out the logic of his argument that by baptism sinners are – have been – united to Christ in his death and resurrection. Through baptism, they died and were raised, in Christ, and with Christ. 'Therefore we have been buried with him through baptism into death, in order that as Christ was raised from the dead through the glory of the Father, so we too might walk in newness of life' (NASB). Again, there is no doubt in the 'might'; note the 'in order that'. Similarly with the 'if' of verse 5, which should be translated 'since'. Again, the 'shall be' of verse 5 is simply Paul working out his argument: 'If... certainly we also shall be'; or, 'since... certainly we are'. As in verse 11: 'Reckon yourselves to be dead indeed to sin, but alive to God in Christ Jesus our Lord'. See Lloyd-Jones: *New* pp29-61.

significance for baptism... Romans 6 is the crucial Pauline reference to baptism as a[113] means of union with Christ.[114]

Again:

The work of Christ is... a once-for-all [time] redemptive event, never to be repeated... The Pauline understanding of baptism, stated most fully in Romans 6, indicates that baptism decisively unites the individual to that redemptive activity of the death and resurrection of Christ, so that what happened in the Christ-event happens in an analogous and derivative way in individual experience through baptism into Christ. Therefore, what happens in baptism is of the same nature as the work of Christ.[115]

Let me repeat some of these words: 'Romans 6:3-4... seems to assert much more than a pictorial significance for baptism... Baptism decisively unites the individual to that redemptive activity of the death and resurrection of Christ'. I agree. And I do so without the slightest reservation. I also agree with Wheeler Robinson: 'The Romans passage implies [Robinson had 'implied'] not merely a symbolic but a realistic union with Christ'.[116] Indeed, I would put it more strongly than Fowler or Robinson. There is no symbolism here at all; it is entirely realistic. There is no 'seems' or 'implication'. It is a stated fact. By baptism we are united to Christ, and with Christ, in his death, burial, resurrection, ascension and being seated in glory.

But the question is (as I keep saying): Which baptism are we talking about? Many Baptists, rejecting sacramentalism, wearing the first pair of glasses, say that Paul was here speaking of water baptism – but as a representation of these things. Not at all! He was

---

[113] Yet again, I ask, why this reticence? If baptism is sacramental, as Fowler maintained, how could he say 'Rom. 6 is the crucial Pauline reference to baptism as *a* means of union with Christ'. *A* means? If baptism is sacramental, 'Rom. 6 is the crucial Pauline reference to baptism as *the* means of union with Christ'.

[114] Fowler: *More* p161. I agree with Fowler, and Armstrong: 'How we understand the biblical-theological argument of texts such as Rom. 6:3-4; Col. 2:11-12 & Gal. 3:26-29, will ultimately determine how we relate to a host of other questions regarding baptism' (Armstrong p163).

[115] Fowler: *More* pp227-228.

[116] Cross: 'Pneumatological' p161.

not speaking of a representation. I can detect no suggestion of it in the text. The apostle was stating a fact, a reality. He was speaking of the substance, not the shadow or sign.

Rightly rejecting this common anti-sacramentalist view that Paul was speaking of baptism as a representation of our union with Christ, Beasley-Murray went on: 'It would seem that Paul speaks of our being involved directly with Christ in his death and resurrection through baptism'.[117] He should have put it more strongly. There is no 'seem' about it. Paul states plainly that by baptism we are united to Christ. As Beasley-Murray himself declared: 'The Christian has died to sin in baptism... Baptism leads to union with the crucified Christ'.[118]

I say again, the question is, however, which baptism are we talking about? Paul does not here call baptism *a picture of* or *a symbol of* union with Christ, or say that it *represents* that union. He says that baptism *unites* to Christ. He states it categorically. The 'representationalists' – that is, the anti-sacramentalists who argue that Paul is speaking of water baptism – have to fight tooth and nail to avoid baptismal regeneration by water. But, on their own premise, they fight in vain. *If* Paul was speaking of water baptism, he *was* teaching sacramental baptism, baptismal regeneration by water. This cannot be avoided – if the baptism is water baptism. The baptism he speaks of unites to Christ. Full stop!

The fact is, however, he was not speaking of water baptism at all. He was speaking of spiritual baptism – regeneration by the Spirit of God.

The context is all-important. It determines, it fixes the meaning. So let us remind ourselves of it; that is, the apostle's lead-up to Romans 6. This in itself rules out the possibility of his speaking of water baptism in this chapter, either as a representation, or as a sacrament.

---

[117] Beasley-Murray: *Baptism in the New Testament* pp135-136. He noted 'the absence from the rest of the New Testament writings of the interpretation of baptism as a dying and rising with Christ' (Beasley-Murray: 'Baptism in the Epistles of Paul' p131. See the earlier extract from Badke. See also the following chapter.

[118] Beasley-Murray: 'Baptism in the Epistles of Paul' pp132,136.

Take the first – baptism as a representation. The notion that Romans 6 is to do with baptism as a symbol fails utterly to come to grips with the flow of Paul's argument. Having, in Romans 5, set out the spiritual *reality* of the headship of Christ, it is incredible to think that the apostle would take his teaching further by talking about a *symbol* of it. Believers are in Christ (Rom. 5); they are in him by baptism – they died, were buried, rose, ascended and were seated in glory with and in him (Rom. 6). Throughout this section of Romans, Paul is speaking of something which happened in eternity in God's decree; in history with Christ in his death, resurrection and ascension; in experience when the sinner comes to faith and repentance; and in the last day when Christ returns.[119] Paul is not talking about a symbol. A symbol (in Rom. 6) – after talking about the reality (Rom. 5)? The suggestion, in light of the context, is incredible. In Romans 6, the apostle is explaining that believers have died and been raised with Christ in spiritual union with him – not a symbol of it!

Indeed, it is stronger than that. Paul wrote Romans 6 because of an objection made to his teaching in Romans 3, 4 and 5. He opened Romans 6 in this way: 'What shall we say then? Shall we continue in sin that grace may abound?' 'Certainly not!', he thundered. 'How shall we who died to sin live any longer in it? Or do you not know that as many of us as were baptised into Christ Jesus were baptised into his death?... For if we have been united together in the likeness of his death, certainly we also shall be in the likeness of his resurrection' (Rom. 6:1-5). And so on. So... if we are to believe that the baptism in Romans 6 is water baptism as a symbol or representation of the spiritual reality, we have to believe that Paul defended and enforced his argument concerning the believer's union with Christ by reference to... by reference to a symbol? Really? The notion is risible.

As for the second suggestion – namely, that Paul was speaking of baptism, not as a symbol but as a sacrament – this has the merit, at least, of realising that the context absolutely rules out, as being woefully inadequate, the notion of a symbol in Romans 6. But was Paul teaching that water baptism actually unites a sinner to Christ?

---

[119] See my *Particular*; *Septimus Sears*.

That it is by water baptism that a sinner dies with Christ, is buried with Christ, is raised, ascended and seated with Christ? No! For this, too, is utterly ruled out by the context. It suffers from the same flaw as the previous suggestion; namely, that if Paul in Romans 6 was talking about water baptism, instead of ascending in his doctrine in this chapter, he was actually descending from the previous lofty heights to... to a rite – a sacramental rite, let it be said, in the eyes of sacramentalists – but a rite, all the same. To speak of salvation by grace through faith, of union with Christ from eternity to eternity (with not the slightest whiff of a suggestion of water baptism), as he did in chapters 3, 4 and 5, and then to descend to a rite – without the slightest intimation that he was thinking in such terms – is, in my view, stretching credibility far beyond all reasonable limits, however elastic those limits. It is ludicrous to think that Paul would quit the ever-rising track of Romans 3, 4 and 5, to descend to a discussion of water baptism – when, as I have shown, he was tackling a direct challenge to his argument in those chapters. The suggestion is as risible as the first. Whatever else Paul was doing in Romans 6, he was further ascending in his argument – not descending.

The Baptist sacramentalist, White, admitted as much. Note his use of 'fatal':

Fatal to a purely sacramental theory is the place which Romans 6 occupies in the argument of the letter. If, in answer to the challenge of [Rom.] 6:1 to justification by faith, Paul really turns from a discussion of faith to argue from the effects of a sacramental rite, then Romans 6 must be dismissed as a gross *non sequitur*.[120]

Excellent. To talk of water baptism in this chapter (even as a sacrament, let alone a representation) is indeed 'a gross *non sequitur*'.

Moreover, White's comment can be broadened. His incontrovertible (and damning) argument against sacramentalism in Romans 6 applies to sacramentalism *as such* – not to what he called 'a purely sacramental theory'.

But, if the sacramentalist continues to insist that Paul was speaking of water baptism in Romans 6, then the inevitable has to be

---

[120] White p219.

faced. The context, the apostle's argument – the very flow of it – means that water baptism plays a vital part in uniting a sinner to Christ. No! That's too weak! It means far more than that! If the sacramentalist is right, water baptism plays a clinching part in uniting a sinner to Christ. Faith, repentance... yes... have their part (Rom. 3 – 5), of course they do, but these only lead to water baptism (Rom. 6). It is water baptism which actually unites the sinner to Christ! Water baptism is the climax of the gospel in its application to the sinner. Water baptism is the vital node in this 'critical path'; water baptism, not repentant faith in Christ. As a consequence, no words can be too strong to describe the place and importance of water baptism. Water baptism ought to be the theme, the high point, when addressing sinners with the gospel. Water baptism! Water baptism! We should hear it everywhere.

Let this sink in. If sacramentalists are right, water baptism is the principal thing. Throughout the New Testament, it should be placarded in addresses to sinners, and feature heavily in discussions of the theology of salvation. Water baptism should be the recurring theme, the resounding theme.

We shouldn't have to hunt for water baptism in apostolic addresses to sinners; it should be written large for all to see. But... is this what we find in the New Testament? Is it? Where? Where in any address to sinners, is water baptism made the pinnacle of the way for a sinner to be saved from his sins? Sinners are called, invited, commanded to repent and believe – and promised salvation if they do. True, they are commanded to be baptised after that – but never commanded to be baptised to be united to Christ. Never. When addressing sinners, water baptism is never made the lynchpin of salvation. Never. The silence is deafening. Therefore the sacramentalist premise regarding Romans 6 must be wrong.

The fact is, Paul was not talking about water baptism at all in Romans 6. Fowler, quoting D.Martyn Lloyd-Jones on Romans 6, summarised the view[121] I am advocating:

---

[121] I would like to say it is the traditional or conventional position. Sadly, I can't. As I have explained, many anti-sacramental Baptists think the passage (and similar passages) refers to water baptism, but gloss it to say that Paul was speaking about baptism's symbolic significance. See earlier where I set out my reasons for strongly disagreeing with this. There is no

Paul speaks in Romans 6 of union with Christ and a baptism which effects this; Paul elsewhere minimizes the significance of water baptism (1 Cor. 1[:13-17]), but he affirms explicitly that believers are baptised by the Spirit into Christ and his body (1 Cor. 12:13); therefore, 'to argue that the apostle has water baptism in his mind in any shape or form here [in Rom. 6] is to give a prominence to [water] baptism that the apostle Paul never gives to it'.[122]

---

hint of a suggestion of the symbolic here. The baptism in this and other passages is effective. The only question is: Which baptism is the apostle talking about?

As for glossing, it is not only non-sacramentalists who gloss. Sacramentalists do it too. Note Pinnock's subtle gloss in his citation of John 3:16: 'God so loves the world that he gives and goes on giving' (Pinnock p8). I have no doubt that God does give and goes on giving his grace – but this manipulation of Scripture is wrong. Pinnock, of course, was preparing the ground for trying to make his case for God's effective giving of grace in the sacraments.

A final word on glossing. I realise, it goes without saying, there is glossing and glossing. See my *Particular*.

[122] Fowler: *More* p171. For Lloyd-Jones' full argument, see Lloyd-Jones: *New* pp29-147. Lloyd-Jones: Sacramentalists 'claim that it is the act of baptising that, in and of itself, unites the person baptised with the Lord Jesus Christ. It is certainly a clear-cut view, but is it [right]? We need not spend much time on it. One over-riding reason for dismissing it at once is this, that according to the New Testament teaching, it clearly... puts the cart before the horse. The teaching of the New Testament is that the people who are to be baptised are those who have already given evidence that they are regenerate' (Lloyd-Jones: *New* pp30-32). Unfortunately, despite this excellent statement, speaking elsewhere Lloyd-Jones was obscure (or worse): 'The sacraments are not only signs, but are also seals of grace. They confirm the grace that we have already received. Yes, but shall we go further? They even *exhibit* it... in a sense they *convey* it'. Citing Acts 2:37-38; 22:16; Rom. 6:3-6; 1 Cor. 6:11; 12:13; Gal. 3:27; Col. 2:12; Tit. 3:5; 1 Pet. 3:21, he said: 'In baptism' – and he meant water baptism – 'in baptism we are cleansed from the guilt of sin... "washing" does partly refer to baptism... it puts us into this position of union', but went on to distance himself from baptismal regeneration. However, more clarity than this is wanted. As he himself said: 'Care is needed' (Lloyd-Jones: *The Church* pp30,37-39, emphasis his). Sadly, he failed to show enough of it here. Let me illustrate why care is essential. In addition to what I have said in my *Infant*, let me show what Baptist sacramentalists make of the misunderstanding 'the seal'. Beasley-Murray: 'In 2 Cor. 1:22; Eph. 1:13;

Nevertheless, as Fowler said: 'If water is in view in this text, then it is more than a symbol'.[123] I couldn't agree more. '*If* water is in view in this text, then it is more than a symbol'. If...!

But there isn't a drop of water in the text or anywhere near it. The baptism of Romans 6:1-11 is spiritual baptism. Sacramentalists disagree with this. You, reader, have to make your choice. In Romans 6, the baptism by which we are united to Christ is either water baptism or Spirit baptism. Which of the two it is, I have no doubt whatsoever. Paul was speaking of spiritual baptism. But whichever we choose, we have to live with the consequences. I do. You do. Romans 6 teaches that all who are baptised are united to Christ and saved for ever. I say that this means that all who are baptised by the Spirit are united to Christ in his death and resurrection, and are everlastingly saved. Will sacramental Baptists say the same for water? Will they live with (and let people die with) the consequences? Are they prepared to face (on the judgement day) those whom they sacramentally baptised with their sacramental interpretation of Romans 6 ringing in their ears – and yet were never converted? Speaking for myself, I am prepared to face any person I had responsibility for baptising (in a non-sacramental way).[124] And I am prepared to say that all who are baptised by the Spirit are everlastingly saved, whereas all who are not baptised by the Spirit are everlastingly damned.

May I return for a moment to the apostle's death-burial-resurrection theme of baptism in Romans 6? Note the question he

---

4:30, we find the idea of the believer being "sealed" with the Holy Spirit. In view of the exhaustive researches of G.W.H.Lampe on the meaning of this conception, it is unnecessary to attempt a further demonstration of its connection with baptism. The central idea appears to be that believers, through faith-baptism, are stamped as God's possession' (Beasley-Murray: 'Baptism in the Epistles of Paul' p142). I strongly disagree. As I say, see my earlier works for my views on the mistaken notion that baptism is a seal.

[123] Fowler: *More* p171.

[124] I hesitate – I realise it is a very serious claim. But whether or not I am prepared to face the consequences of my action, face them I will have to. What made me hesitate was my experience as a young believer (and a young man), when, as the one appointed to carry out the baptising, I was placed in an invidious position by those who should have known better.

asked his readers: 'Do you not know' (Rom. 6:3). Clearly, the idea was self-evident to them.

Let me develop this a little. What I say now may seem to be going off at a tangent, but, reader, please read on. As I have already noted, William B. Badke drew a comparison between Romans 6 and the three questions in 1 Corinthians 1:13-17. I shall return to those three questions in the next chapter, but a most interesting point can be teased out here and now. Quite rightly, Badke noted that in the Corinthian passage, the apostle 'deals with the party spirit in Corinth, which was based on allegiance to human leaders. As part of his argument for unity, Paul contradicts what might have been a misunderstanding in Corinth: Christian baptism does not create allegiance to the baptiser, but is a declaration of allegiance to Christ'. This is important. The point is, Paul did not raise the death-burial-resurrection theme in 1 Corinthians. Why not? The silence is significant. As I will show, in the three Corinthian questions, the issue is not baptism, but allegiance to Christ, and not to men. Badke: 'Here a dying-rising theme linked to baptism would have added great power to Paul's argument. If he could have shown that death and resurrection with the one to whom allegiance was given was integral to baptism, allegiance to the baptiser would have been relegated to second place. Only Christ, after all, could claim a real death and resurrection'.[125] In other words, when talking about baptism in Romans, the apostle raised the (apparently) self-evident concept of death-burial-resurrection, whereas in 1 Corinthians he did not – yet (apparently) it would have suited his argument down to the ground. So why did he not make use of it? Because, whereas in 1 Corinthians 1:13-17, the apostle was speaking of *water* baptism, in Romans 6 he was speaking of *spiritual* baptism.

Let me repeat that. It is very important. Whereas in 1 Corinthians 1:13-17, the apostle was speaking of *water* baptism, in Romans 6 he was speaking of *spiritual* baptism. Spiritual baptism unites to Christ. Water baptism does not.

In conclusion: Since Romans 6:1-5 speaks of spiritual baptism and not water baptism, it therefore cannot possibly teach sacramental water baptism. Water baptism is not in the passage.

---

[125] Badke p25.

What the passage does teach is that the elect by spiritual baptism are united to Christ.

1 Corinthians 6:11

You were washed... you were sanctified... you were justified in the name of the Lord Jesus and by the Spirit of our God.

Fowler thought the verse might allude to water baptism.[126] It doesn't.

Beasley-Murray, however, writing in 1959, had been definite: '1 Corinthians 6:11 certainly relates to baptism'.[127] And again in 1962: 'The voice of scholarship is unanimous in affirming the association with baptism... The majority of exegetes concur in interpreting this statement in the context of baptism'.[128] I cannot speak for the 1960s, but is scholarship still *unanimous* on the point? I think not. Even Fowler, as I have just pointed out, did not seem quite so sure.

He had reason. As I observed when dealing with Christ's words in John 3:5, if Paul had meant 'baptism', he could have used the word. But he didn't. While this may not in itself be conclusive, it is a fact.

I have no doubts about the matter. Paul has no thought of water baptism here. Oh? How can I be so definite? Clearly, the apostle could not more strongly link the believer's washing and his justification and sanctification, than he does in this verse.[129] So, if the 'washing' he speaks of is water baptism, then by water baptism sinners are justified and sanctified. This cannot be evaded by trying to introduce the notion of symbol or representation. Paul is not speaking of washing as a *representation* of justification and sanctification; there is no sense of the symbolic here. The apostle is using figurative language, metaphorical language, yes. But symbolic language? No.[130] The washing and the justification and

---

[126] Fowler: *More* p162.

[127] Beasley-Murray: 'Baptism in the Epistles of Paul' p141.

[128] Beasley-Murray: *Baptism in the New Testament* p163.

[129] See Beasley-Murray: 'Baptism in the Epistles of Paul' pp141-142.

[130] By 'figurative', I mean 'non-literal'. By 'metaphorical', I mean the use of an 'implicit comparison... to describe somebody or something [by] a word or phrase that is not meant literally but by means of a vivid

sanctification come in the same breath. They constitute one act, one work. Therefore, I repeat, if the washing is baptism, then baptism produces – baptism is – a sinner's justification and sanctification. This, for obvious reasons has (to put it mildly) serious consequences. Baptism *is* a sacrament indeed!

But this is *not* what Paul is saying. Not at all. The washing here, is a reference to the cleansing power of the blood of Christ applied by the Spirit – nothing to do with water at all. Indeed, to introduce the notion of 'water', grievously reduces the whole tenor of the apostle's statement. Cleansing, sanctification, justification and... *water?* Water? Not at all! Cleansing, sanctification, justification and... *blood!* Blood! 'The blood of Jesus Christ [God's] Son cleanses us from all sin' (1 John 1:7). When a sinner is washed in *Christ's blood*, he is justified and sanctified. Water indeed!

Gordon D.Fee:

---

comparison expresses something about him, her, or it'. By 'symbolic', I mean representational, the use of a symbol – 'something that represents something else: something that stands for or represents something else, especially an object representing an abstraction' (see *Encarta*).

Let me illustrate. When I say 'it's raining cats and dogs', nobody imagines that felines and canines are literally falling from the sky. Everybody knows it is raining fiercely. To me, it means that the drops, on hitting the surface are splashing as furiously and with as much noise as if cats and dogs were literally hissing and barking, clawing, scratching and snapping at each other. The vivid allusion is meant to add colour to my statement about the intensity of the rainfall. To use it to start a discussion on cats and dogs would be silly. I'm using a metaphor, not a symbol. I'm not talking of literal animals fighting in the street. The picture is all in the mind. The rain is real; the cats and dogs are a metaphor. There are no cats and dogs. Compare talk of the rain coming down in stair rods, or bucketing down. Metaphors, all of them.

Likewise with the 'washing' in 1 Cor. 6:11. It is a metaphor. It is not a symbol. In other words, 1 Cor. 6:11 is not speaking of water baptism with real water as a symbol of spiritual washing, a literal washing in water which represents regenerating grace. Certainly not! It is Paul's way of describing spiritual baptism by means of a vivid comparison between washing and regeneration. But it is a comparison only. The spiritual cleansing is literal, real. The washing is figurative – there is no literal water involved. Just as with my illustration, to talk about cats and dogs is silly, so too with this 'washing'. To start talking about water baptism is silly – and worse.

It is possible, but not as certain as most interpreters [including sacramental Baptists; Fee cited Beasley-Murray] imply, that the verb 'you were washed' is also an allusion to baptism... [But] Paul does not in fact say 'you were baptised', which he was perfectly capable of doing if baptism were his concern. This verb [washed] is not used elsewhere in the New Testament to denote baptism (it is joined to baptism in Acts 22:16, but is not the actual verb for baptism itself)... Regeneration, sanctification and justification... for Paul... are the work of the Spirit in the believer's life, not the result of baptism. [131]

This verse does not teach baptismal sacramentalism.

But, as always, the choice has to be made. Either the washing means water baptism – in which case, by water baptism a sinner is justified and sanctified – or it does not. Reader, what is your opinion?

1 Corinthians 12:13

By one Spirit we were all baptised into one body... and have all been made to drink into one Spirit.

Well, no question of it, here we do have baptism. And, make no mistake, Paul's statement could hardly be more important or dogmatic. Indeed, it is absolute. 'By one Spirit we were all baptised into one body... and have all been made to drink into one Spirit'.

Although I looked at this verse at the start of this chapter, it demands further consideration.

Fowler linked the words with Romans 6: 'If Romans 6 is the crucial Pauline reference to baptism as a means of union with Christ, it might also be said that the crucial reference to the Spirit and the church is 1 Corinthians 12:13'. [132]

Just so. But which baptism is it? Water baptism or Spirit baptism? Fowler was in no doubt, both for himself and the majority of his fellow sacramental Baptists:

Baptist sacramentalists almost universally have interpreted this as a reference to water baptism and an indicator that water baptism is also a

---

[131] Fee: *1 Corinthians* pp246-247.
[132] Fowler: *More* p161.

baptism in the Spirit, and thus a[133] means of union with the body of Christ. It is clear that whatever baptism is in view here initiates individuals into union with the body of Christ, which is to say into union with Christ himself.[134]

I couldn't agree more. 'Whatever baptism is in view here initiates individuals into union with the body of Christ, which is to say into union with Christ himself'. Ah, but which baptism is it? Which pair of glasses should we be wearing?[135]

Beasley-Murray thought the reference in 1 Corinthians 12:13 is to *both* water baptism *and* Spirit baptism: 'The analogy of Galatians 3:27-28 forbids interpreting this saying as implying a Spirit baptism distinct from the experience of baptism in water'.[136] Indeed, he asserted: 'Baptism in water is baptism in the Spirit'.[137]

Well, that's plain enough! 'Baptism in water is baptism in the Spirit'. I could not disagree more strongly. With every fibre of my being, I dispute it.

---

[133] Yet again: Why are Baptist sacramentalists so reticent? The baptism in question cannot be *a* means; either it is *the* means, the only means, or it is no means at all. As Fowler himself said: 'Whatever baptism is in view here initiates individuals into union with the body of Christ, which is to say into union with Christ himself'. If the baptism in question is water baptism, then water baptism it is, and water baptism unites a sinner to Christ. But if it is Spirit baptism, then it is Spirit baptism which unites a sinner to Christ. Note my use of 'absolute' in the main text above, and in what follows. I stand by it. Why do so many sacramentalists baulk at the consequences of their own claims?

[134] Fowler: *More* p161.

[135] Fuller took an interesting – but mistaken – line: 'There are instances in the New Testament in which the word "baptism" does not mean the baptism by water, but yet manifestly alludes to it, and to the Lord's supper as connected with it... In 1 Cor. 12:13... the design may be to illustrate the spiritual union of all true believers in one invisible body, as originating in the washing of regeneration, and as being continued by the renewing of the Holy Spirit. But the allusion is, I conceive, to the ordinances of baptism and the Lord's supper; by the former of which they were initiated into the body of professing Christians, and by the other had communion in it' (Fuller: *Essays* pp857-858). Interesting comment, I repeat, but mistaken. I see no apostolic allusion here to the ordinances of baptism and the Lord's supper.

[136] Beasley-Murray: 'Baptism in the Epistles of Paul' p142.

[137] Beasley-Murray: *Baptism Today and Tomorrow* p56.

Let Fowler bring us back to reality:

The dominant theme of 1 Corinthians 12 is the Holy Spirit. The entire context of the debated verse focuses on the Spirit... The locus of unity in this passage is the Spirit, not baptism... Paul's point in this passage does not depend on any reference to water baptism... It should also be noted that the verse in question refers to the gift of the Spirit in two ways: the first in terms of baptism, and the second in terms of drinking... The second [drinking]... is thoroughly metaphorical, which lends support to the metaphorical sense of the first description [baptism] as well.[138]

In other words, the baptism in question is Spirit baptism; not water baptism.

Fee:

It is often assumed that [in 1 Cor. 12:13] Paul is referring to the sacrament of water baptism, and it is then often argued further [by sacramental Baptists; Fee cited Beasley-Murray] that this text supports the close tie[139] of the reception of the Spirit with baptism itself. But that assumes more than is actually said.[140]

As Fee observed: 'But that assumes more than is actually said'. Water is not mentioned; the baptism is with/in/by *the Spirit*; and, above all, 'one is hard pressed to find an equation between baptism and the reception of the Spirit in Paul's letters'.[141] 'Hard pressed to find'? I go further. I do not find it at all in Paul.

---

[138] Fowler: *More* pp172-173. Fowler: 'As argued convincingly by Gordon D.Fee'. Fowler cited Fee: *God's* pp179-180.

[139] Close tie? I ask yet again: Why this reticence? The text teaches an absolute tie between baptism and the reception of the Spirit. Sacramental Baptists must have the courage of their convictions. If Paul is speaking of water baptism, then water baptism unites to Christ.

[140] Fee: *1 Corinthians* p604. Actually, these sacramentalists are saying *less* than Paul said. Paul did not speak of a *close* tie. He spoke of an *absolute* tie. He said the baptism in question is effective. It does what it says. Moreover, he did not speak of the gift of the Spirit by baptism; he said by baptism the Spirit unites sinners to Christ.

[141] Fee: *1 Corinthians* p604; see also *God's* pp178-180,853-864.

Words matter. Little words often matter most.[142] And their order is important, too. Paul did not say they received the Spirit *by* baptism; he said they were baptised *by* (εν) the Spirit *into* (εις) the body, to drink *into* (εις) the Spirit.

Fee once again:

Paul's usage elsewhere strongly suggests that the prepositions εν and εις should be translated respectively as locative [to do with place] (the Spirit is the 'element' into which they were submerged)... The point is that Paul is not referring to water baptism at all.[143]

Again:

The use of εν with βαπτιζω throughout the New Testament is locative, expressing the element into which one is baptised (see on [1 Cor.] 12:13).[144]

This discussion needs broadening. Paul uses εις. I would translate this as 'into', to denote the element in which the baptism takes place. And the element determines the outcome. Spiritual baptism is baptism in or into (εις) the Spirit which unites to Christ. Water baptism is baptism in or into (εις) water which makes one a professor of Christ.

Now εις is a rich word, capable of a variety of meanings, including 'purpose' or 'object'. In other words, when Paul declares that 'by one Spirit we were all baptised into (εις) one body', he might mean that the Spirit used the baptism for the purpose of uniting us with the body of Christ; that the baptism actually effected its purpose or object. If so, as before, if the element is the Spirit, the purpose of the baptism is to unite the one baptised to Christ; if the element is water, the purpose of the baptism is to make the one baptised a professed believer, a testimony that such a one belongs to the body (the people) of Christ.

Let me re-state it. Paul's words could be taken to mean one of two things. Either he could be saying that the Spirit spiritually baptises sinners into union with Christ; or, the Spirit uses water

---

[142] 'In studying the word of God, we must never underestimate the importance of little words' (Barnhouse p157).
[143] Fee: *God's* pp861-862.
[144] Fee: *1 Corinthians* p445.

baptism to enable believers to make a public profession of Christ. Both are possible. The second, however, is woefully inadequate in the *argument* of the context. What is more, as I have said, there is not a hint of water in that context. The only possible meaning, therefore, is that the Spirit spiritually baptises sinners into union with Christ.

Beasley-Murray, citing εις Χριστον Ιησουν (Rom. 6:3), asked:

What is meant by baptism to Christ Jesus? Frequently εις after the verb βαπτιζειν denotes the goal desired and realised through baptism, [citing εις μετανοιαν (Matt. 3:11); εις αφεσιν αμαρτιων (Acts 2:38); εις εν σωμα) 1 Cor. 12:13]. It would be possible to view 'baptism to Christ Jesus' therefore as baptism in order to be *in* Christ, and so as 'baptism *into* Christ'. This interpretation is strengthened by the related passage, Galatians 3:26-28.

It doesn't take a genius to realise that care is needed here. We must know which pair of glasses we are to wear. The sacramentalist has his! E.Best, for instance. Beasley-Murray went on to quote Best:

The implied suggestion is that those who are 'in Christ' had come 'into him' by [water] baptism, and that therefore εις must carry the social and local meaning of εν.

That is to say, according to Best, water baptism actually unites to Christ – a full-blown sacramental position, of course. But, as Beasley-Murray pointed out:

A difficulty is encountered by this view in that Paul declares the Israelites to have been baptised 'to [into] Moses' (εις τον Μωσην, 1 Cor. 10:2), which can scarcely be said to mean 'into Moses'.

Best had countered this objection by taking Moses as representative of Christ – so that the baptism into Moses was truly an actual baptism into Christ! The paucity of the defence only serves to show the wrongness of the argument. As Beasley-Murray said: 'The Israelites were baptised with respect to Moses... for his allegiance'.[145] Note the 'with respect to... allegiance'. In other words, whereas in spiritual baptism, baptism εις or εν the Spirit actually unites to Christ, in water baptism, baptism εις or εν water is

---

[145] Beasley-Murray: *Baptism in the New Testament* pp128-129, emphasis his.

the profession of Christ, 'with respect to' Christ, allegiance to Christ, commitment to Christ. I agree. If 1 Corinthians 12:13 did speak of water baptism, then being 'baptised into one body' would mean being baptised as a public profession of allegiance to Christ. But this, as I have explained, though possible, falls far short of Paul's statement.

But this must not be taken to mean that Beasley-Murray was retracting his sacramentalist claims. Oh no! Even though he thought it likely 'that when Paul uses the word εν with the verb to baptise, he has in view the element in which baptism takes place', and going on to say that 'the Spirit... is the element in which one is baptised so as to be in the body', he still had no doubt about linking this with water baptism. He dismissed H.T.Andrews[146] for 'daring' to query it:

The question appears naïve from a responsible theologian. The inter-relating of gospel, faith, confession, grace, baptism appears never to have come within the horizon of this writer, nor the idea of baptism as a meeting of God and a penitent sinner on the basis of the Christ event.[147] [Again:] God's gift to baptism and to faith is one: it is his salvation in Christ.[148]

Speaking for myself, I hope I am 'responsible', even though I may be 'naïve' in the eyes of sacramentalists. Leaving that aside, I do dare to question that 'God's gift to [water] baptism and to faith is one', and that this 'gift' is 'salvation in Christ'. I do more than question it. I deny it absolutely. And I respectfully ask to be shown the biblical proof – not mere assertion – of it by 'non-naïve responsible theologians'.

As for assertion, take Cross:

---

[146] And not only Andrews. Beasley-Murray: 'Something similar must unfortunately be said of E.Best's comment on this passage'. Best had written: 'The baptism of 1 Cor. 12:13... is not water baptism but baptism in the Spirit' (Beasley-Murray: *Baptism in the New Testament* p168).

[147] Beasley-Murray: *Baptism in the New Testament* pp167-168.

[148] Beasley-Murray: *Baptism Today and Tomorrow* p37; see also *Baptism Today and Tomorrow* pp27-33). For an assessment of the views of Beasley-Murray, Dunn, Fee, Stott and Lloyd-Jones on 1 Cor. 12:13, see Cross: 'Spirit- and Water-'; O'Donnell. See also Macleod.

The most widely held view of 1 Corinthians 12:13 is that Paul is referring to water baptism which is the means by which the Spirit is given to the believer and by which they [*sic*] are incorporated into the body of Christ.[149]

How do we know this is 'the most widely held view'? And even if it is, the minority are not always wrong; sometimes, but not always.

But, as before, the choice must be made. Either the verse speaks of water baptism or it does not. If it does, then baptism is a sacrament, and it is the sacrament which effectually unites the sinner to Christ. I am convinced there is no water in 1 Corinthians 12:13. The baptism is with/in/by the Spirit. As a consequence, therefore, the verse does not teach sacramental baptism. Rather, it tells us that believers are sinners who, by the Spirit, have been spiritually baptised into Christ, spiritually united to Christ – and all without a hint of water.

Galatians 3:27

For as many of you as were baptised into Christ have put on Christ.

Fowler:

The language of baptism... in Galatians 3:27... The conjunction of εις Χριστον and εν Χριστω seems to indicate that the former phrase... is indicative of movement into saving union with Christ.[150]

I agree. Indeed, I go further. There is no 'seems' about it. In Galatians 3:26-29, Paul is saying that all who have been baptised into Christ have put on Christ. It doesn't matter whether we are talking about Jews or Greeks, slave or free, men or women. Such distinctions have gone for all who have been baptised into Christ – gone for them because they have put on Christ, and they are, all of them, sons of God:

You are all sons of God through faith in Christ Jesus. For as many of you as were baptised into (εις) Christ have put on (ενεδυσασθε) Christ. There is neither Jew nor Greek, there is neither slave nor free, there is neither male nor female; for you are all one in (εν) Christ Jesus. And if

---

[149] Cross: 'Spirit- and Water-' p121.
[150] Fowler: *More* p161.

you are Christ's, then you are Abraham's seed, and heirs according to the promise.[151]

The first question to answer is this: What does the apostle mean by 'put on Christ'? See the Appendix, where I note Helwys and Fuller (along with many others, no doubt) thought that to 'put on Christ' (Gal. 3:27) is to 'make a profession of him'. In other words, by water baptism a believer openly nails his colours to the mast. All very true, of course, but not the teaching of this passage. I cannot see how this would make a fitting climax to such a chapter as Galatians 3. Paul has long since reached higher ground at this stage of his argument. Spiritual inward union with Christ, not an outward profession of allegiance to him, is what Paul is speaking about.[152]

So, yet again, we are faced with the same question as before. In Galatians 3:27, what baptism is Paul speaking about when he says all believers have been baptised into Christ – that is, spiritually united to Christ?

I cannot detect a trace of dampness in the passage. As always, it is the context which is paramount. I find it inconceivable that, in the very letter in which the apostle took such pains to destroy any suggestion that the rite of circumcision could contribute to salvation (Gal. 2:16,21; 3:2-3,5,11; 5:1-6,11-12; 6:12-15), he could teach – without any explanation – that the ordinance of baptism turns sinners into sons of God, clothes them with Christ and makes them heirs of the promise. What is more, if this is so, we have to accept that Paul made this massive claim for water baptism in this one and only reference to the ordinance in his entire letter – and did so without the slightest hint or explanation of it.

This is too much for me to swallow. I do not accept, I cannot accept, that all who have been baptised in water have put on Christ; that is, spiritually united to him. Yet that must be the case, if the apostle was talking about water baptism. But since such a

---

[151] And citizens of heaven, members of the family of God (Eph. 2:19; 3:15; Phil. 3:20).
[152] But whichever interpretation we adopt, all three of us (Helwys, Fuller and me) would have no truck with a sacramental view of water baptism.

conclusion is obviously false,[153] I do not accept that Paul was speaking of water at all. Consequently, neither do I accept that Paul was saying that that all those who, in addition to being baptised in water, have been truly baptised by the Spirit into Christ, have put on Christ. Not at all. There is nothing 'additional' to baptism in the text.

No! The fact is, water baptism is not in the verse or its context. Why, water baptism does not get even a mention in the entire letter! Think about the context; or, as Beasley-Murray called it, 'the drift':

The drift of the passage is clear. It forms the climax of the chapter in which Paul labours to refute the claim of the Judaisers that men become 'sons of Abraham' only through conforming to the law; on the contrary, urges Paul, Abraham's heirs are the 'men of faith'.[154]

Very well. I agree that the verses in question form the climax of a chapter which deals with large and important themes. So how can it be that, according to sacramentalists, we are to understand that Paul, in coming to the *climax* to his argument in such a chapter, in such a book, closes with... water baptism? What an incredible suggestion. The context rules it out.[155]

Beasley-Murray disagreed. He argued that Paul had water very much in mind:

[Water] baptism is the baptism of faith and grace, so that in it faith receives what grace gives. Above all, grace gives Christ, for Christ is the fullness of grace; faith therefore receives Christ in [water] baptism.[156]

Again:

The union [in Gal. 3:27] was realised in [water] baptism. It is evident that baptism into Christ results in being in Christ, which is putting on Christ... [Water] baptism brings unity with Christ and his church. And

---

[153] I take it for granted that no one I am engaging with thinks all baptised people are everlastingly saved. A glance at Acts 8:13,21-23 will soon disabuse anyone who does.

[154] Beasley-Murray: *Baptism in the New Testament* p146.

[155] See my earlier comments on the same point when dealing with Rom. 6.

[156] Beasley-Murray: *Baptism in the New Testament* p151; Fowler: *More* pp185-186.

in that order of precedence... Baptism with faith bestows the status of sons of God in Christ.

Linking Galatians 3:26-27 with 4:6 (the gift of the Spirit), he went on:

The latter relates to what was done once for all in the union with the Son of God in [water] baptism.[157]

Well, reader, as before, the choice is simple and stark. Is it, all who are water-baptised are united to Christ? Or, all who are Spirit-baptised are united to Christ? The choice has to be made. And if the sacramentalists are right, and water baptism accomplishes this union with Christ, let them not equivocate. All who are baptised are the sons of God, united to Christ. There is not a hint of a qualification in Paul's statement. He is categorical. All who are baptised into Christ have put on Christ. If this is water baptism, then all who are baptised by water have 'put on Christ'; they are regenerate.

But Paul was not speaking of water at all. Rather, he was saying, all who have been baptised with the Spirit have 'put on Christ', they are regenerate, and by faith in Christ Jesus they have become sons of God.

Colossians 2:11-12

In [Christ] you were also circumcised with the circumcision made without hands, by putting off the body of the sins of the flesh, by the circumcision of Christ, buried with him in baptism, in which you were also raised with him through faith in the working of God, who raised him from the dead.

Beasley-Murray:

Colossians 2:11ff. provides a significant exposition of the theology... [lying] at the back of Romans 6... [Col. 2:]12 speaks of baptismal participation in the death of Christ... On the comparison of the two passages it may be seen that Colossians 2:11 makes plain the following elements of the theology presupposed in Romans 6:1: (i) The unity of the believer with Christ in his suffering of death on the cross... (ii) The unity of the believer with Christ in his rising from death... (iii)...

---

[157] Beasley-Murray: 'Baptism in the Epistles of Paul' pp138-139.

Participation in Christ's death and resurrection... (iv) The vital part in baptism played by faith.[158]

I agree. The question is, of course, which baptism is Paul talking about?[159]

Since the circumcision spoken of in these verses clearly is not a physical circumcision – it is 'the circumcision made without hands' – it can only be a spiritual circumcision.

What is more, while the Colossian church possibly comprised some converted Jews, it almost certainly[160] was made up mostly of converted Greeks. Yet Paul addressed them all as 'circumcised'. He could not possibly have meant physical circumcision – were the Greeks circumcised?

Then again, Colossians 2:11-15 states that all believers have been both circumcised and baptised, the circumcision and the baptism being one and the same. The one has not superseded the other. Paul declared that the Colossians 'were... circumcised... buried with [Christ] in baptism'. He did not say they were baptised *instead of* being circumcised. He did not say baptism *is the equivalent of* circumcision, nor that it *has replaced* circumcision. He said the Colossians were *both* circumcised *and* baptised. He went further. He did not even use the word *and* between 'circumcision' and 'baptism'. Baptism has not taken the place of circumcision. They were 'circumcised', 'baptised'. In the context the two are *identical*.

What is more, the Greek tense which Paul used was the aorist. He said that the Colossians were circumcised, were baptised, were buried, were raised, all at one and the same time in one finished completed act, one with abiding effect. This shows, again, that the

---

[158] Beasley-Murray: *Baptism in the New Testament* pp152-156. But, it must not be forgotten, as Fowler said, although 'it may be true that Col. 2:11-12 is Paul's commentary on his treatment of baptism in Rom. 6:1-4... neither the Colossians nor the Romans were able to read Paul's teaching in this canonical fashion' (Fowler: *More* p177). They did not have the written New Testament as we do. They could not refer to parallel passages as we can. See the earlier note on Rom. 6:3.

[159] See my *Infant*.

[160] Internal evidence in the book surely suggests it, to put it no stronger. And, after all, the church was in Colosse.

circumcision, the baptism, the burial and the resurrection were one and the same thing. It all took place at one and the same time. They all constituted one event.

It is clear that the circumcision in the passage is not physical. In the same way, nor is the baptism, the burial, or the resurrection. None of it is. It is all spiritual. It all speaks of spiritual union with Christ (Rom. 6:1-11).[161] This is by spiritual baptism; water baptism is not even mentioned in the passage. Note also that Christ is the one who circumcises and baptises – not ministers. If Paul had been talking physically, then ministers would play their part. But he was talking spiritually; ministers do not come into it.[162]

In short, Colossians 2:11-15 teaches that all believers have been united to Christ, having been regenerated by one sovereign act of God, when they were spiritually circumcised, spiritually baptised, spiritually buried and spiritually raised. The aorist is important! Moreover, there is nothing symbolic about any of it. I point out once again, reader, that Paul did not bring in the word 'and'. The circumcision, the baptism in question, are one and the same; they are not separate events. What Paul speaks of has nothing to do with physical circumcision, nothing to do with water baptism.

See also John 3:3-8; Romans 2:28-29; 6:1-11; 1 Corinthians 6:11; 12:13; Galatians 3:26-29; Philippians 3:3; Titus 3:5-6; and so on. In not one of these passages is water baptism or physical circumcision in view.

But as before, we are presented with the usual clear choice: Regeneration and union to Christ comes by water baptism or spiritual baptism; either/or, not both. The choice has to be made. My view is that Colossians 2 does not teach sacramental water baptism.

Reader, what do you say?

---

[161] Although the answer is obvious, the question is important: Had the believers Paul was writing to been *physically* buried and *physically* raised? Of course not. Clearly, Paul was not talking about *physical* burial and resurrection. So, neither was he talking about *physical* circumcision or *physical* baptism. *It was all spiritual.*

[162] 'The baptism with the Holy Ghost, wherewith only Christ and God do baptise' (John Robinson p183; see the extended note on p333). But what about 2 Cor. 3:3? See the extended note on p326.

Hebrews 10:19-22

Therefore, brethren, having boldness to enter the holiest by the blood of Jesus... let us draw near with a true heart in full assurance of faith, having our hearts sprinkled from an evil conscience, and our bodies washed with pure water.

As always, the context is determinative. *And **that** is unequivocal.* Without question, the writer has old-covenant ceremonial sacrifices and washings in mind, and he is showing how the shadow in the old has given way to reality in the new covenant. His entire letter proves it. In particular, in Hebrews 7:11 – 10:18 he has been building to this crescendo: 'Therefore, brethren...' (Heb. 10:19). And what has the writer been pressing home, paragraph after paragraph? The old-covenant sacrifices have been replaced (done away with, fulfilled) by the reality – the sacrifice of Christ himself. That is his point. This means, of course, that the ceremonial washings have gone, have been abolished – by the sacrifice of Christ.

Wait a minute, says the sacramental Baptist. That's not the whole story. When we reach Hebrews 10:19-22, these washings have been replaced, yes, but they have been replaced with... with what? With the reality of... water baptism! Really? According to sacramental Baptists, this is what we are to understand. The old-covenant washing has been replaced by a new-covenant washing in water; that is, the old shadow has been replaced by water baptism.

I fail to see it. Fail to see it? Given the context, it is incredible that one ceremony should have replaced another. Baptism is utterly foreign to the context. Indeed, in light of that context (the fulfilment and end of old-covenant rites including washings *etc.*), the idea that the writer would move to baptism – without any hint or explanation – is fantastic, and shows a remarkable disregard for (or lack of understanding of) what he has said. I simply cannot fathom how anybody could argue for such a 'climax' after the tremendous far-reaching argument set out in Hebrews 7:11 – 10:18.

But Baptist sacramentalists do not think we are talking about water baptism as a symbol. Not at all. They think that the old shadow has been replaced by the real, effective sacrament of baptism. As they see it, sacramental baptism is the real fulfilment of the old-covenant shadow. Staggering! I am afraid I can only use the same word as before and call the suggestion incredible. But Fowler did not think the notion at all incredible. Quite the opposite:

The allusion to baptism is difficult to deny, not only because of the references to water,[163] but also because the exhortation of verse 23 is [as Beasley-Murray said] 'almost certainly an appeal to maintain the confession made in baptism'... It is true that a major theme of the letter is the truth that the death of Christ was the sufficient and final[164] cleansing sacrifice, but the question remains: How does that sacrifice become operative in the individual? How does one enter into the 'full assurance of faith' noted in verse 22? Apparently this occurs through the event indicated in the last clause of the verse; that is, baptism. To quote Beasley-Murray: 'The meeting place of the sanctifying power of Christ's death and the individual is the baptism wherein the believer turns to God in faith for cleansing through Christ'... Baptism is indeed a reminder of the objective cleansing, but the allusion in this text seems to say what other texts say more explicitly, that baptism is not *merely* a reminder.[165]

In other words, according to Fowler, this passage teaches that baptism is a sacrament, an effective means of grace. It is the act through which the believer is washed from his sins, and saved. By an outward washing in water, apparently, the sinner has his heart and conscience cleansed from sin.

And this is supposed to be the climax of the argument from Hebrews 7:11 – 10:18? Remarkable!

Buse:

The writer of the letter to the Hebrews... regards baptism as the point in Christian experience where the results of the death of Christ are made effective by entry into that close fellowship with God which is represented as the Holy of Holies.[166]

---

[163] See above for my views on the 'water' passages.

[164] Final? It was the only sacrifice! Reader, beware of such glosses.

[165] Fowler: *More* p182, emphasis his. Strange, then, that Fowler elsewhere noted that the 'inference from the combination of washing imagery and an aorist participle [in Heb. 10:22] to a baptismal reference is quite common [among sacramentalists] but questionable' (Fowler: 'Oxymoron' p133). It is more than 'questionable'.

[166] Buse: 'Baptism in Other New Testament Writings' p183. Beasley-Murray: 'We draw near to God like the high priest of ancient times, but with the infinitely better cleansing afforded by the sacrifice of Christ, the

Serious claims, indeed. And all are made, please note, on a verse that says nothing – nothing! – explicitly (or even implicitly) about baptism. But if the sacramentalists are right, and the water of Hebrews 10:22 is baptism, then water baptism washes from sin. But if they are mistaken, and water baptism is not in the verse, then it is of no use to them in trying to make their case. Indeed, the harm caused by such an assertion is immense.

John Owen, commenting on the believer's 'boldness' in approaching God, said: 'It is faith in Christ alone that gives us boldness of access unto God'.[167] I agree. Not baptism, not baptism and faith, but faith alone that gives access to God. The Scriptures could not be more explicit.[168] No talk here from Owen of the believer's confidence and assurance given him by baptism (as some sacramentalists claim).[169]

But what about the 'water'? Owen again:

This at first view would seem to refer to the outward administration of the ordinance of baptism... and so it is carried by many expositors. But (1)... Peter tells us that saving baptism does not consist in the washing away of the filth of the body (1 Pet. 3:21); therefore the expression here must be figurative, and not proper.[170] (2). Although the sprinkling and washing spoken of do principally respect our habitual, internal qualification, by regenerating, sanctifying grace, yet they include also the actual, gracious, renewed preparation of our hearts and minds, with respect to all our solemn approaches unto God; but baptism cannot be repeated.[171] (3). Whereas the sprinkling of the heart from an evil

---

power of which is known in baptism' (Beasley-Murray: *Baptism in the New Testament* pp249-250). The anti-climax at the end of this statement is palpable. The high priest... Christ... baptism? Incredible!

[167] Owen Vol.4 Part 1 p511.

[168] See Acts 13:39; Rom. 1:17; 3:27 – 5:2; Gal. 2:16; 3:8-9; 5:4-5; Phil. 3:9, with no mention of water.

[169] In addition to Fowler, Beasley-Murray and Westminster above, see my *Infant*. The notion is unbiblical. I find no hint of a suggestion of it in Scripture.

[170] 'Proper': 'Strictly so-called; genuine, real' (*The Shorter*) – literal, the opposite of figurative. In other words, Owen said: 'The expression here must be figurative, and not literal'.

[171] This is an important point. Let me underline it. Owen had already explained what he understood by 'our hearts sprinkled from an evil conscience'. Two things are involved, he said. There is the original

conscience respects the internal and unknown sins of the mind, so this of washing the body does [that is, respects] the sins that are outwardly acted and perpetrated. And the body is said to be washed from them: *First*, because they are outward, in opposition to those that are only inherent, in the mind. *Secondly*, because the body is the instrument of the perpetration of them... Pure water, wherewith the body is said to be washed, is that which is promised (Ezek. 36:25-26) – the assistance of the sanctifying Spirit, by virtue of the sacrifice of Christ.[172]

Calvin thought it unlikely that baptism is meant in Hebrews 10:22. He put it like this: 'It seems to me more probable that the [writer]... by water... designates the Spirit of God (Ezek. 36:25)'. Gill was certain: 'Not baptismal water, but the grace of the Spirit, which is often compared to water in Scripture'.[173]

There is a further point. Note the word 'pure'; 'our bodies washed with *pure* water'. Why 'pure' water? Isn't baptismal water simply ordinary water – tap, river, stream, lake, well, oasis, pool or sea? How and why is baptismal water 'pure'? But if the verse does speak of literal water in baptism, calling it 'pure' would surely – inevitably – lead to the ridiculous and highly dangerous notion that the water itself has some power.

As I have already noted, the word, καθαρος, is used in John 13:10 where Jesus, having washed his disciples' feet, told them: 'You are clean [καθαροι]'. They had been cleansed outwardly by the physical water, but this is not the point that Jesus was making. As I have already noted, Judas had his feet washed as thoroughly as any of the disciples, but he was not one of the καθαροι. The water,

---

cleansing 'in the communication of regenerating, sanctifying grace'. Then there is the continual cleansing 'in fresh applications of the virtue of the blood of Christ, for the taking away of the defilement by internal, actual sin'. Owen went on to speak of 'fresh applications of our souls unto the efficacy of the blood of Christ for the purification of our hearts'. In this, he was surely right. The question is, of course, how do we get both the original and the continual cleansings? By water baptism? Or...? Since, as Owen pointed out, baptism cannot be repeated, it cannot be baptism. See below for more on the 'conscience' in 1 Pet. 3:21.

[172] Owen Vol.4 Part 1 pp513-514.
[173] Calvin: *Commentaries* Vol.22 Part 1 p237; Gill: *Commentary* Vol.6 p741. W.S.Plumer took the same line quoting Calvin, Owen and Gill (Plumer pp408-409). See also Poole Vol.3 p856.

therefore, while it had cleansed the feet of all the disciples, had not effected the internal cleansing in question for any of them.

Getting back to Hebrews 10:22, and to the claim that the water in that verse refers to baptism, does anybody seriously suggest that the water used in baptism is 'pure' and effectively makes those baptised one of the καθαροι? If so, powerful water indeed!

Reformed sacramentalists down the centuries have had to fend off this claim. Worse still, some of them have actually gloried in the notion of specialness, not to say power, in the water![174] Will Baptist sacramentalists do the same?

If so, may I ask: If the baptismal water is 'pure', how are we to purify it? Where can we find out how to purify it? Does it get its purity as the baptism takes place? Is it still pure after the baptism? What directions for all this do we find in Scripture? The list of such questions is endless.[175] May we have the answers?

None of this! Away with such talk! Such suggestions show the nonsense of taking the water as literal baptismal water. The water – the pure water – is entirely figurative. This is what 'pure' means. I would strengthen Donald Guthrie's words – 'the use of the adjective "pure" would... seem to suggest a symbolic meaning'.[176] I would use the word 'figurative'. And 'pure' more than 'suggests' a figurative use. It is the context again. The old-covenant washing was symbolic and ineffective. The new-covenant washing, however, is effective because the 'washing' is washing in the blood of Christ. Anything less – including baptismal water – will not do.

The fact is, in the context of the letter to the Hebrews, at this point we should not be talking about water baptism at all. The writer was contrasting the ineffectiveness of the old-covenant washings and sacrifices with the purity – the effectiveness – of the washing

---

[174] And still do so. Let me re-quote a part of the extract I included in my *Infant* from Daniel R.Hyde's article in the *Banner of Truth*, May 2008, pp1-8: 'The water of baptism is more than mere water... for the water is so bound to the promise of God that the physical cleansing becomes, if not the instrument, at least the occasion for the spiritual cleansing'.

[175] Compare the difficulties some sacramentalists have got themselves into over the status and disposal of the elements left over after the Lord's supper.

[176] Guthrie p214.

under the new covenant. 'The blood of Jesus Christ... cleanses us from all sin' (1 John 1:7). *This* is what we should be thinking about. That has long been his theme. And how he has repeated it, over and over, hammering it home. Blood... blood... blood (Heb. 9:7ff.). And, keeping *this* in mind, we should be going on to his conclusions: 'Therefore, brethren, having boldness to enter the holiest by the blood of Jesus... let us draw near with a true heart in full assurance of faith, having our hearts sprinkled from an evil conscience, and our bodies washed with pure water'.[177]

All this presents us, once again, with the stark choice. There is only one of two stable positions. Either the water of Hebrews 10:22 is literal in baptism, and is pure and makes effective the sanctifying work of Christ by the Spirit; or it is not, and does not, but is a vivid figurative description of the cleansing power of the blood of Christ applied by the Spirit of God. I have stated my opinion. Reader, what is yours?

1 Peter 3:21

There is also an antitype which now saves us – baptism (not the removal of the filth of the flesh, but the answer of a good conscience toward God).

Fowler admitted that 'this statement occurs in a passage with all sorts of exegetical difficulties'. This, however, has not prevented Baptist sacramentalists making dogmatic claims on the verse. Fowler himself: 'But it clearly asserts that baptism effects salvation... in some way'. Buse: 'The Christian dies with Christ in the waters of baptism, and in that experience he finds salvation'. Beasley-Murray: 'In baptism, affirms Peter, the resurrection of Jesus Christ is a known power. The living Christ is active in it. That is why it is effective'.[178]

Some claims these. Does the passage support these dogmatic assertions?

---

[177] Note the triple 'let us' (Heb. 10:19-25).
[178] Fowler: *More* p164; Buse: 'Baptism in Other New Testament Writings' p179; Beasley-Murray: *Baptism Today and Tomorrow* p32.

Take the 'antitype'. Peter said that baptism is the antitype; that is to say, baptism is the literal fulfilment of a type. The type itself was Noah's flood. The flood literally happened, but it also prefigured or represented – it was typical of – something. What? Peter explains. Noah's flood was a type of baptism; it prefigured baptism: 'There is also an antitype which now saves us – baptism'.

Ah! But which or what baptism? The baptism Peter speaks of is baptism by water, or by the Spirit, or by both (which is, in effect, water baptism). Those who think it is water baptism, offer one of two explanations of Peter's argument, falling as they do into one of two categories; namely, non-sacramentalists and sacramentalists, respectively. Let me glance at the views of these two groups, both of whom think that the baptism in the verse is water baptism. We are talking about the first and second pairs of glasses I mentioned earlier.

*First, **non-sacramental** Baptists who think Peter was speaking of water baptism.* They say the apostle was speaking of water baptism as a *representation* of spiritual baptism; in other words, they wear the first pair of glasses I spoke of at the start of this chapter. But this is wrong. Peter does not here speak of baptism representing anything; indeed, he asserts the opposite – it is the antitype, he says. In other words, the baptism is the literal fulfilment of a type or representation. Noah's flood was the type, the representation. Baptism is the reality. It is not a type of a type. It cannot be a further representation. So Thomas J.Nettles was wrong to claim that the apostle says: 'Baptism represents the confident reliance on the judgement that Christ took for us, which judgement becomes our salvation'.[179] With respect, Peter does not. He speaks of a baptism 'which now saves us', not a baptism which *represents* our salvation.

*Secondly, **sacramental** Baptists who think that Peter was speaking of water baptism.* They say that Noah's flood was a type of water baptism – and water baptism saves us; in other words, they wear the second pair of glasses. There are two points to this. For sacramental Baptists, the baptism in question is not a representation – and in this they are right – the baptism is effective. Secondly – and this is vital

---

[179] Armstrong p38.

– sacramental Baptists say that Peter was talking about water baptism. Noah's flood typified water baptism. That is what they say. Are they right? If so, water baptism saves. No 'if', 'but' or 'maybe'. Water baptism saves. I repeat my question, therefore: Are they right? I think not – but, once again, the familiar choice has to be made. If Peter was speaking of water baptism, typified by Noah's flood, then water baptism is a saving sacrament.

So much for those who say that the baptism Peter was speaking of is water baptism. This leaves those, and I am one of them, who think that Peter was not speaking of water baptism at all; in other words, we wear the third pair of glasses. Peter was saying the flood typified *spiritual* baptism – and it is *spiritual* baptism which saves us. There are not two lots of water in the passage. The only water is Noah's flood – not Noah's flood and water baptism. The baptism, therefore, is spiritual baptism. And spiritual baptism saves! No quibble! No qualifiers!

Of course, lest I should be misunderstood, I state the obvious: Those who are spiritually baptised must be water baptised. But Peter was not talking about *that*.

And what about the 'good conscience'? 'Baptism (not the removal of the filth of the flesh, but the answer of a good conscience toward God)'. In addition to what I said a few moments ago on 'our hearts sprinkled from an evil conscience' (Heb. 10:22), notice that Peter was putting the same thought in a positive way. Those who are spiritually baptised, not only have their hearts sprinkled from an evil conscience, they have a *good* conscience. In fact, he *defined* the baptism in question *as* the answer of a good conscience toward God.

Whether we take 'the answer', επερωτημα, to be 'we have *earnestly sought* a good conscience', 'the *agreement* of a good conscience', 'the *avowal* of a good conscience',[180] or 'the *expression, confession* or *declaration* of a good conscience toward God',[181] this 'having or exercising a good conscience toward God' is one and the same as spiritual baptism.

---

[180] See Thayer.
[181] See Brown: *1 Peter* Vol.2 pp251-252.

As above, lest I should be misunderstood, once again I state the obvious: Those who have or exercise this good conscience toward God must be water baptised. But Peter was not talking about *that*.

So, the question, as always is: Which baptism is the apostle talking about? This baptism saves. It certainly does. 'There is [that] which now saves us – baptism'. The choice has to be made. Is it water baptism or spiritual baptism? And since Peter expressly speaks in spiritual terms – 'not the removal of the filth of the flesh' – I am convinced he was not speaking of water baptism at all. We are saved by spiritual baptism – which was typified by Noah's flood.

* * *

These scriptures, as far as I can tell, are the main passages used by Baptist sacramentalists to make their case. My position is clear: Where water baptism is the subject of the text, there is no sacramentalism attached to it. As for the remaining scriptures – John 3:5; Romans 6:1-5; 1 Corinthians 6:11; 12:13; Colossians 2:12; Hebrews 10:19-22; 1 Peter 3:21 – they do not teach sacramental water baptism simply because they do not refer to water baptism in the first place.

But... if I am wrong on John 3:5; Romans 6:1-5; 1 Corinthians 6:11; 12:13; Colossians 2:12; Hebrews 10:19-22; 1 Peter 3:21, and the sacramentalists are right, and these scriptures do refer to water baptism as the sacramentalists say they do, then all who are baptised with water are regenerated, washed from sin and united to Christ. No qualifiers can prevent it or get round it. It has to be faced; if the verses speak of water baptism, then water baptism saves! There is no talk of a representation in these verses. The baptism actually accomplishes what is being spoken of. And in every case. 'For by one Spirit we were all baptised into one body'; 'all' not 'some', or even 'most', or 'those who prove to be regenerate', but 'all' were. If the verses speak of water baptism, then water baptism saves – and every time: 'We were *all* baptised into one body'; 'all', I stress again. Either water baptism does what is claimed for it, or it does not; a close tie – or a 99.999% success rate – is not good enough. 99.999% is not 'all'. Now we know that Simon (the Samaritan sorcerer) was baptised but not saved by it (Acts 8:13,21-23). This one 'failure', on its own, proves that saving grace does not come by baptism. Therefore the passages cannot speak of water baptism.[182]

* * *

Before I bring this chapter to a close, I would like to take up a weighty point made by Fowler: 'It is... true that more than half of the Pauline letters do not mention baptism, and that the subject is missing from most of the general letters and the Apocalypse as well'. From this just observation, he drew a significant conclusion:

One is forced, therefore, to ask whether baptism is so important after all. Perhaps it is only a flat, simplistic reading of the New Testament which will support this exalted [that is, the sacramental] view of baptism. This [argument]... has some merit, especially in view of the fact that most of the New Testament references to baptism occur only as subordinate propositions used to teach other truths.

Furthermore, Fowler acknowledged 'the relative paucity and brevity of [Paul's] baptismal texts'. So... was Fowler conceding that the sacramentalist's claims don't stand much scrutiny after all? Not at all! Quite rightly noting 'the strength of these texts', Fowler went on to deduce: 'One possible inference is that they simply imply the existence of a widely taught and well understood doctrine of baptismal efficacy which needed little explanation'.[183] In other words, according to Fowler, the very scarcity of baptismal texts, taken in conjunction with their strength, in itself goes to make the sacramentalist's case.

It's time to pause. Let's not get carried away. Fowler's argument from relative silence is remarkable. But we have met it before. If you glance back at the chapter on the history of Baptist sacramentalism, reader – and even more so if you read the full extracts which I there noted from Fowler himself – you will see that this kind of argument from silence played a large role in his attempt to show that there has been a constant stream of Baptist

---

[182] In his 'Baptism in Acts: The Sacramental Dimension', Porter deliberately did not address Simon's case: 'I will not deal with the Simon part of the episode' (Porter p121). Why not? Shouldn't the fact that Simon was baptised, but no grace was conveyed to him, be explained by the sacramentalist?

[183] Fowler: *More* pp177-178.

sacramentalism down the centuries. But, as I have explained, this is not the way to argue from silence. On this basis, the moon is made of green cheese. Why? Because the Bible does not say it is not!

So, then, let's come to the question of baptismal efficacy, and Fowler's deductions from the Pauline texts.

Let me clear the decks. I agree with Fowler's reference as to the fewness of the Pauline texts on baptism. I also agree that these texts are strong. But I quarrel with Fowler's deductions from those texts.

First of all – and it is of the utmost importance to keep it in mind – Fowler was making an assumption. Let me repeat his statement:

> It is... true that more than half of the Pauline letters do not mention baptism, and that the subject is missing from most of the general letters and the Apocalypse as well. One is forced, therefore, to ask whether baptism is so important after all. Perhaps it is only a flat, simplistic reading of the New Testament which will support this exalted [that is, the sacramental] view of baptism. This [argument]... has some merit, especially in view of the fact that most of the New Testament references to baptism occur only as subordinate propositions used to teach other truths.[184]

At the root of this statement lies an enormous assumption.[185] Which is? That these passages refer to water baptism! Fowler might be right in his assumption. I don't think so, as I have argued, but at least we should all recognise that this was what he *assumed*.

Let us start again. I agree that Paul does not often refer to baptism in his letters. Very well. I further agree that in the overwhelming majority of these texts he speaks in very strong terms. But I go further still. He not only speaks in very strong terms, he speaks in absolute terms. But this is where my agreement with Fowler comes to a grinding halt. Whereas Fowler assumed that Paul is speaking of water baptism, I assert that in the Pauline texts where he speaks so strongly of baptism – indeed, where he speaks in absolute terms – *the apostle is not speaking of **water** baptism* at all.

---

[184] Fowler: *More* pp177-178.

[185] I do not use this word in any pejorative sense. I grant that sacramentalists are convinced, believe, are persuaded and argue that the passages speak of water baptism. The same goes for me as far as Spirit baptism is concerned.

Indeed, I maintain, in one leading passage only (1 Cor. 1:13-17)[186] – the passage I will look at in the following chapter – does Paul, in his letters, refer to water baptism. All the other references, I say, are to spiritual baptism (Rom. 6:1-5; 1 Cor. 6:11; 12:13; Gal. 3:27; Col. 2:12; plus Eph. 5:26; Tit. 3:5).[187]

This is a large assertion, I admit. But I have done more than assert it. I have set out my reasons.[188] I fully accept that there are differences of opinion about this. But I have explained why I do not think that Paul in those passages was speaking of water mixed with faith; indeed, why I do not think he was speaking of water at all. I have explained why I think he was always speaking of spiritual baptism. In so doing, I fully accept Beasley-Murray's observation that my view 'might well leave us with virtually no Pauline references to water baptism at all'.[189] Indeed it does. Apart from

---

[186] In addition to the one I have in mind (1 Cor. 1:13-17), there are three other Pauline references to baptism in his letters: 'All were baptised into Moses in the cloud and in the sea' (1 Cor. 10:2). 'What will they do who are baptised for the dead, if the dead do not rise at all? Why then are they baptised for the dead?' (1 Cor. 15:29). 'One baptism' (Eph. 4:5). They do not seem to play any major part in this particular discussion over sacramentalism. But take 1 Cor. 15:29 – which Paul wrote to expose the error of those who deny the resurrection. How would a belief in sacramental baptism prove the resurrection? See Anderson p234.

[187] Anderson listed 'five passages where baptism is doctrinally mentioned' (Rom. 6:3-4; Gal. 3:27; Eph. 4:5; Col. 2:12; 1 Pet. 3:21) (Anderson pp229-230) – four from Paul, one from Peter.

[188] In this chapter and my *Infant*.

[189] See Fowler: 'Oxymoron' p143. But I fail to see why this should mean that 'the idea of baptism as a symbol of death and resurrection appears to be unfounded', as Fowler asserted. Rom. 6 teaches that by spiritual baptism, sinners are united to Christ in his death and resurrection. The entire section in Romans teaches this union with Christ. Now, although I have argued that the overwhelming majority of the Pauline texts do *not* speak of water baptism, but spiritual baptism, and therefore to introduce the notion of representation is a mistake, this does not mean that water baptism does not symbolise the realities of spiritual baptism. That is precisely what it does do. For a start, the obvious play on the word 'baptism' itself makes this evident. Water baptism is a symbol of the spiritual experience of sinners in conversion. Therefore baptism is a symbol of this union. Similarly in the Lord's supper. This symbolic meaning to baptism does not depend on the alleged, but mistaken, reference to water baptism in Rom. 6. It is founded

those references just noted (which do not seem to play a vital role in this discussion), it leaves us with only one! But that single passage is of paramount importance. I will examine it in the following chapter.

Before that, however, let me make a nice point. Allowing for the moment that the sacramentalists are right, and the New Testament does speak of water-baptismal efficacy, what does the relative silence on baptism in Paul's letters – which we have agreed on – mean? Fowler might be right when he asserts that Paul's relative silence on the matter could mean baptismal efficacy was so well known, and so commonly accepted, that it would have been superfluous for him to say much about it. This is possible. But if it is so, and Fowler was right about baptism, may I ask why is there so much in the New Testament about, for example, the efficacy of the blood of Christ? Was that not 'widely taught and well understood'? Why so little about baptism, and so much about the blood, if both are effectual to salvation, and both were 'widely taught and well understood' in New Testament times?

The fact is, the relative silence does not do what Fowler hoped. Not at all! Is it not much more likely that the relative silence in question – the *complete* silence, in my opinion – means that water baptism does not have the sacramental efficacy that these Baptist scholars are trying to maintain, and that nobody thought of it in the early church?[190]

---

on a much broader base than that. Beasley-Murray: John's 'water baptism witnesses to the powerful baptism in [the] Spirit and fire which the Messiah... exercise[s] at his [first] coming' (Beasley-Murray: *Baptism in the New Testament* p48). Just so.

[190] As to Fowler's arguing from silence and by suggestion, take: 'All would agree that the baptism of a confessing believer is a human act of the baptised person [and the baptiser], but the question is whether a divine act is thought to occur also in the event' (Fowler: *More* p181). Quite a suggestion, this – but where are the texts to substantiate it? Compare Fowler's pot-and-kettle talk of 'unwarranted inferences' in 'Baptist critique' of sacramentalism (Fowler: *More* pp204-205), where he points out that although, in Romans and Galatians, Paul draws a contrast between salvation by faith and salvation by law, he draws no such contrast between faith and baptism. Very well. A good observation! And there is an excellent reason and simple explanation for it. Since the believers of Paul's day were

In saying this, I would not be misunderstood. I repeat what I said above. I am not granting Fowler's sacramentalist position. I do not accept his assumption or claim that the Pauline texts in question talk of water baptism at all. I agree that these passages speak very strongly about baptismal efficacy, but they always speak of spiritual baptism. Speak strongly, did I say? Let me repeat what I said a few moments ago. They speak more than *strongly!* They speak absolutely, invincibly and categorically of baptismal regeneration. Let me repeat it. They speak absolutely, invincibly and categorically of baptismal regeneration. But the baptism in question is always by the sovereign Holy Spirit, and nothing to do with water at all.

This is the issue, as I have also said, that we all have to settle. We all hold to baptismal regeneration. All of us do. I do. Reader, you do.[191] The Scriptures teach it (Rom. 6:1-5; 1 Cor. 6:11; 12:13; Gal. 3:27; Col. 2:12; 1 Pet. 3:21). The question is: Is water involved in these passages, or is it not? Are the apostles Paul and Peter speaking of an act performed by a minister, or of a direct act by the Spirit of God? I have made my position clear, and I take the consequences. My aim has been to try to make those I write against (and those who might follow them) face the consequences of their view. We all believe in baptismal regeneration, I say again – but is it by water, or by the Spirit of God (or by water and the Spirit of God)? I re-state my wholehearted agreement with Fowler when, leaving to one side 1 Corinthians 1:13-17, speaking of the Pauline

---

in danger of going back to the law for salvation – and there is abundant corroborating evidence for it – Paul therefore had to write about the subject. Indeed, he and Barnabas travelled all the way to Jerusalem to deal with the issue (Acts 15), having been sent by the church at Antioch to get the matter sorted out. But since there is not a shred of corroborating evidence to show that the early believers were in danger of adopting sacramentalism (baptismal efficacy), is there any doubt as to the reason for Paul's silence on the matter? Since nobody was mixing up baptism and faith with regard to salvation, there was no call to speak about it! If, however, sacramentalists still wish to press the silence argument as proof of the practice, would they say that since Paul never wrote against Mary-worship, transubstantiation and papal infallibility, we may properly deduce that such things were widely taught and well understood in the New Testament? After all, they all come from the same stable.

[191] See my remarks at the start of the Preamble.

(and Petrine – DG) baptismal passages, he remarked on 'the strength of these texts'. Just so. The apostolic passages just cited may be few – but whatever else they are, they are powerful and unequivocal, categorical and sweeping in their claims for the efficacy of baptism. Indeed, they speak absolutely and undeniably in terms of baptismal regeneration. But the question is: Which baptism? If they speak of water baptism, then water baptism regenerates. The question is, I say: Do they speak of water baptism? Baptist sacramentalists say they do. I say they don't.

Finally, let me remind you of the sacramental Baptist's position. According to Fowler, Beasley-Murray, arguing from Romans 10:9-10, saw baptism 'as instrumental in the reception of salvation'. Beasley-Murray himself claimed that 'the relation of the Pauline teaching on salvation by faith and his high estimate of the value of baptism come [*sic*] most nearly to solution in [Rom. 10:10]'. Fowler said that for 'Beasley-Murray... baptism is the means by which faith is translated from attitude into action, and thus the means by which salvation becomes visible and an assured personal reality. Baptism is... an effective sign precisely because it is tied to faith... To assert that baptism saves by virtue of being the vehicle of faith is to take seriously what Paul says about both faith and baptism'.[192]

Let Beasley-Murray himself sum up the Baptist sacramentalist's view of the Scriptures I have looked at in this chapter:

The chief elements have emerged with clarity. With his predecessors and contemporaries, Paul saw in baptism a sacrament of the gospel... Beyond his predecessors and contemporaries, however, Paul saw in baptism the sacrament of union with Christ... Baptism was thus an effective sign; in it Christ and faith come together in the meeting of conversion.[193]

Since by 'baptism', Beasley-Murray meant water baptism, I profoundly disagree. What about you, reader?

All that is left for me to do to bring this book to a conclusion, is to look at the one vital New Testament passage, dealing with baptism, which, I am convinced, puts the final, clinching, nail into the coffin

---

[192] Fowler: 'Oxymoron' pp134-135; Beasley-Murray: 'Baptism in the Epistles of Paul' pp129-130.
[193] Beasley-Murray: 'Baptism in the Epistles of Paul' p148.

of the sacramentalist's case. Indeed, as I have said, this remaining passage is the only cardinal passage in Paul's letters (and in all the New Testament letters) in which he (or any other apostle) raises the subject of water baptism in a way which has any bearing on the subject in hand. It must, therefore, be the principal passage. All of us – sacramentalists and non-sacramentalists – have to come to terms with its teaching.

The Clinching Passage

We now come to the final passage which we need to look at – this being, I am convinced, the only passage relevant to the issue in hand in all Paul's letters.[1]

Now, reader, whether or not you agree with my claim in the previous chapter – that in the other references to baptism in Paul's letters, the apostle speaks about spiritual baptism, not water baptism – surely we must all agree that he *is* talking about water baptism in 1 Corinthians 1:13-17. Everybody accepts *that*... don't they? Of course they do. So, then, let us see what the passage tells us about the ordinance. Does it support the sacramentalist case?[2]

1 Corinthians 1:13-17

Is Christ divided? Was Paul crucified for you? Or were you baptised in the name of Paul? I thank God that I baptised none of you except Crispus and Gaius, lest anyone should say that I had baptised in my own name. Yes, I also baptised the household of Stephanas. Besides, I do not know whether I baptised any other. For Christ did not send me to baptise, but to preach the gospel, not with wisdom of words, lest the cross of Christ should be made of no effect.

Before I come to the main point, a glance at the apostle's second and third questions: 'Was Paul crucified for you? Or were you baptised in the name of Paul?' (1 Cor. 1:13). What can we deduce from the juxtaposition of these two questions – one on the death of Christ, and the other on baptism? Is Paul associating the two? Is he

---

[1] I am omitting 1 Cor. 10:2; 15:29; Eph. 4:5. As I have already noted, I (nor the sacramentalists as I far as I have discovered) do not regard them as crucial in this debate. Eph. 4:5, of course, is important in the connected debate over infant baptism.

[2] Why was this passage not even mentioned in *Christian Baptism*? The silence is significant. This book, so instrumental in the drive for Baptist sacramentalism, with its subtitle, *A Fresh Attempt to Understand the Rite in terms of Scripture, History and Theology*, did not even mention the passage, let alone examine and try to come to terms with its teaching. Why not?

implying – or saying – that the benefits of the crucifixion come to us through baptism? In other words, is he saying that baptism effects union with Christ? If he is, the arguments I used when looking at Romans 6:1-5 and Colossians 2:11-15 clearly do not apply in this case, since, in those passages, Paul was speaking of *spiritual* baptism; here, he is speaking of *water* baptism. So here, in 1 Corinthians 1:13, if he is saying that baptism effects union with Christ, then it inevitably follows – since the baptism in question is water baptism – that he is undoubtedly talking in sacramental terms. And this verse, 1 Corinthians 1:13, therefore, establishes the sacramentalist's case.

But before we get carried away, we must take note of a very important difference between this verse and those other passages – in addition to the baptism he is talking about. In those passages (Rom. 6; Col. 2), Paul *directly* linked baptism and union to Christ in his death and resurrection. Indeed, he stated quite plainly that by baptism we are united to Christ. In 1 Corinthians 1:13, however, there is no such stated link. Indeed, Paul does not *state* anything. He asks two questions. What is more, the only connection here between baptism and the death of Christ (note there is no mention of the resurrection, nor union with Christ, as there was in the other passages) lies in the fact that baptism appears in the first question, and the death of Christ appears in the second. Paul makes no link between the two. He does not say that baptism unites to Christ's death, as he did in Romans 6.

Indeed, I repeat, he does not *say* anything at all. He *asks* two rhetorical questions. Rhetorical? Yes, indeed. A rhetorical question is 'a question asked not for information but to produce an effect'.[3] That is to say, Paul asks these two questions not because he is ignorant and doesn't know the answer – indeed, he is expecting no answer at all (except 'No!') – but because he wants to make his point in a dramatic, open-and-shut way.

And what is his point? It stands out a mile. There is a common factor in the two questions. And it most definitely is not sacramentalism! The common factor is Paul himself: 'Was *Paul* crucified for you? Or were you baptised in the name of *Paul*?' And,

---

[3] *The Concise.*

as I say, the obvious answer to both questions is: No! And, even more obvious – and important – the answer to both questions is... Christ! By asking these two rhetorical questions, Paul makes the Corinthians think about Christ. And this is precisely what he wants.

Furthermore, while sacramentalism has no place at all in the context, division at Corinth is absolutely fundamental to it (1 Cor. 1:10-17). The apostle does not mince his words. You Corinthians are divided. It has to stop. At once! He begins with a plea: 'Now I plead with you, brethren, by the name of our Lord Jesus Christ, that you all speak the same thing, and that there be no divisions among you'. He quickly gets to the heart of the matter. You are making much – far too much – of men. Men? Men! What's all this talk about *men*! Above all, the apostle is enraged at the thought that the Corinthians could divide over 'Paul or Christ'. Paul or Christ? Whatever next! It is Christ! Christ! Christ – not Paul – was crucified for you. It was in Christ's name – not Paul's – that you were baptised. Get this into your heads and hearts. It is Christ! Christ! Stop this inflated talk about men!

This is the context for these questions. The notion that sacramentalism is the link between them is risible. *Christ* is the apostle's theme.

There is no difficulty in proving it. Even in the third chapter, it is still on his heart. Pulling no punches, he tells the Corinthians: 'You are still carnal'. In what way? Just this:

When one says: 'I am of Paul', and another: 'I am of Apollos', are you not carnal? Who then is Paul, and who is Apollos, but ministers through whom you believed, as the Lord gave to each one? I planted, Apollos watered, but God gave the increase. So then neither he who plants is anything, nor he who waters, but God who gives the increase.

He comes to the climax:

No other foundation can anyone lay than that which is laid, which is Jesus Christ... Therefore let no one boast in men. For all things are yours: whether Paul or Apollos or Cephas, or the world or life or death, or things present or things to come – all are yours. And you are Christ's, and Christ is God's (1 Cor. 3:3-7,11,21-23).

And lest the Corinthians should still not get the point, the apostle tells them yet again:

These things, brethren, I have figuratively[4] transferred to myself and Apollos for your sakes, that you may learn in us not to think beyond what is written, that none of you may be puffed up [arrogant] on behalf of one against the other (1 Cor. 4:6).

And as he goes on to the end of his letter, the apostle keeps up the theme. Which is? 'Christ... Christ... our Lord Jesus Christ... Christ Jesus'. In short: 'Christ is all' (Col. 3:11).[5] *This* is the context for Paul's two questions. Not baptism!

The point is further strengthened by noting that the apostle asks *three* questions, not two. Before he reaches numbers two and three, he has already opened in a most peremptory way. You can hear the challenge in his voice, you can weigh the punch and feel the bark of his words: 'Is Christ divided?' And this first question clinches the matter. On the sacramentalist view it plays no part whatsoever. But, taking the line I have set out, it is all of a piece: 'Is *Christ* divided? Was *Paul* crucified for you? Or were you baptised in the name of *Paul*?' 'Christ is all', I say – *this* is Paul's point. In my mind's eye, I can see him thumping the table, or punching the air, as he raps out his questions, driving home his point. And that point, as I noted in the previous chapter,[6] is not sacramentalism. Not at all. It is allegiance – allegiance, not to men but to Christ.

So why do I raise the issue now? Why here? What has it to do with the subject in hand? That is, what has it to do with sacramentalism? Nothing! Nothing at all! So why raise the issue? I do so only because some sacramentalists (both Baptist and infant-baptiser) try to make far more of the verse than is justified. If ever a non-existent, non-sacramental mole-hill was made out to be a sacramental mountain, this is it. Take Beasley-Murray, for instance:

The association imparting Christ as a gift, crucifixion, and baptism, is in harmony with what we have already learned of Paul's teaching in the cardinal baptismal passages [that is, the sacramentalist view of those passages].[7]

---

[4] Paul had drawn illustration from the farmer and the builder.

[5] I shall have more to say on this theme in my *The Pastor: Does He Exist?*.

[6] See the notes connected with Badke's work.

[7] Beasley-Murray: *Baptism in the New Testament* p177.

And the infant baptiser Cullmann certainly did not risk understating his conclusion:

In 1 Corinthians 1:13... baptism is clearly conceived as participation in the cross of Christ... Here the two expressions 'you were baptised' and 'another was crucified for you' are treated as synonymous.[8]

If so, the sacramentalist's case is proved.

But is it 'clearly conceived' that Paul in this verse is saying that to be baptised in water is to participate in the death of Christ? Is that what Paul is saying?

Certainly not! As a matter of fact, as I have observed, the apostle doesn't *say* anything. No! He *asks* two (three) rhetorical questions.[9] It may be a small point, but it is, nevertheless, the truth! And to argue so dogmatically from the juxtaposition of two (three) rhetorical questions, would seem, to say the least, to be going just a little beyond the evidence!

Indeed, Cullmann was flying in the face of the evidence. In the context – see below – Paul quite clearly distinguishes between baptism and the crucifixion (especially, the preaching of it).

Moreover, if Cullman was right, and Paul has linked baptism and the death of Christ – indeed, treated them as 'synonymous' – I find it incredible that he, Paul, could go on – and go on so quickly, hardly drawing breath – to state: 'Christ did not send me to baptise' (1 Cor. 1:17).[10]

According to sacramentalists, we have to believe, apparently, that although baptism accomplishes so very much, the apostle

---

[8] Fee: *1 Corinthians* p61.

[9] As I have said, I freely admit, of course, that by rapping out these three questions, the apostle is, in fact, hammering home his point. Nevertheless, that point is not baptism, but Christ: Christ is all. Christ – not man!

[10] James D.G.Dunn was far too cautious: 'While the association of the two questions... is suggestive, any link between the event of the cross and that of baptism must be based on firmer ground than [1 Cor.] 1:13 affords' (Fee: *1 Corinthians* p61). As a matter of fact, Paul asks three questions, linking all three – and, as I have explained, he tells us what that link is: All our salvation from beginning to end is in and through Christ and not men. Sacramentalism is a million miles away from the passage. So let us stick with what the apostle actually says, and not put words in his mouth. Or, to speak bluntly, stop putting absurdities in his mouth.

rejoiced that Christ did not use him in that work but gave him a lesser task to perform! I, for one, cannot believe it! The anti-climax is fatal to the attempt to make the Baptist-sacramental case based on these two (three) questions.

* * *

Now for the passage itself; in particular, verses 14-17. Before I come to details, let me look at some general comments made by sacramentalists. They make interesting reading.

Beasley-Murray:

If this [passage] is not a minimising of the significance of baptism, it seems perilously close to it. Nevertheless, it is generally recognised that so to read this utterance is to abuse it.

I agree. Paul is not minimising baptism. But that is where my agreement with Beasley-Murray grinds to a halt. He immediately added a few more words: 'It is generally recognised that so to read this utterance is to abuse it *and to misunderstand Paul's sacramental teaching*'. Here I part company with Beasley-Murray. For all the reasons I have set out, I do not accept that Paul's teaching is sacramental.

Then came an intriguing remark from Beasley-Murray:

It may be affirmed with confidence that the man who formulated the baptismal theology reflected in Romans 6:1-11; Galatians 3:26-27; Colossians 2:11-12, did not think lightly of baptism, and would not have wished to give the impression that he did.[11]

There is, of course, a big assumption behind this. Beasley-Murray was taking it for granted that the baptism in all the passages he listed is water baptism. I have set out my reasons for disputing this. Leaving that to one side, the intriguing question is this: How do the *sacramentalists* explain Paul's statement in this Corinthian passage? That is, since they believe that he was speaking so highly of water baptism in the other cardinal passages, yet so differently in this passage, how do *they* explain it? In Romans 6, Galatians 3 and Colossians 2, Paul could not attribute more to baptism than he did;

---

[11] Beasley-Murray: 'Baptism in the New Testament' pp178-179, emphasis mine.

union with Christ, no less! What more could he say? I agree with the sacramentalists, the cardinal baptismal passages do teach baptismal union with Christ. Yes! Indeed, as I have noted, I go further than most Baptist sacramentalists seem prepared to go. Those passages, I say, speak absolutely of the bond – the correlation – between baptism and union with Christ. But – and what a but! – those passages speak of *spiritual* baptism, baptism by the Holy Spirit. In contradistinction, 1 Corinthians 1:13-17 speaks of *water* baptism. Therefore *I* see no difficulty in reconciling 1 Corinthians 1:13-17 (water baptism) with those other passages which speak of spiritual baptism; indeed, no reconciliation is required. They are speaking of two different baptisms. But how do *sacramentalists* reconcile them? In light of their enormous claims for water baptism in the 'cardinal passages', how do *they* face up to this particular passage? Reconcile this passage with the cardinal passages, they must. They cannot dodge the issue.

Fowler made a general comment worthy of note. This passage, said Fowler:

Seems to contradict this [so-called] Pauline respect for the significance of baptism [that is, as alleged by sacramentalists]. [Here] Paul draws a sharp distinction between baptism and the preaching of the gospel... Baptists have argued that although it may appear that Paul was indifferent to the [ordinance], this is a false inference.

Quite. I certainly do not argue that Paul was indifferent to baptism. Not at all! But all this is failing to get to grips with the passage. It is all very well talking about what Paul did *not* say, what Paul did *not* mean, what we should *not* deduce from his words. Very good. But what *did* he say, what *did* he mean, and what *should* we deduce? What do the sacramentalists say about *that*?[12]

Fowler: 'At most the text is a reminder that the gospel embodied in baptism is the heart of the matter, not baptism *per se*'?[13] Really? Is this the *most* that we can deduce from Paul's statement? I think not. I agree with the sentiment, of course. It *is* the gospel – indeed, it is Christ himself, as the context makes clear – not baptism, which is

---

[12] I remind you, reader, that the influential sacramentalist book, *Christian Baptism*, did not even mention the passage!

[13] Fowler: *More* p162.

at 'the heart of the matter'. But I think we can go further than Fowler allowed.

Fowler argued that it was 'a little local difficulty' which prompted Paul's extended statement on baptism in this passage; hence, he seemed to imply, we should not overstretch the apostle's remarks.[14] Oh? While I certainly concur that we should not read more into (or out of) any passage than is justified,[15] Fowler's premise was quite wrong. He failed to recognise the way in which Paul frequently handled things like this. True enough, he often opened with 'a little local difficulty', but, in dealing with that, he would take the opportunity to set out massive principles of universal consequence which apply right throughout the gospel age. I am convinced, it goes without saying, that the Holy Spirit was directing him in this vital work, in accordance with Christ's promise (John 14:26; 16:13; see 1 Cor. 2:12-13).

Let me illustrate. What about 1 Corinthians for a start? Take chapters 3 and 4, where the apostle started with quarrels at Corinth; chapter 5 and its problem of incest at Corinth; chapter 6 and its legal wrangles; chapter 7 and its marriage issues; chapters 8 and 9 and whether or not to eat meat bought in the shambles (the meat market with its connection to idol worship); chapter 10 and its episode from Israel's history; chapters 12, 13 and 14 and the abuse of spiritual gifts; chapter 15 and its misunderstandings about the resurrection; chapter 16:1-2 and the issue of money. And see how in 2 Corinthians 1:12 – 2:4, criticism over Paul's change of plans led him to discourse on the faithfulness of God in his word; and so on. All these passages started life with Paul dealing with 'local difficulties' at Corinth. But who, when thinking about Paul's

---

[14] 'Although some use this text to modify the force of the other baptismal references in Paul's letters, this is not the only solution. The apparent disparagement of baptism is stated in the context of Paul's anguish over divisions within the church at Corinth' (Fowler: *More* p162). As for my 'solution', as I have made clear, it is to observe that 1 Cor. 1:13-17 speaks of water baptism, while the other passages at issue speak of spiritual baptism.
[15] See my comments above on the way sacramentalists read far too much into (and out of) the last two of Paul's three questions in the passage.

deductions from these 'local' issues, would adopt Fowler's way of handling 1 Corinthians 1? Very few, I suspect.

Take two examples. *First*, take that which Paul said about church discipline in 1 Corinthians 5. His words apply to church discipline today – even though, in any particular case, the issue involved may not be precisely that which was local to Corinth nearly 2000 years ago. Paul was writing definitive Scripture for all time. That is the way to treat his arguments from these local problems.

Second, take 2 Corinthians 8 and 9. In course of dealing with a local issue – raising money at Corinth and Macedonia – Paul made one of the most glorious statements of the gospel: 'For you know the grace of our Lord Jesus Christ, that though he was rich, yet for your sakes he became poor, that you through his poverty might become rich' (2 Cor. 8:9). Do not miss the opening 'for'. This statement came directly out of a 'little local difficulty'. Now who would think of playing down this gospel statement because it first saw the light of day when Paul dealt with a problem at Corinth? Nobody! Why, then, should we do anything different with the apostle's comments on baptism in 1 Corinthians 1:13-17?

* * *

So, let's get down to the particulars of the passage.

I thank God that I baptised none of you except Crispus and Gaius, lest anyone should say that I had baptised in my own name. Yes, I also baptised the household of Stephanas. Besides, I do not know whether I baptised any other. For Christ did not send me to baptise, but to preach the gospel, not with wisdom of words, lest the cross of Christ should be made of no effect.

Beasley-Murray, trying to salvage as much as he could from a passage so obviously contrary to his sacramentalist position, spoke of Paul's 'relief that he had baptised few in Corinth' – in that he, Paul, was able to avoid any danger that those he had baptised might have too close a relationship with him. Beasley-Murray also thought that Paul was saying his task was to preach, and to leave baptising to others. Furthermore, the apostle wanted to encourage others to take part, and not hog it all himself. In other words, there is no general principle here after all. It was just that Paul, gazing at his navel, was musing over his own personal, limited concerns.

Let's pause. Beasley-Murray's argument strikes me as a man in desperate straits, clutching at straws. Beasley-Murray himself felt it, it seems, when he graciously continued:

Admitting all that... it yet remains true that 1 Corinthians 1:17 gives the impression that Paul subordinates the administration of baptism to the proclamation of the gospel.

It certainly does!

Nevertheless, grasping at another passing straw, Beasley-Murray went on:

That however is consistent with the nature of baptism itself. For the latter follows the proclamation of Christ, and draws its meaning from the gospel. This we saw to be implicit in the great commission. 'Make disciples of all the nations, baptising them...' presumes the priority of preaching the gospel and the necessity of faith... It could be said that Paul's insistence that he was sent to preach, rather than to baptise, reflected his consciousness of the essential priority of his work if there were to be any baptisms at all!

In short: 'Christ sent Paul to preach the gospel rather than to baptise'.[16]

Full marks for trying, I say, and making the best of a bad job. But that is what it is – making the best of a bad job. Preaching comes before baptism in the order of events! True enough, of course. But how such an obvious point fits the context, I am at a loss to discover.

Why not face up to the only possible conclusion? Preaching, not baptism, is the priority in the New Testament – and not just in the matter of time sequence, the order of events. According to the apostle, preaching has priority over baptism in a far deeper way than mere time. In the context of this particular passage, Paul is comparing – contrasting – preaching and baptism as to their power, their place, their weight, their relative importance... Reader, I am hunting for the right word. Paul is not talking about preaching preceding baptism in time only. He is saying that preaching and baptism are chalk and cheese when it comes to the business of

---

[16] Beasley-Murray: *Baptism in the New Testament* pp179-181. What now of the sacramentalist arguments on Matt. 28:19? See the previous chapter.

fetching sinners out of Adam and bringing them into Christ. Until you have converts, you can't baptise!

In the New Testament, preaching – not baptising – is the means God uses to call sinners to Christ, and apply the benefits of his redemption to them. Yes, indeed! That is what Paul said, and that is what Paul meant.

'I have begotten you through the gospel', Paul declared (1 Cor. 4:15). How does God bring this about? 'Of his own will he brought us forth by the word of truth' (Jas. 1:18). 'The word of truth' certainly means the Scriptures, the gospel (2 Cor. 6:7; Eph. 1:13; Col. 1:5; 2 Tim. 2:15; see also 1 Pet. 1:23 with Heb. 4:12). 'Faith comes by hearing, and hearing by the word of God' (Rom. 10:17).

But I think there is something more. 'Of his own will... the word of truth' also includes God's decree, his authoritative command – as his effective word at creation: 'God who commanded light to shine out of darkness... has shone in our hearts to give [us] the light of the knowledge of the glory of God in the face of Jesus Christ' (2 Cor. 4:6). In short, God uses the preaching of the gospel to regenerate and convert his elect – and he does it in some mysterious, but effective, way like in his fiat at creation: 'Let there be light' – 'and there was light' (Gen. 1:3).[17] 'The law of the LORD [which, in new-covenant terms, is the entire Scripture] is perfect, converting the soul' (Ps. 19:7). As Thomas Manton put it: 'Without grace I cannot be saved; without the word I cannot have grace... The divine grace does all; he begets us; but remember, it is by the word of truth'.[18]

This is why Paul majored on preaching. Preaching is the means God uses to bring sinners to salvation. Not baptism!

Let me offer some further evidence. First of all, glance at the context of Paul's statement in 1 Corinthians 1:13-17; that is, 1 Corinthians 1:1 – 4:21. What do we find? Baptism? Really? Leaving aside 1 Corinthians 1:13-17 for the moment, the suggestion is ludicrous. Paul is writing to the saints – sinners who have been called into union with Christ by regeneration leading to repentance and faith. (To cite individual verses would be superfluous; the entire passage is replete with the point). But how were the Corinthians regenerated? By baptism? As I say, the suggestion is ludicrous. The

---

[17] See Calvin: *Commentaries* Vol.17 Part 2 pp40-44; Johnstone pp82-95.
[18] Manton p119.

opening chapters of 1 Corinthians constitute the greatest declaration in Scripture of the priority of gospel preaching in the calling of sinners. Baptism? No! Not a whiff of a suggestion of it. Preaching? Yes! Just now, I said I agreed with the sacramentalists that Paul was not minimising baptism. Of course not. *But he was maximising preaching!* As he was in 1 Corinthians 15:1-15.

Then again, as he explained, although he had baptised so few of the Corinthians, he had been used to bring many of them to faith (1 Cor. 4:15). They had been baptised, yes, of course. But they were baptised only *after* they had heard him preach, and believed (Acts 18:8).

In light of all this, we need be in no doubt; we should be in doubt. For Paul, preaching and not baptism is the means God uses to bring sinners to a saving experience. Preaching, not baptism!

But it was true not only for Paul. It is true for all of us for all time. And it was the way Christ went about his work. The ultimate end and purpose of his coming into the world was, of course, to offer the one effectual propitiating sacrifice of himself upon the cross. But what was the main thrust and driving force of his life leading up to Calvary? He worked miracles, yes, but above all Jesus was a preacher. It is no accident that Mark opened his account of Christ thus: 'Jesus came to Galilee, preaching the gospel' (Mark 1:14). How did Luke record Christ's first works after his baptism and temptation? 'Then Jesus returned in the power of the Spirit to Galilee... and he taught in their synagogues... So he came to Nazareth... and as his custom was, he went into the synagogue on the sabbath day, and stood up to read... He closed the book... and he began to say to them...' (Luke 4:14-30). And Matthew's testimony could be taken as a summary of Christ's public ministry throughout Israel: 'Jesus went about... teaching in their synagogues, preaching the gospel' (Matt. 4:23). Of course Christ healed the sick. But *preaching* was his work. Christ was first and foremost a preacher. And as for baptism, as far as I can tell, he never baptised anyone; 'Jesus himself did not baptise' (John 4:2), is all we are told about it.

Preaching, therefore, not baptism, is the means God uses to regenerate sinners, bring them to repentance and faith and so to salvation. Baptism has no part in this. Therefore, baptism cannot be sacramental.[19]

Please do not misunderstand me, however. Preaching in itself is not saving. Sinners are not saved merely by attendance at gospel preaching. Nothing less than the 'ordinary' equivalent of Mark 16:20 will do: 'They went out and preached everywhere, the Lord working with them and confirming the word through the accompanying signs'. Above all, sinners have to hear the gospel *and believe* (Rom. 10:8-15). Looking back upon that experience, such sinners can say: 'Now our salvation is nearer than when we... believed' (Rom. 13:11).[20] Not – as a sacramentalist must: 'Now our salvation is nearer than when we... were baptised'.[21]

Getting back to 1 Corinthians 1:13-17, Fee, with consummate understatement: 'It seems clear from this passage that Paul does not understand baptism to effect salvation'.[22] Indeed, it does seem clear. But what an understatement.

Writing elsewhere, Fee got to grips with the passage:

Paul deliberately subordinates baptism to the proclamation of the gospel. This does not mean that he minimises baptism; what he will not allow is that it holds the same level of significance as the preaching of Christ... He specifically associates the reception of the Spirit with his proclamation of the gospel, not with baptism. In Paul's mind, baptism

---

[19] 'Luther reduces all sacraments strictly to one; [namely] faith in the word [of God]; that is, in the promises of God, confirmed to man by the death of his Son – other sacraments, as they are called, are no more than signs and emblems of those promises, instituted to encourage and confirm men's faith' (Brewer Vol.1 p600). Clarification is needed. Baptism confirms *the gospel*, not *us*. Sadly, Luther went back even from what he said here. See above for the way he, Zwingli and Calvin, although they all began well on baptism, when confronted by the biblical teaching of the Anabaptists, collapsed back into the medieval Roman system they had held before.

[20] I have left out '*first* believed' since 'first' is not in the Greek.

[21] In the Bible, the means of salvation is in the active – sinners repent and believe; but for the sacramentalist it is in the passive – 'were baptised'. If anyone is tempted to dismiss this vital distinction as a man of straw, he should re-read both the section on 'conversion as a process', and my *Infant*, and see how Reformed sacramentalists define conversion, draw assurance and seek to promote sanctification based on *passive-infant* baptism.

[22] Fee: *1 Corinthians* p63.

stands on a different level... as [a] response to [the] grace received through the Spirit's coming in connection with the hearing of faith at the time of proclamation. It is nearly unthinkable that Paul could speak so casually of baptism and of his having baptised only two of them (plus one household that he had to be reminded of!), if in fact he understood the Spirit to come at their baptism. [What is more,] in [1 Cor.] 2:1-5, he insists that the Spirit came on them precisely at the point of his ministry, through proclamation, which would hardly be true if it [the gift of the Spirit] came during baptism, since he baptised so few of them, one of whom he had actually forgotten about... One can scarcely imagine Paul to have argued the way he does in 1 Corinthians 1:13 – 2:5, if in fact the Spirit came on believers at baptism... [Take] Galatians 3:2-5... nothing in this text even remotely suggests that Paul presupposes this reception to have taken place at baptism; indeed, his argument loses its point if the reception of the Spirit were simply being transferred from one rite (circumcision) to another (baptism).[23] This could perhaps look like an inconclusive argument from silence were it not for the several texts in which Paul ties his converts' reception of the Spirit directly to his own proclamation of the gospel. For Paul, the Spirit came in the context of his preaching and of their hearing the gospel (1 Thess. 1:5; Rom. 15:16,18-19). By his own admission, he rarely engaged in the actual baptising of converts. Thus, it seems scarcely possible that Paul himself understood the reception of the Spirit to be in response to their baptism in water. For him it would have been exactly the opposite... What... this evidence... suggest[s] is that the close tie[24] of water baptism to the Spirit does not come from a close reading of Paul, but stems from reading back into Paul the later experience of the church.[25]

Fee was not quite strong enough here. 'It seems scarcely possible that Paul himself understood the reception of the Spirit to be in response to their baptism in water... What... this evidence... suggest[s]...'. Surely we can put it more dogmatically than that – and should put it more dogmatically. The passage utterly rules out the notion that water baptism conveys the Spirit. The evidence is incontrovertible.

---

[23] See my comments on Gal. 3:27 in the previous chapter. Fee was not saying the Spirit came through circumcision, of course.

[24] 'Close tie'. Interesting use by Fee. See the previous chapter for my comments on the weakness of this language by sacramentalists.

[25] Fee: *God's* pp862-863. 'The later experience of the church' – that is, the corruptions foisted on the church by Christendom.

Preaching, then, not baptism, was Paul's emphasis when, in the immediate context, he said: 'It pleased God through the foolishness of the message *preached* to save those who believe. For Jews request a sign, and Greeks seek after wisdom' – and, I cannot help observing, sacramentalists demand baptism – 'but we *preach* Christ crucified' (1 Cor. 1:21-23).

And this is not the only place. Paul forced the issue on the Galatians when he challenged them: 'Did you receive the Spirit by the works of the law' – and I cannot help accommodating the text: 'Did you receive the Spirit by baptism?' – 'or by the hearing of faith?' (Gal. 3:2). In all his instructions to Timothy and Titus – books so relevant for church practice – not once did the apostle mention baptism, but repeatedly referred to preaching and teaching (1 Tim. 1:3; 2:7; 3:2; 4:6,11,13,16; 5:1,17; 6:2-5,17; 2 Tim. 1:11; 2:2,14-15,25; 3:10,16; 4:2,17; Tit. 1:3,9,13; 2:1-10,12,15; 3:1,8-9; see also 1 Thess. 2, for instance).

I repeat the sentiment already expressed: I am not for a minute suggesting that the apostle minimised baptism, nor am I going back on the earlier extract from Spurgeon preaching on Ananias, but I am saying that sacramentalists give a place to baptism, give an efficacy to baptism, which is totally unwarranted by Scripture, and which flies in the face of this passage we are looking at. Whereas Paul maximises preaching, sacramentalists maximise baptism. But do not miss the difference. Paul is writing Scripture. If he maximises preaching, and sacramentalists do not, they must be distorting the apostolic model – and that must destroy their case.

Let me summarise: 1 Corinthians 1:13-17 is the only major passage in Paul's letters which deals with water baptism as far as it concerns the subject in hand. As such, it must play a very important role – indeed, the all-important role – in determining how we view the ordinance. From this passage, it is quite clear that preaching – not baptism – is that which God has established as the means of calling sinners to Christ. A huge, unbridgeable chasm yawns between Paul and the sacramentalists here. Sacramentalism is bound to reverse the roles of preaching and baptism. It is logically bound to reverse their order, too. But the reversal of the priority – let alone the order – of preaching and baptism, is fatal to sacramentalism in that it so plainly contradicts the apostle in this passage. Baptism, therefore, whatever else it is, cannot be sacramental. The sacramentalists must be wrong. 1 Corinthians 1:13-17 is conclusive. It is, indeed, the clinching passage.

If, despite this fact, sacramentalists have their way and sacramentalism gets a hold, then baptism must be in the driving seat. That being so, as I have argued, promiscuous infant baptism, at the earliest possible time for the baby, must inevitably follow. And it will be fatal to all who end up thinking they are saved because they have been baptised.

And this leads me to what I want to say by way of bringing this book to a conclusion.

Conclusion

In bringing this book to a conclusion, I want to move away from the history of Baptist sacramentalism, move away from looking at individual passages, to broaden the focus and glance at the overall New Testament picture. We need to stand back. The detailed study in which we have been engaged is essential, of course, but if we left it there, we would miss the whole picture. By concentrating on a few detached trees, we would miss the forest. And the forest is important.

What do I mean? Just this: When describing salvation and the way to it, does the New Testament – as a whole – speak of baptism? Or does it speak of preaching which leads to repentance and faith? What overall impression would a man from Mars get if he read the New Testament? Furthermore, sacramentalists admit the fewness of baptismal texts. How can this be accounted for if baptism assumes such importance as they claim? Again: Are there any passages – indeed, whole books – where salvation is ascribed to faith and repentance, with no mention of baptism? Of course there are. But, if the sacramentalists are right, this could not possibly be so. Such silence on baptism is deafening. Talk about the dog which didn't bark in the night![1]

W.T.Conner:

To interpret [those] passages [which, sacramentalists say, teach sacramentalism] literally – that is, in such a way as to make baptism a condition of salvation – is to make the New Testament fundamentally a self-contradictory book. This would introduce an inconsistency into the very heart of its doctrine of salvation. This is evident if we look at the numerous passages in the New Testament where it is plainly taught that the only conditions of salvation are spiritual. It is abundantly set forth in the New Testament that repentance and faith are the only conditions of salvation – conditions that are primarily and only spiritual. Salvation is a spiritual transaction and depends on spiritual conditions alone.[2]

---

[1] Once again, I am not belittling baptism in saying this, but just noting that saving faith and repentance – not baptism – is always the issue for the salvation of sinners.

[2] Fowler: *More* p204.

261

Just so. Sacramental baptism introduces 'an inconsistency into the very heart of [the] doctrine of salvation'. A serious charge indeed. And one I agree with.

But can it be right? Can I really argue that sacramental baptism ruins the doctrine of salvation (or justification) by faith?

Let me raise an objection. If sacramental baptism ruins the doctrine of salvation by faith, how is it, as Fowler asserted,[3] that, despite *their* sacramentalism, *Reformed* infant-baptisers have, down the centuries, been able to maintain that very doctrine? Surely this fact alone proves that a sacramental view of baptism does not threaten – let alone ruin – salvation by faith. So it is claimed.

Let me answer the objection. I will tackle it head-on. I will not mince my words but say at once that I do not accept the conclusion. Why not? Because it begs the question.

First, as I have shown, some Reformed teachers – a growing number, as far as I can tell – unashamedly assert baptismal regeneration, and claim (with some cogency, in my opinion) that this is consistent with their Reformed standards. And what else does baptismal regeneration do but ruin salvation by faith!

Leaving such teachers and their teaching to one side, I admit, of course, that in their Confessions, in their sermons, in their books, most Reformed infant-baptisers maintain salvation by faith. *That*, it would be utterly foolish to question, let alone deny. What is more, as I have explained, when, in their Confessions and books, Reformed teachers do make their strong claims for sacramental infant baptism, they almost always immediately make contradictory statements in terms of their usual 'qualifiers', to the effect that baptism does not certainly save. So far, so good, it might be thought. The doctrine of salvation by faith has not been compromised.

But this does not substantiate the objection. For, as I have also argued, how can we know how many, in Reformed congregations, believing the statements about the efficacy of baptism, have chosen to ignore the warnings, or have not understood them? We cannot tell. We simply cannot tell, I say. None of us can. And this includes the sacramentalists themselves. The day of judgement – and that day alone – will declare whether or not the sacramental view of infant

---

[3] Fowler: *More* p204.

baptism promulgated by the Reformed has led to any being deceived, or how many. On that great day, the question will not be whether the Confessions or the books were right! Every individual soul will be searched as to his or her personal saving repentance and faith in Christ, and the life lived as a consequence. Confessional statements, yes; but what about the sinner sitting in the pew? What does he take home with him?

I am not, I hasten to add, pre-judging the issue. Not at all. Indeed, my point is, sacramentalists must not pre-judge the issue! I am simply observing that the outcome of all our doctrines and practices (including mine) will be known absolutely only on the day of judgement.

I ask sacramentalists – not least Baptist sacramentalists – to bear this in mind. They do not always seem to do it. Take Fowler. He asserted that 'among the Reformation traditions, Lutheran theology has taught both the strongest form of justification by faith alone and the highest view of baptismal efficacy'. Very well. But it remains to be seen whether or not Fowler was right to go on to maintain that when people like me say that 'the idea that salvation by faith alone is incompatible' with this Lutheran sacramental view of baptism, that this 'is at least historical nonsense'.[4] From where I'm standing, I think it anything *but* 'historical nonsense'.[5] But we shall only find out the ultimate truth of the matter when the fire of the day of the Lord destroys the dross to leave the precious (1 Cor. 3:10-15). Speaking from where we are now, it is all a question of conviction based on faith. We all have to decide now whether we are building with gold or stubble. But the crucial test awaits *that* day. It is not merely a 'historical' question. We, ourselves, our doctrine and our practice, not only have to stand the test of history; we await God's searching verdict – which he will give on the great final day.

Now to contradict my opening paragraph to this chapter. Having taken a glance at the general panorama of the New Testament, there is one passage which, to my mind, towers above the rest, and must

---

[4] Fowler: *More* p204.
[5] In Lutheran sermons I have listened to (2010/11), I have heard no call for personal conviction of sin, no call for personal turning to Christ in repentant faith; only the repeated mantra – 'through holy baptism'.

dominate our overall view of this present discussion. I refer to Matthew 28:19-20. This passage, it seems to me, stands prominent in the New Testament – setting out, as it does, Christ's manifesto for the church in its efforts to spread the gospel. Having already looked at it in some detail, I now return to the verses in this general sense. I do so by recalling an earlier extract from Hodge:

The commission was: 'Go into all the world and preach the gospel to every creature'. This does not mean that baptism was not included, but it does mean that baptising was very inferior to preaching. It is subordinated in the very form of the commission: 'Go therefore, make disciples of all nations, baptising them' *etc.* The main thing was to make disciples; recognising them as such by baptism was subordinate, though commanded.

I now quote Hodge a little further. He went on to say:

During the apostolic age, and in the apostolical form of religion, truth stood immeasurably above external rites. The apostasy of the church consisted in making rites more important than truth. [In 1 Cor. 1:17] the apostle's manner of speaking of baptism in this connection as subordinate to preaching is, therefore, a wonder to those who are disposed unduly to exalt the sacraments.

Hodge concluded by saying: 'While therefore it is unscriptural to make baptism essential to salvation or a certain means of regeneration, it is nevertheless a dangerous act of disobedience to undervalue or neglect it'.[6] Quite! I should think so! Nothing I have said could be construed as playing down this ordinance of Christ. But my purpose now is to underline three of Hodge's statements:

---

[6] Hodge: *1 Corinthians* p17. I note, once again, the sacramentalist's hesitancy. Hodge was a Reformed sacramentalist. Why are sacramentalists loathe to stand by their convictions? Why all these qualifying adjectives? 'A certain means'? *A* certain means? A *certain* means? As I have pointed out several times already, if baptism is *a* means, it is *the* means; and if it is *the* means, it is *the certain* means. Of what? Of regeneration! So why don't sacramentalists assert it and have done with it? Let them put an end to their waffling! But with Hodge's main sentiment, I heartily agree. Indeed, this is my very point about baptism – it is an ordinance of Christ, and it is sinful disobedience for a professed believer to remain unbaptised. Even so, baptism is not saving!

First, 'the main thing was to make disciples; recognising them as such by baptism'. Baptism does not *make* disciples, please note; it *recognises* them, declares them to the world.

Secondly, in 1 Corinthians 1:17, 'the apostle's manner of speaking of baptism in this connection as subordinate to preaching is, therefore, a wonder to those who are disposed unduly to exalt the sacraments', the very thing sacramentalists are bound to do. First, the sacraments are made an effective accompaniment of preaching; then baptism becomes the more important; and, finally, like the outcome in the fable of the camel's nose, baptism installs itself comfortably in the warm, while preaching shivers in the cold outside the tent. This is what Baptist sacramentalism will lead to.

Thirdly, I repeat Hodge's just observation: 'The apostasy of the church consisted in making rites more important than truth'. Historically it was so with the Fathers, and has been ever since. And if Baptist sacramentalism triumphs, history will repeat itself among the Baptists.

As for the history of sacramentalism, let Verduin spell it out:

It was... inevitable that, with the coming of 'Christian sacralism', preaching was crowded aside by act. In the place of salvation by believing response to the preached word, came salvation by act, by sacramental manipulation. The two have been in competition with each other ever since. In sacramental Churches, preaching atrophies; in preaching churches, the sacraments [ordinances] are secondary. Attempts have been made to combine the two 'means of grace', but one or the other is always *primus inter pares* [top dog]. No Church has been able to achieve in practice the equality to which it in theory holds. As the one increases, the other decreases.

That's the history. But what of today? Verduin went on:

Just now [1964-1980] we witness a heightening of sacrament in many Protestant churches; this could be illustrative of what we say; the word has been discredited... Hence the sacrament receives the attention which once went to the word.[7]

---

[7] Verduin p136.

See my *Infant* for proof that this is going on among Reformed sacramentalists. I say this, even though I am sure it will be met with howls of protest. Are there not many fine Reformed preachers? Indeed there are, the latest in a long line stretching back 400 years or more. But I still say that sacramentalism and preaching are, in the final analysis, mutually contradictory. And the history of the past 1500 years makes it clear which of the two has the greater staying power in the struggle for mastery. What is more, current trends among the Reformed indicate the way the wind is blowing.

May I offer an observer's opinion? Have the Reformed, in the main, sublimated their sacramentalism down the years? I think so. But, as I have fully documented, in recent times the lid has been taken off, and Reformed teachers are now going back to their sources (Calvin, Westminster, and so on), and re-discovering their sacramentalism – which has been suppressed for so long. Throwing off their inhibitions, Reformed scholars, teachers, writers and preachers are beginning to promulgate their sacramentalism, unashamedly and with vigour – and increasingly so. Reformed congregations haven't begun to scratch the surface of what this will lead to. In my view, if the Reformed allow their sacramental logic to have full play, they will unleash the dire consequences I speak of here.

The same goes for sacramental Baptists. If they get their way, and Baptists swallow sacramentalism, they, too, will not be able to avoid the consequences. It is inevitable. Indeed, as I write it is going on. Full-blooded sacramentalism is on the agenda. In 2006, the Baptist sacramentalist, Barry Harvey wrote:

The God of Israel summons the church to a way of life and language that stands in marked contrast to the practices of the establishment. This life and language, however, is only evidenced by a people who have been gathered together by the Spirit, *principally through the sacramental celebrations of baptism and eucharist.* These signs and seals of God's rule... baptism and eucharist... are... not just the means but also the media of grace.[8]

---

[8] Harvey pp97,102, emphasis mine. Originally published in 2003; re-published in 2006.

Amazing words for a Baptist, are they not? 'Baptism and eucharist... are... the media of grace'? So, according to this Baptist, baptism communicates grace. Really?

One of the consequences of sacramentalism is that it will oust preaching. It is already doing so. Note the 'principally' in the above from Harvey: 'The Spirit' gathers together the elect 'principally through the sacramental celebrations of baptism and eucharist'. What place now for preaching? Not much, I should say. I therefore disagree with Haymes: 'A theology that is sacramental produces a strong theology of preaching... a non-sacramental theology diminishes preaching'.[9] Haymes could not be more wrong. History has proved, and will yet again prove him wrong. The truth is quite the opposite to what he asserted! Above all, for the reasons I have given, I am convinced that the New Testament disproves the notion that sacramentalism produces strong preaching. Paul (in 1 Cor. 1:10 – 2:16, in particular) could not speak in higher terms for preaching – and all without a hint of sacramentalism.

Now, as I have said, and said repeatedly, we have to make a choice. Either we think baptism is a sacrament, or we think it is not. Which is it? Baptism conveys grace, or it does not. It is one or the other. Reader, which do you think it is? Large consequences follow from the choice. Let me spell them out. Before I do, let me quote myself – words which I wrote right at the opening of this book: 'I do not look upon sacramentalism as a peripheral issue. Far from it. Sacramentalism is ruinous to the gospel. It is pernicious, a poison injected into the jugular of the Christian religion. And, as such, it is disastrous to the souls of men'.

Let me set out five ways in which this is so.

First, adopting the sacramentalist view will radically alter the way we address sinners, and how we hope to see them converted. Surely the New Testament way is by preaching the gospel – which the Spirit is pleased to use to regenerate and convert sinners. If sacramentalism wins the day, however, this will no longer be the case. The sacrament of baptism will inevitably take over from preaching the gospel. And not only shall we end up with a very

---

[9] Haymes p264.

different method to the New Testament, we shall end up with a very different result. Why, Pinnock even thought that 'those who have the living experience of the baptism in the Spirit often can communicate it to the seeker'.[10] I find this suggestion absolutely incredible. How can I, as a regenerate man, communicate – convey – regeneration to a natural man? By baptising him? If the impossible is possible – that I as a believer can communicate the Spirit to an unbeliever – surely it must play havoc with what we understand, from Scripture, by conversion, and the way to it. What place now for preaching?

John Howard Hinton:

Let it be supposed that there is introduced into the gospel system the element of baptismal regeneration, or the idea that baptism has an efficacy to confer spiritual benefits, and the whole scene is changed. Now the entire community is to be addressed from the first in language totally different. Instead of being solemnly told that they are sinners, and warned of the wrath to come,[11] they must be assured that in their baptism they were justified, and brought graciously by God into his family, while at the same time that most blessed change, spiritual regeneration, took place upon them.[12]

I agree.

In this regard Baillie raised a pertinent question for all sacramentalists. *A* pertinent question? *The* pertinent question:

Should we expect or demand, in the case of those who have been brought up from infancy within the Christian faith and fellowship and 'in the nurture and admonition of the Lord', a single decisive experience of readjustment such as can be called conversion? We must now try to answer that question as clearly as we can.

Quite! So what was Baillie's clear answer? This:

---

[10] Pinnock p17.

[11] There is far more to preaching the gospel to sinners than this, however. Inviting, commanding, exhorting, persuading them to trust Christ, must come into it. See my *Offer*; *Particular*; *Septimus Sears*.

[12] Fowler: *More* p79. For more on this fatal re-defining of conversion, and the contrast between the biblically *active*, and the sacramentally *passive*, means of salvation, see the chapters 'Baptist Sacramentalism – the Drivers' and 'The Clinching Passage'.

We shall all agree that nobody should or can be called a Christian until he has been adjusted to the new situation brought about by the coming of God to man in the flesh and by the preaching of the Christian gospel. On this all parties think alike.[13] The disagreement is only between those who hold that in the case of those brought up within the Christian Church this adjustment should normally be... 'a continuous process', gradually accomplishing itself as the child grows into adolescence and manhood... and those who affirm... that 'no one is, or should be called, a Christian', or has made a 'beginning of real Christian life', until a crisis of readjustment has been experienced by him.

Baillie left no room for doubt about his own view:

Real Christian life begins when an infant is received by baptism into the Christian community. Such an infant... is already a Christian infant... The desirable and proper course of events is that the seed of Christian life thus sown should mature steadily and gradually into Christian adolescence and manhood or womanhood. It is expected of every Christian child that, as he grows up, he should more and more become confirmed in the faith, sealing by his own deliberate decision the commitment which was made for him in his infancy... I should... very much deprecate any teaching which makes everything hinge upon a single conversional readjustment... Such teaching has had several unfortunate consequences.

Well, that's clear enough! I, for my part, argue the other way, and do so with all the power I can muster. The sacramental process-conversion notion has appalling consequences – even eternal consequences.

To go on. In support of his position, Baillie quoted Alec Vidler, speaking in 1938 on 'Do we need Conversion?':

Christian conversion is a process, a life-long process. It is not a sudden event that can be finished and done with. It is a gradual transformation of personality through the love of God in Christ.[14]

Here we have it! This is what sacramentalism leads to.

As I have shown, although – at present – they might still reject infant baptism (but for how long?), in company with all sacramentalists, Baptist sacramentalists must view – and do view – conversion as a process and not a crisis. And that process begins

---

[13] I hope so!
[14] Baillie pp100-112.

with water baptism. As a consequence, Baptist sacramentalists will not only have to re-define baptism and conversion, they will have to alter the way of addressing sinners. And radically! Instead of 'repent, believe and be baptised', sinners will be told to 'be baptised'. Indeed, as I have argued, promiscuous infant baptism will ultimately follow, so that sinners won't be addressed at all; the parents of infants will be told to 'have them baptised'.[15] And this for salvation. Where in the New Testament can support be found for *that*?

Secondly, following on from the first point, adopting the sacramentalist view will radically affect the way we determine who is or who is not regenerate.[16] I have already spelled out the consequences of infant baptism in this regard.[17] What now of *Baptist* sacramentalism? If you are in any doubt, reader, glance once again at the section on the re-defining of conversion in the earlier chapter on the drivers of Baptist sacramentalism. The outcome of the sacramentalist view of baptism must be (it is!) – when challenged as to their conversion – for sinners to say: 'I have been baptised'. Look at my remarks on Romans 13:11 in the previous chapter. And churches will have to (they do!) accept this statement of fact as evidence of regeneration, and receive such people, including infants, as members.

Thirdly, following on from the previous point, to adopt the sacramentalist view of baptism will have a far-reaching effect on continuing church life, church membership and church discipline. Just as the Fundamentalist rebuts all challenges to his lack of

---

[15] When my grandson was born, I was urged by a prominent Reformed preacher to 'get him under the covenant, brother – get him under the covenant!'. I had no intention of doing anything of the sort, of course. Even if I had wanted it, what right did I have to overrule the parents' wishes? I am glad to be able to record that, as I write, this very day, almost 17 years later, he is to be baptised (immersed) as a believer. By the way, wasn't he supposed to be already 'in the covenant' by reason of his birth?!? Hmm!

[16] And, of course, we must not forget the growing tendency to taboo this sort of question – all in the name of 'not judging others' – based on a misguided interpretation of Matt. 7:1.

[17] See my *Infant*.

spirituality – or downright disobedience to the law of Christ – by the claim: 'I made a decision', 'went forward', forty years ago, or whatever, so the sacramentalist will reply: 'But I have been baptised!'.[18]

Fourthly, to adopt the sacramentalist view of baptism will have a far-reaching effect on the way we address, and deal with, genuine saints. As I have shown, sacramentalists argue that a saint gets his assurance, resists temptation, and so on, by recalling his baptism. As I have also shown, this is completely at odds with the New Testament. Where, in Scripture, do we read the text: 'Remember your baptism!'? I have heard it preached by a prominent Strict Baptist minister, but I have never read it in the Bible. I do not for a moment deny that there is spiritual nourishment to be found in obedience to Christ in his ordinances, but let us be biblical in our talk – loose talk will soon lead to loose thinking, and worse. Take Freeman's closing climax to his chapter on the Lord's supper:

A sub-Zwinglian orthodoxy will not satisfy the soul's hunger. Yet there is a way from a low view of the Lord's supper as private devotion, obligatory ordinance, real absence and mere symbol to a rich communion worship of common prayer, life-giving practice, real presence and powerful signs. All God's people are invited to be nourished at the Lord's table where is spread a spiritual meal of divine grace to feed upon by faith. Come and dine![19]

Note the pejorative adjectives in the first half of the sentence, and the glowing ones in the last half. As I have said, taking the supper as a memorial need not be the same as making it meaningless.[20] More than that, I would like to know what scripture would justify the last invitation, command or exhortation. Note the subtle gloss. The gospel call to come to Christ is likened to coming to a feast (Isa. 55:1-3; Matt. 22:1-14; Luke 14:15-24; John 6:27–59; 7:37-39; Rev. 22:17). Where is this kind of language ever applied to Christ's

---

[18] What a contrast to the New Testament. See below. See my *Infant* for the man who rebuffed all gospel overtures by retorting: 'My father was in the covenant'. See the note just above.

[19] Freeman p210.

[20] See Newman p215 quoting George on the Anabaptists.

ordinances? I am not nit-picking. As I said, loose talk today leads to loose practice tomorrow, which leads to...

Fifthly, worst of all, in the end, sacramentalism takes away from Christ. Oh yes, it does! I can hear the howls of protest. Even so, I stand by what I have said. Sacramentalism takes away from Christ. Consider Rome – as the most highly developed of all the sacramental systems. Can you find Christ hidden by all the clutter of priestly paraphernalia, water-baptismal regeneration, the Mass, gaudy robes and buildings, incense, statues, Mariolatry and saint worship? And it all started with sacramentalism!

Leaving aside the Church of Rome – although, as I have shown, for those sharp-eyed enough to discern it as the ecumenical train thunders down the track, 'Rome and Beyond' is stamped on its destination-board – for regeneration, for assurance, for comfort, for spiritual nourishment, instead of looking to Christ, men will look to their baptism and the Lord's supper. In my *Infant* I have given abundant evidence of it among the Reformed. It will arise among the Baptists, if sacramentalism triumphs among them (us). And it is a tragic error. I remind you, reader of Grebel's words:

The Scripture describes baptism for us thus: That it signifies that, by faith and the blood of Christ, sins have been washed away for him who is baptised, changes his mind, and believes before and after; that it signifies that a man is dead and ought to be dead to sin and walk in newness of life and spirit, and that he shall certainly be saved if, according to this meaning, by inner baptism he lives his faith; so that water does not confirm or increase faith, as the scholars of Wittenberg say, and [does not] give very great comfort [nor] is it the final refuge on the death bed. Also baptism does not save, as Augustine, Tertullian, Theophylact and Cyprian have taught.[21]

In short, if we adopt a sacramentalist view of baptism, we shall have to change our hymn book: 'Nothing in my hand I bring – except my baptismal certificate'. More important, we shall have to change

---

[21] Grebel in G.H.Williams pp80-81. For Grebel, 'baptism signifies the forgiveness of sins, an inner transformation of mind and heart, and a pledge of a life of discipleship. He affirmed that the "water does not confirm or increase faith, as the scholars at Wittenberg say... Baptism does not save, as Augustine, Tertullian, Theophylact and Cyprian have taught"' (Estep: *Anabaptist* p151).

Romans 8:33-39 to answer the questions: 'Who shall bring a charge against God's elect... Who is he who condemns?... Who shall separate us from the love of Christ?', not in the way the apostle did: 'It is Christ', but by the blanket response: 'I have been baptised'.

Sacramentalism will lead to these five wretched consequences. Our addresses to sinners, our view of conversion, our concept of church life, of the way of the edification of believers, and, above all, of the glory of Christ, will all be grievously altered and diminished. Our views and concepts will become unbiblical. *We* shall become unbiblical. If we go down the sacramentalist route, we shall end up with a different gospel – a different gospel to that of the New Testament. To adopt the sacramentalist view of baptism will lead to Paul's strictures:

You are turning away... to a different gospel... There are some who trouble you and want to pervert the gospel of Christ.

I go further, as Paul does. With the apostle, I say:

If we, or an angel from heaven, preach any other gospel to you than what [the apostles] have preached to you, let him be accursed... I say again, if anyone preaches any other gospel to you than what you have received, let him be accursed (Gal. 1:6-9).

And, whatever precise explanation is adopted of Paul's words in Galatians 5:11-12 and 6:12, their relevance to the subject in hand is clear – to me, at least:

If I... preach circumcision... the offence of the cross has ceased. I could wish that those who trouble you would even cut themselves off... As many as desire to make a good showing in the flesh, these would compel you to be circumcised, only that they may not suffer persecution for the cross of Christ.

Paul was here tackling those who wanted to make circumcision a part of the gospel, and who were doing their utmost to promote the rite among the Galatians. He knew it was no peripheral matter. Therefore he wrote to the Galatians to put a stop to the dangerous – spiritually lethal – nonsense. Having expressed himself as forcefully as he knew how in writing his letter, as he drew to a close, sensing the issue might still hang in the balance, he pulled out all the stops in a last-ditch effort to clinch the vital point. Let me repeat his words. They bear repetition:

If I... preach circumcision... the offence of the cross has ceased. I could wish that those who trouble you would even cut themselves off... As many as desire to make a good showing in the flesh, these would compel you to be circumcised, only that they may not suffer persecution for the cross of Christ.

Leaving aside the mistaken connection many make between circumcision and baptism, the principles Paul set out in his final appeal to the Galatians resonate with what I say in this book. Sacramentalism, whether Reformed or Baptist, is toxic. The drive toward it is, as I said at the start, horrific to me. I am not casting aspersions on the motives of those I oppose, but their teaching I do oppose. I am convinced that if sacramentalism wins the day, we shall end up with a very different gospel. The gospel of Christ carries offence with it. Sacramentalism – salvation by a ceremony – will do away with that offence. *And it will do away with salvation at the same time!* This is what Paul saw as the result of adopting circumcision. And this is why he was so vehement. Salvation by works or ceremony, or salvation by faith in Christ on the basis of grace – that is the choice I have set before you, reader. For nearly 2000 years, Paul's letter to the Galatians has played a pivotal role in maintaining the doctrine of justification by faith, and more.[22]

Of course, the gospel is offensive, offensive to the natural man. I am a condemned sinner. I cannot save myself. I can contribute nothing, do nothing, earn nothing, deserve nothing, merit nothing, observe nothing... to save myself. No priest, pastor or minister can do anything to me, or for me,[23] to save me. No amount of water, no

---

[22] I will have more to say on this in my book on the law. I am convinced Galatians is about more than justification by faith. The motive for both justification and sanctification, the spur to it, the standard to be reached – none of these comes by the law. All comes by and in Christ. *That* is the theme of Galatians.

[23] See the letter printed in the *Evangelical Times*, October 1994. The letter from 'a sin-sick soul' was a virtual confession of sin to 'the pastor' with the urgent request that 'the pastor' should pray for this 'sin-sick soul'. The writer could not even address 'the pastor' by his name! The letter and what it represented boiled down to unadulterated priestcraft! Confession of sin to

mumbo jumbo, no rite can save me. I have to cast myself entirely and unreservedly by faith and in repentance upon the sacrificial death of Christ, his blood and righteousness, and trust myself completely to him, his death and resurrection, his intercession and coming again, to save and keep me and bring me to everlasting glory. And this, to the natural man, is offensive. He finds the gospel ridiculous (1 Cor. 1:23; 2:14). He hates it (Rom. 1:28; 8:7).

But... bring in the notion of priests and ministers, bring in sacramental water, bring in rite and ceremony, then 'the offence of the cross has ceased'. And if 'the offence of the cross has ceased', we are left with something other than the gospel. The fact is, unwelcome though it is to many to say it, unless we preach a Christ and a gospel which is offensive in the way I have described, we are failing to preach the gospel of Christ. And unless we have received the New Testament Christ through the New Testament gospel which is thus offensive, whatever else we have accepted, it is not the Christ, nor his gospel!

Offence! There is no way of avoiding 'offence'. If we are a friend of the world, we are an offence to God (Jas. 4:4). But if we are pleasing to God, then we are an offence to the world (John 15:19). Offence! How that word grates in many churches today! We live in times when making 'the offence of the cross to cease' has become a work of art. What am I talking about? Inclusivism. Inclusivism? What's that? It is perhaps the besetting curse of the churches today – inclusivism. I will not digress to expand on it here – but it is important! – so please see the extended note on p327.

The offence of the gospel! Paul closed his letter to the Galatians, speaking of how men in his day tried to get round 'the offence of the

---

'the pastor'? Desire for 'the pastor' to pray; could the man (or woman) not pray for himself? Christ was not mentioned once! And the man knew what was wrong in his life but instead of putting it right, he shuffled his responsibility onto God and 'the pastor'. The letter, and its publication, was an offence to all those who reject Popery, or it ought to have been. So this is what 'the pastor' business comes to. Pastor and priest are not so very different in spelling, and when men and women hold the kind of views illustrated by the letter just quoted, pastor and priest are virtually the same in more ways than mere spelling. See my forthcoming *The Pastor: Does He Exist?*.

cross'. They have been at it ever since. The apostle's words ring with relevance today.

Brown:

It is this which makes genuine Christianity so much disliked by natural men... – the insisting on relinquishing every ground of hope but one, and that one the death of Jesus Christ on a cross. Whenever Christianity has been so modified as to get quit of this most repulsive principle, it has ceased to excite very strongly the antipathies of natural men. But it is this doctrine which gives Christianity all its peculiar efficacy; and when 'the offence of the cross' ceases in any other way than by the eyes of the mind being opened to behold its glory, the triumph of Christianity ceases also. The Jews had no great objection that Jesus should be allowed to be the Messiah, if, *at the same time*, the law of Moses was admitted to be the only way of salvation; and there are multitudes who are ready enough to admit that Jesus was a divine messenger, if they may be but permitted to depend for salvation on anything but his obedience to death... The death of Jesus Christ on the cross, as the expiation of human guilt – the only ground of human hope, superseding everything else as the foundation of acceptance with God. It was this doctrine which was peculiarly unpalatable to the unbelieving Jews – leading, as it plainly did, to a renunciation of all the expiatory rites of the mosaic law as utterly useless, and indeed impious and criminal, if used as affording a method of obtaining the divine favour.

As a consequence: 'Let our religion... not [be] an external and ritual service, however simple or however imposing'.[24] In particular, let it not be water baptism!

Richard N.Longenecker: 'The preaching of circumcision is antithetical to and entirely nullifies the preaching of Christ crucified'. Ben Witherington III, quoting this, concluded:

The words [of Paul in Gal. 5:7-12]... show how passionately Paul cared about his converts, and how much he despised the actions of those who, in his view, were trying to corrupt them with a non-gospel (*cf.* the similar language in Phil. 3:2-3). He knows that his audience has a choice whether to follow their advice or his, and the decision now hangs in the balance. Therefore all the rhetorical stops must be pulled out to try and persuade the Galatians to pursue a certain [the right] course.[25]

---

[24] Brown: *Galatians* pp278,359-360,362 emphasis mine.
[25] Witherington pp374-375.

Reader, too big for my boots I may be – but that is precisely the pressure I feel, and it is why I have written as I have. I do not apologise for my strong language. Not at all! I feel the force of the words I chose as the epigraph for this work: 'Blow the trumpet in Zion, and sound an alarm in my holy mountain!' (Joel 2:1). 'If the trumpet makes an uncertain sound, who will prepare himself for battle?' (1 Cor. 14:8). I have not taken up my pen to dispute over mere words. I have not been trying to score points in some kind of theological chess game. Far from it! I have been contending as earnestly as I know how 'for the faith which was once for all delivered to the saints' (Jude 3). I have been contending for the souls of sinners and their eternal welfare. Reader, I have been contending for the everlasting good of *your* soul.

Let me stress Witherington's words: Paul was afraid that false teachers would 'corrupt [the believers in Galatia] with a non-gospel'. Indeed, said Witherington, the apostle 'despised the actions' of those false teachers. James Kidwell Popham: 'Error in doctrine produces error in practice'.[26] In particular, sacramental baptism is an error – a grievous error – with eternal consequences.

That is why I have written, and why I have written in the way that I have.

To bring this volume to a close, let me set out, in the words of Scripture (in an eclectic translation), the issue which lies at the root of all this:

How then can a man be righteous before God?... A righteousness from God... has been made known... This righteousness from God comes through faith in Jesus Christ to all who believe... All [who believe]... are justified freely by his grace through the redemption that came by Christ Jesus, whom God displayed publicly as a propitiatory sacrifice by his blood, through faith... He did it to demonstrate his justice or righteousness at the present time, so as to be just and the justifier of the one who has faith in Jesus... 'Abraham believed God, and it was accounted to him as righteousness'... The words, 'it was accounted to him', were written not for him alone, that it was imputed to him, but also for us, to whom God will impute righteousness – for us who believe in him who raised Jesus our Lord from the dead... Therefore, since we have been justified through faith, we have peace with God

---

[26] *Gospel Standard* 1929 p125.

through our Lord Jesus Christ, through whom we have gained access by faith into this grace in which we now stand... For just as through the disobedience of the one man [that is, Adam] the many were made sinners, so also through the obedience of the one man [that is, Christ] the many will be made righteous... Don't you know that all of us who were baptised into Christ Jesus were baptised into his death? We were therefore buried with him through baptism into death in order that, just as Christ was raised from the dead through the glory of the Father, we too may live a new life... Therefore, there is now no condemnation for those who are in Christ Jesus.[27]

The choice, as I have said repeatedly, is clear. Here we have the most vital question of all: 'How then can a man be righteous before God?' Reader, I must put it personally to you: 'How then can *you* be righteous before God?'

At the heart of the New Testament answer to this most vital of all questions – lies baptism. Baptism? Yes, baptism. Read the extract again. Christ has accomplished the necessary redemption, he has offered the propitiatory sacrifice to his Father, and God is satisfied. 'Therefore, there is now no condemnation for those who are in Christ Jesus'. Yes, but how does the sinner receive the benefit? By faith, of course! Yes, it is by faith, but, more precisely, it is by union with Christ through faith. So how does the sinner become united to Christ? By faith, yes. But more precisely, through baptism. Baptism unites to Christ? Yes indeed:

Don't you know that all of us who were baptised into Christ Jesus were baptised into his death? We were therefore buried with him through baptism into death in order that, just as Christ was raised from the dead through the glory of the Father, we too may live a new life.

But we must be clear. Let me stress it even more: ***But we must be clear***. Baptism unites to Christ. There is no sign or symbol in any of this. The sinner is by nature under the wrath of God; *this* is no symbol. Christ did propitiate the wrath of his Father and accomplish redemption; *this* is no symbol. The sinner who believes is justified; *this* is no symbol. None of it symbolic. All of it literal, real, actual, spiritual.

---

[27] Job 25:4; Rom. 3:21-26; 4:3,23-24; 5:1,19; 6:3-4; 8:1.

The same goes for the lynchpin in all this – baptism. Baptism cannot be a symbol here. It must be literal, real, actual, spiritual.

So, it must be a sacrament! No, not at all! With the utmost vigour I can marshal, baptism is not a sacrament! If to introduce water baptism as a symbol in this chain of argument is ludicrous – as it is – then to introduce water baptism as a sacramental rite is equally ludicrous. Water baptism is not in view here at all. The baptism Paul speaks of must be – can only be – an effective baptism. Not a symbol. Not a sacrament. And that real, spiritual baptism can only be the baptism with/in/by the Spirit:

Don't you know that all of us who were baptised into Christ Jesus were baptised into his death? We were therefore buried with him through baptism into death in order that, just as Christ was raised from the dead through the glory of the Father, we too may live a new life.

Surely Paul was speaking of regeneration and union with Christ by the Holy Spirit – without any thought of water.

Nevertheless, the choice, I say it yet again, is clear cut. The baptism in question unites to Christ, and therefore brings the sinner into all the benefits of Christ's redemption. If this is water baptism, then water baptism is the great essential. Let us preach it as such. Let us water-baptise as many as we can to unite them to the Lamb. Faith? Yes, of course, let us preach for faith. But, above all, let us preach for water baptism. We must! And let us assure all who are water baptised that they are for ever justified, and free from condemnation. *That is, if the baptism is water baptism.*

But if the baptism is spiritual baptism... ***and it is***... then let us preach the necessity of regeneration by the Spirit, the necessity of repentance towards God and faith in our Lord Jesus Christ, with all the assurance that he who is regenerated and trusts Christ in repentant faith is for ever united to the Lamb, and is justified – and justified without the slightest quibble or question. Having trusted Christ, then, and only then, should that believing sinner be water-baptised – not as a sacrament to make something happen, but as a symbol to declare what has happened to him. And all this in submission to Christ as Lord and Saviour.

As for me, I take the latter course. Reader, which is it for you?

Appendix

Thomas Helwys published *The Mystery of Iniquity* in 1612, having written it the year before. The copy I have used is that produced in 1935 by The Baptist Historical Society, being a replica of the original black-letter edition – indeed, a replica of the very copy presented by Helwys to king James. In the extracts which follow, I have transcribed this edition to the best of my ability, making, as usual, such changes in spelling and punctuation as necessary, without altering the sense. I have indicated where I have been unable to decipher the text.

Why have I devoted an Appendix to Helwys? For one thing, any work written by Helwys, which has any bearing on the subject in hand, must be of interest. After all, Helwys was one of the original early 17th-century Baptists. What is more, in his *Mystery*, in part an answer to John Robinson, he used arguments which have resonance today.

But the main reason for this Appendix lies in the works of the Baptist sacramentalists I am opposing. As I noted when dealing with the way Baptist sacramentalists try to appeal to 17th century history, Philip E.Thompson claimed Helwys showed a sacramental view of baptism in his *Mystery*. As I said, I dispute this. I find no trace of sacramentalism in it whatsoever. And so I want to let Helwys speak for himself – and at large. But before I let him loose, as it were, I would like to draw attention to the following points.

1. Although he used 'sacraments' when quoting others, Helwys himself spoke much of the 'ordinances of Christ'.

2. Helwys strongly denied that baptism is a seal.

3. When he talked of 'put on Christ by baptism' (Gal. 3:27), I am convinced Helwys meant to 'make a public profession of Christ', 'owning Christ before men'.[1]

---

[1] Fuller was of the same mind. Commenting on Gal. 3:27, he said: 'The allusion is to the putting on of apparel, as when one that enters into the service of a prince puts on his distinguishing attire; and the design of the

4. When Helwys spoke of 'regeneration and the new birth', he seemed to be distinguishing between the two. If so, he was, in my opinion, doing something similar to what Charles Stovel would do in the 19th century,[2] who thought regeneration is the secret inward work of God by his Spirit, and the new birth is the start of an open profession of Christ before men. I have indicated my disagreement

---

sacred writer is to remind those of them who had before professed the Jewish religion [or had been pagans], that by a solemn act of their own they had, as it were, put off Moses [or their paganism], and put on Christ. There is a putting on of Christ which is internal, and consists in relinquishing the former lusts, and being of the mind of Christ; but that which is here referred to appears to be an *open profession* of his name, to the renouncing of everything that stood in competition with him... The amount is: *That as many as were baptised in the primitive [apostolic] ages were voluntary agents, and submitted to this ordinance for the purpose of making a solemn and practical profession of the Christian faith...* Such, brothers, is the profession we have made. We have not only declared in words our repentance towards God, and faith towards our Lord Jesus Christ, but [we] have said the same things by our baptism... We have confessed him...'. Again: The 'putting on Christ' of 'Gal. 3:27... is analogous to a soldier on his enlisting into his [or her] Majesty's service putting on the military dress. The Scriptures lay great stress upon "confessing Christ's name before men" (Matt. 10:32); and baptism is one of the most distinguished ways of doing this. When a man becomes a believer in Christ, he confesses it usually in words to other believers; but the appointed way of confessing it openly to the world is by being baptised in his [that is, Christ's] name... Baptism is an act by which we declare before God, angels and men, that we yield ourselves to be the Lord's'. Again: 'Baptism is that divine ordinance by which we are said "to put on Christ", as the king's livery is put on by those who enter his service; and, by universal consent throughout the Christian world, is considered as the badge of a Christian. To admit a person into a... church without it, were equal to admitting one into a regiment who scrupled to wear the soldier's uniform, or to take the oath of allegiance' (Fuller: *Practical* p728, emphasis his; *Essays* pp854,857).

Excellent! But not the teaching of Gal. 3:27. As I have made clear, I am convinced the verse speaks of spiritual baptism, whereas Helwys and Fuller thought it speaks of water baptism. I disagree. I cannot see how water baptism marking a public profession of Christ would make a fitting climax to such a chapter. But both men were convinced that to 'put on Christ', in this verse, meant to 'make an open profession of Christ'. In other words, neither man was in the least sacramental on this point.

[2] See the main body of this book where I look at Stovel's views.

with this distinction; but the point is, in making this distinction, Helwys was not being a sacramentalist.

5. Helwys was not writing a treatise on baptism. Rather, he was answering Rome, the Puritans (particularly the Presbyterians), the Brownists and the Separatists – especially John Robinson, who, by arguing from the Old Testament, and making ridiculous comparison with Judah, Israel and the Philistines, distinguished between a true church, a false church and no church at all. By means of such 'logic', Robinson regarded the Churches of Rome and England as churches, though false and therefore defective. From this, Robinson argued that their baptism was valid, right in the essential matter, though not complete,[3] calling it a 'naked baptism'. Helwys, rightly

---

[3] This, of course, as I have explained, was pure Calvin (and Augustine). The Anabaptists denied Calvin's claim that baptism by Rome was a true baptism. 'Against these absurdities' – as Calvin dismissingly called the Anabaptist arguments – 'we shall be sufficiently fortified if we reflect that by [Roman] baptism we were initiated not into the name of any man, but into the name of the Father, and the Son, and the Holy Spirit and, therefore, that baptism is not of man, but of God, by whomsoever it may have been administered. Be it that those who baptised us were most ignorant of God and all piety, or were despisers, still they did not baptise us into a fellowship with their ignorance or sacrilege, but into the faith of Jesus Christ, because the name which they invoked was not their own but God's, nor did they baptise into any other name... The objection that baptism ought to be celebrated in the assembly of the godly [which Rome is not! – DG], does not prove that it loses its whole efficacy because it is partly defective'. And, right to the end, in his last and unfinished work, Calvin was still maintaining his stance on the acceptability of Roman baptism, even though performed in so corrupt a system: 'In the Papacy, such declension has grown up through many ages, that they have altogether denied God. Hence they have no connection with him, because they have corrupted his whole worship by their sacrilege, and their religion... differs in nothing from the corruptions of the heathen. And yet it is certain that a portion of God's covenant remains among them, because... God remains faithful... God's covenant with [the Jews] is [was?] not abolished, although the greater part of the people had utterly abandoned God. So also it must be said of the Papists... although with regard to themselves... they are without it [the covenant], and show by their obstinacy that they are the sworn enemies of God. Hence, it arises, that our baptism [which we received from the Papists] does not need renewal, because although the devil has long reigned

dismissing Robinson's basic threefold 'philosophy' (true, false and no church), argued that there is no such thing as a 'naked' baptism. Just because a baptism is carried out with Robinson's 'essentials' – water and the 'right' formula (Helwys argued there is no such 'formula') – this does not make it right. For a true, biblical baptism – the ordinance of Christ – the Holy Spirit must also be present:

And here is the true matter wherewith men must be washed; which is, water, and the Holy Ghost, that is pure from an evil conscience [that is, a conscience cleansed from sin and condemnation], and washed with water. Therefore, can you not [you cannot] divide the water and the

---

in the Papacy, yet he could not altogether extinguish God's grace; indeed, a Church is among them... The Church is indeed among them; that is, God has his Church there, but hidden and wonderfully preserved; but it does not follow that they are worthy of any honour; indeed, they are more detestable, because they ought to bear sons and daughters to God, but they bear them for the devil and for idols' (Calvin: *Institutes* Vol. 2 p521; see also pp313-314; *Commentaries* Vol.12 Part 1 pp120-121). See also Calvin: *Letters* pp215-216.

Pace Calvin, this is nothing but absurdity! – even though he was here following his mentor, Augustine. But Calvin, for once, fell out with Augustine over a corollary. The Donatists' view that 'bad ministers' make the sacraments ineffective, Beckwith dismissed as the 'error' which 'led Augustine to develop the *ex opere operato* teaching on the sacraments' (Beckwith p92) – which (that is, *ex opere operato*) Calvin abhorred. The important point I wish to make is this: In addition to Calvin's preoccupation with 'the minister' and 'the formula' – if an ordained man baptises using the right words, the baptism is effective (note the 'efficacy'), even if he does it in the Church of Rome – observe how Calvin here destroyed many of the arguments for infant baptism – a parent being a believer, the covenant, households – unless he was saying Rome comprised believers, men and women in the covenant. Of course he did not think that! 'They are without it... sworn enemies of God', he declared. In other words, by allowing – justifying – Roman baptism by an ordained minister using the right words, Calvin was, in fact, allowing – justifying – the promiscuous baptism of infants, regardless of the state of the parents – even to the extent that 'their religion... differs in nothing from the corruptions of the heathen'! *This* is the point which has to be faced by those who advocate Calvin's teaching on the 'sacraments'! And, of course, by accepting Roman baptism, he was gathering fuel for the ecumenical fire being fed by many of his followers today. I have little doubt they will eagerly and increasingly latch on to Calvin and Augustine in this!

Spirit in this baptism. Christ has joined them together, and he that denies washing, or is not washed with the Spirit, is not baptised; and he that denies washing, or is not washed with water, is not baptised, because we see that the baptism of Christ is [for a man] to be washed with water and the Holy Ghost.[4]

And as for infant baptism:

Under the old covenant, infants were circumcised in the flesh; so under the new covenant, [you allege] infants must be baptised in the flesh. What ignorance is this?... There is no such baptism in the New Testament, as baptism in the flesh... The baptism of the New Testament must be a spiritual baptism of water and the Spirit (John 3:5), with which baptism infants cannot be baptised... You confess that all infants must be regenerate and born again or else they cannot enter into the kingdom of heaven. And our Saviour Christ, the Saviour of us[?] all says, that they that are born again must 'be born of water and the Spirit'. To what end then is the baptising of infants? – they not being regenerate thereby.[5]

In saying this, Helwys was not being sacramental. Rather, he was maintaining that for a true baptism, a man must *first* have been regenerated by the Spirit (which is shown, of course, by repentance and saving faith), and *then* (and only then) be washed in water – and in that order! Leaving aside the order, Helwys argued, water alone, even with the 'right' formula as Robinson saw it, will not suffice. Infants, of course, who cannot show the necessary marks of regeneration, cannot be baptised.

6. Wheeler Robinson, in his 1935 'Introduction' to Helwys' book, drew no sacramental conclusion – which is inexplicable if he had found the slightest trace of sacramentalism in it. Such a reference would have been manna for the sacramentalist Wheeler Robinson. Wheeler Robinson's silence says more than that of Helwys.[6]

Before I quote at large from Helwys himself, consider this extract from Wheeler Robinson's 'Introduction':

---

[4] Helwys p139.
[5] Helwys p174.
[6] Note the date, 1935. See my look at history in the main body of this book.

The third part [of Helwys' book] (pp84-123) is directed against the inconsistencies of Puritanism. Why not follow out to its true issue – separation – the reformation you profess to seek? Your presbytery [Presbyterianism] is no better than prelacy... A true church must have a true government... but you rob Christ of his power by your false method of government. Leave your bondage! Come forth from your Egypt!

The fourth and longest part (pp123-212) deals with the Separatists themselves, and especially with the outstanding figure of John Robinson... The main point of the argument... [is] the inconsistency of retaining as the basis of church membership a baptism that had been derived from an admittedly false Church,[7] and the further inconsistency of baptising infants, incapable of the repentance and faith which the New Testament requires as a prior condition of baptism...[8]

It is important to remember that John Smyth – with whom Helwys had been closely associated – had drawn up the first Baptist Confession in 1609, which Confession had included:

The church of Christ is the society of believers who have been baptised after confession of faith and of sins, on which [society] the power of Christ has been bestowed... Baptism is the external symbol of the remission of sins, of death and renewal of life, and therefore does not belong to infants.[9]

From this, Wheeler Robinson[10] rightly argued:

---

[7] I draw attention to Wheeler Robinson's point. When talking about 'put on Christ' by baptism, Helwys was referring to church membership. See the earlier note.

[8] Wheeler Robinson: 'Introduction' vi-vii.

[9] 'The church of Christ is a company of the faithful, baptised after confession of sin and of faith, endowed with the power of Christ... The church of Christ has power delegated to themselves of announcing the word, administering the sacraments... Baptism is the external sign of the remission of sins, of dying and of being made alive, and therefore does not belong to infants... The Lord's supper is the external sign of the communion of Christ, and of the faithful among themselves by faith and love... The ministers of the church are, not only bishops (επισκοποι), to whom the power is given of dispensing both the word and the sacraments, but also deacons, men and widows, who attend to the affairs of the poor and sick brothers' (Lumpkin p101). Although this Confession spoke of 'sacraments', there isn't a trace of sacramentalism in it.

[10] Wheeler Robinson: 'Introduction' x-xii.

These two articles underlie the argument of Helwys in *The Mystery of Iniquity*, though he also criticises the Separatist acquiescence in *any* baptism received from a Church which they had subsequently repudiated. A somewhat similar controversy had disturbed the ancient [patristic] Church; was the baptism administered by schismatics to be regarded as valid? Cyprian of Carthage said: 'No'; Stephen of Rome said: 'Yes', and the latter view eventually prevailed.[11] Helwys was thus, without knowing it, on Cyprian's side so far as the present argument went. Your baptism, he says to the Separatists in general, is 'a worldly baptism brought out of the world, and not the baptism and ordinance of Christ'.[12] Thus you 'retain your first badge and chief mark of Babylon, which is your baptism'...[13] Helwys treats with contempt John Robinson's argument that there is a distinction between a false church and no church, since a false church is no church. Similarly, he rejects as a scholastic splitting of hairs the distinction between the essence of baptism (washing with water into the name of the Father [*etc.*]) and the particular circumstances of its administration.[14] If there is a true Anglican baptism, then there is a true Roman baptism; 'you all have brought... your baptism from Rome, and so are you all Christians and believers by succession from Rome'.[15] Thus Helwys clears the ground for what is really his main position – that baptism belongs to believers only. It is futile, he says, to claim that baptism is properly extended to the infant children of believers; in practice, it is given also to the infant children of unbelievers [that is, by you to Papists], and [in any case] Christians cannot beget Christians by [natural] generation.[16] It is equally idle to allege the parallel with circumcision, for that belongs to the old covenant which has been disannulled. Baptism, according to the teaching of the New Testament, was never intended for infants; *their* conscience cannot be purged by it, and they cannot amend their ways [repent] and believe before receiving it, as the New Testament requires. Why then baptise infants, if they are not regenerated by baptism?[17] The

---

[11] See my *Infant* for Augustine on this.
[12] See Helwys p125.
[13] See Helwys p127.
[14] See Helwys p140.
[15] See Helwys p157.
[16] See Helwys p172.
[17] A very important point. If – an enormous 'if', I might add – *if* infants are regenerated by baptism, then we have an excellent reason for baptising them; indeed, we *must* baptise them – and that as soon as possible. Moreover, if baptism does regenerate, we have the *only* reason for baptising them. Anything less than baptismal regeneration proves to be a hindrance,

true holy seal is that of the Spirit [not baptism], which is given to faith alone. No meritorious faith of the parents can be substituted for the faith of the baptised. The truth is that infant baptism saves the trouble of teaching and training; hence its popularity. You must repent of this sin of infant baptism before you yourselves can be forgiven.[18]

As can be clearly seen, Wheeler Robinson saw no trace of sacramentalism in Helwys.

For these reasons, I say, Thompson was mistaken when he claimed Helwys as a sacramentalist.

Now to let Helwys speak for himself:

If you follow not Christ in the [way of] regeneration; that is, if you be not 'born again of water and of the Spirit, and so enter the kingdom of heaven', all is nothing, as you see by the example of [Nicodemus]. And Cornelius (Acts 10), if he had not been baptised 'with the Holy Ghost and with water', for all his prayers and alms, he had not, nor could not have entered into the kingdom of heaven...

This only is the door which Jesus Christ has set open for all to enter in at, that enter into his kingdom (John 3:5)... No other way of salvation has Christ appointed but that they first believe and be baptised (Mark 16:16)...

There is no way for them that are of the world, who are not in Christ, but enemies to Christ, as all that are of the world are, there is no other way to join and come to Christ, but only to 'amend their lives [repent], and be baptised' (Acts 2:38) and (Gal. 3:27): 'All that be baptised into Christ have put on Christ'... Infidels and unbelievers have no other way to come, and be joined to Christ, but only by believing and being baptised...[19]

Unbelievers... and... all infidels... there was, nor is, any way for you to join unto Christ, but to 'amend your lives [repent] and be baptised', and by 'baptism to put on Christ'... The Holy Ghost teaches that infidels or unbelievers must 'amend their lives [repent] and be baptised, and by baptism put on Christ'. And our Saviour Christ (Mark 16:16) giving a

---

producing confusion at the point of conversion. But it all depends on the 'if'. That is why there are only two stable positions – sacramental baptismal regeneration, or symbolic baptism. See my *Infant*.

[18] See Helwys p181.

[19] Helwys pp122,124. For John Robinson's reply to Thomas Helwys on the necessity or otherwise of baptism, see the extended note on p332.

general direction to his disciples to preach the gospel to all, gives likewise a general direction, what all unbelievers must do, if they will be saved. 'They must believe and be baptised'... We hope you will not say that there may be a church of unbaptised Christians...[20]

Now for Helwys on John Robinson's 'logic' in trying to distinguish between a false church and no church. Helwys:

The Spirit of God teach[es] us that a false church is no church, but a synagogue of Satan; and false apostles are no apostles; so then are false sacraments no sacraments, and 'false' and 'none' in God's ordinances are all one [that is, they are the same], and you cannot distinguish nor put a difference between them...[21]

Having thus showed you by evidence of truth that you [Mr Robinson], bringing your false baptism out of a false church (both which yourselves confess), your baptism is no baptism, and *that* false church [the Church of England or Rome] is no church. This being made plain, as the indifferent [unbiased, neutral?] may judge, we will try Mr Robinson's ground for this retained baptism [from the Church of England or Rome], who be will found to make haste to deceive with as many windings and turnings as - --,[22] and be not altogether trusting to bring his baptism from Israel [that is, the true church], he strives withal deceitful still to prove that their baptism is true in one respect, though brought from Babylon [that is, from the Church of England and Rome], and this matter he understands after this manner, in his book *Of Justification of Separation* pp184-185. He commends unto the reader a distinction of a twofold respect: Baptism, says Mr Robinson, is to be considered first nakedly [simply], and in the essential causes, the matter water. The simple washing with water in the name of the Father *etc.* These are the essential causes of Mr Robinson's naked baptism. In this respect, he confesses true baptism both in [the Church of] England and Rome. Mr Robinson, shall we speak angrily to you, and mourn for the hardness of your heart, and great blindness and ignorance? Have you lost the beginning of knowledge in the mystery of godliness? Is all light shut from your eyes, and all truth debarred from your understanding, that you should argue thus? That water, and washing, and words are the essential causes of matter of baptism! If you had known Christ, of whose baptism you pretend to speak, you would never have written

---

[20] Helwys pp125-126,129. Note 'a church'. This confirms my earlier comment. Helwys was talking about saving faith leading to public confession of Christ and joining a church.

[21] Helwys pp133-134.

[22] Badly printed in my copy. Could be 'a die'; today 'a dice'.

thus. Do you [not] know that Christ's kingdom is a *spiritual* kingdom, his ordinances *spiritual* ordinances? And will you confess this with your tongue, and with your tongue and deeds deny it? Which, that it may appear plainly you do, consider with yourself, and let all that seek the Lord in spirit and truth consider, with what understanding you can say, that *naked* water, washing and words, are the essential causes of a *spiritual* baptism! Thus do you spoil men through philosophy and vain deceit, in which iniquity you abound. Away with your naked respect, and be counselled to buy white raiment that you may be clothed, and that your vile nakedness do not appear. Know you not that all they that are baptised into Christ have put on Christ? And do you, with your philosophy to teach simple souls a naked baptism, and make it good with respects? The Lord give you grace to see your great evil herein, and the Lord deliver his poor people for these your deceitful ways, and so the Lord give them to learn, to know, from the word of God, that there is but one baptism of Christ (Eph. 4:5).[23] And that whosoever is baptised into Christ has put on, or is clothed with, Christ (Gal. 3:27), and therefore whosoever shall wash with your naked baptism shall be found naked at the day of Christ's appearing, though you piece it and patch it with green leaves. And for your effectual causes, lay down [set out] plainly what baptism you speak of, and you shall be convinced in yourself, as thus: If you say of Christ's baptism which is *spiritual*, that the essential matter thereof is *earthly* water, would not your ignorance easily appear? The like of your form [of baptism], if you should say that the form of *spiritual* baptism is *bodily* washing only [accompanied] with bare words, your own understanding would reprove you.[24] It were to be wished, and you have often been required to lay away your school terms [scholasticism] in the causes of God, whereby you do for the most part but hide the truth, and blind the eyes of the simple. How do you think the simple should understand you in the essential causes and matter, and form of baptism? Do the Scriptures show that any of the

---

[23] The point is, in Scripture there is only one water baptism – not two. There is no such thing as one water baptism which is 'naked', and another which is complete; one which is essentially right but wrong, and another which is wholly right. Similarly, there are not two sets of requirements (as infant baptisers claim), one for the baptism of infants and the other for the baptism of believers. The fact is, there is no such thing as one baptism for infants, and another for believing adults. *There is only one water baptism.* Rightly, Helwys made this point repeatedly.

[24] Helwys here was showing as plainly as could be that he was anti-sacramentalist – not merely non-sacramentalist. He did not allow anything spiritual to be made effective by water.

holy men did ever thus distinguish? If your art had been good and profitable, could not our Saviour Christ have used it for the manifestation of his truth, and would he not have endued his apostles with that gift? Indeed, the Lord endued them with the most excellent gifts, for the evident declaration of his truth, whereof logic and philosophy was none; which vain sciences, if you had not used, you could never have forged so many deceits as you have in your book. And now we desire you to know that the Scriptures teach not any baptism that is in one respect true, and in other respect false. There is no such thing in the whole word of God. These are but your own devices, wherein you divide Christ, to serve your own turns [ends] to deceive, persuading men that they are in one respect truly baptised, and in another respect falsely baptised, and if they will come and wash in your water, and join your societies [churches], you can make that part which was false, true. What popery is this to take upon you to dispense with the false administrations of the ordinances of Christ? Thus do you run into dark places while you forsake the lantern that should light your paths, which light of truth teaches you, and all men, that the baptism of Christ 'is the baptism of amendment of life [repentance], for the remission of sins' (Mark 1:4). And our Saviour Christ says: 'Except a man be born of water and the Spirit, he cannot enter the kingdom of God' (John 3[:5]); and: 'Let us draw near with a true heart in assurance of faith, our hearts being pure from an evil conscience [that is, a conscience cleansed from sin and condemnation], and washed in our bodies with pure water' (Heb. 10:22).

Here is the true baptism set down, which is the baptism of amendment of life for the remission of sins. And here is the true matter wherewith men must be washed; which is, water, and the Holy Ghost; that is, [they must be] pure from an evil conscience [that is, a conscience cleansed from sin and condemnation], and washed with water. Therefore, can you not [you cannot] divide the water and the Spirit in this baptism. Christ has joined them together, and he that denies washing, or is not washed with the Spirit, is not baptised; and he that denies washing, or is not washed with water, is not baptised, because we see that the baptism of Christ is [for a man] to be washed with water and the Holy Ghost.[25] And to take away [to remove, deal with] a subtle exception

---

[25] As I have explained, Helwys was not being sacramental. He was saying that water is not enough. The person being baptised must be regenerate before baptism. Thompson argued the wrong way round. It is not that the water leads to the Spirit, but, rather, that when a man has the Spirit, he may be (must be) baptised in water. The Spirit's work is the condition of baptism, not its consequence. Indeed, in Helwys' illustration which

[that you might raise against this teaching – the fact is, that] if a man be in prison, or any place, and be converted to the Lord, and would be baptised with water but cannot, he is accepted with God, 'who accepts the will for the deed' (2 Cor. 8:12), and herein is the Lord's mercy equal with his justice, for if a man's heart consent to evil, he is guilty before the Lord, although he do it not (Matt. 5:27-28).[26]

Thus much [have I written] to discover [that is, display] the great deceitfulness of your way in the first respect of your false distinction, wherein you would [try to] prove, only, the essential *matter* [of baptism] water, and [try to prove] washing with water, and words, [to be] the essential *form* [of baptism]. We pass by your form of words, because we think you will not stand upon it, in that you see there is no certain form of words held (Acts 10:48; 19:5) [that is, there no set formula laid out in Scripture for use in baptism]. And take this with you to consider of, that if there were any truth in your distinction and respect, then were *any* washing with water, with [that is, if accompanied by] those words, the true matter and form of Christ's baptism.[27] And if one [that is, if any] child baptised another with water and [repeated] those words, it is [that is, the baptised child has been baptised with the] true baptism in *that* respect [by use of the formula], and let that child come and join to you, and you can make it good in *all* respects. Pass not these things over as you have done, for you are not able to answer them with any true understanding from God's word. And so we come to your second respect...[28]

In the section which follows, Helwys answered what he called Robinson's 'second respect', in which he, Robinson, had alleged that neither the baptism of Rome or the Church of England was a truly complete baptism – it was only a 'naked' baptism. Robinson argued this because, he said, for a truly complete baptism it needs 'a lawful person by whom [the baptising is done], a right subject upon which [the baptism is carried out], a true communion wherein it [baptism] is to be administered and dispensed'. Robinson thought Rome and the Church of England failed in this respect and so, said

---

followed, he makes it abundantly clear that the essential thing is regeneration, not baptism.

[26] Helwys could not have been more plain. When push comes to shove, the only baptism that matters is spiritual baptism, not water baptism. This statement, on its own, proves that Helwys was no sacramentalist.

[27] Helwys was here showing that Robinson was getting close to *ex opere operato*. See my *Infant* for Calvin's wriggling on this hook.

[28] Helwys pp136-140, emphasis his.

Helwys, addressing Robinson: 'You do not approve it to be true baptism within Rome or [the Church of] England' in the second respect – though you do approve of it in the first respect.[29] So, according to Robinson, such a baptism was both true and false at one and the same time. Helwys rightly gave this short shrift:

The spirit of error leads you to justify that a baptism, where there is neither the 'Spirit of God, lawful minister, right subject, nor true communion', is the true baptism and ordinance of Christ in the essential parts thereof...[30]

If this your ground were true, then a Turk [a Muslim] baptising a Turk [a Muslim] with water, and [using] those words [that is, the so-called formula], in any assembly whatsoever, is the true baptism of Christ in the essential parts thereof. See what rocks you run upon, while you forsake the way of truth. It may now appear no marvel, though you would have baptism to be nakedly considered, you have made a most naked baptism and ordinance of Christ of it. First, where there is 'no Spirit of God, no lawful minister, no right party' to be baptised, 'no true communion', [yet you say] it may well be called a naked baptism, and [doing so] you [show yourself to be] a naked man[31] of all grace and godly understanding [because you continue] to maintain it for a true baptism and ordinance of Christ in any respect...[32]

And thus do you deceive natural men, and yourself, as in this point in hand, because with your carnal eyes and ears you see and hear water and washing, with such words, to be used in the administration of the Lord's baptism, therefore you, according to your natural understanding, judge these things to be the essential causes of spiritual baptism, and teach simple souls that these things being once truly done, they are not to be repeated or done again,[33] when they are wholly natural actions, and profanely done, as you confess, and therefore can in no respect be

---

[29] Helwys p140. For John Robinson's reply to Thomas Helwys on the 'double consideration' of baptism, see the extended note on p333.

[30] Helwys pp140-141.

[31] Helwys was indulging in ironical word play. Robinson proposed a 'naked' baptism – which is foolish. In proposing such a thing, Robinson was showing he was a 'naked' man – ignorant!

[32] Helwys p141.

[33] Echoes of Calvin and the Anabaptists over re-baptising. The Anabaptist denied they re-baptised – their first baptism was no baptism at all, they said. Calvin, unwilling to concede a micron on the issue, denied all re-baptism, even to the extent of allowing his prejudice to warp his exegesis of Scripture.

said to be the baptism of Christ, which is a wholly spiritual action, and ought holily to be performed and done. Thus do you make the ignorant believe that you can put the Spirit of grace into natural actions formerly and profanely done, and make the same actions spiritual and acceptable to God...[34]

This then is your rule (deny it if you can) – every washing with water in the name of the Father *etc.*, is the true baptism and ordinance of Christ, in the essential causes thereof, by whomsoever administered, and upon what person, or thing, soever. This may be good logic and philosophy, but this is blasphemous cursed doctrine in divinity...[35]

[Since, contrary to your teaching,] no distinction, nor difference can be made between a false church and no church, but they are both one... your whole false building is at once fallen to the ground, for a false church being no church, then [the Church of] England being by you adjudged to be a false church, is no church. So is your baptism brought out of no church; and your false baptism is no baptism. And thus shall the simplest among you be able to say to you: 'Is our baptism that we had in [the Church of] England a false baptism? Then is it no baptism, then are we not baptised'. And to this you shall never be able to answer them... [As] a false church is no church, as a false God is no God, a false Christ no Christ, a false apostle no apostle, so is a false ordinance no ordinance of Christ, a false baptism no baptism of Christ... God has no false ordinances...[36]

As we have said to you called Brownists in this point, so say we to [the Church of] England, and to the Presbyterians: If the Pope and they of that profession be believers in Christ Jesus, and be truly baptised into his name, then have you of [the Church of] England, and all the nations of the earth, sinned greatly to separate from Rome, in that you were all of one body, and members one of another, and, being believers in Christ Jesus, they are your brothers, and you ought to walk towards them as brothers, and ought not to separate from Rome as you have done, and build new churches every one upon several [various, different, separate] foundations. If you of [the Church of] England, and the Presbyterians, and you called Brownists, did make any conscience to walk by the rules of Christ herein, you would not walk towards Rome as you do. If you hold them believers in Christ Jesus, and truly baptised into his name – which if they be, then are all the scriptures that are applied against Rome to prove her Babylon... all these scriptures are misapplied to Rome – these cannot be applied to any persons or people that are

---

[34] Helwys pp142-143.
[35] Helwys p143.
[36] Helwys pp152-153.

believers in Christ Jesus, and have put on Christ by baptism. And there is no voice of the Lord that calls you to come out from believers in Christ Jesus. The Scriptures teach no such thing. Therefore, Brownists must return to the Church of England, and the Church of England and the Presbyterians must return to Rome, and be all sheep of one sheepfold, and repent of your unjust separation from the body whereof you were and are all members. We say 'are all members' because by one Spirit you are all baptised into one body, and though you say you are not of the body with the Church of Rome, are you therefore not of the body (1 Cor. 12:13,15)? You have and do all by one baptism put on Christ, and you all have brought... your baptism from Rome, and so are you all Christians and believers by succession from Rome, and you account Rome believers in Christ. Therefore, though you say you are not of one body with Rome, yet you are all members of one body with Rome.[37]

Helwys then moved on to Robinson's claims for infant baptism:

You of [the Church of] England, and the Presbyterians, sin, in accounting [the Church of] Rome and all them of that profession, Christians... These you account Christians upon this ground, and from this root, because when they are infants, they are washed with water in the name of the Father *etc.*, and you approve that they are baptised when they are infants because they are the seed of Christians and of the faithful.[38]

What words might we take to ourselves to make your madness, and the madness of the world, herein to appear, who pretend that all the seed of Christians and of the faithful are to be baptised only, and that under this pretence baptise, and approve of the baptism of all the seed of all the wicked and ungodly in these parts of the world [that is, Papists], indeed those that have been wicked to the third and fourth generation, and to the tenth generations enemies of God...[39] The seed of all these are baptised, and by reason of this baptism they are all held and accounted Christians by you... Do you set down a law to yourselves that the infants of the faithful are to be baptised, and do you approve of the baptising of the infants of the enemies of God [that is, Rome], that fight

---

[37] Helwys pp156-157.

[38] Helwys pp161-162.

[39] Excellent point. See my *Infant* on baptising infants on the basis of the covenant – a thousand generations. How do infant baptisers square this with Ex. 20:5?

against the Lamb, and the infants of some also that have not so much faith as the devils [– they, at least,] who believe and tremble?...[40]

The Church of England and the Presbyterians do allow of [that is, they accept] the baptising of all the infants of Rome, whose Pope and Cardinals and all their whole ministry that administer the baptism, and the parents of the infants that are baptised, and those infants being already come to be men of years, would destroy their kings, and princes and countries, and all of them, for professing Christ as they do – are *these* the seed of the faithful?... It is apparent [therefore]... whatsoever you say, that you hold that all infants – whether their parents be faithful or unbelievers – shall be baptised. Your rule then is, that both the seed of the faithful and unfaithful shall be baptised, and that is your practice. What warrant can be found for this? Or it is [that is, is it] no matter whether there be warrant or not?...[41]

Under the old covenant, infants were circumcised in the flesh; so [you allege] under the new covenant, infants must be baptised in the flesh. What ignorance is this?... There is no such baptism in the New Testament, as baptism in the flesh... The baptism of the New Testament must be a spiritual baptism of water and the Spirit (John 3:5), with which baptism infants cannot be baptised... You confess that all infants must be regenerate and born again or else they cannot enter into the kingdom of heaven. And our Saviour Christ, the Saviour of us[?] all says, that they that are born again must 'be born of water and the Spirit'. To what end then is the baptising of infants? – they not being regenerate thereby.[42]

Furthermore, you frame your consequence [reasoning] with these words: 'As infants were sealed with the seal of the covenant under the law, so they must be sealed with the seal of the covenant under the gospel'. We demand of you, is washing with water a seal? If it be a seal, it is a seal in the flesh. Where, then, is the print or impression thereof? It has none; therefore it can be no seal. Oh how blindly are the wise men of the world carried away in these things, contrary to all understanding, to imagine that washing an infant with water is a seal. Are they not vain inventions, without ground of Scripture, reason, or commonsense? Can you walk thus and think to please God? Will God be pleased with you when you walk in those ways that best please your own ends? Be not deceived, God will not hold you guiltless for thus using his name and ordinance in vain. If you will examine the New

---

[40] Helwys p162, emphasis his.
[41] Helwys p163. See earlier note on promiscuous infant baptism.
[42] Helwys p174. Helwys was making a powerful point. See earlier note on the reason for infant baptism.

Testament throughout, you shall find no seal, nor none sealed, but they that believe, 'who are sealed with the Holy Spirit of promise' (Eph. 1:13).[43] By which 'Holy Spirit we are all baptised into one body' (1 Cor. 12:13). And there is but 'one Spirit, one baptism, and one body' (Eph. 4:4-5). Which holy seal of the Spirit seeing infants cannot have, they cannot be baptised with that one baptism, into that one body.[44] So is your consequence [argument, reasoning] for the baptising of infants directly contrary to the covenant and ordinance of God; the covenant of the Lord being that they 'which believe and are baptised shall be saved', and the ordinance being 'the baptism of repentance for the remission of sins'...[45]

The covenant of the New Testament is a covenant of life and salvation only to all that believe and are baptised (Mark 16:16). The seal of that covenant must be answerable to that holy covenant; a seal of life and salvation only to them that believe and are baptised (Eph. 1:13-14; Rev. 2:17,28).[46] The apostle here [writing] to the Ephesians shows that 'after they believed, they were sealed with the Holy Spirit of promise'. Let all then confess, with whom there is any uprightness, that infants, who cannot believe – 'for faith comes by hearing, and hearing by the word of God' (Rom. 10:17) – cannot be sealed with the seal of this covenant. It is not in the power of parents to set this seal upon their infants, as it was in their [that is, the Jews in the old covenant] power to set the sign[47] of circumcision upon their flesh...[48]

---

[43] See my earlier works.

[44] Helwys was not saying that water baptism unites a man to Christ; rather, water baptism joins the believer to the body of Christ, the church, by public profession. Although I do not agree with Helwys – as I have made clear, I think the baptism of 1 Cor. 12:13 is spiritual baptism and *that* does unite to Christ – nevertheless, Helwys was far from being sacramental. After all, he was saying that until a man is sealed with the Spirit (which follows saving repentance and faith), he cannot be baptised.

[45] Helwys pp174-175.

[46] In other words, as above, until a man is sealed with the Spirit – which comes only after repentance and saving faith (Eph. 1:13) – he cannot be baptised. Naturally, this means that infants are excluded from baptism altogether.

[47] Note this – a 'sign' – Helwys deliberately avoided calling circumcision a seal for the Jews. For one man only – Abraham – is it ever said that circumcision was a seal. Far too many Baptists unthinkingly concede the unbiblical claim by infant baptisers that it was a seal for all Jews. In doing so, as I have explained elsewhere, they are allowing infant baptisers to go on to make unbiblical deductions based on the original unbiblical basis.

We confess with Mr Robinson that 'we are all by nature the children of wrath, conceived and born in sin', but we desire to know of Mr Robinson whether he holds not that all children are alike children of wrath, and alike begotten in sin? Or [does he think] that some parents confer grace by generation more than others?[49] And if they do not (as we assure ourselves you will confess), but that all infants are alike in themselves the children of wrath, then let us see, not after a sort, but directly, by what evidence of Scripture it can be proved (their sins being all alike in themselves) that God should execute the justice to *condemnation* upon some children, for the *sins* of their parents, and show mercy to *salvation* upon others for the *faith* of their parents, seeing the just God has said that 'everyone shall receive' salvation or condemnation 'according to that which *he* has done in the flesh', and not according to that which *his parents* have done... We pray Mr Robinson and all men to consider the words of the Lord (Ex. 20[:5]) who says 'he will visit the sins of the fathers upon the children of them that hate him', which hatred is shown by the breach of his commandments. But do infants hate God and break his commandments? You all confess with the prophet (Ezek. 18:14-17) (notwithstanding these words in Ex. 20[:5]): 'That if a wicked man beget a son that sees all his father's sins, which he has done, and fears, neither does such like, he shall surely live'. Then must you grant that the infants of wicked parents that do not such-like sin as their parents do, shall not die. [In other words, parents cannot transmit grace to their children.] Thus much to stop Mr Robinson...[50]

And now let the covenant of the Lord stand firm and good against all the adversaries thereof, which covenant is 'they which believe, and are baptised, shall be saved'. The words whereof being spoken by him that made it, do with authority convince to the consciences of all that will hear them, that this covenant is made only with them that 'believe and are baptised, which is with them that [are] of the faith of Abraham' (Rom. 4:12-16), and not they that are of the children of the flesh of Abraham... (Rom. 9:8). How ignorant and obstinate are men become, whom no word of God can persuade, but they *will* have the children of the *flesh* to be the children of the *promise*, and the seed. For they will have the seed of the faithful – that is all the children begotten of their bodies – to be the children of the promise, and the seed with whom the covenant is made, saying: 'The covenant is made with the faithful and their seed', meaning all the children begotten of the flesh. Yet as(?) the

---

[48] Helwys pp175-176.
[49] See my *Infant*.
[50] Helwys pp178-179, emphasis his.

apostle says: 'The children of the flesh are not the seed'. But the apostle's testimony will not serve the turn [that is, it will not convince those who are determined to baptise infants. Why not? Because] the Pope says it is not so; and the bishops and Presbyterians (having learned it of the Pope) say it is not so; and the Brownists (having learned it of the bishops) say it is not so. Here are many witnesses, and they have long and ancient custom, and the script[51] is fair to look upon, and pleasant to the eye and mind, that infants are begotten and born Christians. The most wicked and profane parents that are [alive in the world], like this well, that they be accounted to beget Christians, and that their children may be made members of the body of Christ, when they are new born. The best men like this well. And the worst like it well. This pleases all flesh in these parts of the world. There was never any one doctrine of Christ, nor of the apostles, that ever was so acceptable to all men.[52] It must needs be acceptable, because so good a thing is so easily come by. What a grievous thing it would be if one might not be a Christian, and member of Christ's body, before they had learned Christ, and to believe in him! This would trouble children if they should be forced to learn to know Christ before they could be admitted to be his disciples, and to be baptised! And this would be a great trouble to parents that their children should not be baptised before they had carefully 'brought them up in the instruction and information of the Lord'! And this would be a great burden to bishops and priests, if they should have none admitted members of their Church, until by their diligent and faithful preaching of the gospel, they were brought to knowledge, faith and repentance, and 'to amend their lives [repent] and be baptised'!...[53]

Neither can it follow that because infants were circumcised with circumcision in the flesh under the law, therefore infants must of necessity be baptised with the baptism of repentance under the gospel, with which baptism they cannot be baptised, as all of any understanding must needs confess; and [as I keep reminding you] there is but one baptism... [Mr Robinson,] forsake this root of error which overthrows the covenant, the gospel of Jesus Christ, in the first foundation thereof, bringing in the seed of the *flesh* of the faithful, by *carnal* generation, for

---

[51] The text, as far as I can decipher it, reads 'scuyt'.

[52] Helwys, of course, was not conceding that infant baptism is the 'doctrine of Christ'. Rather, the nonsense put forward by men gets ready credit, but the truth of Christ is believed by few. Bad news travels faster – and further – than good.

[53] Helwys pp179-181, emphasis his. Helwys, once again, was being ironical.

the seed of *promise*, instead of the seed of the faith of *Abraham* by *spiritual* generation, making the infants that are begotten of the faithful after the flesh members of the body of Christ, and heirs of the covenant of the New Testament (which is the covenant of faith and repentance), through the faith of their parents, and by this means you have [brought], and do daily bring, all the wicked and ungodly in these parts of the world to be members of Christ's body, and heirs of the covenant by natural birth, which our Saviour Christ says (John 3[:5]; [see also John 1:12-13]) can no way be, but by new birth; that is, 'by being born again of water and the Spirit' [John 3:5], which is by 'believing and being baptised' [Mark 16:16]. Thus do you utterly destroy and overthrow the holy covenant of the Lord, the holy baptism, and the body of Christ making them common to all young and old wicked and profane, blasphemers, persecutors, murderers, adulterers and witches, and all their children. But let all know this, such as the members are, such is the body, and such is the baptism, and such is the covenant, the covenant of death and condemnation unto all that are under it, and not the covenant of life and salvation, which is only made with them that believe and are baptised...[54]
You all justify the baptising of infants... [Indeed,] would you not with your last breath justify... that the baptising of infants is a holy ordinance of Christ? But if it be no ordinance of Christ...[55]

In conclusion, addressing all whom he had had in his sights when writing his book:

The Lord give them the Spirit of wisdom to direct them to the true understanding and meaning of God in the Scriptures, that they might be able... to attain to the true knowledge – then shall all that seek after Christ strive to enter into his kingdom by regeneration and new birth, 'being born again of water and the Holy Ghost', then shall men learn to know the true baptism of Christ, which is 'the baptism of repentance for the remission of sins', and be therewith baptised, 'and put on Christ', and not satisfy themselves with childish baptism, in which baptism they have not, nor could not, put on Christ; and without which baptism of repentance for the remission of sins, they cannot put on Christ; and then shall the elect of God not be deceived by the multitude of false prophets with all their lying wonders.[56]

---

[54] Helwys pp184-185, emphasis his.
[55] Helwys p201.
[56] Helwys p204.

Extended Notes

Extended note from p29
All sacral societies have their rites of passage, their sacraments
Even the Nazis. 'They tried to develop a liturgy. The Nazi publishing house put out a pamphlet describing "forms of celebrations of a liturgical character which shall be valid for centuries". The main service consisted of "a solemn address of 15-20 minutes in poetical language", "a confession of faith recited by the congregation", then the "hymn of duty"; the ceremony closed with a salute to the Führer and one verse of each of the national anthems. The Nazi creed, used for instance at harvest festivals, ran: "I believe in the land of the Germans, in a life of service to this land; I believe in the revelation of the divine creative power and the pure blood shed in war and peace by the sons of the German national community... I believe in an eternal life on earth of this blood that was poured out and rose again in all who have recognised the meaning of the sacrifice and are ready to submit to them [*sic*]... Thus I believe in an eternal God, an eternal Germany, and an eternal life". Essentially, then, Nazism, unlike communism, was not materialist; it was a blasphemous parody of Christianity, with racialism substituted for God, and German "blood" for Christ. There were special Nazi feasts, especially Nov. 9th, commemorating the *putsch* of 1923, the Nazi passion and crucifixion feast, of which Hitler said: "The blood which they poured out is become the altar of baptism for our Reich". The actual ceremony was conducted like a passion play. And there were Nazi sacraments. A special wedding service was designed for the SS [the armed wing of the Nazi party]. It included runic [old German alphabet or magical] figures, a sun-disc of flowers, a fire bowl, and it opened with a chorus from *Lohengrin*, after which the pair received bread and salt. At SS baptismal ceremonies, the room was decorated with a centre altar containing a photograph of Hitler and a copy of *Mein Kampf*; and on the walls were candles, Nazi flags, the Tree of Life and branches of young trees. There was music from Grieg's *Peer Gynt* ("Morning"), readings from *Mein Kampf*, promises by the sponsors and other elements of the Christian [Christendom's] ceremony; but the celebrant was an SS officer, and the service concluded with the hymn of loyalty to the SS. The Nazis even had their own grace before meals for their orphanages, and Nazi versions of famous hymns. Thus: "Silent night, holy night,/All is calm, all is bright,/Only the Chancellor steadfast in fight,/Watches o'er Germany by day and night,/Always caring for us". There was also a Nazi burial service' (Johnson pp486-487).

Even anti-God societies have rites of passage! The communists were no laggards. Take the Soviet bloc in the last half of the 20th century. God and religious rites were officially abolished, but 'having eliminated religion from the public life of the nation, Soviet planners recognised the importance of creating rituals and events that fostered social cohesion and a sense of identity. These were often deliberately conceived as alternatives to their "Christian" [my quotation marks – DG] counterparts... Once invented, these rituals became part of normal Soviet life'. These rites and events, aping those of the 'banned' Russian Orthodox Church, included special days, anniversaries, and such like. Not least, the Soviets replaced infant baptism, and subsequent confirmation, with events to mark the birth of a child and, later, its admission to the Communist Party. And when the Soviet Union collapsed? Surprise, surprise, there was a massive return to the Russian Orthodox Church: 'With the fall of the Soviet Union, these rituals and cults were replaced by a renewed commitment to those of the Russian Orthodox Church' (McGrath: *Twilight* pp267-268).

Extended note from p42

More on the unbiblical dependence of the 'ordinary' believer on explanations supplied by the professionals

I have claimed that sacramentalism leads to sacerdotalism. One aspect of this is the encouragement it gives to the ever-present tendency for 'ordinary' believers to want a 'pope'. In saying that, I am not talking about Rome! Many believers like to be told (in a nice way, of course) by their 'leader' (pastor, elder or whatever) what's what. In some circles, it is more than 'told'; it can mutate into 'heavy-shepherding'. Even where this is not the case, it is not altogether unknown for leaders to prefer a people who compliantly accept their pronouncements rather than think for themselves and – dare I say it – ask awkward questions! I know of a Reformed (Grace, Strict) Baptist church where the church members have been refused all public discussion – not only of the way the pastor and elders have formulated church policy in a vital area, but of the policy itself – the leaders making no room for any open consultation of the church members. 'Touch not the Lord's anointed' is the (often unspoken) mantra in such cases. But I am afraid the relationship all too often is symbiotic. 'An astonishing and horrible thing has been committed in the land: The prophets prophesy falsely, and the priests rule by their own power; and my people love to have it so. But what will you do in the end?' (Jer. 5:30-31).

I assert that sacramentalism does nothing to diminish this tendency. Let me prove it. Take, for instance, Curtis W.Freeman: 'Of course the doctrine of [the] real absence [in the Lord's supper] is more common in populist rhetoric than in careful theology' (Freeman p203). Let me translate: 'Ordinary people' (see *The Concise*) (perhaps unthinking or ill-taught), with their simplistic approach might hold to the symbolic view of the supper, but theologians know better! I have met this kind of talk before. How many Roman Catholics, when confronted on a point of faith or doctrine, reply with effect that how are they supposed to know? They leave that to the priest. Mother Church tells them what's what. Now, however, we are being told that ordinary *Baptist* folk should leave it to *their* professionals to tell them what to believe. Indeed, in a discussion on a disputed issue with a Strict (or Grace) Baptist lady of many years experience, when I asked her to tell me what she thought a certain text meant, what did it say to *her* – she replied that we have ministers to tell us that!

Sacramental Baptists certainly seem to see the need for professional interpreters for the 'ordinary' Christian – a large step along the sacerdotal road. See Elizabeth Newman's extended exploration of philosophy and the philosophers who point 'us in helpful direction in re-evaluating the real/symbol dichotomy in... "post-critical" philosophical and theological reflections' (Newman pp220-227). (By Newman I mean Elizabeth Newman not J.H.Newman, whom – where there is any ambiguity – I always specify by including his initials). And, in general, note how Cross and Thompson's *Baptist Sacramentalism* moves from sacramentalism to sacerdotalism in its closing three chapters: 'The Sacramental Nature of Ordination: An Attempt to Re-engage a Catholic Understanding and Practice'; 'Towards a Baptist Theology of Ordained Ministry'; 'Towards a Sacramental Understanding of Preaching'. Such statements as: 'I would plead... that we move beyond anxieties about offending Protestant shibboleths in order to engage in an urgent discussion concerning the nature of Christian ministry... That the element of human act (or outward sign) in any sacramental rite is both a prayer and a promise, I find illuminating; to consider the sacrifices and rites of the Old Testament, along with the ecclesial [Church] sacraments of the New Testament... Paul Fiddes, in his recent discussion of the pastoral implications of an understanding of the trinity, can speak of a pastor as "a living sacrament, embodying the accepting and healing love of God"' (Colwell pp232,237,245). 'Can we... find resources within a Baptist account of ecclesiology to account for the apparently "permanent" nature of ordination... or for the practice of gathering tasks of liturgical (and sacramental) presidency...?... By the Spirit, the Church participates in the priestly ministry of Christ by participating in his final and complete priestly offering by faith through the sacrament' (Holmes pp248,256-257). 'A theology that is sacramental produces a strong theology of preaching... a non-sacramental theology diminishes preaching' (Haymes p264).

I will return to this last statement from Bryan Haymes. For now, let's take a glance at the sort of sacramental 'explanation' which the 'professionals' give us. Take Freeman, quoting Neville Clark and Paul Fiddes, speaking of 'energised elements', 'doors into the dance of *perichoresis* in God' (Freeman p209) Perichoresis? I take it to mean 'neighbouring' or 'participating' in God. Reader, if you don't like that, try this for size from Wikipedia: 'Perichoresis (or circuminsession [is *that* any better?]) is a term in Christian theology first found within the Church Fathers but now reinvigorated among contemporary figures... It refers to the mutual inter-penetration and indwelling within the threefold nature of the Trinity, God the Father, the Son and the Holy Spirit'. I wonder how many 'ordinary' Baptists sitting under their sacramentalist teacher-and-baptiser understand *that*? I think it more than possible that some will think it must be right just because they don't understand it. But are we really to believe that Christ set up his church, its ministry and ordinances, on such a philosophical basis that ordinary folk need professionals to explain it all to them? It is said of the Saviour: 'The common people heard him gladly' (Mark 12:37). No wonder – look at the simplicity of his style and language, for a start!

To end this extended note on a somewhat lighter – but still very serious – note, let me relate two anecdotes. A friend of mine attended a meeting in England at which a hyper-Calvinist did not mince any words in spelling out the doctrine of double predestination; that is election and reprobation. A lady he knew went up to the speaker after the meeting and thanked him for his discourse, But, as my friend said, if she had understood what he was saying she would have hated every word of it! The second anecdote concerns a lady leaving a preaching service in Scotland. She said how much she liked what she heard. On being asked if she understood it, she replied: 'I wouldn't presume to understand such a learnèd man as he'!

Extended note from p50

Sacramentalism skews the biblical order of faith before baptism

Sacramentalism skews – to put it mildly – the biblical order; namely, faith before baptism. The infant baptiser, Oscar Cullmann, argued for baptism before faith. Fowler, though he agreed with Cullman on sacramentalism, asked: 'But how does all this correlate with the New Testament passages which call for faith prior to baptism?' Quite. Fowler summarised Cullman's black-is-white argument thus: 'What is demanded by baptism is *subsequent* faith' (Fowler: *More* p212, emphasis his). How wrong can you be? I am afraid I cannot work out what Fowler really thought of this. His fellow-Baptist-sacramentalist, S.I.Buse, made his own position clearer, however: 'Cullmann goes to desperate lengths in an attempt to prove that faith follows rather than precedes baptism' (Buse: 'Baptism in the Acts' p126). As Beasley-Murray said: 'Faith is needful before baptism... Baptism is administered to converts. This is commonly recognised now [in 1962. Beasley-Murray cited Roman Catholics, Lutherans, Anglicans, Reformed, Congregationalists, Methodists], though not by all. [H.] Cremer has many successors. His statement: "Faith must be the *effect* [emphasis original] of our baptism, if the latter has effected anything at all", is manifestly constructed on the basis of infant baptism as the norm of baptismal practice... [and] is anachronistic in the consideration of New Testament teaching' (Beasley-Murray: *Baptism in the New Testament* p274; see also *Baptism Today and Tomorrow* pp38-41). Beasley-Murray was not quite right. This distortion – the utter turning-up-side-down of the New Testament – is not only because of infant baptism. He himself pointed out Cremer's reference to baptism *effecting* something. This is the core of the problem. If it is granted that baptism is a sacrament – that is, it *effects* something, it *produces* something – all sorts of nonsense follow. Sacramentalism is the root of the trouble, as I keep saying, and shall keep saying. Naturally, if baptism effects or produces something, that 'something' must follow baptism. So, if baptism produces faith, baptism must precede faith. But baptism does not produce anything! Let me re-state the obvious in the New Testament: Faith precedes baptism!

Extended note from p51
Baptism and local church membership
For Spurgeon on this, see Spurgeon: *Early* pp125,145-152; Grass and Randall pp60-62. Acts 8:38 could be cited against me; similarly, Acts 9:18. But not every detail in Acts (and the Gospels) should be taken as normative for church practice – see below when I examine Baptist-sacramentalist views on specific scriptures – the letters are designed for that purpose. Acts was a transition period, a time of explosive spiritual power when extraordinary things were going on – some unique in the history of the church. And I mean unique, never (whatever some may claim) to be repeated. Just as hard cases make bad law, so to use extraordinary – unique – events as normative for the church today, is far from sensible. Consider, for instance, the immediacy of New Testament baptism. If I may speak personally, while I acknowledge that excessive delay of baptism is the mistaken norm in some circles, as one who has had the responsibility for baptising, I have felt the need in our culture, blighted by centuries of Christendom, for more caution than seems warranted by the practice in Acts – which practice was carried out under very different social and religious conditions to our own. Compare the rapid funeral arrangements in Acts 5:1-11 with ours today. I will return to this point about the extraordinary.

Getting back to the two verses I suggested might be cited against my view of church membership, in addition to what I have said about the extraordinary nature of Acts, considering Acts 8:38, it is hard to see what Philip could have done with an individual convert who was travelling back to North Africa where there was no other believer – let alone a church. If similar circumstances should occur today, no doubt a like baptism would take place. But we are talking about the other 99.9999% of cases. Let us not legislate for such an isolated instance. As for Acts 9:18, note how, upon baptism, Paul immediately joined the disciples at Damascus, and started preaching there (Acts 9:19-20). And, in course of time, he became a member at Antioch (Acts 11:25-26; 13:1-3; 14:26-28; 15:1-3,22-23,30-35,40; 18:22-23). In any case, as for the connection between baptism and church life as found in the Gospels and Acts, Matt. 28:18-20 is unassailable for the former, and Acts 2:41-42 for the latter. See Fuller: *Essays* p857. I will return to how Baptist sacramentalists find the common practice of open-membership Baptist churches useful to them in making their case.

Extended note from p52
More on strict or closed communion
J.C.Philpot: 'If strict communion is according to the precept of Christ and the practice of the apostles, no arguments against it, drawn from other sources, are admissible. For if once we admit any reasons to prevail over the testimony of God in his word of truth, we reject divine revelation, we deny that the Scriptures are a perfect rule of faith and practice, we turn our back upon the teachings of the Holy Ghost on that particular point, and we open a wide door for the introduction of every error. If baptism is an ordinance of Christ, it stands upon his authority. It is not to be slighted as unnecessary, still less to be rejected with contempt. Nor can a child of God safely shelter himself under the names of great and good men who have not seen, nor submitted to that ordinance. Highly esteemed though they are to be for their work's sake, they are not our Lord; they did not die for our sins, nor rise for our justification. They were [as we all are] but men, fallible men, and in many things offending all, though beloved of God, and blessed in their work. If the principles and practices of the churches founded by the apostles were not those of strict communion, let it be unceremoniously discarded; but if, as I fully believe, and as I think I have proved in the following pages [of his book], the churches set up by the Holy Ghost immediately after the day of Pentecost were strict baptist churches, those that reject that order are guilty of [misunderstanding, ignorance or] disobedience... I put the question wholly upon scriptural precept and scriptural practice. Let the practice of strict communion stand or fall by the unerring testimony of God' (Philpot pp3-4). See Fuller: *Essays* pp852-859. Since I quoted Spurgeon above, it is only fair to point out that he did not hold with a closed table. But, like Philpot, while saying good men may differ, I can only state my own opinion, whoever disagrees with it. Reader, you must do the same.

Wood noted the 1951 statement of the Baptist Union (even though the BU was and is 'open table'): 'We believe that, although there is no statement on the point in the New Testament, our brethren who belong to "close-communion" churches are undoubtedly right in maintaining that membership of the... church (and therefore presumably participation in the Lord's supper), seems in the earliest [that is, apostolic] days to have been confined to persons who were baptised upon profession of faith. We honour the sincerity and earnestness of those who have contended for this aspect of the truth, sometimes under very great difficulties. We believe the church of Christ today would be infinitely poorer had it not been for their witness' (Wood, unnumbered pages, but taken from the final page of the text). In 1996, the Baptist Union published *Believing and Being Baptised: Baptism, so-called re-baptism, and children in the church.* In the historical introduction, John Briggs admitted that Baptist Union churches have 'changed' from following the 'clear [biblical] logic... that valid baptism had to precede communion, and hence the closed-communion position'. And he further admitted that 'it is not clear that we [the BU] have developed a theology... sufficient to justify' the change (baptist.org.uk).

Extended note from p63
Evidence for my summary of Fowler's (and others') method
As evidence for my summary of Fowler's way of arguing, I refer to such of his statements as: 'The exact relationship was not spelled out in detail... The language... as it stands might mean... This imprecision regarding what exactly happens in baptism is characteristic of much Baptist literature of the 17th century, because the writers were in most cases concerned... only to a limited degree about the sacramental issue... The... connection... was not stated explicitly... The language suggested... Baptism... was... although not (explicitly at least)... The typical Calvinistic view is almost never stated explicitly... It is not clear that the omissions... imply denial... It would appear that the Calvinistic concept of baptism as a seal... continued to shape the way in which Baptists described the efficacy of the baptism of professed believers. However, this understanding was largely unelaborated, due to the necessity... There was no explicitly sacramental language... The evidence is minimal and undeveloped... He did not use this language explicitly. Baptists of the 18th century generally avoided this terminology, partly because... Although the 18th century writers did not use the term "sacrament", there was no explicit rejection of the term... The retreat from the designation of baptism as a seal is as difficult to analyse as the retreat from sacrament... Baptists emphasised that baptism was not necessary for salvation in a way that muted their Calvinistic sacramental heritage... It is true that the Baptist literature of this period spoke more directly about baptism in relation to spiritual re-birth, but it was usually written in reaction to Anglo-Catholicism, and this reactionary process tended to formulate baptismal theology in a reductionistically non-sacramental direction... His answer was negative, but it is clear that what he was negating is... The... quotation shows the primary concern... was to refute... Is it possible that... [he] actually embraced a sacramental sense of baptism in the end, and that his initial statement was limited by the context? Probably not... It would be hard to imagine a more powerful rejection of baptismal regeneration... [but] one should not draw hasty inferences... His rhetoric does not sound as if he

would feel comfortable with a concept like baptism as the "seal of regeneration", but he did not directly address the issue... In a less polemical context... [he] might have provided a positive [sacramental] baptismal theology' (Fowler: *More* pp12,13,15,18,20,31,50,55,57,59,68,79,82,83).

This, reader, is the sort of thing I am talking about. Please read the entire section in Fowler. And if this is the best evidence, I am reminded of my father, reprimanding me as a teenager over some display of my ignorance, and comparing it to my school report: 'If you're one of the best, don't show me the worst!'.

Again: Note how Fowler glossed the words of the sacramental Baptist A.W.Argyle (in *Christian Baptism* in 1959): 'He [Argyle] chronicled what he interpreted as the descent of the early [patristic] Church into superstitious views of baptismal efficacy... and he traced the rise of infant baptism as a corollary of this shift' (Fowler: *More* p120).

I pause. I am grateful for this observation, since I have argued – both here and in my *Infant* – that sacramentalism is *the* issue; *that* bushel having been swallowed, the grain of infant baptism follows. But my point here is Fowler's 'what he [Argyle] interpreted'. Did the early (patristic) church *not* descend into superstition over sacramentalism? Is it only a question of 'interpretation'? Is it not an indisputable fact? Fowler claimed that Argyle, although he denied baptismal regeneration, 'was like many earlier Baptists who, when they denied baptismal regeneration, were not rejecting the idea that God conveys spiritual benefits (indeed, the Spirit himself) through baptism' (Fowler: 'Oxymoron' p137). As far as 'many earlier Baptists' are concerned, this needs proof.

Again, Fowler used Baptist hymns in making his case, as I do. But this, I suggest, needs treating with care. Poetic licence, and all that. Having said as much, I freely admit that for most believers the hymn book plays a very significant part in forming their theology – more important, in not a few cases, than the Bible itself.

Fowler was not alone in arguing from history. Thompson, in his much briefer attempt to establish a historic Baptist sacramentalism, took the same route as Fowler. Clutching at straws, arguing from silence, and by association, Thompson asserted: 'There is ample evidence that early Baptists regarded the sacraments as means of grace... to strengthen and increase faith unto salvation'. With respect, I find this a somewhat ambiguous statement; are the sacraments a means of grace to nourish and increase faith – or are they a means of grace unto salvation? I don't want to fault a man for a word, but precision is vital here. Furthermore, I question that there is 'ample evidence that early Baptists...'. There is *some* evidence that *some* early Baptists did make *some* sort of sacramental statements. What is more, the examples Thompson culled from Benjamin Keach, the Midlands General Baptists and John Bunyan – 'those gospel ordinances called sacraments, which do confirm us in this faith', 'sacraments to nourish us in the church', 'such as help man's salvation' – are hardly ringing endorsements of the kind of sacramentalism Baptist sacramentalists wish they could produce. And to claim that, because the 1689 Confession said that 'by... baptism and the Lord's supper, prayer and other means appointed of God, [faith] is increased and strengthened', and to claim that sacramental 'understanding was present even in Confessions that did not employ explicit sacramental terminology', strikes me as a man trying to defend a desperate case; or, to change the figure, clutching at the merest straw for support. The same goes for Thompson's argument from the way the 17th century Baptists, though they rejected the idolatrous State Church – Anglicanism – still held to the sacraments or ordinances. Naturally, they still held on to baptism and the supper – but that didn't make them sacramentalists! In addition, of course, I admit – and regret – that some of them called the ordinances 'sacraments' – though 'ordinances' was far more common – but just because they spoke of baptism and the supper, this does not prove 'the Baptists... did not reject the sacramental idea', and did not deny that 'the locus of... God's freedom... to mediate grace unto salvation, was the church and sacraments'! And to claim that 'Baptists realised that the sacraments had to be not mere[!] symbols, but truly sacraments that mediate the free grace of... God', is unwarranted. Granted that Luther said that 'faith hangs on the water', but to go on to claim that 'this is, perhaps surprisingly, not far from the early Baptists' views... Early Baptists believed that Christ was present in baptism by the power of the Holy Spirit, and so was salvifically active in the rite' (Thompson: 'Sacraments' pp38-49), I find incredible. Can we be given some unequivocal, direct statements of these Baptists saying that baptism mediates saving grace to sinners?

Cross supplied some extracts from Keach. Citing various scriptures, Keach stated: 'See what great promises are made to believers in baptism'. Certainly! Baptism is of great benefit to *believers*, to those who are already regenerate and show it by their faith and obedience. But, 'outward water cannot convey inward life. How can water, an external thing, work upon the soul in a physical manner[?]. Neither can it be proved that ever the Spirit of God is tied by any promise to apply himself to the soul in a gracious operation when water is applied to the body... Baptism is a means of conveying grace when the Spirit is pleased to operate with it'. Let me pause. Keach's opening remarks in these extracts are anything but sacramental. But here we do get to the nub of the thing. 'Baptism is a means of conveying grace when the Spirit is pleased to operate with it... for it is the sacrament of regeneration'. I pause again. Well, this certainly looks like sacramentalism; indeed, it looks like baptismal regeneration! But wait a minute. Keach had already said that baptism is for believers; that is, the regenerate who show it. So he could not have been saying, now, what it looks like at first glance. Let Keach go on: 'Baptism is a means of conveying grace when the Spirit is pleased to operate with it... for it is the sacrament of regeneration, as the Lord's supper is of nourishment... Faith only is the principle of spiritual life, and the principle which draws nourishment from the means of God's appointments' (Cross: 'Dispelling' p372). While Keach was prepared to use language that I certainly would not, it seems to me he was saying no more than that both baptism and the Lord's supper have been appointed by God to nourish believers, and that as believers obey Christ they find great benefit. I do not concede that Keach was a Baptist sacramentalist.

As for Thomas Helwys (c1550?/c1575?-c1616), I dispute Thompson's sacramental inference when he stated: 'Helwys argued that in Christ, the water of baptism and the Holy Spirit are bound together inseparably', citing Helwys: *Mystery* pp137-139. See the Appendix for extended extracts from Helwys, and my comments. And Helwys merits a closer look. He was, after all, one of great Baptist pioneers of the early 17th century. If anybody, therefore, should be a star witness for the sacramentalist case, *he* should! Is he? In brief here: Thompson admitted that Helwys rejected the notion of the seal (Thompson: 'Sacraments' pp39,48). He certainly did! And though Helwys quoted others (particularly John Robinson) talking about 'sacraments', Helwys himself spoke at large about the 'ordinances of Christ'. What is more, it is significant that Henry Wheeler Robinson, in his 'Introduction' to the 1935 (the date is important– see the following chapter) replica of *Mystery*, drew no sacramental comfort whatsoever from the work. And Kevan felt able to cite Helwys as out-of-step with the notion that sacramental Baptists were re-discovering a historical stream of sacramentalism among the Baptists (Fowler: *More* pp128-129). Far from being a star witness for the sacramentalists, Helwys is no witness at all for them.

Moving on the best part of a century, I admit the 1689 Particular Baptist Confession had a Calvinistic, sacramental view of the Lord's supper, based heavily on the Westminster Confession, which had stated: 'Worthy receivers... do... inwardly by faith, *really and indeed*, yet not carnally and corporally, but spiritually, receive... Christ crucified... the body and blood of Christ being... not corporally or carnally, in, with, or under the bread and wine; yet, *as really*, but spiritually, present to the faith of believers in that ordinance, as the elements themselves are to their outward senses' (Westminster p119, emphasis mine). The 1689 Confession included the first of the emphasised phrases but not the second (Lumpkin p293; *The London* p52). I cannot explain this. Michael A.G.Haykin's suggestion – 'possibly it was thought that Luther's view [that is, consubstantiation] was not entertained by any in the Calvinistic Baptist community during the 17th century, and it was thus omitted so as to avoid encumbering the Confession with needless statements' (Haykin pp179-180) – fails to satisfy me, I'm afraid. After all, in the same section, the 1689 denied transubstantiation – to which, presumably, Haykin's suggestion could also be applied. See Lumpkin p292; *The London* p52. See also Freeman p200. Newman was wrong to cite the 1689 as 'affirming [the] real presence in a manner found in other Reformed bodies' (Newman p216). This is precisely what it did *not* do! And what about the 1644 Particular Baptist Confession? The only mention of the Lord's supper was in later editions of that Confession where the words 'and after to partake of the Lord's supper' were added to the conclusion of the opening statement on baptism: 'That baptism is an ordinance... persons professing faith... who upon a profession of faith, ought to be baptised *and after to partake of the Lord's supper*' (Lumpkin p167). There is not a whiff of sacramentalism in the 1644. As in other matters, the 1644 did not toe the Reformed line of the times, contrary to the 1689, which did. The 1689 was, in my view, an attempt by the Calvinistic Baptists to show their 'political correctness'. I hope to say more about this in my book on the law.

On a general note, reading all these repeated claims by sacramental Baptists reminds me of another episode from my schooldays. My mathematics master, explaining why he kept teaching us the same geometry theorems every year, said something along the lines of: 'We work on the principle of throwing mud at a wall', he said. 'The more we throw, the more often we throw it, the more chance we have of getting some to stick'. In other words, if sacramental Baptists keep repeating that the early Baptists were sacramentalists, saying it loudly and often enough, one day we might dinned into believing it. If not that, people will start to use the language and absorb the notion by osmosis. People generally mimic what they hear – often subconsciously. Take one example. Who was the first to use 'absolutely' instead of 'yes' when replying to a question? Nowadays, to get an answer 'yes' is a rarity indeed. And sacramentalists do not tire of making their claim. For example: 'Recent research indicates that the kind of Baptist thinking represented by Kevan differs significantly from the first century of Baptist thought which was often sacramental' (Fowler: 'Oxymoron' p145). I dispute this, as I have said.

Extended note from p69
The leading part in Baptist sacramentalism played by Henry Wheeler Robinson
Cross: 'The person who did more than anyone else to help Baptists rediscover[!] the sacramental understanding of baptism, certainly in 20th century Britain, was Wheeler Robinson' (Cross: 'Pneumatological' p174; see also his p154). Underwood: 'Largely under the influence of the writings of Dr H.Wheeler Robinson, many English Baptists have abandoned [the symbolic view of baptism] in favour of a sacramental interpretation of believer's baptism' (Underwood pp268-269; Cross 'Pneumatological' p174). Note Underwood's admission. Baptists until the 20th century were

non-sacramental. Cross wrongly talked of 'rediscovering' sacramentalism, whereas Underwood rightly spoke of the 'abandoning' of the (biblical – DG) interpretation for (the unbiblical – DG) sacramentalism.

Wheeler Robinson's influence extended beyond the subject in hand. His works were open to criticism for taking 'the modern approach to the Bible... opening up important new approaches both to Old Testament religion and to Christian theology'. Nevertheless, they had a great influence. According to Payne, 'his volume on Deuteronomy and Joshua... appeared in 1907... It... has been a help to many students... Of much more importance for his growing reputation was the appearance in 1909 in *Mansfield College Essays*, presented to Dr Fairbairn for his seventieth birthday, of the important paper "Hebrew Psychology in relation to Pauline Anthropology"... Competent judges were in no doubt as to the novelty and importance of its psychological approach... "Comprehensive" and "masterly" were adjectives frequently applied to the book. "It is", wrote James Denney... "of quite unusual interest, power and importance... Take it for all in all, the book is one of the finest contributions which has been made for [a] long [time] to biblical and philosophical theology"... *The Christian Doctrine of Man*... has proved among his best known and most used. *The Religious Ideas of the Old Testament* was published in 1913... In 1911... "Baptist Principles before the rise of Baptist Churches" [appeared]. It offered an important defence and interpretation of Baptist witness, linking baptism with the gift of the Holy Spirit, and arguing for the recognition of the sacramental principle. Often reprinted... the essay has become widely influential for modern Baptist apologetic' (Payne: *Henry Wheeler Robinson* pp53-55). There is no doubt about it. To put it mildly, Wheeler Robinson played a big part in the (unbiblical) development of sacramentalism (and other things) among Baptists in the 20th century. See Payne: *Baptist Union* pp231,253.

Extended note from p69
Henry Wheeler Robinson and John Henry Newman
See Robinson's lecture 'John Henry Newman' in Payne: *Henry Wheeler Robinson* pp110-131, delivered at the Friends' Meeting House, York, in 1913. Robinson could hardly have spoken of Newman in more glowing terms, predicting that he would be recognised as 'the most striking figure' in 19th century Church history. But how did Robinson cope with Newman's casuistry? How did he cope, for instance, with *Tract XC* in which Newman had tried to argue that when the Anglican 39 Articles condemned 'the sacrifices of Masses', they did not condemn the sacrifice of the Mass itself? Robinson excused his hero, thus: 'It is surely possible for a man so constituted as Newman to deceive himself by the very subtlety of his intellect, without any breach of good faith'. Really? Robinson went on to explain. Newman's great get-out was to argue from the limited power of

reason (which, of course, is a perfectly correct assertion), to the need for an infallible authority – which he came to find in the Church of Rome. In particular, 'Newman was for a long time repelled from the Church of Rome by the position ascribed in that Church to the Virgin Mary'. He could not allow this veneration – since it detracts from the glory of the One True God. So how did Newman come to accept Roman dogma on Mary, and how did he justify her worship? Simply because he accepted 'the divine right of the Catholic Church to guarantee such tradition as truth'. What did Wheeler Robinson say of that? The need to recognise in 'the very subtlety of his... intellect... an essential feature of the real Newman, the man whose limitations we must frankly confess, that we may admire his true worth the more whole-heartedly'. Robinson quoted Henry Bonner: Newman's 'search was for a Church, not for a religion. He believed in dogma from the first; he never had any doubt about it. He believed in a revelation, that there is a Church of God on earth, with a deposit of truth, and with rites and sacraments. His one question was: "Where is this Church?"'. The answer Newman eventually came up with was, of course, Rome. The process for Rome owning Newman a Saint [in Roman terms] is gathering momentum. In Birmingham, on Sept. 19th 2010, Benedict XVI took the next step and beatified him.

Contrast the Baptist, Wheeler Robinson's, 20th century view of *Tract XC*, with that of some in the Church of England in the 1840s. C.P.Golightly read it 'with horror'. Four Oxford tutors, J.Griffiths, A.C.Tait, T.T.Churton and H.B.Wilson, 'declared in ugly English that *Tract XC* was dangerous because it mitigated the serious differences which separated the Church of England from the Church of Rome... All the heads of houses except [four]... resolved to censure the tract... The vice-chancellor published... a declaration of the hebdomadal [weekly] board that the Tracts were in no way sanctioned by the university, and that the suggested modes of interpretation evaded the sense of the articles, and were inconsistent with due observance of the statutes of the university... Conservatives wanted to stop these opinions being lawful within the established Church'. Some Bishops also opposed the tract. Owen Chadwick summarised their comments as including 'condemned the tract as evasive... condemned nine specific interpretations... the author [Newman] wanted to reconcile the Church of England to the Church of Rome... The most dishonourable efforts of sophistry [clever but flawed argument] ever witnessed in theological discussions... jeering at the Church of England'. 'The provost of Oriel refused testimonials to ordinands if they would not repudiate *Tract XC*'. Chadwick concluded: 'The battle over *Tract XC* ended Newman's usefulness to the Church of England' (Chadwick pp181-189). But not, it seems, for the Baptist, H.Wheeler Robinson, 70 years later.

Spurgeon's reaction to Tractarianism is a byword. See Murray: *The Forgotten* pp116-137. Fowler owned it (Fowler: *More* p86).

Extended note from p76

More on Baptist sacramentalists and history

In the previous chapter, I showed how Baptist sacramentalists have accused their critics, and those they opposed, of a lack of historical awareness. Fowler took this line with Kevan and Gill, (and 20th century Baptist sacramentalists!), describing their contribution as symptomatic of 'the distressing and ongoing Baptist tendency to ignore the work of previous Baptists as if there were no Baptist tradition at all'. Fowler somewhat patronisingly dismissed those he had in mind: 'It is unfortunately possible to dogmatise about alleged Baptist distinctives while being relatively ignorant of the actual history of Baptist thought' (Fowler: *More* p129; 'Oxymoron' p145). Shades of pot and kettle, I think. Fowler cited Beasley-Murray to the effect that 'Baptist tradition needs to be seriously examined before anyone makes sweeping statements as to who are the faithful heirs of that tradition, if in fact there is a consistent tradition'. Very well. But such an admission would seem to destroy much of Fowler's own thesis; namely, that there has been a Baptist-sacramental stream since the 17th century. Significantly, as Fowler went on to say: 'Unfortunately, he [Beasley-Murray] did not take the time to uncover the evidence of this tradition [which doesn't exist!] which would have supported his case' (Fowler: 'Oxymoron' p148). Can we be sure it was just a shortage of time – or, rather, a failure of will and commitment? Might it be that the evidence is not there, however much time is devoted to trying to unearth it? How could Fowler conclude his essay with: 'Recent research indicates that the kind of Baptist thinking represented by Kevan differs significantly from the first century of Baptist thought which was often sacramental... If the critics [of *Christian Baptism*] had understood the history of Baptist thought, especially the formative period of the 17th century, then they would have recognised that "Baptist sacramentalism" is not an oxymoron' (Fowler: 'Oxymoron' pp145,150)? Pretty rich, this, to dismiss Kevan (as one among others) as ignorant of 17th century Baptist history! See the previous chapter for my comments on this alleged (sacramental) Baptist tradition and the appeal (or lack of appeal) to it by sacramentalists. To my mind, Fowler's approach smacks of special pleading.

Extended note from p86

More on Fowler's view that unless we think of baptism as a sacrament, we have no adequate marker of conversion

Fowler was wrong. The New Testament does not allow us to confine this 'adequate marker' of conversion to baptism – although baptism is surely a part of the testimony to it – in the spirit, perhaps, of 1 Tim. 6:12. But more than baptism is required. Consider Matt. 7:15-23; John 13:35; 2 Cor. 5:17, for instance. Of course, I admit that these markers are to be lived out over the rest of the life, increasingly so (2 Pet. 1:1-11; 3:18), but when a sinner is converted there must be – and there will be – credible signs of the new spiritual life. The regenerating power of the Spirit, leading to conversion, will inevitably show itself. Conversion is a crisis. The new life of the new creation begins at once! Speaking personally, if anyone tells me they would like to be baptised, I ask them: Why? Their answer reveals a great deal. I will have more to say on this.

Referring to Charles Grandison Finney and his use of the 'anxious seat', Fowler argued: 'It is thus recognised in practice that if union with Christ is to be an experiential reality, then the entrance into that union calls for some event which translates the attitude of faith into a personal act' (Fowler: *More* p251). Leaving Finney and his innovation to one side, can we be given any scriptures for Fowler's call for 'some event', such as he had in mind?

Extended note from p89
The events connected with Rome from 1960 on
For an overall summary of events connected with Rome from 1960-1988, see Jackson pp115-132,147-155. For the broadening of this summary of the move from Rome to other religions during the years 1960-1994, see Morrison pp525-588.

For the events during the years 1945-1981, and the resistance offered by Lloyd-Jones when confronted by the ecumenical movement and its involvement with Evangelicals, Baptists, Pentecostalists, Charismatics, Anglo-Catholics, Roman Catholics, mass evangelism (particularly the Billy Graham Crusades), Vatican II, and so on, all leading to re-union with Rome, see the index entries 'Ecumenical Movement' and 'Roman Catholic/Catholicism/Church of Rome' in Murray: *The Fight*. As early as 1945, Lloyd-Jones had spotted the trend, and gone public about it. He wrote that he had given three talks in Welsh on the radio: 'I enjoyed analysing and trying to answer the current issues that characterise the present phase – Barthianism, ecumenicity, sacerdotalism...'. But, in assessing Lloyd-Jones after his death, Murray had to confess that 'only slowly had his [Lloyd-Jones'] conviction deepened that the older denominations were committed to the vision which had gathered such momentum since the World Council of Churches was formed at Amsterdam in 1948, and that union with Rome was the intention of the ecumenical movement'. However, 'Lloyd-Jones' public co-operation with the leaders of' 'the Anglican Evangelical party' was 'brought to a final end' with the 1970 publication of *Growing into Union* – 'written by four Anglican clergy who had all been involved in recent ecumenical discussions'. 'What made the book of special significance was that here two professing Anglo-Catholics... were co-authors with two Evangelicals, C.O.Buchanan and J.I.Packer. The four men gave their proposals [as to] how *both* views not only could but *must* be contained within a future united Church. Their professed intention was to attempt to demonstrate the truth of the words of Michael Ramsey... "Catholicism" and "Evangelicalism" are not two separate things'. The book itself contained such statements as: 'Tradition... is the handing on to each Christian of the riches of the Father's house to which he became entitled by his baptism... The bishop must be seen to be what he is in the liturgical life of the Church, the sacramental expression of the headship of Christ... Only the children of communicants would qualify for baptism. They would then be eligible for admission to communion with their parents... The [episcopal] ministry... [is] the sacramental expression of the continuing headship of Christ over his Church' (Murray: *The Fight* pp128-129,559,656-657, emphasis his). For Lloyd-Jones' views in 1967, see his 'Luther' pp38-44. He set out the three leading questions. What is a Christian? How does one become a Christian? What is a church? He was categorical: 'There is no possible compromise for the Evangelical with a belief in baptismal regeneration: it is impossible'. He was explicit: 'The ecumenical movement... is not only heading to Rome, it is heading also towards an amalgamation with the so-called world religions, and will undoubtedly end as a great World Congress of Faiths'.

For a fuller, wider and deeper account of the years 1950-2000, including baptism, the charismatic movement and corporate salvation, see Murray: *Evangelicalism*.

Extended note from p90

Sacramental Baptists are in the forefront of this drive to Rome

As can be seen by a glance at this from George: 'Vatican Council II... Roman Catholics and many conciliar [of or concerning a Church Council – see *The Concise*] Protestants...'; 'if, with the Council of Trent, we can...'; 'for those who believe in purgatory... *sursum corda* [that is, a short sentence spoken by a priest during Mass] in the liturgy...'; and so on. George described 'the second phase of the Reformed-Roman Catholic dialogue in the document: "Towards a Common Understanding of the Church" (1984-1990)' as 'the most helpful effort' in handling 'the kerygmatic [preaching] and sacramental understandings of the Church'. He also stated: 'The Blessed Virgin Mary [capitals original] can indeed be *mater ecclesiae* [Mother of the Church] for Baptists and Evangelicals no less than for Orthodox and Roman Catholic Christians'. He referred to 'the Pentecostal-Roman Catholic Dialogue... the Evangelical-Roman Catholic Dialogue on Mission (ERCDOM)... (1977-1984)... Cardinal Joseph Ratzinger [later to become Benedict XVI]... Vatican Council II... In the 1984 Apostolic Exhortation: *Reconciliatio et Paenitentia*, Pope John Paul II delineated three ways in which the Church can be spoken of as sacrament' (George pp21-35). Grenz: 'The Roman Catholic theologian Regis Duffy might even find echo among Baptists when he describes a sacrament'

(Grenz p90). Freeman commented on 'the bilateral Catholic-Baptist discussions on grace' (Freeman p196; see below). Newman: 'A more sacramental understanding of the Lord's supper would bring Baptists closer to the Church universal, in the sense that Catholic, Orthodox and many Protestants (for example, United Methodists, Episcopalians, Lutherans) regard this practice as a sacrament... In light of Roman Catholic belief and practice, is transubstantiation... as a theory of real presence fully catholic, since only the Roman Catholic Church has embraced this position? Might there be a 'reformed' way to understand the Lord's supper as sacrament that is at the same time catholic and consistent with God's word?' (Newman p214). Stephen R.Holmes: 'The recent decision by the Baptist Union... to include youth specialists and evangelists on the list of accredited ministers could be interpreted as an attempt to return to a form of such patristic practice'. He developed his argument for the sacramental ordained minister so that 'no other should preach or celebrate [note the word] the sacrament, while insisting that this role is not separable from the ministry of the Church, and so the gathered faithful have their own proper but subordinate part to play in the celebration of the liturgy. This would lead to an account similar to that advanced by the Second Vatican Council... where there is a particular "priesthood of the laity"'. The actual document stated that 'the common priesthood of the faithful... join in the offering [note the word] of the eucharist by virtue of their royal priesthood' (Holmes pp 260-261). I think such extracts fairly make the point that sacramental Baptists are in the van of the drive to Rome.

A final observation. Sacramental Baptists claim that 19th century anti-sacramentalism among the Baptists was as a result of their reaction against the Romanising, Anglo-Catholic movement of the time. I disagree. I am convinced that anti-sacramentalism went deeper than that. But, for sake of argument, let us accept the Baptist-sacramentalist claim. Doing so, note the highly significant difference between the anti-sacramental Baptists of the 19th century and these present-day sacramental Baptists. The former rejected Rome as heretical and an enemy of the gospel; the latter approach Rome with open arms and an open (or, rather, an already-committed) mind.

Extended note from p90
Sacramentalists and all religions

Beasley-Murray was pleased to quote 'Old Catholic, Anglican, Reformed, Roman Catholic and Baptist' writers to make his case for sacramentalism (Beasley-Murray: *Baptism in the New Testament* pp265-266).

In 1996, Peter Kreeft, one-time Dutch Reformed Protestant who attended Calvin College, but who, at the age of 21, 'converted' to Rome, published his *Ecumenical Jihad: Ecumenism and the Culture War* (stfrancismagazine.info/ja/EcumenicalJihad). In this book, Kreeft looked forward to an eternal ecumenism which will embrace Protestants,

Romanists, Orthodox, Jews, Muslims, Buddhists, Hindus, New Age
followers, occultists, agnostics and atheists. What did he see as the power
to bring this about? 'The power that will reunite the Church and win the
world is eucharistic adoration... The distinctly Catholic devotion of the
eucharist (and to Mary) may prove to be the key to victory in ecumenism
and in the "culture war"'. Kreeft's book was endorsed by Chuck Colson
and James I.Packer (njiat.com/media/Ecumenical).

See Pinnock's admission of debt to 'Catholic, Orthodox and Protestant
traditions' (Pinnock p8). 'God is everywhere and in everything... Even in
the myths of the world's peoples, he has made himself known'. Pinnock
cited Joseph Martos 'Sacraments in all Religions'. In particular, he argued
from God's 'election of Israel and [how he] blessed her with sacramental
structures'. Pinnock, having spoken of the sacramental benefits of *all*
religions and myths, went on to speak of the greatest revelation of
sacraments; namely, 'supremely for Christians' (Pinnock pp11-12). In other
words, the gospel is just one of a line of sacramental religions – the best, to
be sure, but all of a piece with the rest. And sacramentality is the key. As
Pinnock had said: 'General sacramentality underlies Christian
sacramentality and heralds it'.

In passing, I point out that the reference to Israel is a singularly bad
example for the sacramentalist to choose. Grace, inward grace, was
expressly *not* conveyed by the signs God gave Israel (Acts 13:39; Rom.
8:3; Heb. 7:18-19; 9:9-14; 10:1-4). I therefore disagree with White who
spoke of 'the undoubted truth that in proselyte baptism something was
expected to be achieved; it was no empty performance, no merely
traditional ceremony' (White p72; Porter p119). In light of the passages just
above, I fail to see it. Spurgeon could hardly have thought so. He spoke of
'Jewish proselyte baptism, whether it originated before, or, as many
eminent infant-baptisers believe, after apostolic times'. 'An attempt to
prove the rightful subjects of Christian baptism from God's word *and*
[emphasis mine] Jewish proselyte baptism, is to imitate the popish appeal to
Scripture and tradition. Besides, no man upon earth *knows* [emphasis his]
that proselyte baptism had an existence in apostolic times'. Spurgeon went
on to speak of the apostles who 'must have understood Christ [in Matt.
28:18-20], on account of the baptism they had already witnessed and
practiced. They knew not, so far as we are aware, any other baptism than
John's, and that of Jesus through themselves [that is, Christ using them to
baptise]. Were we to bind with the Bible all the rabbinical lumber and all
the condemned (or approved) Jewish traditions that the world contains, we
should, while dishonouring the sufficiency of inspired writ, be in the same
destitution of evidence that the apostles knew of any other baptisms than
those recorded in the oracles of God' (Spurgeon: *On Baptism* pp11,13,18).

Extended note from p95
Evangelical and Reformed return to the Fathers
The path has long been marked out by Calvin: 'Calvin's explicit references to the early Church Fathers number more than 3200; some 1700 of them are references, often with extended quotations, to Augustine. The numbers are greatly increased when echoes and allusions are taken into account' (Gerrish p291). I fully recognise that Calvin gave prime place to Scripture, and not the Fathers, but such Reformed qualifiers (compare on baptism) can so easily get missed, be misunderstood or ignored. The unwary who play with matches don't always escape unburnt!

In addition to what I have said in the body of the book, as further evidence of a return to the Fathers today, see, for instance, McGrath's biography of James Packer. 'Packer tends to see himself as standing in the main Christian stream – the "great tradition"... which starts with the Fathers, which was partly (though not totally) de-railed during the Middle Ages, which recovered its balance and identity through the work of the Reformers (especially Calvin) and subsequently continued through the Puritans (especially Jonathan Edwards). As a representative of what he styles "great-tradition Christianity", Packer is able to affirm the importance of patristic and medieval writers – such as Athanasius, Augustine, Anselm and Aquinas, to limit ourselves merely to those whose names conveniently begin with the first letter of the alphabet – while at the same time recognising the importance of the Reformation. For Packer, the Reformation corrected "skewed western understandings of the church, the sacraments, justification, faith, prayer and ministry"; nevertheless, that correction "took place within the frame of the great tradition, and did not break it"' (McGrath: *To Know* pp183-184,248-255,284). In light of this, it can come as no surprise that Packer did not have much time for the Anabaptists. Furthermore, nobody should be surprised at the way Packer's thought and practice developed, and where it ended up.

Then again, I have detected a growing tendency for Reformed and Evangelical (not excepting Baptist) books and magazines to put Papist or Orthodox paintings on the cover. And more! Why, as I am in the final stages of preparing this book for the press (Sept. 9th 2010), I have came across the following from a Reformed Baptist stable: 'Michael Haykin's new book, *Rediscovering the Church Fathers: Who They Were and How They Shaped the Church*, is due out Spring 2011'. Haykin: 'The book seeks to stimulate a thirst for the Fathers and to reveal how rich the Fathers are in theology and piety... and hopefully stir up interest and make the Fathers increasingly a known land... Many of our Evangelical forebears read the Fathers and that reading enriched their lives and thought. We need to do the same to help us meet some of the great challenges of our day' (andrewfullercenter.org).

Oh dear! The writing on the wall gets bigger and clearer by the day! Is it true that we never learn from history? Some Anglicans went to the Fathers in the 1830s and 40s, and look where they ended up! Will some Reformed Baptists and others repeat the mistake today? That, down the years, the Reformed (not excluding Baptists) have quoted the Fathers, I do not for a moment deny, but we should not ignore the warnings given by such men as John Owen, John Gill and J.A.Wylie. See, for example, Owen: *Causes* in Works Vol.4 p227; Gill: *Cause* (Part 4) pp220-221. Owen pointed out that the Fathers 'so disagree among themselves'. Gill observed that 'the purest writers of the first ages were not free from considerable mistakes and blemishes, and deviations from the word of God, and doctrines of the apostles'. He also commented on the many interpolations and 'many spurious pieces' which make it 'difficult to know their [the Fathers'] true and real sentiments... They do not appear to have very clear and distinct notions of the doctrines of [the Christian religion]; at least, [they] are not very happy in expressing their sentiments of them... They were but children in comparison of some of our European divines since the Reformation'. Wylie: 'As we pass from Paul to Clement, and from Clement to the Fathers that succeeded him, we find the gospel becoming less of grace and more of merit. The light wanes as we travel down the patristic road, and remove ourselves farther from the apostolic dawn. It continues for some time at least to be the same gospel, but its glory is shorn, its mighty force is abated... Seen through the fogs of the patristic age, the gospel scarcely looks the same [as that] which had burst upon the world without a cloud but a few centuries before' (Wylie p6). I cannot find that Fuller was much of an advocate for the Fathers. What he would think about a website, which bears his name, advocating a return to the Fathers, is not hard to imagine.

As for a return to the Fathers, in Oct. 2010, on reading of the proposed Banner of Truth publication, for children, of the lives of some of the Fathers, I sent an email to the publishers, expressing my astonishment. I received no reply. I have not been able to see these works before going to press, but I hope they will play fairer than the 1999 Christian Focus publication on Augustine – which seemed to accept the invented hierarchy in the Catholic Church, and made no mention whatsoever of Augustine's seminal and appalling promulgation of baptismal regeneration, let alone giving a warning against it.

Extended note from p98
The New Perspective and justification
Peter Slomski: The New Perspective teaches 'that justification is God's acknowledgement [that] you are already in [the covenant], rather than the Reformed [biblical] understanding that it is God's declaration that you are not guilty, and that you are righteous in Christ. [According to the New Perspective,] faith is just a badge of membership, rather than the instrument

by which we enter into union with Christ and are saved. Note also that our faith is in Christ as Lord, not as Saviour. Sin and God's wrath are downplayed, and so there is no place here for the atonement of our sin; in fact, we appear to be able to enter into God's covenant literally for free. [Of course, salvation is free to the sinner – the cost was borne entirely by Christ]. The whole point of Christ's death is extremely unclear and obscure in New Perspective teaching. What does seem clear is that there is no apparent place for penal substitution – Christ being punished in our place. Nor is there room for the imputation of Christ's righteousness'. Slomski went on to ask: 'If faith is simply a badge of your membership, how do you actually get in? The New Perspective appears to teach it is by baptism... You enter into the covenant community here on earth by baptism (with faith being simply a badge of that membership), and you stay in and then eventually enter into heaven by a good life... In summary, the New Perspective appears to teach: Grace (God chooses you)... baptism (you enter)... faith... good works... heaven'. Slomski quoted Maurice Roberts: 'There are serious ccumenical implications attached to these [New Perspective] views'. Slomski linked this with the Federal Vision (a modern Reformed infant-baptiser approach to the sacraments – which, as I have shown in my *Infant*, its advocates cogently argue they find in Calvin *et al.*), which he summarised as: 'God's gracious choice... baptism (you enter)... faithfulness in good works... heaven'. Slomski claimed that both the New Perspective and the Federal Vision 'are semi-Pelagianist [Arminian]... [which is] the teaching that Roman Catholicism promotes' (Slomski pp283-289).

Extended note from pp110,131
The quickening of the Baptist pace towards infant baptism
In this extended note, I repeat some extracts I have already set out in the main text. I do so for completeness here.
In 1926, the Baptist Union replied to the Lambeth Appeal of 1920: 'In our judgement, the baptism of infants incapable of offering a personal confession of faith subverts the conception of the church' (Payne: *Baptist Union* pp280-281; Underwood p262).
Wheeler Robinson, in 1927, while advocating sacramentalism, had conceded no ground whatsoever to the practice of infant baptism. He was very clear: In the New Testament, 'all who were baptised were already believers... Indeed, it was the very divorce of baptism from personal faith which has made "sacramentarianism" [sacerdotalism] possible'. He quickly got on to his agenda: 'Baptists have been reluctant to recognise... "baptismal grace", just because, in their judgement, it is utterly misrepresented and distorted when ascribed to unconscious infants. The reaction from a false doctrine of divine grace in [infant] baptism has made them suspicious even of [what Robinson called] the genuine

sacramentalism of the New Testament' (Wheeler Robinson: *The Life* pp176-177). Cross summarised Robinson's view: 'The rite of infant baptism lends itself to a mechanical and quasi-magical conception of faith and grace... "Believer's baptism is the logical and effective safeguard against such parodies of scriptural truth"... "There is no risk at all for Baptists to teach the baptism of power, whatever there may be for those who practice infant baptism"' (Cross: 'Pneumatological' pp167-168). Whatever else was amiss, there was no truck with infant baptism in Wheeler Robinson here!

In 1955, Payne, though not so strong as the Baptist Union and Wheeler Robinson thirty years before, was still very suspicious of infant baptism. He spoke of 'the stricter wing of the Baptist movement which has, on the whole, been dominant; the wing, that is, which hesitates about full Church fellowship with those who practice infant baptism'. Payne referred to 'attempts to recognise both forms of baptism' in Ceylon and North India at the time, which he described as an 'ingenious' way that was being tried to get round the problem. 'Most Baptists feel deeply hesitant about admitting that the baptism of infants is really Christian baptism' (Payne: 'Baptist-Congregational' pp102-103). Here was a noticeable shift towards infant baptism.

Beasley-Murray, in 1959, though cautious, wished – but feared he would not see – the triumph of Baptist sacramentalism, which would lead infant baptisers to what he considered a better practice: 'Here Baptists and infant baptisers come to a decisive issue. To [Baptists], it seems clear that whether one thinks of baptism as a sacrament of the gospel, or a sacrament of union with Christ, in either case faith is integral to it. The gospel exercises its radical influence in a man's life when he receives it in faith; he becomes one with Christ when he submits to him in faith; for Paul, the decisive expression of such faith is baptism... Accordingly it appears to us to do violence to exegesis when the Pauline teaching concerning the baptism of believing converts is applied to infants who are incapable of such faith. Nor is there [any] evidence that Paul possessed another baptismal theology which he applied to infants. Not a few infant-baptist scholars recognise this, particularly commentators. Some of them concede that infant baptism involved a fall from the heights of Paul's conception of faith. But is it necessary for the church to persist in a lowered baptismal practice and theology? It needs a baptism which can convey the fullness of meaning which... [the] apostle ascribed to it. To regain such a baptism would require adjustment on the part of all the Churches, including the Baptists, although theirs is an easier task compared with the revolutionary measures which the infant-baptiser churches would have to take to secure it. Though there is no prospect on the horizon of any such revolution taking place [in 1959!], it remains that it will be a great day for the Church if she finds enough

courage to regain the treasure of baptism according to the teaching of Paul'
(Beasley-Murray: 'Baptism in the Epistles of Paul' pp148-149).

In 1962, Beasley-Murray, clearly alarmed by what he considered loose talk
of (a contemporary) acceptance of infant baptism by some fellow Baptist
sacramentalists, did what he could to put a stop to it. Even so, on behalf of
his fellow sacramentalists, he extended the olive branch to infant baptisers:
'I think it right to disabuse the minds of any who have been led by the
utterances of some of my Baptist colleagues to imagine that a change of
view on this matter [of infant baptism] is taking place in Baptist circles;
there is strong resistance to any such change among British Baptists [in
1962], and the mere voicing of it is looked on with astonishment among
Baptists in the rest of the world, who form the bulk of our people... There is
more, however, to be said on this matter. It lies in the power of Baptists to
take a significant step towards the establishing of closer relations with the
other Churches... Could we not refrain from requesting the baptism of those
baptised in infancy who wish to join our churches, and administer baptism
to such only where there is a strong plea for it from the applicant?... This
step would be a small one for the English Baptists to take, since their policy
of having "open-membership" churches has long since been established'
(Beasley-Murray: *Baptism in the New Testament* p392).

In 1966, Beasley-Murray, although he spoke of 'some painful encounters'
between Baptist and others, even so welcomed a growing rapport between
Baptists and infant baptisers: 'There have been undoubted gains, and there
is promise of more fruitful exchange of ideas in the future' (Beasley-
Murray: *Baptism Today and Tomorrow* p113). (This, however, was not the
final word from Beasley-Murray on the subject. See below for the comment
made by Cross on Beasley-Murray's work in 1994).

By 1977, the pace towards infant baptism had quickened considerably. In
that year a Baptist and an Anglican, Donald Bridge and David Phypers,
jointly published a book on baptism: 'Concerning the nature of baptismal
grace, we have urged a middle way. Baptism does not bring salvation
automatically, by the work being worked [*ex opere operato*], but neither is
it merely symbolic. It is a sacrament which brings grace through faith. It is
part of the obedience of faith. The act of baptism demonstrates that faith is
active for salvation... If the infant-baptiser clergyman... moves, perhaps
unconsciously, to a position nearer to his Baptist counterpart, cannot the
Baptist minister, for his part, join him in accepting some form of Christian
household baptism, and thus himself move closer to the infant-baptist
position?' (Bridge and Phypers pp181,203).

I have already referred (with regard to closed communion) to the 1996
Baptist Union report: *Believing and Being Baptised: Baptism, so-called re-
baptism, and children in the church*. A curate's egg, in part it showed a
strong commitment to 'traditional' Baptist teaching, but it also made
serious concessions. Driven by 'the ecumenical context', the report touched

on many of the issues I am raising – ecumenism, infant baptism, re-baptism of those baptised as infants, salvation as a process, water baptism and Spirit baptism, a common baptism, and sacramentalism. Clearly, there were tensions within the committee; 'a significant minority' wanted 'to regard the infant rite as truly baptism'. There were, however, reservations about applying to infants the full benefit of what the committee regarded as the sacramental aspect of baptism which, they thought, properly applies only to the baptism of believers; namely, when talking of believers, 'the New Testament associates baptism in water with baptism in the Holy Spirit, or immersion into the realm of God's Spirit'. As to the mode of that baptism, however, it is only 'preferably by immersion'. As for children, the report concluded that while they cannot be members of the body of Christ, they can be in the body of Christ, and it spoke of 'the blessing of children' in a special service. Under 'Final Hopes', admitting that 'Baptists often seem to be awkward ecumenical partners over the issue of baptism', the committee pleaded 'for Baptists to think more seriously about the place of children in the church; we urge that the act of "presentation and blessing of infants" among Baptists be understood more clearly as a part of a journey of growing relationship with God' (baptist.org.uk).

I now want to go back to what I said a moment or two ago, and re-quote Cross (in 1999) on what Beasley-Murray said in 1994. 'The greatest surprise to Baptists is the modified position on infant baptism adopted by George Beasley-Murray. In his most recent work [1994] he explores the "possibilities" of a rapprochement between believer's baptism and infant baptism when infant baptism is seen as attesting "the commencement of the work of grace within the baptised with a view to its blossoming into fullness of life in Christ and his body the church as the individual's life progressively opens to Christ". This could be supported... especially if focus was placed on "initiation"; that is, the whole process of leading individuals to Christ and into the church. He asks "that churches which practice believer's baptism should consider acknowledging the legitimacy of infant baptism, and allow members in infant-baptiser churches the right to interpret it according to their consciences". In practice, this would involve believer-Baptist churches refraining from "re-baptism". Beasley-Murray's cautious optimism has received the support of [the infant baptiser] David Wright... Beasley-Murray and Wright... seek to establish a *modus vivendi* in which there is mutual recognition of each other's convictions and a striving after the possibility of a rapprochement. As such, this position is to be highly commended as a most fruitful way forward, and also, given the present state of the debate, quite probably the most realistic. The Church today desperately needs such a *modus vivendi*, and I applaud such work, which could well lead to an acceptable common theology of baptism' (Cross: 'One Baptism' pp205-206).

Finally, I turn to the 2008 Baptist Union report: *Baptists and Ecumenism*. Having sketched the history of Baptist 'ecumenical commitment', the report came to 'the issue of baptism', stating: 'There continue to be those who hope and seek to build deeper ecumenism on the basis of a common baptism, but this is always likely to be problematic for Baptists. That is not to say ways forward cannot be found... Baptists will tend only to look for minimum agreement in order to recognise, talk and work with others... Baptists will look for only minimum agreement in order to recognise, talk and work with others'. No, I didn't make a mistake and type the same sentence twice! Tensions there certainly are among the members of the Baptist Union, but nobody can doubt the hoped-for destination. Nor how they hope to get there! The report stated that 'we need, for example, the calling of the Orthodox to draw us back into the universal song of unending praise to God, or the Church of England to help us express a vocation to serve the life of the nation... Ecumenism is an inescapable reality for all of us' (baptist.org.uk).

Unpacking all this, it is clear that the great issue is sacramentalism. If both parties – Baptists and infant baptisers – could agree on *that*, progress would be made. Sacramentalists used to have doubts this would happen. Today, talk of sacramental ecumenism leading to a common baptism is rampant!

By the way, notice how one step off the right road so easily leads to another. Instead of insisting on a baptised regenerate church-membership, Baptist churches begin to allow non-baptised believers to become members. Then the question of infant baptism comes up. Because the first step away from the New Testament has been taken, it is relatively easy to accept baptised infants as members. The ultimate step will be to accept non-regenerate members – some baptised as infants, some baptised in their teens, and some not baptised at all. And, no doubt, Calvin's mistaken view of the parable of the tares will be called on to justify it all. But it won't work! See my *Battle*; *Infant*.

Extended note from p135

Efforts to reconcile Anglicans and Baptists during the first half of the 20th century

In 1889, the Baptists did not proceed with an exploratory letter from the Archbishop of Canterbury; 'their view of baptism required that it be preceded by personal repentance'. But twenty years later, John Howard Shakespeare, Secretary of the Baptist Union 1898-1924, who did not show his hand at first, was prepared to accept episcopacy and some kind of re-ordination of Baptist ministers by an Anglican bishop in order to achieve reunion. For this, he met with a frosty reception from his fellow Baptists when going public in 1918. The Anglicans tried again in 1920, but 'suspicion of where they were being led caused many members of the Baptist Union Council to revise their attitude to some of the wider ecumenical developments which were taking place... Tension on the question of Christian unity continued... among British Baptists'. In 1939, however, the Baptist Union accepted the invitation to join the World Council of Churches (which, because of the War, was not inaugurated until 1948). In the early 1940s, a Free Church Federal Council was set up, and a British Council of Churches with the Archbishop of Canterbury as President. In 1946, Archbishop Geoffrey Fisher suggested '"intercommunion" if the Free Churches would "take episcopacy into their systems"'. Things moved slowly, however, and, in 1948, discussions between the Baptists and the Churches of Christ produced the pamphlet *Infant Baptism Today* which 'drew attention to the disquietude regarding the theology and practice of infant baptism, which was becoming evident in both Reformed and Anglican churches'. In 1952, at the Lund Third World Conference on Faith and Order, 'there was general agreement that baptism and the Lord's supper are more closely related in the New Testament than had been recognised... and that a study of their relationship might provide a new and fruitful line of ecumenical advance'. In 1953, in the Baptist Union, 'the various decisions regarding relationships with other Churches were arrived at in most cases without the tension and division among Baptists which had accompanied the "conversations" a quarter of a century earlier'.

In all this, considerable movement in a sacramental direction among the Baptists can be traced:

'The New Testament law of baptism requires a profession of faith in the Lord Jesus Christ as a pre-requisite' (1889).

'Baptism... [is a] means of grace to all who receive [it] in faith... The ordinance of baptism is administered among us to those only who make a personal confession of repentance and faith... This symbolic representation... In our judgement, the baptism of infants incapable of offering a personal confession of faith subverts the conception of the church... [To] the place given to sacraments by the Lambeth Appeal... we cannot assent... It will be gathered from this reply that union of such a kind as the bishops have contemplated is not possible for us' (1926).

'But when [these pre-requisites] are fulfilled (as in the baptism of believers), the rite becomes a true sacrament, in which the believer, obeying the ordinance of God, receives from God in response to his faith, a fuller measure of the Holy Spirit' (1938).

'Baptism... this sacrament. The New Testament clearly indicates a connection of the gift of the Holy Spirit with the experience of baptism which, without making the rite the necessary or inevitable channel of that gift, yet makes it the appropriate occasion of a new and deeper reception of it' (1948).

Finally, it is enlightening (or, rather, it is depressing for those, like me, who think the old is closer to Scripture) to compare these changes with the 17th century Particular Baptist Confessions, where baptism is described as an ordinance, a sign, and there is no talk of sacraments or means of grace or gift of the Spirit. See Payne: *Baptist Union* pp145-146,169,185-187,197-199,218-221,250-253,262,271-303; *Fellowship* pp87-89,126-162; 'Baptists and the Ecumenical Movement' pp120-129; Underwood pp248-255,261-274; Lumpkin pp143-171,235-295.

Extended note from p228
A look at 2 Cor. 3:3

'You are a letter of Christ ministered by us, written not with ink but by the Spirit of the living God... on tablets of flesh; that is... the heart'. Paul was saying that he needed no letter of recommendation to the Corinthians – the Corinthians themselves were all the letter he needed. Christ himself wrote it; that is, by his Spirit he had regenerated the Corinthians and brought them into a living union with himself through their repentance and faith. Nevertheless, said Paul, Christ had used him as an amanuensis. Christ did the work by his Spirit, but Paul was the hand that he used, and this was the proof that Paul was indeed a minister of Christ. See also 1 Cor. 9:1-2. But what was this amanuensis-work which the apostle had in mind? Could it be baptism? Was baptism the hands-on work that Paul did so that Christ regenerated as he, the apostle, baptised? This, indeed, would have been a literal hands-on ministry. Is it right? Does Col. 2:11-12 fit in here? Broadening the point, is baptism the hands-on work that ministers do today so that Christ regenerates as they baptise?

Not at all. Such a suggestion – were it to be made – would be a leap far too far. Let us look at the context of 2 Cor. 3:3 – I mean from 2 Cor. 1:1 – 6:2, not forgetting, above all, 1 Cor. 1:10 – 4:21. What do we find? Baptism? The suggestion is ludicrous. I will return to 1 Cor. 1 (where Paul destroys the notion that he is talking about baptism in 2 Cor. 3:3). So, what about the context of 2 Cor. 3:3? Baptism is not mentioned. *But preaching is mentioned – indeed, stressed – over and over again* – 2 Cor. 1:18-20; 2:12,14-17; 4:2-5,13; 5:11,18-21; 6:1-2 – and this as the means of bringing sinners to Christ. Neither ministers or water baptism are in Col. 2:11-12, nor baptism in 2 Cor. 3:3. Therefore the claim, if it were to be made – namely, that by linking Col. 2:11-12 with 2 Cor. 3:3, we may say that Paul was speaking of baptism by ministers – would be baseless. Indeed, the boot is on the other foot. Sacramental baptism cannot justly be got out of the passages, nor should it be foisted upon them. In fact, the proper reading of the passages in their context is destructive of sacramentalism.

The truth is, Christ uses any of his saints as ministers (servants) – not just 'ministers' – to regenerate his elect under their preaching (using the biblically-wide definition of both minister and preaching). As for 'ministers', as the word is commonly misused – 'ordained ministers' – I shall have more to say on this in my forthcoming *The Pastor: Does He Exist?*. I mention this now because sacramentalists are usually very shy of allowing 'ordinary' believers to get involved in 'sacramental' duties, except under the most limited of circumstances – this would hinder the drive to sacerdotalism!

Extended note from p275
Inclusivism
In addition to what I say here, see my forthcoming book on Sandemanianism. To avoid being misunderstood in what follows, although I refer to what I have read or heard from others, in the main I am speaking of what I have personally observed – almost entirely among Reformed and Evangelical churches which baptise believers.

Let me state the problem. We want unbelievers to attend our services, hear the preaching, and be converted. Yes. There is no question of it. But... and here's the rub, the very act of unbelievers sitting among us, and joining in our services, compromises at once what we are trying to do. Let me explain. We welcome unbelievers to our meetings. We do so at the door, in the 'notices', and, increasingly, on a sheet of paper which we hand them. We include them in our prayers: 'O God, *we* worship you, *we* praise you'. We include them in our hymns: 'Amazing grace, how sweet the sound, that saved a wretch like *me*'. We include them in our readings: 'I consider that *our* present sufferings are not worth comparing with the glory that will be revealed in *us*'. We cannot help it. However carefully we preface these exercises, the unbelievers present are part of it. They mouth the words, they are made to feel included. Indeed, they are included. *But until they are converted, they are **not** part of it, and they should know and feel they are not part of it!* I have wrestled with this dilemma, as I know others have, and I recognise that good men have differed over the way to deal with it.

But there has been a sea change in recent years. Today, most churches seem blissfully unaware that there is any such problem at all! The predicament most churches wrestle with is not how to deal with unbelievers so as to avoid deceiving (and eternally ruining) them, but how to attract and hold them, how to make them feel part of what we do. Indeed, it sometimes seems as though this constitutes our *raison d'être*. So much so, inclusivism now seems to be determining *policy* of most Evangelical churches. Everything has to bow down at its altar. Carnal means are used to get unbelievers to attend. The music is deliberately chosen to appeal to them – especially the young. Having got the unregenerate to come, nothing must be said or done to cause them the slightest offence. Quite the opposite! The over-arching mood is friendliness at all costs. Unbelievers must be made to feel comfortable, at home; nothing must be allowed to disturb them. Services are carefully structured to avoid upsetting them. Anything and everything which might embarrass or disturb is studiously avoided. Any hint of controversy, anything pointed, everything negative is taboo. The offence of the cross is muted – if not eradicated. Softly-softly is the mantra.

What used to be called 'divine service' has been reduced, in many cases, to little more than 'man service', a cheery social gathering tinged with religion, 'needs-oriented' – by which I mean the promise to satisfy human desire for a pain-free, happy, fulfilled, successful life – with every relationship guaranteed as much bliss and sparkle as the most optimistic yellow-back romance.

In churches where inclusivism has gained firmest hold – from the opening bright and breezy remarks after the 'leader' has bounced onto the dais, or into the pulpit (if there still *is* a pulpit), to the closing chat over a cup of tea (a chat often about yesterday's football, the latest shopping bargain, or last week's holiday; rarely over spiritual matters) – everybody is treated and addressed as a believer. The Alpha course sums it up. According to press releases, 'it is relaxed, non-threatening, low-key, friendly and fun. It is supported by all the main Christian denominations, particularly Roman Catholics' (uk.alpha.org). The current climate of user-friendly, anti-confrontational, 'non-directive' psychological counselling, which sets out to build up self-esteem in man and, consequently, reduces God – with its promise of the penny and the bun – live as you like now and heaven hereafter – has much to answer for. Names, places and ideas such as Carl Rogers, Abraham Maslow, Larry Crabb, Bill Hybels and Willow Creek, Rick Warren and Saddleback, *The Purpose Driven Church*, the emerging church movement, come to mind. See E.S.Williams; Adams. See also the Engel Scale and the Gray Matrix (internetevangelismday.com/engel-scale.php).

Grievously, even in not a few Reformed and Evangelical churches which still retain a vestige of solemnity, and take some thought about these issues, things have reached a parlous state. I am afraid that many who would throw up their hands in horror at any thought of such things as I have mentioned, have, nevertheless, been influenced – subtly – by the underlying ethos. I fear that most contemporary churches are affected to a lesser or greater degree.

As I see it, this, or something very like it, sums up what goes on in many Evangelical churches. Any other approach is considered 'unhelpful', a threat, which 'drives the fish away', and works against what the present-day church is looking for. (I have been accused of it. It is, of course, based on a misunderstanding of Matt. 4:18-22. The fishing Christ was talking about was not with fly or float – but, rather, with the drag net, scooping up as many as possible. I am not saying skill is not required in the use of the drag net, but the notion of out-smarting the fish with lure, bait, deception and stealth, is far removed from the illustration). Many contemporary churches, contemporary in more ways than one, design their 'programme' with the attraction of unbelievers uppermost in their thoughts. The days of Acts 2:43; 5:5,11-13; 1 Cor. 14:24 are long gone.

I know the motive is good. It is to get unbelievers to attend services so as to 'evangelise' them. But the cost is prohibitive. Cost? *Prohibitive* cost? Yes, indeed! Carnal means used to attract sinners, and carnal means used to make them feel at home among us, actually ruins the gospel we should be preaching to them, and runs directly counter to the experience they desperately need – to be convicted of sin, and converted to Christ; to leave their idols and turn to Christ in repentance and faith (1 Thess. 1:4-10, for instance). This ruination is the cost of inclusivism.

Inclusivism. Take the children. Children today are often allocated a principal part – a prominent part – in the service, making them feel important. In the 'children's talk', they are frequently addressed as virtual believers. How often a biblical passage, written to believers, is directly applied to children who, addressed as 'little Christians', are encouraged to produce Christian graces.

Inclusivism. Take the preaching. Above all, take the preaching for (and usually it is 'for' and not 'to' – there is a *big* difference between the two) those who remain after the children have gone out. The preacher, treating the congregation almost from start to finish as believers, avoids all eye-contact, asks few if any open-ended questions, makes little or no *pointed* application, and rarely if ever uses 'you', but nearly always talks in terms of 'us', 'we' and 'them'. Inclusivism through and through. 'User-friendly' is the watchword! Be genial! Polished professionalism is what is wanted, a jokey and anecdotal style of service and preaching, gentle and non-threatening, platitudinous, a 'light touch'. There might be a phrase or two at the end of the sermon, such as 'if you are not trusting Christ' – or some reference to it in the prayer – but the sermon has been so heavily inclusive, that such token gestures count for little. Hymns, prayers, readings – above all, the preaching – the whole shooting match, the complete ambience of the meeting – has been telling all and sundry that they are Christians. And, never forget, the message and the method are inextricably linked. Indeed, the method dominates what the hearers perceive as the message. *How* the message is presented almost certainly has a greater effect upon them than *what* is presented. (If 1 Cor. 9:19-23 is called on to justify such an approach, it can only be done at the expense of misunderstanding the passage).

Inclusivism. The Lord's supper is increasingly being observed as the central part of the 'family service', with insufficient, if any, safeguards put in place against participation by children and unbelievers. Indeed, as for the former, more and more are children being welcomed at the table.

Inclusivism. Take marriages and funerals. Even 'serious' (not excluding Reformed) churches are becoming liberal – and increasingly so – in their terms upon which and for whom they will offer such services – and about what they will say and do at such services. And I am talking about marriages and funerals for unbelievers! I speak of what I know! Above all, bear in mind that it is not what the 'ministers' *say* about what is going on in such services; it is what 'ordinary' people *think* is going on that counts!

As a consequence of all this inclusivism, many churches have in their congregation old people who have attended for years, been treated as virtual believers, addressed as such, feel totally at ease and comfortable in a semi-detached sort of way, and who know they will, after death, be treated as though they had been believers – and are yet unconverted! And not only old people! It is an utter disaster, Christendom with a vengeance. But... if anybody dares to question this contemporary inclusivism...!!! 'Don't you believe in evangelism?'! 'Evangelism' – a word not found in the Bible! – has become one of the chief gods of the age (I am well aware that I am punching an entire battery of red buttons in what I say).

Lloyd-Jones opened his ministry in South Wales in February 1927. Although some of the following is obviously dated, its thrust is relevant still. On March 20th, his preaching must have startled the congregation: 'Our Christianity has the appearance of being an adjunct or an appendix to the rest of our lives, instead of being the main theme and the moving force in our existence... We seem to have a real horror of being different. Hence all our attempts and endeavours to popularise the church and make it appeal to people. We seem to be trying to tell people that their joining a church will not make them so very different after all. "We are no longer Puritans", we say, "we believe that they over-did things and made Christianity too difficult for people. They frightened people with their strictness and their unnecessarily high standards. We are not so foolish as to do that", we say, and indeed we do not do so. Instead, however, we provide so-called "sporting parsons", men of whom the world can say that they are "good sports" – whatever that may mean. And what it does so often mean is that they are men who believe that you can get men to come to chapel and church by playing football and other games with them. "I'll fraternise with these men", says such a minister. "I'll get them to like me and to see that I'm not so different from them after all, and then they'll come to listen to my sermons". And he tries it, but thank God, he almost invariably fails, as he richly deserves. The man who only comes to church or chapel because he likes the minister as a man is of no value at all, and the minister who attempts to get men there by means of that subterfuge is for the time being guilty of lowering the standard of the truth which he claims to believe. For this gospel is the gospel of salvation propounded by the Son of God himself. We must not hawk it about in the world, or offer special inducements and attractions, as if we were shopkeepers announcing an exceptional bargain sale... The world expects the Christian to be different and looks to him for something different, and therein it often shows an insight into life that regular church-goers often lack. The church organises whist-drives, fetes, dramas, bazaars and things of that sort, so as to attract people. We are becoming almost as wily as the devil himself, but we are really very bad at it; all our attempts are hopeless failures, and the world laughs at us. Now, when the world persecutes the church, she is performing her real mission, but when the world laughs at her she has lost her soul. And the world today is laughing at the church, laughing at her attempts to be nice and to make people feel at home. My friends, if you feel at home in any church without believing in Christ as your personal Saviour, then that church is no church at all, but a place of entertainment or a social club. For the truth of Christianity, and the preaching of the gospel, should make a church intolerable and uncomfortable to all except those who believe, and even they should go away chastened and humble' (Murray: *The First* pp141-142; see also his pp131-151,215).

Some of the above is, as I say, old hat. Things have moved on. And how! Whist drives, musical concerts, fish-and-chip suppers are far too tame these days. Many Reformed and Evangelicals have moved up market with a vengeance. We can, we vainly think, out-world the world! Banquets, with a glitzy after-dinner speaker, are commonplace. Clay-pigeon shooting, jousting tournaments, boule contests, cricket matches, Victorian evenings, river trips, bbqs, theatre trips, pub breakfasts... I could go on. And on. I know – I know, I say – where a prospective pastor was thought to be 'the man for us' because of his ability to organise such events. And in the Grace Baptist church which did secure him, he and his wife have lost no time in confirming their catering credentials. When I recently asked an (unsympathetic) observer how things are going, I was told that there would be little fear of numbers dropping as long as the standard of the food is kept up. I am afraid there is more than a grain of truth in such sarcasm.

The buzz word is 'community'. The church must be a 'community church'. The pastor must be the leading light in the 'community'. We must reach out to and be part of the 'community'. Of course, as private individuals, we should use our social contacts to seek to spread the gospel. But I am talking about the church – the church of *Christ*, after all; the church of *Christ* – he who has made his mind known in Scripture. Too often the one word to describe a modern Evangelical church is 'social'. In the New Testament it is 'spiritual'. I repeat my challenge to the churches and their elders – get rid of the social crust, and replace it with the spiritual (Acts 2:42, for example), and see what happens to the attendance. See my *Battle*. Would to God that churches today obeyed Artaxerxes' positive stipulation for the returning Jews (Ezra 7:21), and, on the negative side, followed their Master himself when he cleansed the temple of all its worldly clutter (Matt. 21:12-13; Mark 11:15-17; Luke 19:45-46; John 2:14-17; see also Mal. 3:1 – 4:6)!

Finally, I am reminded of my youth. 'Separation' was a word and notion much in vogue in those days; rightly so. Nowadays it is hardly ever heard. Is it thought about? Is it practiced? To 'encourage' us young people to stay clear of the world, our mentors told us the salutary tale of the earnest young man, recently converted, who thought he would go to the dance hall and witness for Christ. Taking the girl in his arms and waltzing out onto the floor, he addressed her thus: 'I'm a Christian'. 'What are you doing here, then!', came the immediate rebuff.

And in the 18th century, dissenters used to speak of the church as 'a garden enclosed' (Song 4:12). Isaac Watts' hymn – 'Zion's a garden walled around,/Chosen and made peculiar ground;/A little spot, enclosed by grace/Out of the world's wide wilderness' (*Gospel Hymns* number 820) – encapsulated the idea. See also Thomas Kelly's, 'Lord behold us in thy grace' (*Gospel Hymns* number 819). Thus it used to be said that the church is in the world. Nowadays, the world is in the church. Indeed, like the closing page of *Animal Farm*, it is getting increasingly difficult to sort out the Orwellian which is which – the church and the world act so much alike, they meld one into the other. The great day (1 Cor. 3:9-15) will mark the reckoning.

Two American correspondents (Nov. 14th 2010) told me of their experience of Reformed Baptist churches in the States. They spoke of 'a shallow belief... younger people who are beginning to come to the doctrines of grace, but really don't know exactly what they believe... Their testimony... is very shallow. Their lack of knowledge of Scripture, their love of contemporary religious music, casual dress, casual attitude toward worship is something they bring with them, and it is a big influence on the church as a whole. Compromise in one area affects all areas of the worship. If these concerns are mentioned to the [leaders], those who have the concerns are seen as old fashioned, unloving and judgmental. Pressure is put on by these newcomers and new members to compromise the music, and worship in general. Many of the professing non-members are included in various programs of the church – outreach ministries that represent the church *etc*. And when new visitors come to the church, these non-members are often seen greeting the visitors, and assuming a position the same as the members, and they are often very forward. The true meaning of membership has been downgraded. It is in these things that we see inclusivism as a dangerous trend and a threat to the stability and health of Christ's true church'.

Extended note from p287

John Robinson's reply to Thomas Helwys on the necessity or otherwise of baptism

Robinson: 'It is not true [as] he [Helwys] says, that none can come and be joined to Christ without baptism. The Scriptures testify that so many as believe in Christ, receive him, are engrafted into him, having him living in them, and dwelling in their hearts (John 1:12; Rom 11:20; Gal. 2:20; Eph. 3:17). Which faith is before baptism, in some men a longer time; in some, a shorter; and, in some, also dying unbaptised (Matt. 8:10; 15:28; Acts 10:4,35; Luke 23:40 *etc*.). And, according to this, was the tenor of Christ's commission to his apostles, by teaching to make disciples or Christians, and to bring men to believe, and afterwards to baptise them (Matt. 28:19; Acts 11:26; Mark 16:16). And to baptise any of years, but [that is, unless] being before joined to Christ by actual faith, and so making manifestation, were to profane God's ordinance. Neither is it Paul's meaning, where he tells the Galatians that "they which had been baptised into Christ, had put on Christ", that they were not joined to Christ before their outward baptism, but to show that their baptism was a lively sign of their union with, and incorporation into, Christ, and participation in the washing of his blood and Spirit, as also an effectual means more and more to apply the same unto them; being all their life long to put on the Lord Jesus Christ, and the new man, as the same apostle teaches (Rom. 13:14; Eph. 4:24). And [as] for Acts 2:38, it shows, indeed, that they who believe and repent are to be baptised; that is, being unbaptised before, as they then were, and as we [that is, John Robinson's company] now are not; God having also added to the outward washing or baptism, though in the false church, the inward washing of the Spirit to repentance and amendment of life' (John Robinson p166). (By 'the false church', did Robinson mean the nation of Israel? – if so see my *Infant* and my forthcoming book on the law where I deal with this mistaken notion that Israel was the church. Or did he mean Rome? I think the latter).

I make three points. *First*, Robinson was an infant baptiser – though, judging by the above, you would hardly believe it! There is a hint of it, however. But elsewhere he was a very clear advocate of infant baptism. See the following extended note for instance. Putting that to one side, observe how well Robinson put the biblical case for the baptism of believers only. Out of his own mouth... *Secondly*, just to point out once more that I disagree with both Helwys and Robinson when they take Gal. 3:27 to refer to water baptism. *Thirdly*, Robinson misunderstood Helwys. Helwys knew full well that it is by faith a man is saved – that if baptism is impossible, a believer's lack of it does not un-save him – as he himself plainly stated. The 'joining to Christ' both men were talking about was the public owning and confession of Christ.

Extended note from p292

John Robinson's reply to Thomas Helwys on the 'double consideration' of baptism

What follows is, I am afraid, complicated. Robinson made it so. Here goes...

Robinson, replying to Helwys, summarised the 'double consideration [he, Robinson,] put [made] of baptism: The one [consideration] taking it, in itself, and as I speak nakedly, and in the essential causes or parts – namely, washing with water in the name of the Father, Son and Holy Ghost; the other [consideration], in respect of the manner of administering it; namely, the minister by, and the person upon whom, and the communion wherein it is administered. In the former respect, I affirm the baptism true, both in [the Church of] England and Rome; but not so in the latter [respect], but on the contrary, [it is] false and idolatrous, as being against the second commandment, which forbids... idolatry and false worship'.

I pause. I will be brief. I hear echoes of Calvin, and it is unadulterated nonsense. Apparently, baptism is complete (or whatever the word is) if it is carried out with the right formula in the right Church, but it is OK – yet not complete – (or whatever the words are) if carried out with the right formula in the wrong Church. I say it once again; unadulterated nonsense.

To let Robinson go on. Taking up Helwys' point about 'one baptism' (Eph. 4:5), Robinson said that baptism 'has in it two parts – the sign, and the thing signified – either of which is also in the Scriptures called baptism – the one, the baptism with water, wherewith John baptised (Matt. 3:11; Mark 1:8), and wherewith all ministers do baptise; which is the outward baptism, and sign of the inward; the other, the baptism with the Holy Ghost, wherewith only Christ and God do baptise... The outward and inward baptism are joined together by Christ, and so ought not by men to be separated, but joined together in their time and order'.

I pause. On spiritual baptism – 'the baptism with the Holy Ghost, wherewith only Christ and God do baptise' – excellent; see my comments on Col. 2:11-12. As for the rest, Robinson was badly mistaken. Badly! *First*, baptism does not have two parts – water and the Spirit. No! These are two distinct baptisms! *Secondly*, he was also wrong on the order of the two. Water baptism must follow Spirit baptism. Not the other way about. *Thirdly*, Christ did *not* join the two baptisms. Joining them is precisely what he did not do! As I have shown, Christ most decidedly distinguished between the two baptisms. *Indeed, he contrasted them.* And we must always separate them! In these three particulars, Robinson got things very badly wrong. And, as a consequence, he appeared to be saying that water baptism leads to Spirit baptism; in other words, teaching baptismal regeneration. I concede he was not, because he recognised that a person could be baptised in water and not be spiritually baptised. Even so, Robinson *was* playing with fire, giving the impression he *was* teaching baptismal regeneration.

That is not all. Robinson then made a ridiculous assertion. He went on to 'deny that... where the inward baptism by the Spirit is not actually manifested, as in the infants of believers, there the outward [baptism] is not to be ministered'. I pause again. What nonsensical speculation! Indeed, what *dangerous* speculation. The two baptisms – spiritual baptism and water baptism each must keep to its proper place, order and time. Quite right! Robinson himself had said as much. And the New Testament teaches that water baptism can only take place after evidence of spiritual baptism. This, of course, rules out both sacramentalism and infant baptism. So where did Robinson go wrong? There are two points I need to make. *First*, was Robinson claiming that the babies of believers have the inward baptism of the Spirit by reason of their birth? If so... And, *secondly*, let's avoid the double negatives. Robinson was saying that although the inward baptism by the Spirit cannot be outwardly manifested in the babies of believers (assuming it to exist!), nevertheless they can be baptised! In other words, the biblical order is baptism by the Spirit followed by baptism in water, but in the case of the babies of believers, said Robinson, we baptise them in water, even though we cannot tell if they have been inwardly baptised by the Spirit! Why? Is it because they *are* already baptised by the Spirit, or so that they might *be* baptised by the Spirit? And what about the point at issue – namely, baptism in a false church? 'I', said Robinson, 'deny that... baptism... being administered unlawfully in apostate churches... is no outward baptism at all, nor spiritual in itself, though carnally used, nor to be held upon repentance [that is, upon the one baptised leaving the false church for a true church], without repetition'; that is, getting rid of the double negatives yet again, under the circumstances envisaged, the first baptism need not be repeated – though carried out carnally in an apostate church. And whatever did Robinson mean by an outward baptism being 'spiritual in itself'?

Robinson again: 'I conclude, therefore, that there is an outward baptism by water, and an inward baptism by the Spirit, which though they ought not to be severed, in their time, by God's appointment [note Robinson's unbiblical claim and his unbiblical order!], yet many times are [severed] by men's default; that the outward baptism in the name of the Father, Son and Holy Ghost, administered in an apostate church, is false baptism in the administration, and yet in itself, and own nature, [it is] a spiritual ordinance, though abused; and whose spiritual uses cannot be had without repentance [that is, the one baptised coming to his senses, leaving the apostate church and joining a true church]; by which repentance, and the after-baptism of the Spirit, it is sanctified, and not to be repeated'. In other words, someone who was baptised in a false church, on his leaving the false church and joining a true church, and being baptised by the Spirit, all will be well, and there is no need to re-baptise! And this goes for an infant, too (John Robinson pp181-185). Phew!

One further thing. Did Robinson mean that when someone, baptised in a false church, comes to his senses and joins a true church, he is inevitably baptised with the Spirit? Or did he allow that there can be members of a true church who have been baptised in a false church, come to their senses about that, yet are still not regenerate? I am afraid I am unable to unravel Robinson any further. Why, on re-reading this (time and again), I still have to scratch and shake my head! What complications arise when we depart from the simplicity of Scripture!

Source List

Act 3 Review, Vol.15, no.2, 2006, Carol Stream.

Adams, Jay E.: *The Biblical View of Self-Esteem, Self Love, Self-Image*, Harvest House Publishers. Eugene, 1986.

Anderson, Robert: 'Christian Baptism and Baptismal Regeneration', being an Appendix to *The Bible or the Church?*, London, 1908.

Anon: *Sanderson of Oundle* (The Macmillan Company, New York, 1928), archive.org/details/sandersonofoundl009661mbp

Armstrong, John H. (ed.): *Understanding Four Views on Baptism*, Zondervan, Grand Rapids, 2007.

Atkinson, Basil F.C.: *Valiant in Fight: A Review of The Christian Conflict*, The Inter-Varsity Fellowship, London, 1950.

Badke, William B.: 'Baptised into Moses – Baptised into Christ: A Study in Doctrinal Development', in *Evangelical Quarterly*, 1988.

Baillie, John: *Baptism and Conversion*, Oxford University Press, London, 1964.

Barnhouse, Donald G.: 'The Meaning of the Term "Baptism"', in Stevenson, Herbert F. (ed.): *The Ministry of Keswick*, Second series, Marshall Morgan and Scott, London, 1964.

Beasley-Murray, G.R.: *Baptism Today and Tomorrow*, Macmillan, London, 1966.

Beasley-Murray, G.R.: *Baptism in the New Testament*, The Paternoster Press, Exeter, 1962/1972.

Beasley-Murray, G.R.: 'Baptism in the Epistles of Paul', in Gilmore, A. (ed.): *Christian Baptism...*, Lutterworth, London, 1959.

Beckwith, Francis J.: *Return to Rome: Confessions of an Evangelical Catholic*, Brazos Press, Grand Rapids, 2009.

Beeke, Joel R.: 'Calvin on Piety', in McKim, Donald K. (ed.): *The Cambridge Companion to John Calvin*, Cambridge University Press, Cambridge, 2004.

Bernard, J.H.: 'The Cyprianic Doctrine of the Ministry', in Swete, H.B. (ed.): *Essays on the Early History of the Church and the Ministry by Various Writers*, Second Edition, Macmillan and Co., Limited, London, 1921.

Boorman, David: 'Reformers Before the Reformation', being a paper given at The Westminster Conference 1973: *Adding to the Church*.

Brewer, J.S.: *The Reign of Henry VIII...,* ed. James Gairdner, John Murray, London, 1884.

Bridge, Donald, and Phypers, David: *The Water that Divides: The baptism debate,* Inter-Varsity Press, Leicester, 1977.

British Reformed Journal.

Brown, John: *An Exposition of the Epistle of Paul the Apostle to the Galatians,* The Sovereign Grace Book Club, Evansville, Indiana, 1957.

Brown, John: *Expository Discourses on 1 Peter,* The Banner of Truth Trust, Edinburgh, 1975.

Bruce, F.F.: *The Spreading Flame,* The Paternoster Press, London, 1958.

Buchanan, Colin, and Vasey, Michael: *New Initiation Rites...,* Grove Books Limited, Cambridge, 1998.

Buse, S.I: 'Baptism in the Acts of the Apostles', in Gilmore, A. (ed.): *Christian Baptism...,* Lutterworth, London, 1959.

Buse, S.I: 'Baptism in Other New Testament Writings', in Gilmore, A. (ed.): *Christian Baptism...,* Lutterworth, London, 1959.

Calvin, John: *Institutes of the Christian Religion,* A new translation by Henry Beveridge, James Clarke & Co., Limited, London, 1957.

Calvin, John: *Calvin's Commentaries,* Baker Book House, Grand Rapids, 1979.

Carson, D.A: *Matthew 13-28,* Zondervan, Grand Rapids, 1995.

Carson, H.M.: *Farewell to Anglicanism,* Henry E.Walter Ltd., Worthing, 1969.

Carson, H.M.: *Dawn or Twilight? A study of contemporary Roman Catholicism,* Inter-Varsity Press, Leicester, 1976.

Carson, H.M.: *The New Catholicism,* The Banner of Truth Trust, London.

Castelein, John D. in Armstrong, John H. (ed.): *Understanding Four Views on Baptism,* Zondervan, Grand Rapids, 2007.

Chadwick, Owen: *The Victorian Church, Part 1: 1829-1859,* SCM Press Ltd., London, 1971.

Clark, Neville: 'The Theology of Baptism', in Gilmore, A. (ed.): *Christian Baptism...,* Lutterworth, London, 1959.

Colwell, John E.: 'The Sacramental Nature of Ordination: An Attempt to Re-engage a Catholic Understanding and Practice', in Cross,

Anthony R., and Thompson, Philip E. (eds.): *Baptist Sacramentalism*, Wipf and Stock Publishers, Eugene, 2006.

Cross, Anthony R.: '"One Baptism" (Ephesians 4:5): A Challenge to the Church', in Porter, Stanley E., and Cross, Anthony R. (eds.): *Baptism, the New Testament and the Church*, Sheffield Academic Press, Sheffield, 1999.

Cross, Anthony R.: 'Dispelling the Myth of English Baptist Baptismal Sacramentalism', in *The Baptist Quarterly*, Oct. 2000.

Cross, Anthony R.: 'Spirit- and Water- Baptism in 1 Corinthians 12:13', in Porter, Stanley E., and Cross, Anthony R. (eds.): *Dimensions of Baptism*, Sheffield Academic Press, Sheffield, 2003.

Cross, Anthony R.: 'The Pneumatological Key to H.Wheeler Robinson's Baptismal Sacramentalism', in Cross, Anthony R., and Thompson, Philip E. (eds.): *Baptist Sacramentalism*, Wipf and Stock Publishers, Eugene, 2006.

Cross, Anthony R.: 'The Evangelical sacrament: *baptisma semper reformandum*', in *Evangelical Quarterly*, July 2008.

Cross, Anthony R., and Thompson, Philip E. (eds.): *Baptist Sacramentalism*, Wipf and Stock Publishers, Eugene, 2006.

Cross, Anthony R., and Thompson, Philip E.: 'Introduction: Baptist Sacramentalism', in Cross, Anthony R., and Thompson, Philip E. (eds.): *Baptist Sacramentalism*, Wipf and Stock Publishers, Eugene, 2006.

Curtis, Geoffrey: 'Baptism and the Quest of Unity', in: *Mirfield Essays in Christian Belief by members of the Community of the Resurrection*, London, 1962.

Dawkins, Richard: *A Devil's Chaplain: Reflections on Hope, Lies, Science, and Love*, books.google.co.uk

Douglas, J.D. (general editor): *The New International Dictionary of the Christian Church*, The Paternoster Press, Exeter, 1974.

Downing, Victor K.: 'The Doctrine of Regeneration in the Second Century', in *Evangelical Review of Theology*, The Paternoster Press, Exeter, April 1990.

Douglass, Jane Dempsey: 'Calvin in Ecumenical Context', in McKim, Donald K. (ed.): *The Cambridge Companion to John Calvin*, Cambridge University Press, Cambridge, 2004.

Eaton, Michael: *The Gift of Prophetic Preaching: A Charismatic Approach*, New Wine Press, Chichester, 2008.

Ellis, Christopher: 'A View from the Pool. Baptists, sacraments and the basis of unity', being a consultation paper on 'The Sacramental Dimension of Baptism', in *The Baptist Quarterly*, July 2001.

Encarta Dictionary from the internet.

Estep, William R.: *The Anabaptist Story*, William B.Eerdmans, Grand Rapids, 1975.

Estep, William R.: *Renaissance and Reformation*, William B.Eerdmans, Grand Rapids, 1986.

Estep, William R.: *Revolution Within the Revolution,* William B.Eerdmans, Grand Rapids, 1990.

Evangelical Times.

Fee, Gordon D.: *The First Epistle to the Corinthians*, William B.Eerdmans Publishing Company, Grand Rapids, reprinted 1991.

Fee, Gordon D.: *God's Empowering Presence: The Holy Spirit in the Letters of Paul*, Hendrickson Publishers, Peabody, 1994.

Flinn, P.Richard: 'Baptism, Redemptive History, and Eschatology: The Parameters of Debate', in Jordan, James B. (ed.): *The Failure of the American Baptist Culture*, in *Christianity and Civilisation*, Geneva Divinity School, Tyler, 1982.

Fowler, Stanley K.: *More than a Symbol: The British Baptist Recovery of Baptismal Sacramentalism*, Wipf and Stock Publishers, Eugene, 2006.

Fowler, Stanley K.: 'Is "Baptist Sacramentalism" an Oxymoron?: Reactions in Britain to *Christian Baptism* (1959)', in Cross, Anthony R., and Thompson, Philip E. (eds.): *Baptist Sacramentalism*, Wipf and Stock Publishers, Eugene, 2006.

Freeman, Curtis W.: '"To Feed Upon by Faith": Nourishment from the Lord's Table', in Cross, Anthony R., and Thompson, Philip E. (eds.): *Baptist Sacramentalism*, Wipf and Stock Publishers, Eugene, 2006.

Friesen, Abraham: *Erasmus, the Anabaptists, and the Great Commission*, Wm. B.Eerdmans Publishing Co., Grand Rapids, 1998.

Fuller, Andrew: *The Practical Uses of Christian Baptism*, in *The Complete Works of... Andrew Fuller...*, Henry G.Bohn, London, 1866.

Fuller, Andrew: *Essays, Letters, &c. on Ecclesiastical Polity*, in *The Complete Works of... Andrew Fuller...*, Henry G.Bohn, London, 1866.

Ganoczy, Alexandre: 'Calvin's Life', in McKim, Donald K. (ed.): *The Cambridge Companion to John Calvin*, Cambridge University Press, Cambridge, 2004.

Gay, David: *Battle For The Church*, Brachus, Lowestoft, 1997.

Gay, David H.J.: *Particular Redemption and the Free Offer*, Brachus, Biggleswade, 2008.

Gay, David H.J.: *Infant Baptism Tested*, Brachus, Biggleswade, 2009.

George, Timothy: 'The Sacramentality of the Church: An Evangelical Baptist Perspective', in Cross, Anthony R., and Thompson, Philip E. (eds.): *Baptist Sacramentalism*, Wipf and Stock Publishers, Eugene, 2006.

Gerrish, B.A.: 'The Place of Calvin in Christian Theology', in McKim, Donald K. (ed.): *The Cambridge Companion to John Calvin*, Cambridge University Press, Cambridge, 2004.

Gill, John: *A Complete Body of Doctrinal and Practical Divinity; or, A System of Evangelical Truths, Deduced from the Sacred Scriptures*, W.Winterbotham, London, 1796.

Gill, John: *The Cause of God and Truth*, W.H.Collingridge, London, 1855.

Gill, John: *Gill's Commentary*, Baker Book House, Grand Rapids, 1980.

'Gill's Archive' (pbministries.org/books/gill/gills_archive.htm).

Gilmore, A.: 'Jewish Antecedents', in Gilmore, A. (ed.): *Christian Baptism...*, Lutterworth, London, 1959.

Gillies, Donald: *Unity in the Dark*, The Banner of Truth Trust, London, 1964.

Google Books.

Gospel Hymns, The Strict and Particular Baptist Society, Robert Stockwell, Ltd., London, 1915.

Gospel Standard.

Grace Hymns, Grace Publications Trust, London, 1978.

Grass, Tim, and Randall, Ian: 'C.H.Spurgeon on the Sacraments', in Cross, Anthony R., and Thompson, Philip E. (eds.): *Baptist Sacramentalism*, Wipf and Stock Publishers, Eugene, 2006.

Gregg, Pauline: *Free-Born John: A Biography of John Lilburne*, Phoenix Press, London, 2000.

Grenz, Stanley J.: 'Baptism and the Lord's Supper as Community Acts: Toward a Sacramental Understanding of the Ordinances', in Cross,

Anthony R., and Thompson, Philip E. (eds.): *Baptist Sacramentalism*, Wipf and Stock Publishers, Eugene, 2006.

Griffiths, D.R.: 'Baptism in the Fourth Gospel and the First Epistle of John', in Gilmore, A. (ed.): *Christian Baptism...*, Lutterworth, London, 1959.

Guthrie, Donald: *The Letter to the Hebrews...*, Inter-Varsity Press, Leicester, 1983.

Haldane, Robert: *Exposition of the Epistle to the Romans*, The Banner of Truth Trust, London, 1958.

Harrison, Graham: 'Becoming A Christian – in the Teaching of John Calvin', being a paper given at The Westminster Conference 1972: *'Becoming A Christian'*.

Harvey, Barry: 'Re-membering the Body: Baptism, Eucharist and the Politics of Disestablishment', in Cross, Anthony R., and Thompson, Philip E. (eds.): *Baptist Sacramentalism*, Wipf and Stock Publishers, Eugene, 2006.

Haymes, Brian: 'Towards a Sacramental Understanding of Preaching', in Cross, Anthony R., and Thompson, Philip E. (eds.): *Baptist Sacramentalism*, Wipf and Stock Publishers, Eugene, 2006.

Haykin, Michael A.G.: '"His soul-refreshing presence": The Lord's Supper in Calvinistic Baptist Thought and Experience in the "Long" Eighteenth Century', in Cross, Anthony R., and Thompson, Philip E. (eds.): *Baptist Sacramentalism*, Wipf and Stock Publishers, Eugene, 2006.

Haykin, Michael: 'A plea for solid reflection on the meaning of baptism' (andrewfullercenter.org/'Baptist Life & Thought'/'A plea for solid reflection on the meaning of baptism', posted May 4th 2009).

Hedegård, David: *Ecumenism and the Bible*, The Banner of Truth Trust, London, 1964.

Hendriksen, William: *The Gospel of Matthew*, The Banner of Truth Trust, Edinburgh, 1974.

Hendriksen, William: *The Gospel of Mark*, The Banner of Truth Trust, Edinburgh, 1975.

Helwys, Thomas: *The Mystery of Iniquity*, The Baptist Historical Society, London, 1935.

Hill, Christopher: *The Experience of Defeat: Milton and Some Contemporaries*, Bookmarks, London, 1994.

Hodge, Charles: *A Commentary on Romans*, The Banner of Truth Trust, London, 1972.

Hodge, Charles: *An Exposition of the First Epistle to the Corinthians*, The Banner of Truth Trust, London, reprinted 1964.

Holland, Bernard G.: *Baptism in Early Methodism*, Epworth Press, London, 1970.

Holmes, Stephen R.: 'Towards a Baptist Theology of Ordained Ministry', in Cross, Anthony R., and Thompson, Philip E. (eds.): *Baptist Sacramentalism*, Wipf and Stock Publishers, Eugene, 2006.

Hyde, Daniel R.: 'A Catechism on the Holy Spirit – 4: The Work of the Holy Spirit Upon the Church', in *Banner Of Truth*, May 2008.

Jackson, Bill: *The Final Flock. The Final Gathering of Satan's False Religions...*, Colonial Baptist Press, Louisville, 1988.

Johnson, Paul: *A History of Christianity*, Penguin Books Ltd., Harmondsworth, 1976.

Johnstone, Robert: *A Commentary on James*, The Banner of Truth Trust, Edinburgh, 1977.

Jones, Hywel R.: *Gospel and Church: An evangelical evaluation of ecumenical documents on church unity*, Evangelical Press of Wales, Bryntirion, 1989.

Kruse, Colin G.: *John*, Inter-Varsity Press, Nottingham, 2003.

Lane, Anthony N.S.: 'Baptism in the thought of David Wright', in *Evangelical Quarterly*, April 2006.

Laning, James: 'Do We Hold to Kuyper's View of Presupposed Regeneration?', in *The Standard Bearer*, Vol.75, no.2, Grandville, Oct. 15th 1998.

LeBruyns, Clint: 'The Evangelical Advantage: A New Engagement with the Petrine Ministry', in *Act 3 Review*, Vol.15, number 2, 2006, Carol Stream.

Lloyd-Jones, D.Martyn: *Romans: An Exposition of Chapter 6. The New Man*, The Banner of Truth Trust, Edinburgh, 1975.

Lloyd-Jones, D.Martyn: *Romans: An Exposition of Chapter 8:5-17. The Sons of God*, The Banner of Truth Trust, Edinburgh, 1974.

Lloyd-Jones, D.Martyn: 'Luther and his Message for Today', in Jones, Hywel R. (ed.): *Unity in Truth: Addresses given by Dr D.Martyn Lloyd-Jones at meetings held under the auspices of the British Evangelical Council*, Evangelical Press, Darlington, 1991.

Lloyd-Jones, D.Martyn: *The Church and the Last Things*, Hodder & Stoughton, London, 1998.

Lord, F.Townley: 'The Holy Communion in Congregational and Baptist Churches', in *The Holy Communion, A Symposium*, SCM, 1947.

Lumpkin, William L.: *Baptist Confessions of Faith*, Judson Press, Valley Forge, Sixth Printing, 1989.

Macleod, Donald: *The Spirit of Promise*, Christian Focus Publications, Fearn, 1986.

Malia, Martin: *History's Locomotives: Revolutions and the Making of the Modern World*, Yale University Press, New Haven, 2006.

Manton, Thomas: *An Exposition on the Epistle of James*, The Banner of Truth Trust, London, 1962.

McGrath, Alister E.: *Understanding Doctrine: Its Purpose and Relevance Today*, Hodder & Stoughton, 1990.

McGrath, Alister: *To Know and Serve God: A Life of James I.Packer*, Hodder & Stoughton, London, 1998.

McGrath, Alister: *The Twilight of Atheism...*, Rider, London, 2004.

Montgomery Hyde, H.: *Norman Birkett*, Hamish Hamilton, London, 1964.

Morrison, Alan: *The Serpent and the Cross. Religious Corruption in an Evil Age*, K&M Books, Birmingham, 1994.

Murray, Iain H.: *The Forgotten Spurgeon*, Second Edition, The Banner of Truth Trust, London, 1973.

Murray, Iain H.: *David Martyn Lloyd-Jones: The First Forty Years 1899-1939*, The Banner of Truth Trust, Edinburgh, 1982.

Murray, Iain H.: *David Martyn Lloyd-Jones: The Fight of Faith 1939-1981*, The Banner of Truth Trust, Edinburgh, 1990.

Murray Iain H.: *Evangelicalism Divided. A Record of Crucial Change in the Years 1950 to 2000*, The Banner of Truth Trust, Edinburgh, 2000.

Murray, John: *Redemption Accomplished and Applied*, The Banner of Truth Trust, London, 1961.

Newman, Elizabeth: 'The Lord's Supper: Might Baptists Accept a Theory of Real Presence?', in Cross, Anthony R., and Thompson, Philip E. (eds.): *Baptist Sacramentalism*, Wipf and Stock Publishers, Eugene, 2006.

Newton, Benjamin Wills: *The Doctrine of Scripture Respecting Baptism Briefly Considered*, Lucas Collins, London, 1907.

O'Donnell, Matthew Brook: 'Two Opposing Views on Baptism with/by the Holy Spirit and of 1 Corinthians 12:13. Can Grammatical Investigation Bring Clarity?', in Porter, Stanley E., and Cross, Anthony R. (eds.): *Baptism, the New Testament and the Church*, Sheffield Academic Press, Sheffield, 1999.

Owen, John: *An Exposition of Hebrews*, 7 Volumes in 4, Sovereign Grace Publishers, Evansville 13, Indiana, 1960.

Owen, John: *The Causes, Ways and Means of Understanding the Mind of God as Revealed in His Word...*, in *The Works of John Owen*, Vol.4, edited by William H.Goold, The Banner of Truth Trust, London, 1967.

Packer, J.I.: *Keep in Step With the Spirit*, Inter-Varsity Press, Leicester, 1984.

Packer, J.I.: 'Foreword', in Cross, Anthony R., and Thompson, Philip E. (eds.): *Baptist Sacramentalism*, Wipf and Stock Publishers, Eugene, 2006.

Payne, Ernest A.: *Henry Wheeler Robinson...*, Nisbet & Co., Ltd., London, 1946.

Payne, Ernest A.: *The Fellowship of Believers: Baptist Thought and Practice Yesterday and Today*, The Carey Kingsgate Press, Ltd., London, 1952.

Payne, Ernest A.: *The Baptist Union: A Short History*, The Baptist Union of Great Britain and Ireland, London, 1959.

Payne, Ernest A.: 'Baptist-Congregational Relationships', in *Free Churchmen, Unrepentant and Repentant, and Other Papers*, The Carey Kingsgate Press Limited, London, 1965.

Payne, Ernest A.: 'Baptists and the Ecumenical Movement', in *Free Churchmen, Unrepentant and Repentant, and Other Papers*, The Carey Kingsgate Press Limited, London, 1965.

Payne, Ernest A.: 'Baptists and Church Relations', in *Free Churchmen, Unrepentant and Repentant, and Other Papers*, The Carey Kingsgate Press Limited, London, 1965.

Philpot, J.C.: *Two Letters... Strict Communion... Were Christ's Disciples Baptised?... Extracted, with Corrections from the Gospel Standard for 1840*, Gospel Standard Publications, London, 1967.

Pink, Arthur W.: *Exposition of the Gospel of John: Three Volumes... in One*, Zondervan Publishing House, Grand Rapids, 1978.

Pinnock, Clark H.: 'The Physical Side of being Spiritual: God's Sacramental Presence', in Cross, Anthony R., and Thompson, Philip E. (eds.): *Baptist Sacramentalism*, Wipf and Stock Publishers, Eugene, 2006.

Plumer, William S.: *Commentary on... Hebrews*, Baker Book House, Grand Rapids, 1980.

Poole, Matthew: *A Commentary on The Holy Bible*, Vol.3, The Banner of Truth Trust, Edinburgh, reprinted 1975.

Porter, Stanley E.: 'Baptism in Acts: The Sacramental Dimension', in Cross, Anthony R., and Thompson, Philip E. (eds.): *Baptist Sacramentalism*, Wipf and Stock Publishers, Eugene, 2006.

Porter, Stanley E., and Cross, Anthony R.(eds.): *Baptism, the New Testament and the Church: Historical and Contemporary Studies in Honour of R.E.O.White*, Sheffield Academic Press, Sheffield, 1999.

Praise!, Praise Trust, Darlington, 2001.

Protestant Truth.

Riddle, J.E.: *A Manual of Christian Antiquities...*, John W.Parker, London, 1839.

Robinson, H.Wheeler: *The Life and Faith of the Baptists*, Methuen & Co., Ltd., London, 1927.

Robinson, H.Wheeler: 'Introduction', in Helwys, Thomas: *The Mystery of Iniquity*, The Baptist Historical Society, London, 1935.

Robinson, John: *Of Religious Communion, Private and Public*, in *The Works of John Robinson...*, Vol.3, John Snow, London, 1851.

'Rome sweet home?', being a review article in *Protestant Truth*, July-Aug. 2009.

Ross, J.M.: *The Theology of Baptism in Baptist History*, in *The Baptist Quarterly*, July 1953.

Russell, David S.: 'Michael John Walker: An Appreciation', in Walker, Michael J.: *Baptists At The Table: The Theology of the Lord's Supper amongst English Baptists in the Nineteenth Century*, Baptist Historical Society, Didcot, 1992.

Sandlin, P.Andrew: 'The Importance of Being Catholic', in *Act 3 Review*, Vol.15, number 2, 2006, Carol Stream.

Schaff, Philip: *History of the Christian Church*, Hendrickson Publishers, Peabody, 1996.

Schrotenboer, Paul (ed.): 'An Evangelical Response to "Baptism, Eucharist and Ministry"', in *Evangelical Review of Theology*, The Paternoster Press, Exeter, Oct. 1989.

Shaw, Jane: 'Face to faith', being an article in *The Guardian*, Saturday Oct. 6th 2007.

Sibbes, Richard: *A Fountain Sealed*, in *Works of Richard Sibbes*, Vol.5, The Banner of Truth Trust, Edinburgh, 1977.

Slomski, Peter: 'Should We Adjust Our Eyesight? The New Perspective on Paul and the Federal Vision', in *Bible League Quarterly*, Oct.-Dec. 2009.

Snyder, C.Arnold: *Anabaptist History and Theology: Abridged Student Edition*, Pandora Press, Kitchener, 1995.

Soper, Charles: 'More Downgrade in the FIEC', in *Bible League Quarterly*, July-Sept. 2009.

Spurgeon, C.H.: *The New Park Street and Metropolitan Tabernacle Pulpit... 1861*, Vol.7, Passmore and Alabaster, London, 1862.

Spurgeon, C.H.: *The Metropolitan Tabernacle Pulpit*, Vol.21, Passmore and Alabaster, London, 1876.

Spurgeon, C.H.: *The Metropolitan Tabernacle Pulpit*, Vol.23, Passmore and Alabaster, London, 1885 (surely 1878?).

Spurgeon, C.H.: *The Metropolitan Tabernacle Pulpit*, Vol.31, The Banner of Truth Trust, London, 1971.

Spurgeon, C.H.: *Second Series of Lectures to my Students...*, Passmore and Alabaster, London, 1885.

Spurgeon, C.H.: *Speeches... at Home and Abroad*, Passmore and Alabaster, London, 1878.

Spurgeon, C.H.: *The Early Years 1834-1859*, The Banner of Truth Trust, London, 1967.

Spurgeon, C.H.: *Spurgeon on Baptism*, Henry E.Walter Ltd., Worthing, being a reprint of the Appendix he published with Watson, Thomas: *Body of Divinity*, and omitted by the Banner of Truth Trust.

Spurgeon, C.H.: *The Sword and the Trowel...*, edited by C.H.Spurgeon, Passmore and Alabaster, London, 1867.

Thayer, Joseph Henry: *A Greek-English Lexicon of the New Testament...*, Baker Book House, Grand Rapids, 1991.

The Concise Oxford Dictionary of Current English, Eighth Edition, BCA, London, 1991.

The London Baptist Confession of Faith and Keach's Catechism, Gospel Mission, Choteau.

The Shorter Oxford English Dictionary on Historical Principles, Third Edition, Guild Publishing, London, reprinted 1988.

The Daily Telegraph.

Thompson, Philip E.: 'Sacraments and Religious Liberty: From Critical Practice to Rejected Infringement', in Cross, Anthony R., and Thompson, Philip E. (eds.): *Baptist Sacramentalism*, Wipf and Stock Publishers, Eugene, 2006.

Tidball, Derek: 'A Baptist perspective on David Wright, *What has Infant Baptism done to Baptism?...*, in *Evangelical Quarterly*, April 2006.

Toon, Peter: *Born Again: A Biblical and Theological Study of Regeneration*, Baker Book House, Grand Rapids, 1987.

Underwood, A.C.: *A History of the English Baptists*, The Carey Kingsgate Press Limited, London, 1947.

Verduin, Leonard: *The Reformers and Their Stepchildren*, The Paternoster Press, Exeter, 1964.

Walker, Michael J.: *Baptists At The Table: The Theology of the Lord's Supper amongst English Baptists in the Nineteenth Century*, Baptist Historical Society, Didcot, 1992.

Walker, Williston: *A History of the Christian Church*, T.&T. Clark, Edinburgh, revised 1959.

Wallis, J.: *Japhia. Another Jazer: An Answer to... J.Irons on the Subject of Baptism*, London, 1824.

We Believe: A Guide for Church Fellowship, National Assembly of Strict Baptists, Devizes, 1974.

Westminster Documents: *The Confession of Faith* and other documents of the Westminster Assembly, The Publication Committee of the Free Presbyterian Church of Scotland, 1967.

White, R.E.O.: *The Biblical Doctrine of Initiation*, Hodder & Stoughton, London, 1960.

Williams, E.S.: *The Dark Side of Christian Counselling*, The Wakeman Trust & Belmont House Publishing, London and Sutton, 2009.

Williams, George Huntston (ed.): *Spiritual and Anabaptist Writers*, SCM Press Ltd., London, 1957.

Wilson, A.N.: *The Victorians*, Arrow Books, London, 2003.

Witherington III, Ben: *Grace in Galatia: A Commentary on... Paul's Letter to the Galatians*, T.&T.Clark, Edinburgh, 1998.

Wood, E.J.: *The Two Ordinances*, Strict & Particular Baptist Trust Corporation, Caterham, 1968(?).

Wright, David F.: 'One Baptism or Two?...', in *Evangelical Review of Theology*, The Paternoster Press, Exeter, Oct. 1989.

Wright, David.F.: *What has Infant Baptism Done to Baptism? An Enquiry at the End of Christendom*, Paternoster Press, Milton Keynes, 2005.

Wright, David: 'Christian baptism: where do we go from here?', in *Evangelical Quarterly*, April 2006.

Wylie, J.A.: *The History of Protestantism*, Vol.1, Cassell & Company, Limited, London.

http://archives.sbts.edu

www.andrewfullercenter.org

www.baptist.org.uk

www.internetevangelismday.com/engel-scale.php

www.njiat.com/media/Ecumenical

www.pbministries.org/books/gill/gills_archive.htm

www.regent-college.edu/events/conferences/index.php

www.scborromeo.org/ccc.htm

www.stfrancismagazine.info/ja/EcumenicalJihad

www.wheaton.edu/Calendars/events.html

www.uk.alpha.org

Index of Scripture References

Lightning Source UK Ltd.
Milton Keynes UK
21 March 2011

169659UK00001B/4/P